Scubadivers and Chrysanthemums

Scubadivers and Chrysanthemums

§

Essays on the Poetry of Araki Yasusada

edited by
Bill Freind

Shearsman Books

Published in the United Kingdom in 2012 by
Shearsman Books Ltd, 50 Westons Hill Drive, Emersons Green
Bristol BS16 7DF

Shearsman Books Ltd Registered Office
30–31 St. James Place, Mangotsfield, Bristol BS16 9JB
(this address not for correspondence)

www.shearsman.com

ISBN 978-1-84861-184-9
Copyright © the individual authors, 2012.
All rights reserved.

Acknowledgements & Permissions

'Can I Get a Witness?' by Eliot Weinberger, from *Karmic Traces*, copyright © 1997 by Eliot Weinberger. Reprinted by permission of New Directions Publishing Corp., New York.

'In Search of the Authentic Other: The Poetry of Araki Yasusada' by Marjorie Perloff. Originally published in *Boston Review*, Vol. 22: no. 2, 1997.

'Review of *Doubled Flowering: From the Notebooks of Araki Yasusada*' by Forrest Gander. Originally published in *The Nation*, 13 July 1998.

'Hyper-Authorship: The Case of Araki Yasusada' by Mikhail Epstein. Originally published in Yasusada, Araki. *Doubled Flowering: From the Notebooks of Araki Yasusada*. Ed. and Trans. Tosa Motokiyu, Okura Kyojin, and Ojiu Norinaga. New York: Roof Books, 1997.

'The Strange Case of Araki Yasusada: Author, Object' by Eric R.J. Hayot. Originally published in *PMLA* Vol. 120, No. 1, Jan., 2005. Reprinted by permission of the Modern Language Association.

'Doubled Flowering: Charles Yu, Araki Yasusada and the Politics of Faking Race' by Paisley Rekdal. Originally published in *Western Humanities Review*, Vol. 62, No. 1, 2008.

'The Authentic Poet in the Late 20th Century: Ted, bp, and Araki Yasusada' by David Rosenberg. Originally published in *Fascicle*, No. 3.
http://fascicle.com/issue03/main/issue03_frameset.htm

'Illegible Due to Blotching: Poetic Authenticity and its Discontents' by David Wojahn. Originally published in *Notre Dame Review*, No. 9, Winter 2000.

'Letter to Araki Yasusada' by Hosea Hirata. Originally published in *Also, With My Throat, I Shall Swallow Ten Thousand Swords: Araki Yasusada's Letters in English*. Cumberland, RI: Combo Books, 2005.

When essays in this collection cite these articles, the parenthetical citation gives the page number both in the original source and in this collection.

Contents

Bill Freind
    Araki Yasusada and Beyond   7

Eliot Weinberger
    Can I Get A Witness?   16

Marjorie Perloff
    In Search of the Authentic Other:
    The Poetry of Araki Yasusada   23

Forrest Gander
    Review of *Doubled Flowering:*
    From the Notebooks of Araki Yasusada   51

Mikhail Epstein
    Hyper-Authorship: The Case of Araki Yasusada   58

Kent Johnson
    Some Thoughts on Araki Yasusada the Author   76

Brian McHale
    The Yasusada Notebooks and the Figure of the Ruined Text   86

Paisley Rekdal
    Doubled Flowering: Charles Yu,
    Araki Yasusada and the Politics of Faking Race   107

Jenny Boully
    "Here is the offering of a sacred name which is
    [illegible, eds.]": The Necessity of Anonymity in
    the Entity of Araki Yasusada   129

Alex Verdolini
    Desert Music, Hiroshima:
    The Poetics and Politics of Pseudonymity   165

Eric R. J. Hayot
    The Strange Case of Araki Yasusada: Author, Object   180

Jacob Edmond
    Araki Yasusada and Conceptual Writing   205

Martin Corless-Smith
    Three Dialogues between Real and Imaginary Poets   220

Farid Matuk
    "A Displacement of the Main Reed into the Other"   239

David Rosenberg
    The Authentic Poet in the Late 20th Century:
    Ted, bp, and Araki Yasusada   252

David Wojahn
    Illegible Due to Blotching:
    Poetic Authenticity and Its Discontents   286

Hosea Hirata
    Letter to Araki Yasusada   312

Dan Hoy
    This Is a City with No Person: Authorial Voids
    among the Mess of Meta-Hyperawareness   316

Bill Freind
    After Yasusada   326

Biographical Notes   337

Araki Yasusada and Beyond

Bill Freind

In some ways, an introduction to the work of Araki Yasusada (and Tosa Motokiyu) is unnecessary for anyone planning to even skim this volume, since most of the essays provide their own overview of the controversy. But since presenting the history of the Yasusada scandal is almost as obligatory as the epic invocation to the muse, I'll give a quick summary of the scandal; however, rather than concentrating on the issues that were central to the discussion of the text in the 1990s, my concern is why Yasusada's work remains relevant, and how it has been enriched and augmented by the work Kent Johnson has published after *Doubled Flowering: From the Notebooks of Araki Yasusada*. In other words, this is less of an introduction than an e-duction: instead of offering an overview or analysis of Yasusada's work, it seeks to show how the Yasusada project anticipates and contextualizes Johnson's later work.

First, the quick summary: Araki Yasusada, allegedly a survivor of the atomic bombing of Hiroshima, had his work published posthumously and in translation in the mid-1990s. The work was widely praised and seemed to fuse traditional Japanese forms and themes with more innovative North American techniques and a sprinkling of French critical theory. However, Yasusada was an invention, and while no one claimed responsibility for the work, most readers agree that Kent Johnson was the creator, although Johnson insists the actual author is Tosa Motokiyu, the pseudonym for an unnamed writer who is now dead.

To oversimplify somewhat, the initial debate about Yasusada essentially fell into two camps. Those who praised Yasusada saw the poems as an empathetic and moving testament to the atrocity of the bombing of Hiroshima and, by extension, Nagasaki. Others in the pro-Yasusada camp called attention to the work's heteronymy, a word most closely associated with the work of the Portuguese poet Fernando Pessoa, who created dozens of fully formed personae, in whose voices he wrote. For his celebrators, Yasusada constituted an aesthetically liberatory gesture, since in spite of the pronouncements of Barthes and Foucault, the figure of the author still dominates many modes of reading. Recasting the author as a figure who is simultaneously present and fictive can be a way of undermining that domination, of not eliminating the author but textualizing him or her as another type of literary character.

Those critical of Yasusada often emphasized the ethical questions surrounding an author of (presumably) European descent not only appropriating the voice of a *hibakusha*, or survivor of the atomic bombing, but also employing some of the more familiar stereotypes of East Asia in general, and Japan in particular. For instance, Juliana Chang, Walter K. Lew, Tan Lin, Eileen Tabios, and John Yau write:

> Like most hoaxes, Johnson's is fueled mainly by the potential for self-gain. And like all hoaxes it is complex—his act of yellowface at once plays into an existing and apparently vigorous orientalist fantasy, exposes American ignorance of both Japanese poetry and recent Japanese history, and levels a critique against an experimental writing community to which the author also seeks to ingratiate himself. In this last respect, Johnson's act is doubly disturbing: he wants the taint of scandal without having to take responsibility for the stereotypes he celebrates. (Chang)[1]

This is a nuanced claim: Chang, et. al., suggest that part of Yasusada's "yellowface" is in fact a critique of the insularity of contemporary North American poetics. At the same time, they claim that that critique constitutes a career move by Johnson, since it would allow him an entrance into the post-avant community. To do that, Johnson must walk a very fine line: he needs to employ racist and orientalist stereotypes without either endorsing or explicitly mocking them. The clear implication is that Johnson's motivation is mostly or even merely cynical. But the claim that the Yasusada project was "fueled mainly by the potential for self-gain" seems, simultaneously, both completely self-evident and unsupported by any evidence whatsoever. Obviously, almost all writers are fueled by the potential for self-gain: they're looking for some kind of approbation, even in the tiny, fractured worlds of contemporary Anglophone poetry. At the same time, to leap

---

[1] I wanted to include this essay in the collection, but one of the authors refused permission to reprint it.

to unsupported speculation about authorial intention more than a half century after Wimsatt and Beardsley published 'The Intentional Fallacy' seems to be a peculiar move. As I noted above, many readers (including me) have suggested that the poems in *Doubled Flowering* evince a striking empathy for the fictive *hibakusha* of the poems. Does it matter if those poems stem from a cynical careerism or an "authentic" compassion for the victims? And how could we tell the difference?

The importance of the Yasusada work has become clearer with the subsequent publications of Johnson's poetry. If one of the central concerns of *Doubled Flowering* is the construction of the author(s), much of his later work concentrates on the construction of authority in both official verse culture and various otherstream poetries. In *Epigramititis: 118 Living American Poets*, Johnson resuscitates the epigram, that formerly venerable form that often served as the perfect poetic medium for praise, spite, and/or vindictiveness. Each epigram includes a drawing or photograph on the facing page, but they're metaphorical, not literal representations of the poet who is the subject of the epigram. For instance, the epigram to Robert Pinsky, which is paired with a photo of an inept-looking used-car salesman, reads:

> I, too, dislike him,
> though I'm not sure why (Epigramititis 37).

As poet laureate, and now as *de facto* poet laureate emeritus of the United States, Pinsky, as Johnson notes, continues to play a role in which he is required to bemoan the irrelevance of poetry in the US, while coming up with solutions (or, some might say, gimmicks) to change this state of affairs. The epigram, which reworks Marianne Moore's widely anthologized 'Poetry,' suggests that as poet laureate Pinsky is the visible face of poetry in the United States, while the image contends that Pinsky has attempted to foist poetry to a largely uninterested public, just as a sleazy car salesman might use the hard sell to move a lemon off the lot. I think Pinsky operates as a kind of shorthand for other poetry salesmen such as Ted Kooser, another former laureate; John Barr, the investment banker who presides over the more than $100 million endowment at the Poetry Foundation; and Dana Gioia, the former VP of marketing at General Foods who formerly directed the National Endowment for the Arts.² Each of these men has explicitly called for marketing poetry as if it were a product.³ That's where the irony of the photo really comes into focus: even a dismal used car salesman has a better sales record than these guys. The problem isn't only that poetry has become a business; it's that it has become a spectacularly unsuccessful business, as Pinsky, Kooser, Barr, et. al., attempt to foist a mediocre product on an indifferent market.

While Johnson certainly revels in controversy, it is wrong to dismiss him as merely a provocateur. When Charles Bernstein condemned the Yasusada project as "an expression of white male rage" (Bernstein 213), or when Arthur Vogelsang, former editor of *American Poetry Review*, called the Yasusada project "essentially a criminal act" (Nussbaum 82), those comments served as clear demarcations of the limits of what Bernstein himself has called "official verse culture." Submitting poems to a journal without indicating that the "author" is a heteronym is not only poetically unacceptable; in Vogelsang's eyes, it constitutes an actual violation of the law. Despite Bernstein's unmistakable commitment to some types of innovative writing, he believes that a white author writing under the heteronym of a *hibakusha* must be motivated by racially-based, or even explicitly racist anger. Johnson recognized those comments were instructive enough to use as blurbs: Bernstein's appears

---

[2] Johnson's epigram 'The Poet Laureate' continues this conflation of those who would serve as spokespeople for poetry:

> I can't quite recall his or her name presently.
> Is it Robert, Rita, or Billy?
> Or is it Ted? No . . . Ted Hughes is dead.
> He wears a helmet of hair in Hell.
> I'm so silly (167).

The accompanying photo is of Laura Bush, who has attempted to promote both reading in general and poetry in particular. The poem suggests that the attempt to domesticate poetry for public consumption puts the American laureate in a position that's analogous to the British laureate, whose job is to write verse for state occasions. The position of laureate makes these different poets indistinguishable from each other, and from the first lady, and suggests that they are at least tacitly complicit in the actions of the government that employs them.

[3] For an excellent analysis of the strategies of Kooser, et. al., see Evans, Steve. 'Free (Market) Verse,' 29 July 2007 http://www.thirdfactory.net/freemarketverse-all.html.

in *Also, With My Throat, I Shall Swallow Ten Thousand Swords*, while Vogelsang's appears both in that volume and in *Doubled Flowering*.

This was not to be the last time that Johnson was accused of violating the law. In *A Question Mark above the Sun: Documents on the Mystery Surrounding a Famous Poem "by" Frank O'Hara*, Johnson suggests that Frank O'Hara's famous poem "A True Account of Talking to the Sun at Fire Island" (itself a reworking of Mayakovsky's 'An Extraordinary Adventure Which Befell Vladimir Mayakovsky in a Summer Cottage') may have been written by O'Hara's friend Kenneth Koch. Koch has stated that he found the poem after O'Hara's death, and Johnson somewhat tentatively proposes that Koch could have written the work as a tribute to his friend. As Johnson admits, the evidence is somewhat circumstantial, and he himself believes that O'Hara probably is the author. Nonetheless, even that was enough to elicit the threat of a lawsuit. Before *A Question Mark* was even published, Richard Owens, whose Punch Press was about to release the volume, received a certified letter from the Kenneth Koch Literary Estate threatening legal action. According to Johnson, the letter states "Alfred A. Knopf (publisher of both Koch and O'Hara), Maureen Granville-Smith, executor of the Frank O'Hara Estate, and poets Bill Berkson, Ron Padgett, Jordan Davis, and Tony Towle [. . .] all are strongly convinced that this publication is a malicious hoax, one that denigrates Kenneth Koch's character and dishonors his work" (Latta). It seems to me that this response is the most important aspect of *A Question Mark*. There's an absurd disjuncture between the funny, irreverent writing of both Koch and O'Hara, and the spurious threat of a lawsuit. I would guess that one of the central purposes of Johnson's claim was to see just how excessively the guardians (self-appointed or otherwise) of Koch's and O'Hara's reputations would respond to a fairly tentative thesis published in a small press book. And clearly, their response was excessive. While the signatories of the letter had close, personal relationships with Koch and/or O'Hara, the threat of legal action for "dishonoring" Koch's work seems more typical of a large corporation seeking to protect its reputation. Koch becomes essentially the same as Coke: he is a brand whose name must be protected. Perhaps this is the inevitable result of the author-fetish in late-capitalism: the name of the poet becomes a commodity even in the almost non-existent market for contemporary poetry.

Johnson's post-Yasusada work is often more explicitly political than *Doubled Flowering* which, in spite of its subject, does not even allude to the larger military or historical issues that surround the bombing. For instance, 'Lyric Poetry After Auschwitz, Or: "Get the Hood Back On,"' published in his collection *Homage to the Last Avant-Garde*, provides a striking example of this political engagement. In the poem, various American service members introduce themselves with stereotypical small-town American affability, then reveal the people to whom they're speaking are Iraqis they are about to torture:

> Welcome, Kamil, I'm an American girl, nineteen, pregnant, my Dad is an alcoholic, but my Mother is in recovery, with her own Daycare, and I'll be taking it over after the Army, I've always wanted to have my own business, and I'm going to expand beyond just one location, I'm not thinking small. And since I believe it is always important to say what one means and not beat around the bush, I want you to know something: I'm going to hold a pistol to your head and tell you to jack-off, while you recite the Koran as fast as you can, you heathen, Hell-bound fuck, and then I'm going to look at the camera with a cigarette dangling from my sultry, teenage lips, giving the thumbs up. By the time you get to MI, you'll be softened up, and you'll tell us where the missing evil Baathists are. (120–121)

The poem resists an easy demonization: the unnamed speaker is a not untypical "American girl" (in her formulation), and she claims she believes "it is always important to say what one means and not beat around the bush." But what follows is a description of the torture and sexual, physical, and spiritual humiliation that Kamil (whoever he might be) will endure. We have no way of knowing if Kamil actually knows where the "missing evil Baathists are," so this torture could be as pointless as it is savage. This brings us back to the title of the poem, which alludes to Theodor Adorno's (in)famous pronouncement that to write a poem after Auschwitz is barbaric. But the poem fundamentally reworks Adorno's dictum: each of the sections begins with a seemingly hospitable introduction, then goes into a chronicle of savagery. The juxtaposition is jarring, even terrifying, and the implication is that a political poem written after Auschwitz must itself enact barbarism as a way of addressing that barbarism. Contra Hannah Arendt, this evil is not so much banal as endemic, since these affable, salt-of-the-earth American soldiers almost effortlessly slide into atrocity.

However, Johnson's willingness to imaginatively address atrocity is not "witness," at least not in Carolyn Forché's already dated sense of the word.[4] Both poet and readers are not passive viewers but are instead already implicated:

> Hi there, Madid, I'm an American poet, twentyish, early to mid-thirtyish, fortyish to seventyish, I've had poems on the *Poets Against the War* website, and in *American Poetry Review* and *Chain*, among other magazines, and I have a blog, and I really dig Arab music, and I read Adorno and Spivak, and I'm really progressive. I voted for Clinton and Gore, even though I know they bombed you a lot, too, sorry about that, and I know I live quite nicely off the fruits of a dying imperium, which include anti-war poetry readings at the Lincoln Center and the Poetry Project, with appetizers and wine and New World Music and lots of pot. And because nothing is simple in this world, and because no one gets out unscathed, I'm going to just be completely candid with you: I'm going to box your ears with two big books of poems, one of them experimental and the other more plain speech-like, both of them hardbound and by leading academic presses, and I'm going to do it until your brain swells to the size of a basketball and you die like the fucking lion for real. You'll never make it to MI because that's the breaks; poetry is hard, and people go up in flames for lack of it everyday. By the time any investigation gets to you, your grandchildren will have been dead over one thousand years, and poetry will be inhabiting regions you can't even begin to imagine. Well, we did our best; sorry we couldn't have done better… I want you to take this self-righteous poem, soak it in this bedpan of crude oil, and shove it down your pleading, screaming throat.
>
> Now, get the hood back on. (122)

---

[4] It's interesting to note that Forché praised the Yasusada project, writing: "Yasusada's writing is an entry into a spiritual space . . . It is a work of art in the largest sense." (Johnson and Nagahata).

Scubadivers and Chrysanthemums

One of the potential drawbacks to political poetry is that it can offer both poets and readers the consolation of righteous anger and/or a kind of voyeuristic thrill that stems from the suffering of others. This poem works against those readings, suggesting that poetry, at best, changes nothing, and at worst is implicated in the very structures it would critique. Political poetry changes nothing, and not infrequently slides into a self-congratulatory complacency. But refusing poetry is not a possibility; as Johnson writes in '33 Rules of Poetry for Poets 23 and Under':

> Write political poems. But remember: The politics you are likely protesting are present, structurally, inside poetry, its texts and institutions. Write political poems with a vengeance. (72)

One of things that makes Johnson's work so compelling is its acute sensitivity to the power structures that are present both in the realms of geopolitics and in the insular worlds of contemporary poetry. His attention to the latter suggests one of the most important aspects of Johnson's work, which is its strong metapoetic and conceptual quality. His poetry continually returns to the question of how poetic reputations are made, of what poems count and why. This is a question that is central to the Yasusada project, since the initial success of the poems was due in large part to the fact that they so perfectly fulfilled the desire for an author who was simultaneously foreign and familiar, who perfectly encapsulated the *poète maudit* who died unrecognized, only to be discovered after his death. In other words, the Yasusada project presents an implicit critique to its own success, and to an endeavor such as this collection.

Works Cited

Bernstein, Charles. 'Fraud's phantoms: a brief yet unreliable account of fighting fraud with fraud (no pun on Freud intended), with special reference to the poetics of Ressentiment.' *Textual Practice* 22.2 (2008): 207–227.

Chang, Juliana et al. 'Displacements.' *Boston Review* 22.3–4 (1997): 34.

Johnson, Kent. *Epigramititis: 118 Living American Poets*. Buffalo: BlazeVOX, 2006.

Johnson, Kent. *Homage to the Last Avant-Garde*. Exeter, UK: Shearsman, 2008.

Johnson, Kent and Akitoshi Nagahata. 'The Yasusada Affair—Ethics or Aesthetics? . . . the Kent Johnson / Akitoshi Nagahata letters.' *Jacket* 2. http://jacketmagazine.com/02/yasu.html. Accessed 3 January 2011.

Latta, John. *Isola di Rifiuti*, 'Update: Kent Johnson's *A Question Mark*.' http://isola-di-rifiuti.blogspot.com/2010/09/update-kent-johnsons-question-mark.html Accessed 3 January 2011.

Can I Get a Witness?

Eliot Weinberger

Though the story is scarcely believable, the example is apt: an early explorer reported that an African tribe had only one song that had only one line: "The King has all the power." Whether this was all the community had to express or all that they were allowed to express, the message is the same: political poetry is as old and as varied as poetry itself, and as intrinsic to poetry as fertility, love, and death.

For most of this century, the image of political poetry was restricted to that which was plainly written to further a specific movement or goal (revolution, collective liberation, peace). Then, as the ideologies unraveled, academic theory began insisting on an amorphous "political" reading of everything: the silences implicit in the poem about a daffodil. Like much of what is called "theory," it was both perfectly true and a self-evident generality that was all too easy to reiterate in complex ways.

Lately, a new subgenre has been invented to stand for the whole in this ideological interregnum: the poetry of "witness." Anti-New Critical with a vengeance, witness poetry is entirely dependent on biographical background, and is ultra-empirical in a way perhaps unprecedented in literary history. It is a poetry where you had to have been there.

The Qur'an of the witness subgenre is Carolyn Forché's popular anthology, *Against Forgetting*. Limited to the twentieth century, poets in the book qualify as witnesses if they have been combatants or civilians in a war, prisoners or exiles, or citizens of a totalitarian regime (regardless of one's life under that regime). More dubiously, also included are journalists or visitors in a war zone, even for a short period, and non-white residents of the United States. (White people, presumably, do not witness injustice in this country.) Others, including those whose poetry is normally considered "political" by any other standards—Allen Ginsberg, for one—might as well have spent their time composing pantoums at the club.

This taxonomy, like the Hindu caste system or editorial policy anywhere, has subtleties of distinction that are impossible for outsiders to grasp. Tadeusz Borowski is a witness of the Holocaust because he was interned in Auschwitz and Dachau. Nelly Sachs is a witness of the Holocaust because she wrote poems about the Holocaust from her exile in Sweden. Irena Klepfitz is a witness of the Holocaust because she was born in Warsaw in 1941 and was hidden in the countryside, emigrated to the United States as a small child, and wrote poems about the Holocaust in New York City. Charles Reznikoff, however, is not a witness of the Holocaust because he was born in the United States and wrote poems about the Holocaust in New York City.

Such literalness and hair-splitting historicism is, incredibly for a poet, a surprisingly absolute denial of imagination. (One hardly demands similar evidence from other writers: snapshots of Laura or Beatrice, or of the poet holding his shoes on Dover Beach.) The "poetry of witness," as a concept—not the poets themselves, but the box they have now been put into—has become a branch of the poetry as auto-therapy that is currently being promoted on public broadcasting television and in countless writing schools. A poetry where one's autobiography is primary, incidents of victimization are the salient features of one's life, and writing is seen as the way to heal those psychic wounds. (This last feature is the best evidence that this has nothing to do with poetry at all. Poetry does not close wounds or answer questions; it opens them.) *Against Forgetting*, with its organizing principle of biographical "extremity," is not all that different from a book published a few years ago in Spain, a fat international and historical volume with an ominous black-on-black cover: *The Anthology of Poets Who Committed Suicide*. Once upon a time, it was enough for poets to think, dream, and write, and their first-person was usually a persona. Now they must submit a résumé to be validated for sincerity.

The inherent value of "witnessing" as a measure of poetry is evident in two recent publications. The first is *Outcry from the Volcano*, edited and translated by Jiro Nakano, an anthology of tanka written by Hiroshima survivors, mainly amateur poets, in the years immediately following the devastation. It is both a moving document and of practically no interest as poetry. (And one reads it with amazement: did not one of these poets feel that the tanka's five lines and counted syllables were somehow inadequate to their experience?) The second is the poems of Araki Yasusada, a postal clerk whose family was erased by the bomb, but who lived on to 1972. His strange and wonderful notebooks were discovered years after his death; lately they have been appearing in translation in *Conjunctions*, *Grand Street*, and other magazines, where they have provoked considerable interest.

Scubadivers and Chrysanthemums

The problem is that Yasusada is the pseudonym of an anonymous, possibly American poet, who has brilliantly written all the work, complete with slightly awkward bits of translationese. A telling case: had rumors of Yasusada's identity not begun to circulate, he would have become "our" primary poet-witness of nuclear disaster—much as the greatest witnessing of plague is Daniel Defoe's entirely fictional first-person account.

Witness poetry, a sign of the times, reduces, yet again, the political to the personal, and confines the act of writing to a factual narcissism. It should be remembered that legal witnesses are not automatically presumed to be reliable. Poets are no more or less credible, regardless of the greatness of the work. Speaking of Hiroshima, here is one of the masters, William Carlos Williams, in a letter to another poet, Byron Vazakas, dated August 7, 1945: "The day following the atomic blast—the poor Jews who accomplished it. Now we'll hate them worse than ever." And here is another master, Lorine Niedecker, three months later:

> New
> Reason explodes. Atomic split
> shows one element
> Jew

Postscript: I Found a Witness

The preceding was published in the *Village Voice Literary Supplement* in July 1996 and was the first public declaration of the pseudonymity of Araki Yasusada. A few weeks later, the *American Poetry Review* published an issue with a special supplement featuring Yasusada. *APR*, whose trademark is photos of the poets often larger than the poems themselves, represented the witness poet with what appeared to be the blurred xerox of a xerox of a xerox of a mug shot of some low-level yakuza.

The coincidence led to an article in *Lingua Franca*, a gossip magazine for academics, in which an *APR* editor called the poems a "criminal act," a proof that they publish poets, not poems. This, in turn, led to one of those momentary media frenzies that now routinely accompany any novelty: articles in the *Wall Street Journal*, *The Guardian*, the *Sydney*

Morning Herald, and the *Financial Times* of London; a front-page story in the *Asahi Shimbun*, Japan's largest newspaper; a conference in Utrecht; symposia in the *Boston Review*, the *Denver Quarterly*, *Stand* in England, and in various places on the Internet—all before the poems were published in book form.

The first order of speculation was, of course, whodunit. A poet I vaguely know called me out of the blue—he had never called before—to ask point-blank if I was Yasusada; he had a long list of entirely persuasive reasons. An editor at one of the magazines that had published the poems thought it was her old boyfriend. Various names were raised and debated, with the likeliest suspects being the primary purveyors of the Yasusada manuscripts: Javier Alvarez, a prominent Mexican composer living in London, and Kent Johnson, an instructor at a community college in Illinois and the editor of anthologies of American Buddhist and contemporary Russian poetry.

In response to the journalists, Alvarez and Johnson said the poems were the work of one Tosa Motokiyu, who had been their roommate in Milwaukee in the 1970s. "Motokiyu" was, almost needless to say, also a pseudonym, and the person attached to that name had recently died; Alvarez wrote a moving account of his last hours.

Meanwhile, in a further complication, the Russian critic Mikhail Epstein rather brilliantly demonstrated that Yasusada could be the work of either of two well-known Russian writers, Andrei Bitov and Dmitri Prigov, or a collaboration between them. Both had previously invented authors—one of them Chinese, another Polish-Italian-Japanese—and both had long-announced, mysteriously unpublished "Japanese" projects. Moreover, in true conspiratologist fashion, Epstein located both writers at a conference in St. Petersburg with none other than Kent Johnson.

In the proliferating discussions, the identity of the author had become so refracted that it approached the condition of We Are All Yasusada. Perhaps it is best to call him/her/them the Yasusada Author, much as we refer to a Renaissance painter as the Master of the X Altar.

The Yasusada debate rather predictably fell into the categories of politics, literary politics, and theory. The political reading was based on the assumption that the author was a white American male, and thus the poems were a cruel, racist, imperialist joke. This was based on the (racist and imperialist) assumption that anyone who is not a white Euromale wants to speak only in an "authentic" voice. It was inconceivable that the Yasusada Author could be a young woman in Chiapas. (In the beginning of the century, there was a Japanese memoirist and novelist, Onoto Watanna, who was a best-selling writer in the West; she turned out to be a half-Chinese Eurasian who lived in Hong Kong.)

In the political debate, Edward Said's *Orientalism* was inevitably cited, much as medieval discussions always deferred to the authority of Isidore of Seville. But, as Said himself says in passing, his dissection of the Orientalism of the "Near" and "Middle" East (those geographical dislocations) becomes less applicable as one goes further East. Western scholars, poets, and philosophers never idealized Arab civilization as the Source of Wisdom in the way that the Enlightenment imagined China or Romanticism India. When one reaches twentieth-century Japan, a First World imperialist nation, Said's book hardly applies at all. The Yasusada Author, even if a white American male, is no more an agent of colonialism than a Japanese country & western singer.

The literary-political response centered on two points, both true. One was the current cult of celebrity that has expanded to engulf literature: we now like to have authors attached to books, preferably attractive people or ones with sad lives (or best of all, both). The other was the general ignorance and lack of interest in nearly all foreign poetry. Thus, it was only Yasusada's tragic life, not his poetry that got him published in leading magazines. And if the poetry seemed radical, it was only because few were familiar with twentieth-century Japanese poetry. (In fact, for a far more complex reaction to the war, see Takamura Kotaro's *A Brief History of Imbecility*.)

Finally, the theory-minded raised the banners of those other Isidores of Seville, Foucault and Barthes, to connect Yasusada to "the death of the author," an advertising campaign that was wildly successful in the academic market, but had limited appeal to readers and writers. It was true that the Yasusada Author refused to step from behind the curtain—at the opposite extreme from Joyce Carol Oates, who writes "pseudonymous" books that are labeled, on the cover, "Joyce Carol Oates writing under the name of ...."—but pseudonymous authorship, even when fractured into heteronyms (Pessoa) still assigns production to a single named source. True invisibility—the "text itself"—could easily be achieved by publishing every book and every magazine contribution under a different name. Writers, as far as one knows, have never practiced it; if one were that egoless, one wouldn't be a writer.

Yasusada had appeared at a moment when the Eng. Dept. had split into two contradictory "postmodernisms": multiculturalism and deconstruction (and its spin-offs). One side wanted to hear the stories that hadn't been told, and the other doubted that stories could be told; one side promoted authenticity, and the other inauthenticity. The former embraced Yasusada and then violently rejected him when his identity became questionable—the precise moment when the latter embraced him.

Finally, for all the talk of Orientalism and "Japonoiserie," no one has discussed Yasusada as the latest chapter in the American invention of Japanese poetry. The Yasusada poems are very much written in the style, not of Japanese poetry, but of American translations of Japanese poetry, including some witty intentional infelicities and bits of translationese. Moreover, they could only have been written in recent years, for they owe a great deal to the work of Hiroaki Sato.

Sato, the most prolific contemporary translator of classical and modern Japanese poetry has, since the 1970s, vigorously promoted the idea of translating haiku and tanka (and by extension, renga) as single English sentences without line breaks—the way the poems are written out in Japanese. Sato's work has been widely and unjustly reviled by the academics, but it is precisely Sato's form of presentation—not necessarily the Japanese poems themselves—that were clearly determining for the Yasusada Author. (Some have mistakenly attributed the Yasusada prose-poem line to Ron Silliman's so-called "new sentence," which is comparable but not the origin.)

Yasusada, regardless of authorship, is very much an American Japanese poet: a product of the specifically American tradition of translating Japanese poetry. (It is stylistically highly unlikely that the Author is Russian or Spanish or French.) While it is true that the initial reception was due largely to the biography—and in that sense the work was exploitative of the publishing climate and the poems a "hoax"— the creation of the work is clearly an act of empathy and compassion. The Yasusada Author has merely taken the invention of a first-person narrator of a novel one step further: along with speaking, thinking, seeing, feeling, this fictional character now writes. In many ways, the work is far more interesting, full of brilliant details, after one knows that Yasusada is an invention. He is both the greatest poet of Hiroshima and its most unreliable witness.

In Search of the Authentic Other:
The Poetry of Araki Yasusada

Marjorie Perloff

The July/August 1996 issue of *American Poetry Review* featured a special supplement called 'Doubled Flowering: From the Notebooks of Araki Yasusada.' Translations of this Japanese poet had already appeared in such leading periodicals as *Grand Street*, *Conjunctions*, *Aerial*, *First Intensity*, and Jon Silkin's British poetry journal *Stand*. According to Yasusada's three translators—Tosa Motokiyu, Okura Kyojin, and Ojiu Norinaga—all three, like the poet, from Hiroshima—Yasusada's notebooks were discovered by his son in 1980, eight years following the poet's death. These fourteen notebooks contained dozens of poems, drafts, English class assignments, diary entries, drawings, letters, and recordings of Zen dokusan encounters. None of this material, it seems, had been published during Yasusada's lifetime. The following biographical note, prepared by the translators, appears, with slight variation in each of the periodicals cited above:

> Yasusada was born in 1907 in the city of Kyoto, where he lived until 1921, when his family moved to Hiroshima. He attended Hiroshima University sporadically between 1925 and 1928, with the intent of receiving a degree in Western Literature. Due, however, to his father's illness, he was forced, in the interests of the family, to undertake full-time employment with the postal service and withdraw from his formal studies.
>
> In 1930 he married his only wife Nomura, with whom he had two daughters and a son. In 1936, Yasusada was conscripted into the Japanese Imperial Army and worked as a clerk in the Hiroshima division of the Military Postal Service. His wife and youngest daughter, Chieko, died instantly in the atomic blast on August 6. His daughter Akiko survived, yet perished less than four years later from radiation sickness. His son, Yasunari, an infant at the time, was with relatives outside the city.
>
> Yasusada died in 1972 after a long struggle with cancer. (*APR* 23; *Doubled* 10)

We are further told that Yasusada was active in avant-garde groups of the pre-War period like *Soun* [*Layered Clouds*] and the experimental renga circle *Kai* [*Oars*] and that in the sixties he "discovered" Jack Spicer and Roland Barthes (*APR* 23; *Doubled* 10). A 1967 letter to his renga collaborator Akutagawa Fusei, included in the *APR* selection, talks enthusiastically of Barthes's *Empire of Signs* (*APR* 24; *Doubled* 79), and the translators further comment that there are undated haiku that "unmistakably bear the stamp of the famous poet, and Holocaust survivor, Paul Celan," whose work "was read by the Layered Clouds group and critically discussed by them" (*APR* 26; *Doubled* 93).

The poems—of which more in a moment—have aroused great interest and enthusiasm. In response to the *Conjunctions* portfolio, the poet Ron Silliman told his friends and fellow poets on the Buffalo Poetics List that the journal had introduced "a poet whose work simply takes my breath away." Citing the short 'Telescope with Urn,' which begins with the line "The image of the galaxies spreads out like a cloud of sperm," Silliman remarks, "There's an elevation of tone in these poems that reminds me more of Michael Palmer than Spicer, perhaps because the translators are all Hiroshima poets (one of whom seems to spend half of each year in Sebastapol [CA], although I don't know if he's known to [David] Bromige or to Cydney Chadwick). These works kept me up last night and probably will again for another night or three. I recommend them highly" (Silliman).

Yet even as the Yasusada poems were prompting this sort of response, the word was leaking out that there was no Yasusada, that indeed the whole Yasusada publication was an elaborate hoax, perpetrated, most probably, by one Kent Johnson, a young poet-professor at Highland Community College in Freeport, Illinois. Johnson, the co-editor, with Stephen M. Ashby, of an anthology of New Russian poetry called *The Third Wave* and, with Craig Paulenich, of an anthology of contemporary American Buddhist poetry called *Beneath a Single Moon*, still doesn't admit to inventing Yasusada; he now declares that the "real" author is the Yasusada translator Tosa Motokiyu (a pseudonym, in its turn, of yet another unknown poet who is safely dead). But when *American Poetry Review* and *Stand* recently demanded the return of their author's payment, it was to Kent Johnson they addressed their letters. And since he is at the very least the middleman and facilitator of the "hoax," as a matter of convenience, I shall refer to him here as its author.

According to *Lingua Franca*, which ran an article on 'The Hiroshima

Poetry Hoax' in its November 1996 issue, Arthur Vogelsang, one of the three editors of *American Poetry Review*, went so far as to call Johnson's deception a "criminal act" (Nussbaum 82).[1] Wesleyan University Press, which had contemplated publishing a volume of Yasusada poems, immediately dropped the project: an anonymous reader, whose report was made available to me by Kent Johnson, expressed great admiration for the poems but felt queasy at the suggestion that the manuscript might be a hoax, it being out of bounds, in the reader's estimation, for anyone to impersonate a figure as *ipso facto* tragic as a Hiroshima survivor.

While these editors and publishers have taken issue with what they perceive as the immorality of the hoax, scholars have objected to its inaccuracy. "This is just Japanized crap," John Solt, a professor of Japanese culture at Amherst College, told *Lingua Franca*'s Emily Nussbaum. "It plays into the American idea of what is interesting about Japanese culture—Zen, haiku, anything seen as exotic—and gets it all wrong, adding Western humor and irony." (Nussbaum 83). Yet this estimate may also be a simplification. For Solt, like *APR*'s Vogelsang and the anonymous reader for Wesleyan, are assuming that Kent Johnson (or whoever the "real" Yasusada turns out to be) produced as accurate a simulation as possible, whereas the fact is that the author has put in, surely not unintentionally, any number of clues that raise questions as to Yasusada's authenticity. Consider the following:

1) The name Araki Yasusada means, in Japanese usage, that Araki is the family name, Yasusada the first name. Araki is indeed a common family name in Japanese.[2] Yet the "translators" regularly refer to the poet as Yasusada, which would be equivalent to referring to Roland Barthes as Roland. By the same token, the poet's wife's name, Nomura, is in fact a family name, not a first name, so the reference given would be like Robert Lowell referring to his wife as Hardwick. Again, "Motokiyu" is a misspelling for "Motokiyo" and "Ojiu" should be 'Ogyu." So the author is, at the very least, playing fast and loose with Japanese names.

---

[1] In the September/October issue of *American Poetry Review*, the editors published a recension of the Yasusada 'Special Supplement,' and apologized to their readership for the fraud.

[2] I owe this and subsequent bits of information about Japanese usage to Dr. Akitoshi Nagahata of Nagoya University.

2) It is hard to accept the explanation that Yasusada, who was supposedly active in avant-garde groups in the 1920s and 30s, never tried to publish any of his postwar poems and that they were entirely unknown in his native Japan, where he seems to have had the liveliest of correspondences with his fellow poets.

3) Yasusada, we are told, "attended Hiroshima University sporadically between 1925 and 1928, with the intent of receiving a degree in Western Literature." His attendance must have been sporadic indeed since Hiroshima University was not founded until 1949. As for studying Western Literature, there would have been no such subject. English Literature, French Literature—these were and are academic subjects, but the idea of Yasusada studying "Western" literature looks like an American representation of what a Japanese might do.

4) Yasusada ostensibly came under the influence of Jack Spicer in the mid-60s, which is to say when Yasusada was in his late fifties. This is implausible on a number of counts. First, Jack Spicer was an unknown coterie poet at the time; indeed, he is still largely an unknown coterie poet, whose work does not appear in any of the major anthologies. It is, of course, conceivable that the poet's friend Natsume Kuribayashi brought the book *After Lorca* (1957) back to Hiroshima from a visit to San Francisco. But if so, Yasusada must have been the only poet in Japan who took an interest in Spicer.

5) Roland Barthes is listed as a second major influence. But *The Empire of Signs*, which Yasusada supposedly pored over in 1967, wasn't even published in French until 1970. The U.S. edition dates from 1982. There is thus no way Yasusada could have read this book, and Barthes' earlier works were, like Spicer's, only very little known outside France.

6) Paul Celan, ostensibly read and studied by the *Soun* group before World War II, did not start publishing—and then in German— until 1952. So the notion that he was closely studied in the Japan of the thirties is totally absurd.

7) Finally, there is a wonderful clinamen in the November 7, 1967 letter to the poet's collaborator, Fusei. "Besides Spicer," writes Yasusada, "there are interesting new books here waiting for you by poets named Gary Snyder, Bob Kaufman, Kenneth Rexroth, Howard McCord, Robert Creeley, Helen Adams [*sic*], and Lawrence Ferlinghetti. Kuribayashi tells me that they were strongly recommended to him by

McCord, the owner of City Lights Bookstore, a popular bookseller in San Francisco" (*APR* 26; *Doubled* 78). Now we can, with a stretch of the imagination, accept the fact that the sixty-year old Hiroshima survivor, whose poetic habits would most probably have been formed much earlier, would interest himself in the newest Beat poets from the U.S. But the give-away in the list is Howard McCord, not a Bay Area poet at all but a poet-professor from Bowling Green University who was Kent Johnson's college mentor. Hence the sly footnote provided by Yasusada's translators: "Yasusada is confused here, as the real owner of the City Lights Bookstore is Lawrence Ferlinghetti" (*APR* 26; *Doubled* 79).

Clearly, if the inventor of the Yasusada persona had wanted to cover his tracks, he need never have mentioned Howard McCord or the influence of Celan on Yasusada, much less the Japanese poet's reading of Barthes's *Empire of Signs*. We can only conclude that the "real" author wanted his readers to find something perplexing in the Yasusada archive, that he purposely set the stage for suspicion. The very first poem in the *APR* Supplement, for example, is represented as a "modest gathering of haiku" sent to Yasusada's friend, the haiku master Ogiwara Seisensui.[3] The poem is dated March 30, 1925 and goes like this:

> iris moon sheaths
> scubadivers chrysanthemums also
> deer inlets dream
> oars this earth
> geese lined bowl
> shard so horizon
> cod dried dawn
> bones sky written
> lichened space rock
> fossils celebrating investors
> crematorium shared persimmon
> hyacinth clustered strangers
> cranes three words (*APR* 24; *Doubled* 50)

This looks rather like a page of ideogram transcriptions from the Ernest Fenollosa notebooks that Ezra Pound used when composing his *Cathay*:

---

[3] Seisensui is a real haiku master, although again the name is reversed; the family name is Ogiwara.

> gathering gathering fixed clouds
> pattering pattering temporary rain
> eight surface same dark
> flat road this wide & flat[4]

But what are those "scubadivers" doing between the chrysanthemums and the iris? The technology of scuba diving was not invented until World War II, which also gave "Yasusada" the word "crematorium." As for "investors" in line 10, this reference to capitalist activity does not exactly belong to the haiku discourse radius of hyacinths and persimmons, cranes and lichen. The perspective is rather like Pound's in the *Homage to Sextus Propertius* (1917), where the lines "My cellar does not date from Numa Pompilius, / Nor bristle with wine jars," is followed by the startling, "Nor is it equipped with a frigidaire patent" (Pound 206). What such overlays do is to take the material in question out of its temporal and spatial frame, problematizing its representation and tone. And this, for Johnson-Yasusada, as for Pound-Propertius, is clearly intentional.

Why, then, given such obvious clues as "scubadivers" and "crematorium," have editors and readers so quickly assumed that they are dealing with an "authentic" Hiroshima poet? We cannot just dismiss these disseminators as ignorant, for they include editors and writers as varied as they are talented. Bradford Morrow, for one, came to *Conjunctions* as an Ezra Pound scholar and editor; he published, for example, the excellent facsimile editions of the Pound-Wyndham Lewis Vorticist magazine *Blast*. Rod Smith's *Aerial* has played a central role in the introduction of radical new poetries: the issue that includes Yasusada's works also contains a preview of Joan Retallack's *Musicage* as well as Cage's own piece "Art Is Either A Complaint Or Do Something Else" and Jackson Mac Low's *Merzgedicht* for Kurt Schwitters.[5] And there are few contemporary poets more widely read, engaged, and intellectually lively than the poet-editor-critic Ron Silliman, who declared that Yasusada's memorable phrases kept him awake at night.

---

[4] See Kenner, p. 207. The passage transcribes the Chinese poem "The Unmoving Cloud" by To-Em-Mei.

[5] In conversation, Rod Smith has told me that he suspected all along the manuscript he received was a hoax, but he found it so charming and apropos he decided to publish it.

II

To understand why Silliman and Morrow, Jean Stein of *Grand Street*, and Jon Silkin, the longtime editor of the British radical quarterly *Stand* were "taken in" by the Yasusada manuscripts, we must look at the larger issues of multicultural and cross-cultural reception on the current poetry scene. The Yasusada case, I shall argue here, can be understood as a reaction formation experienced by a literary community that no longer trusts the individual talent to rise above mass culture and hence must find a poetry worthy of its attention in increasingly remote and improbable locations. "Excellence," now largely dismissed as an essentialist concept, is subordinated to issues of agency and positionality, the master text here no doubt still being Michel Foucault's famous 1969 essay, "What Is an Author?"

Foucault's central position, which has come to be *de rigueur* in the academy, is that it is the culture that constructs or *writes* the author, not vice-versa: "the essential basis of . . . writing is not the exalted emotions related to the act of composition or the insertion of a subject into language. Rather, it is primarily concerned with creating an opening where the writing subject endlessly disappears" (Foucault 116). Disappears because, far from being "free" to write whatever he or she wishes, the writing subject can only work within the limits of the dominant discourse and hence is no more than a function of the discourse within which it circulates. No longer then do we ask "What has [the author] revealed of his most profound self in his language?" The question is rather, "Where does [this discourse] come from; how is it circulated; who controls it? What placements are determined for possible subjects?" (Foucault 138). Who, in other words, is empowered to speak and from what position? And, once these questions become central, emphasis falls on those who have, thus far, not been empowered to speak—in earlier centuries, women and lower-class writers; in our own moment, the victims of oppression of whatever stamp: Colonialist, racist, sexist, homophobic, and so on.

In practice, of course, these questions of positionality and empowerment have become very complicated. In the case of Yasusada, it would be a simplification to suggest that the editors and readers who responded so warmly to the work did so only—or even primarily—

because the poet was that rare thing, a previously unknown Hiroshima survivor, a witness to the events of August 6, 1945. But certainly the Hiroshima witnessing is a central factor in the equation. Let me explain.

From the fifties to the late eighties when the Cold War came to an end, and with it, the urgency of world-wide protests against the production and testing of nuclear weapons, an appreciable number of Japanese poetry books and anthologies appeared on the horrors of Hiroshima and Nagasaki. A recent such anthology is Jiro Nakano's *Outcry from the Inferno: Atom Bomb Tanka Anthology*.[6] The preface is by the leading tanka poet Seishi Toyota, a Hiroshima survivor who suffered from radiation poisoning and declared that "writing and reading atomic bomb tanka are my karma and life-long work" (xiii). The typical tanka in the anthology goes like this:

> Like a demon or ghost
> a man runs away
> staggering—
> with both hands
> hung loosely in front of him. (2)

or,

> A crowd of ten thousand
> are standing in despair
> with skins hanging
> from red sores—
> the scorched land of Hiroshima. (51)

Or, occasionally more polemically:

> Mothers, wives, sisters
> and grandmothers—
> remember your losses,
> Stand up and fill those prisons.
> Defy the draft! (18)

---

[6] According to Earl Miner, "*Tanka* is a Japanese form originating in the 7th century which consists of 31 morae (conventionally construed syllables) in lines of 5, 7, 5, 7, and 7. Hypersyllabic but not hyposyllabic lines are allowed." "It is," says Miner, "the definitive literary form in Japanese poetry" (1265).

These tanka are obviously more notable for their subject matter than for their poetic quality. A more sophisticated version of Japanese atomic bomb literature is found in Richard Minear's *Hiroshima: Three Witnesses*. Minear's three are the fabulist Hara Tamiki, the novelist Ota Yoko, and the poet Toge Sankichi. Toge is probably the key figure in Hiroshima literature: his *Poems of the Atomic Bomb*, written in 1951 when he was already dying from a radiation-related illness, has gone through more than forty printings. Instead of the haiku and tanka he had used in his pre-war poetry, Toge here uses free verse, with much rhetorical variation: onomatopoeia, repetition, elaborate sound play. Here is the opening of 'Dying' (in Minear's translation), a poem that Jerome Rothenberg and Pierre Joris have chosen for inclusion in the second volume of their *Poems for the Millennium*:

> Loud in my ear: screams.
> Soundlessly welling up,
> pouncing on me:
> space, all upside-down
> Hanging, fluttering clouds of dust
> smelling of smoke,
> and, running madly about, figures.
> "Ah,
> get out
> of here!"
> Scattering fragments of brick,
> I spring to my feet;
> my body's
> on fire. . . .
> (308)

And the poem concludes with a passage in which extinction is represented not only verbally but metrically, four one-word lines culminating in the silence of the final line, which contains no more than a single question mark:

> Why here
> by the side of the road
> cut off, dear, from you;
> why

>   must
>   I
>   die
>   ?
>   (310)

Toge is probably the most noted realist chronicler of the Hiroshima tragedy: over and over again, he records the chaos and suffering of ordinary people in the fire storms of August. A short poem of his called 'Give the People Back' appeared in a 1985 *American Poetry Review* portfolio on Hiroshima poets, in which Suneko Yoshikawa presents four poems (one of them her own), translated by the Canadian poet Steven Forth. Here a full page of background information is followed by two short pages of poetry. These poems are again straightforward and often polemic monologues, as in the case of Hara Tamiki's "Water Please," with its lines like "Help me help me / Water / Water/ Somewhere / Someone" (8).[7]

But although the testimonials of the *hibakusha* (atomic bomb survivors) continue to play a central role in Japanese culture, and although there has been a definite market for Hiroshima-witness poems, especially in the West, the fact is—and this will shed light on Yasusada's position—that contemporary Japanese poets have been reluctant to write about Hiroshima or, for that matter, about the culture of nuclear weapons. No doubt, memories of a war that the then wholly nationalist, autocratic, and bellicose Imperial Japanese government had initiated are too painful; for those born after 1945, moreover, these memories no longer seem directly relevant. "It is difficult," the young poet-scholar Nagahata Akitoshi remarked in a letter to me (January 15, 1997), "for us to talk about Hiroshima / Nagasaki, because to do so would always make us question our subjectivity. We are sons and daughters of the people who were bombed, but at the same time of the oppressors. We

---

[7] An interesting recent Hiroshima memoir is Hideko Tamura Snider's *One Sunny Day: A Child's Memories of Hiroshima*. Tamura Snider was ten years old the day of the attack and her account of the devastation is very vivid and moving. But for her and her characteristically apolitical family (a family living at a time when the government ruled by decree and there were no opposition parties), Hiroshima essentially meant the loss of one's nearest and dearest (Hideko Tamura lost her mother), and how the populace coped with that loss. The issues are not construed as "political."

could blame our fate on the politicians at the time (i.e., militarists) or on the war in the abstract. But I think this is an evasion."

Nagahata's observations are confirmed by the literature. Open any volume like Leith Morton's *Anthology of Contemporary Japanese Poetry* and you will find an extraordinarily colloquial, often casual, postmodern poetry that deals with every aspect of sexuality, with themes of longing and frustration, memories of childhood, contemplation of urban congestion and natural beauty, with self-interrogation and remorse, the relation of private to public, individual identity to culture and to the natural world—in short, pretty much all the themes that would characterize our own poetry[8]. Six of the sixteen poets in Morton's anthology are women—and very emancipated women at that. The performance poet Shiraishi Kazuko (b. 1931), for example, has a poem written for her friend Sumiko's birthday that is called "Penis" (*Dankon*) and begins:

> God is not here but he exists
> Also he is funny so
> He's like a certain type of person
> This time
> Bringing a gigantic penis above
> The horizon of my dream
> He came for a picnic
> By the way
> I'm sorry
> I didn't give anything to Sumiko for her birthday
> The seed of the penis that God brought if only that
> I want to send into
> The delicate small sweet voice of
> Sumiko on the end of the line (Shiraishi 197)

Shiraishi had worked closely with Kenneth Rexroth: her mode is a ribald version of Beat or San Francisco Renaissance poems, going back, perhaps, to the bitter-sweet erotic free verse poems of Apollinaire.

---

[8] Another excellent anthology is *Modern Japanese Poetry*, trans. James Kirkup, ed. A. R. Davis (St. Lucia, Queensland: University of Queensland Press, 1978). Kirkup's range is wider than Morton's—he includes eighty-three poets as compared to Morton's sixteen—but thematically, tonally, and prosodically, the poems are quite similar.

Scubadivers and Chrysanthemums

Another free-verse poem, this time by a younger woman poet, Ito Hiromi (b. 1955), is called 'Don't Squash Them,' and begins:

> I make some dumplings out of rice-flour and bring
> Them to my man
> Boil sugar and make a syrup
> Immerse the cooked dumplings in it
> Refrigerate them
> Pack them into an air-tight container
> And bring them along
> The dumplings stick to the bottom of the container
> The skin of the dumplings remain stuck
> The round
> Shape is distorted
> He scoops them out with a spoon
> Hey
> Watch out
> Scoop them up
> Without squashing them!
> (Tanikawa 367)

And the rest of the poem wittily relates the dumpling-eating incident to their subsequent love-making. Throughout, the poet's tone is one of detached bemusement, a tone we find most fully developed in the work of the celebrated postwar poet Tanikawa Shuntaro, who has a predilection for short riddling lyrics or fables like 'The Poet':

> If there is a mirror the poet will always look into it
> He makes certain whether or not he is a poet
> Even if he reads poetry he doesn't know whether or not he's a poet
> He firmly believes that if he looks at his face he can tell with a
>   single glance
> The poet is dreaming that one day
> His face will be put on a stamp
> He says he wants if possible to have his face on a really cheap
>   stamp
> Then he can have lots of people lick him
> While his wife is frying some noodles
> She has a sour puss (LM 358).

Tanikawa, Ito, Shiraishi—these are hardly well-known poets in the U.S. Indeed, the very *American Poetry Review* that published Yasusada and then called the submission of the manuscript a "criminal act," has, in the past fifteen years, published no other translations of contemporary Japanese poetry with the exception of the Hiroshima portfolio I cited above. Bengali women poets, underground Chinese, Polish and Rumanian, Nicaraguan, and South African poets—all these appear in the pages of *APR* as does a feature on two medieval Japanese women court poets, as translated by Jane Hirschfield and Mariko Aratani, and a special supplement on the Zen Master Muso (Muso Sosei, 1275–1351) translated by W.S. Merwin with the help of Soiku Shigematsu. But the new Japanese poets, whose brilliance and variousness are extremely impressive, are not sought out. And I have noticed the same trend in the other periodicals under consideration.

Why this neglect of contemporary Japanese poetry? Why the equation of "Japanese" with the courtly or Zen tradition of the distant past? Perhaps because modern, or rather postmodern Japan is too close to our own advanced capitalist world, too similar in its First World obsession with technology, urban and ecological problems, and so on. To put it another way, Japanese poetry—most of it in free verse and, like the poems above, in colloquial, up-to-date idiom—will not allow itself to be patronized; it is neither a poetry of victims nor of the oppressed, and it defines itself as a poetry very much of the present rather than of the historical imagination.

III

How Japanese, then, is Yasusada's lyric? And how does that lyric relate to our own late twentieth-century paradigms? Let me begin with the poem that so impressed Ron Silliman, 'Telescope with Urn' from *Conjunctions*:

> The image of the galaxies spreads out like a cloud of sperm.
> Expanding said the observatory guide, and at such and such
>   velocity.
> It is like the idea of the flowers, opening within the idea of the
>   flowers.

> I like to think of that, said the monk, arranging them with his papery fingers.
>
> Tiny were you, and squatted over a sky-colored bowl to make water.
>
> What a big girl! cried we, tossing you in the general direction of the stars.
>
> Intently, then, in the dream, I folded up the great telescope on Mount Horai.
>
> In the form of this crane, it is small enough for the urn.
>
> (CON 69; *Doubled* 32)

Compared to the Japanese poems I cited a moment ago, 'Telescope with Urn' is elliptical and fragmentary. Each line, set off from the next by double spacing, is a separate sentence, and the sentences, while straightforward syntactically, tend not to connect. Reference, moreover, is often unclear as in "I like to think of that, said the monk, arranging them with his papery fingers," where we know neither what "that" is nor what "them" the monk is arranging. The poem's ellipsis is coupled with syntactic inversion, as in "Tiny were you" and "What a big girl! cried we," with the Zen-like repetition of such phrases as "It is like the idea of the flowers, opening within the idea of the flowers," and with the circumlocution of "squatted over a sky-colored bowl to make water."

The effect of such devices is that the poem has a reassuringly "archaic," "oriental" feel; its reticence, dignity, and elusiveness, its references to Mount Horai, flowers, and stars, bring to mind the ritual and stylization of Noh and Bunraku. At the same time, the "Japanese" nature imagery is eroticized in a distinctly modern way, and the "scientific" reference to the "velocity" of the expansion of the galaxies reminds us that this is an up-to-date lyric. And not just any up-to-date lyric but one about Hiroshima: "Telescope with Urn" refers to the death of the poet's young daughter in the nuclear raid. The urn with the crane on it is hers, and the poem contrasts the enormity of the macrocosm (the galaxies) with the terrifying microcosm of the life reduced to ashes inside the small urn.

Kent Johnson has thus found a perfect recipe for a new Orientalism, conceived in the best American tradition of Emerson's doctrine of "natural" hieroglyphic language, Pound's *Cathay*, and, most recently,

Marjorie Perloff

Kenneth Rexroth's *Love Poems of Marichiko* (1978), presented by the poet as translations of the erotic lyrics of an actual Japanese woman although Rexroth later admitted he had made them up entirely himself.[9] The *Love Poems of Marichiko*, which Johnson surely knew, provided him with a blueprint for the fusion of concrete sexual imagery and "Buddhist" reticence.

But in the wake of the disjunctive poetry of the eighties and nineties, the demand is for greater obliquity, fragmentation, dislocation. For these, Johnson evidently turned to one of Rexroth's contemporaries, the Jack Spicer who produced the exotic *After Lorca*. Here is a sample:

> In the middle of my mirror
> A girl is drowning
> The voice of a single girl.
> She holds cold fire like a glass
> Each thing she watches
> Has become double.
> Cold fire is
> Cold fire is.
> In the middle of my mirror
> A girl is drowning
> The voice of a single girl. (Spicer 46–47).

Spicer's poem is not as fragmented as Yasusada's but it has the same simple declarative sentences, the concrete imagery, the direct, naive tone, the delicate obliquity and ellipsis, as in "Cold fire is / Cold fire is." Like Spicer, Yasusada is obsessed by images of death, but, as Johnson has understood, in the post-Cold War era, there is little calling for the realistic descriptions of dismemberment favored by, say, Toge Sankichi. At the same time, Western guilt about the dropping of the bomb is such that the reader is programmed to find Yasusada's muted references to the Hiroshima "tragedy" moving, especially when these references are matter-of-fact and stoic.

'Telescope and Urn' thus satisfies our longing for a Japan, rather like that of Barthes' *Empire of Signs*, an imaginary Japan that is gentler

---

[9] See Robert Kern's excellent *Orientalism, Modernism, and the American Poem*. The classic discussion of orientalism as a Western discourse is, of course, Edward Said's in *Orientalism*.

and more dignified than the brash West, a world of grace, ritual, and transience, of elegant calligraphy and Zen gardens, a world in which the wrapping of packages is an art and chopsticks delicately separate bits of food, unlike those Western knives and forks which brutally cut up slices of meat. "It is like the idea of the flowers, opening within the idea of the flowers." Those delicate flowers, perhaps, that emerge from little paper balls dropped into a glass of water.

Consider another Yasusada poem, this one published in the little magazine *First Intensity* under the title 'Mad Daughter and Big-Bang' and subtitled 'December 25, 1945*,' the mock footnote explaining that "In the aftermath of the bombing, many survivors moved into the hills, surrounding Hiroshima. This was the case with Yasusada and his daughter. –eds."

> Walking in the vegetable patch
> late at night, I was startled to find
> the severed head of my
> mad daughter lying on the ground.
> Her eyes were upturned, gazing at me, ecstatic-like . . .
> (From a distance it had appeared
> to be a stone, haloed with light,
> as if cast there by the Big-Bang.)
> What on earth are you doing, I said,
> you look ridiculous.
> Some boys buried me here,
> she said sullenly.
> Her dark hair, comet-like, trailed behind . . .
> Squatting, I pulled the
> turnip up by the root. (*First* 10; *Doubled* 11)

Here the reference is again to the death of the poet's daughter in the Hiroshima raid. But the technique is somewhat different: for the elliptical and dislocated sentences of 'Telescope and Urn,' Johnson here substitutes narrative—a kind of "magic realist" narrative in which events are displaced and transformed. The hallucinatory presence of the dead child, transformed into a "mad daughter," the speech of the "severed head," the Maenad-like image of "dark hair, comet-like, trail[ing] behind," and the title's ironic allusion to "Big-Bang" theories—these give the poem the semblance of a dream, or rather a nightmare. At the same time, the daughter's "sullen" explanation that "Some boys buried me," is literally quite true if we take the "boys" to be the U.S. military. Again, in the poem's conclusion, the surreal image of "Squatting, I pulled the turnip up by the root," is accurate enough if we read it as a reference to the easy removal of the charred and rotten corpse from the ground in which the live body was "rooted." Such images play into the residual guilt of contemporary American readers, even as the poem's multiple ironies temper that guilt, allowing us to concentrate on the effectiveness of Johnson's fiction, especially the immediacy of the terse dialogue between father and daughter.

One would be hard put to find actual Hiroshima witness poems (or even later Japanese re-enactments of Hiroshima poems) that are characterized by such irony and restraint, such self-consciously surreal, oblique images. Rather, the matter-of-factness of the disconnected sentences, both here and elsewhere in the Yasusada manuscript, recalls such long prose poems as Ron Silliman's *Tjanting*. A Yasusada poem in *Grand Street* #53 (1995), for example, begins with the line "The sake shop hisses with its pleasures, all boiled up," and continues with such sentences as "Here is a black-haired man with a black-haired man," or "There are two sticks and a cup in Spring" (*GS* 25; *Doubled* 48). The relationship of these present-tense, simple declarative sentences to those that compose Japanese renga is taken up in a piece which was evidently Yasusada's American debut, the "tape-essay" called 'Renga and the New Sentence,' conducted in Madison, Wisconsin, December 1989, by Tosa Motokiyu, Ojiu Norinaga, and Okura Kyojin—the three familiar Yasusada translators-editors—and published in *Aerial*. The dialogue takes up the issue of what Ron Silliman, in a well-known essay by that name, defined as "The New Sentence," a "sentence" that is the building block of the new "poetic" prose, even as the line is the basic unit of the conventional poem. Tosa Motokiyu and his collaborators cite Silliman's definition (see *New* 91) verbatim:

1. The paragraph organizes the sentences;
2. The paragraph is a unit of quantity, not logic or argument;
3. Sentence length is a unit of measure;
4. Sentence structure is altered for torque, or increased polysemy / ambiguity;

> 5. Syllogistic movement is (a) limited; (b) controlled . . .
> (*Aerial* 54)

Silliman, they note, claimed that the only precursor of the "New Sentence" was the William Carlos Williams of *Kora in Hell*, but, as they demonstrate, the "New Sentence" has a more significant source in "the Japanese haikai/renga—forms that anticipate by more than four centuries a number of the principles underlying 'new sentence' approaches to composition" (*Aerial* 52). As Motokiyu explains it, renga, like the "new sentence," is animated by "the faith that non-syllogistic movement may open onto alternate forms of perception" (*Aerial* 52). In twentieth-century experimental renga, moreover, "the stanzas shatter their prosodic constraints and move brazenly into prose," forcing "the written into new conceptual territory" (*Aerial* 52). And Kyojin cites Earl Miner's definition of renga in *Japanese Linked Verse*:

> (T)he renga is no single thing. It has been practiced in short versions of two stanzas and in long versions up to ten thousand . . . (T)he art of linked poetry involves adding stanzas in such a fashion as to keep something but to change the meaning of what might be called the stanza itself and the stanza in connection with its predecessor. In such fashion the sequence is truly sequential and a sustained plot is impossible. (*Aerial* 52, ellipses are the author's).

Modes of linking, according to the translators, include "flat linking," "mosaic linking," "linking through paragram," "linking through assonances," and so on, all these devices "generating a prismatic and collective textuality" (*Aerial* 52, ellipses are the author's). And they cite a traditional renga written by Matsuo Basho and Shita Yaba, which begins:

> (MB) At a fragrance of plums, a blob, the sun, appears on a mountain path.
> (SY) here and there a pheasant call rises
> (SY) he begins repairing his house while there's nothing to do in spring
> (MB) news from Kansai raises the price of rice
> (MB) in the evening there was some pattering—now the moon among clouds

(SY) talking with a bush in between—the autumn, the
  loneliness
(*Aerial* 53)

The American Language poets now get a slight slap on the wrist because "they have not begun, really, to seriously move outside the ideologically constructed parameters of single-author composition"; indeed, with rare exceptions like *Legend* (written by Bruce Andrews, Charles Bernstein, Ray Di Palma, Steve McCaffery and Ron Silliman), they have insisted on "self attribution" and "personal ownership" of texts" (*Aerial* 55). They should, according to our Japanese discussants, experiment more fully with depersonalized Buddhist sensibilities, should eschew ownership of their verse. And now we are introduced to a renga by three Hiroshima poets: Araki Yasusada, Ozaki Kusatao and Akutagawa Fusei.

This renga, ostensibly of the 1930s, is introduced by a defensive letter of June 1937 from Yasusada to Ogiwara Seisensui, the head of the *Soun* avant-garde group. Yasusada defends the "impure" linking used in their renga and argues that "*dissonance*" is its "deep measure." A footnote on the part of the translators tells us that this letter is "among the over 100 carbon copies of Yasusada's letters in our possession. It is interesting that Yasusada and his friends were very influenced by the American poet Jack Spicer; indeed, a few of their renga are dedicated to him" (*Aerial* 59). And they insert another letter, this one to Fusei, dated November 17, 1965, in which Yasusada describes his enthusiasm for the "new" California poets whose books his friend Natsume Kuribayashi has brought to Hiroshima: Robert Duncan, Alex [sic] Ginsberg, John Wieners, Brother Antoninus, Philip Lamantia, and especially Jack Spicer, whose *Billy the Kid*, and *Heads of the Town Up to the Aether* are declared to be kindred works (*Aerial* 59).[10]

There are a number of incongruous details here. Why, to begin with, would such "experts" as Tosa Motokiyu and his friends rely on the American scholar Earl Miner's definition of renga? And how could the footnote to the 1937 letter refer to the Spicer influence, Spicer then being twelve years old! Neither the editor of *Aerial* nor the journal's

---

[10] Note that this list overlaps with that in the November 7 letter, also to Fusei, (*APR* 26, *Doubled* 93).

readers seem to have been bothered by these lacunae, evidently because the affiliation of the "new" Language poetry with the "old" renga seemed so appealing, giving Silliman's own poems a new authority. Here are the first nine lines of the renga itself:

> Happening to notice the willow leaves in the garden, a braille page of words
> The voices of the sorority girls sing of fucking in a plaintive way
> Dressing their frail bodies in armor are the young widows of the prefecture of
> It was there we saw the trace ruins of an ancient dog-shooting range
> So running after me was the young child whose name is Manifold
> A screen of moonflowers and creeping gourds, with a thicket of cockscomb and goosefoot, evoking cocks and cunts
> She told me that the master of the house had left for a certain location in town and that I had better look for him there pronto, if I desired to speak to him
> Everybody was fucking overjoyed to see him, as if he had returned from the dead
> Terrified by these words he walked straight into the province of Kaga
> (*Aerial* 57–58)

The translator Okura Kyojin comments: "Similarities with 'new sentence' writing seem compelling. The hokku unit is now extended out into pure prose utterance. As Fusei says elsewhere: 'no easy messages, no intention to share self-emotion; no lyrical intensity—percussive soundings within patterns of harmonic and dissonant chords. Utterance as autonomous fact *and* its saturation in context. *This* tension. Gaps now as intrinsic to such grammar. . .'" (*Aerial* 58, ellipses the author's).

What could sound more contemporary, more late twentieth-century American than the frank sexual references to the "sorority girls" who "sing of fucking," and to "cocks and cunts" as well as to the slang of "Everybody was fucking overjoyed" or "I had better look for him there pronto." And yet all the Japanese properties are here: the "willow leaves in the garden," the "screen of moonflowers and creeping gourds," the "master of the house," the young girls' "frail bodies" the "province of Kaga." The layering of language registers reminds me of nothing so much as Pound's *Elektra*, where the poet brings Sophocles' great tragedy into his own post-World war II orbit (the play was written with Rudd Fleming while Pound was incarcerated in St. Elizabeth's) by juxtaposing lines of the original Greek (especially in Electra's speeches) to the Western twang of Orestes' revenge speech:

> This is what we're agoin' to do,
> listen sharp and check up if
> I miss any bullseyes . . .
> you nip into this building, find out everything that's
> being done there, and keep us wise to the lot of it. Snap. (*Elektra* 4)

or the flat vulgarities of Clytemnestra, here presented as a vindictive shrew:

> You've shot off a lot of brash talk
> to a lot of people,
> a lot more than was so
> about how forward I am, how unjust
> insulting you and your gang. (*Elektra* 23)[11]

In thus deconstructing the expected linguistic registers, Pound found a way of relating Elektra's ancient tragedy to his own situation as a condemned war traitor.

In inventing a Japan to satisfy contemporary American fantasies as to a less complicated, more orderly society—a society at once highly refined and yet quite frank about sexuality—Johnson uses one other form of layering that deserves mention. In all the Yasusada portfolios published to date, the poems are embedded in a larger archive, that consists of letters, English assignments, commentaries, and elaborate footnotes. The model would be the palimpsestic notebooks of George Oppen, where drafts of poems are surrounded by extracts from Heidegger and other philosophers, by letters, autobiographical notes, source material, and so on.[12] Clearly, contemporary readers have a

---

[11] See Carey Perloff's commentary on the complexities of language, (*Elektra* ix–xxv).

[12] On the "palimpsestic" text as quintessentially postmodern, see Michael Davidson, 'Palimtexts: Postmodern Poetry and the Material Text.'

predilection for this sort of documentary material. Yasusada, telling Kusatao in April 1965 that he has been in the hospital for a "couple stays" (would any Japanese translator use this slang expression?), informs his friend that "The difficulty, as you know, is the sickness after treatment." "Luckily," Yasusada adds, "the hospital wing they have me in looks out on the pine-covered hills of Mount Asano" (*APR* 25; *Doubled* 60). How authentic! How vivid! What a reminder of the Hiroshima tragedy! And Yasusada has an English teacher, Mr. Rogers, who advises him to study the writer James Joyce, "who is famous for a form of writing called 'streams [sic] of consciousness'" (*APR* 25; *Doubled* 69). Again, how quaint and charmingly incorrect, at least when we don't probe too carefully into the conundrum that Yasusada might not know Joyce although he does know Spicer.

IV

Kent Johnson has, I think, done a brilliant job in inventing a world at once ritualized and yet startlingly modern, timeless yet documentary, archaicized yet *au courant*—a poetic world that satisfies our hunger for the *authentic*, even though that authentic is itself a perfect simulacrum. To call his Yasusada impersonation a hoax, much less a "criminal act," is of course absurd: the pseudonym is a time-honored device in literature, and from James Macpherson's *Ossian* to the present, writers have invented fictional personae and passed them off as the real thing.

Still, there is something deeply troubling about the uncritical reception of these "Japanese" poems and prose pieces, with their brash distortions of literary and political history and their questionable conjunctions of jarring verbal registers. Why is it, one wonders, that none of Yasusada's editors sought out the guidance of bona fide Japanese poets, scholars, or translators? That they didn't read these "newly found" and never before published works against the well-known brilliant poetries of, say, Tanikawa Shuntaro? And that, once exposed as having been "taken in" by the hoax, they have put the blame on everyone but themselves? Let me try to summarize the reasons why the "hoax" has worked so well, and why, so I believe, similar inventions will occur with increasing frequency as we move toward the millennium.

Marjorie Perloff

First, most academics today (and most poets and editors, after all, now hold academic posts) pay lip service to the Foucaultian notion of cultural construction, of discourse networks that discipline the individual talent. Hence the search for novel and interesting cultural positioning, as in the case of Araki Yasusada, that rare Hiroshima survivor to have turned up so conveniently so late in the day, with such a fascinating cache of never-before-published poems and documents. Never mind Araki Yasusada the individual: it is his identitarian self that matters, his occupation of the position of avant-gardist who is also victim, disseminator of Jack Spicer, Roland Barthes, and the Language poets, who is also a traditional renga and haiku poet, purveyor of dissonant chords and gaps in grammar who also has something centrally important to say about atomic warfare, and quintessential neglected genius who is also a communitarian, believing that there is no such thing as "ownership" of one's writings.

Yasusada thus satisfies, as fully as possible, the current disciplinary demand. Yet, despite the continuing predilection for viewing individual poetry as the fruit of such cultural construction, there is another demand, this one deep-seated and instinctive, for individual authenticity, for uniqueness, for the Benjaminian aura that comes only in the presence of the Real Thing, not its copies. Look at that letter written from the Hiroshima hospital in 1965! Look at the elegiac lines written to a particular wife and daughter! Look at the correspondence with his very own English teacher and the mistakes that Yasusada makes in his assignments, misspelling words like "him" ("Hime"), "sky" ("skye") and "patrolling" ("patroleing") in ways, so my Japanese sources tell me, no Japanese student of English who was as far along as Yasusada would possibly make. These ancillary documents, in any case, humanize the situation; they give Yasusada a particular habitation and a name and make his work more accessible for the readers of *American Poetry Review* or *Grand Street*.

Accessibility, in this case, has much to do with the paradox that even as Yasusada's poetry satisfies an American reader's demand, his work *makes no demand on us*. We can empathize with the "tragedy" in which Yasusada was caught up in the prime of his life (he was thirty-eight at the time of the nuclear attack), without having to think through the ethical issues involved in any serious way. The Yasusada archive puts forward no choice we would have to make, triggers no moral or psychological debate we might engage in. Rather, the work's mode is, as I remarked earlier, Orientalism, "that Western style," in Edward Said's words, "for dominating, restructuring, and having authority over the Orient" (Said 3)—an Orient represented since antiquity as "a place of romance, exotic beings, haunting memories and landscapes, remarkable experiences" (1). And the great irony of the current situation in American letters is that the New Multiculturalism, far from countering the Orientalism Said decried as long as twenty years ago, has turned out to be its inadvertent promoter.

How did we get ourselves into this bind? Partly, no doubt, because our current skepticism, indeed cynicism, as to the power and efficacy of government (that is, *our* government) is generally coupled with an uncritical—or at least unquestioning—attitude toward the governments of other nations. The Cold War, as it is currently represented in the literary and visual arts, is almost invariably *our* Cold War, the bombing of Hiroshima, *our* infamy. The complexities and contradictions of geopolitics thus take a back seat to moral outrage on the one hand, fictional construction on the other.

As I was completing this essay, I happened to come across a front-page article in *The New York Times* (January 22, 1997) titled 'A Japanese Generation Haunted by Its Past,' the first of a series of articles on 'Main Street, Japan: Wounds of War.' The reporter, Nicholas D. Kristof, interviewed a group of old men in the small farm town of Omiya, 200 miles southwest of Tokyo. The men he spoke to are haunted by memories of fifteen years of brutal warfare, from the invasion of Northern China in 1931 through World War II. They recall thrusting bayonets through the chests of Chinese infants, committing acts of torture, massacring civilians, raping young girls almost everywhere they went—and even committing cannibalism. As a young soldier, Shinzaburo Horie recalls, he ate the flesh of a 16-year old Chinese boy. "It was only one time," he says, "and not so much meat, but after 60 years I can't put it behind me":

> Mr. Horie and his buddies had eaten some rare fresh meat that had suddenly become available in the local market in northeastern China one day in 1939, he recalled. Then the

kempeitai, the Japanese secret police, came around asking whether anyone had bought that meat in the market.

"Some Japanese soldiers who were hungry had killed the boy and eaten some of his meat and sold the rest to the Chinese merchant, and we bought it from that merchant," Mr. Horie said. He added that he had heard that the Japanese soldiers had been punished for the killing and the cannibalism. (Kristof A6).

The paradox, as Kristof puts it, is that men like Shinzaburo Horie are now "unfailingly courteous, gentle and honest. They are deeply respected in their communities, and everyone knows they would never think of cheating anybody or losing their tempers. Yet they collectively killed 20 million or 30 million people" (A6).

You won't find such paradoxes in the gentle, elegiac lyric of Araki Yasusada, any more than you will in the angry anti-war poems of Toge Sankichi. The war memories are too painful and, for the young, too remote. The *Times* article reports that many teenage students, expert at algebra and biology, cannot answer the question, "What country dropped the atomic bomb on Japan?" "Hmmmmm," muttered Naruki Orita, "a 13-year old boy who is known as a good student in Omiya Junior High School," "I'm not really sure. I don't know." "Naruki," writes Kristof, "said he knew that his grandfather had died in the war, but he did not know where" (A6).

Kristof's is not, of course, the last word on this subject, and it may be that the attitudes of young Japanese students to World War II and Hiroshima are much more complex and varied than he allows. But, whatever the validity of the newspaper account, the questions Kristof raises are suspended in Yasusada's poetry, dealing as it does with personal memory and rather than with the harder questions about responsibility and guilt. The work thus responds to the Romantic tenet that the poet (and by extension the poet's audience) is committed to *feeling* rather than *knowing*, to perception and intuition rather than philosophy and history. Indeed, the common prejudice that poets, as well as their readers, are exempt from the pursuit of complex ideas, dies hard: witness the division, still standard in American universities, between the departments of "English Literature" and "Creative Writing," the names implying that scholarship and critical theory are not "creative," even as "creative writing" does not need to be informed by theory or scholarship.

In forcing us to think about these questions, Kent Johnson has, whether intentionally or not, performed an invaluable service. His Yasusada manuscript challenges many dubious notions: for example, that the "new sentence," as conceived by Ron Silliman and his friends, has no precedent in poetry, that certain "tragic" events cannot be the "subject" of surreal or parodic treatment, and that literary influence (Spicer and Barthes on Yasusada) exists if and when the influenced author claims it does. Like Pound's *Homage to Sextus Propertius*, the Yasusada notebooks force us to go back to the "originals," so as to see what they really were and how they have been transformed. One can argue, of course, that Pound did write *Propertius* in his own name; he did not, as Johnson does, pose as someone else. But the fact is that Pound was already famous when he wrote his Latin "translation" and so he could afford to be Ezra Pound, whereas the unknown Kent Johnson, writing in what is an increasingly glutted and cut-throat poetry market, had no such alternative. Johnson took, in other words, the *Ossian* route rather than the route of Pound or of the Goethe of the *West-Oestlicher Divan*. But just as Macpherson's *Ossian* brought on a valuable reconsideration of the *medieval*, so "Yasusada" may prompt us to familiarize ourselves with the actual Hiroshima memoirs of the fifties and sixties, as well as with Japanese postwar poetry in its specific articulations. What we need are not more "authentic" and "sensitive" witnesses to what we take to be exotic cultural and ethnic practices, but a willingness, on the part of poet as well as reader, to look searchingly and critically at what is always already there.

Works Cited

Barthes, Roland. *Empire of Signs*. Trans. Richard Howard. New York: Hill and Wang, 1982.

Davidson, Michael. 'Palimtexts: Postmodern Poetry and the Material Text.' In *Postmodern Genres*, Ed. Marjorie Perloff. Norman: University of Oklahoma Press, 1989 (75–95).

Davis, A. R., Ed. *Modern Japanese Poetry*, trans. James Kirkup. St. Lucia, Queensland: University of Queensland Press, 1978.

Foucault, Michel. 'What Is an Author?', in Foucault, *Language, Counter-Memory, Practice: Selected Essays and Interviews*, ed. Donald F. Bouchard, trans. Donald F. Bouchard and Sherry Simon. Ithaca: Cornell University Press, 1977.

Hara Tamiki. 'Water, Please,' trans. Steven Forth. *American Poetry Review* 14.4 (1985).

Johnson, Kent and Stephen M. Ashby, Ed. and trans. *The Third Wave*. Ann Arbor: University of Michigan Press, 1992.

Johnson, Kent and Craig Paulenich. *Beneath a Single Moon*. Boston and London: Shambhala, 1991.

Kenner, Hugh. *The Pound Era*. Berkeley and Los Angeles: University of California Press, 1971.

Kern, Robert. *Orientalism, Modernism, and the American Poem*. Cambridge and New York: Cambridge UP, 1996.

Miner, Earl. "Tanka." In *The New Princeton Encyclopedia of Poetry and Poetics*, ed. Alex Preminger and T. V. F. Brogan. Princeton: Princeton UP, 1993.

Motokiyu, Tosa, Ojiu Norinaga, and Okura Kyojin. 'Renga and the New Sentence.' *Aerial* 6/7, 1991: 52–59.

Nakano, Jiro, Ed. and trans. *Outcry from the Inferno: Atomic Bomb Tanka Anthology*, Special Double issue of *Bamboo Ridge, The Hawaii Writers Quarterly*, 67/68 (1995).

Nussbaum, Emily. 'Turning Japanese: The Hiroshima Poetry Hoax,' *Lingua Franca* 6.7 (1996): 82–84.

Pound, Ezra. 'Homage to Sextus Propertius,' in *Personae: The Shorter Poems of Ezra Pound*. Ed. Lea Baechler and A. Walton Litz. New York: New Directions, 1990: 203–204.

Pound, Ezra and Rudd Fleming. *Sophokles' Elektra, a Version by Ezra Pound and Rudd Fleming*. Introduction and Production Notes by Carey Perloff. New York: New Directions, 1990.

Rexroth, Kenneth. 'Love Poems of Marichiko.' In *The Morning Star*. New York: New Directions, 1979.

Said, Edward. *Orientalism*. New York: Random House, 1978.

Shiraishi Kazuko. 'Penis.' In Leith Morton, ed. and trans. *An Anthology of Contemporary Japanese Poetry*. New York and London: Garland, 1993.

Silliman, Ron. 'Great Poet.' Buffalo Poetics List Archive, 21 December 1994. http://listserv.buffalo.edu/cgi-bin/wa?A2=ind9412&L=POETICS&P=R1 0133&D=0 Accessed 3 January 2011.

——————. *The New Sentence*. New York: Roof Books, 1987. 63–69.

——————. *Tjanting*. Cambridge: Salt Publishing, 2002.

Snider, Hideko Tamura. *One Sunny Day: A Child's Memories of Hiroshima*. Chicago and LaSalle: Open Court, 1996.

Spicer, Jack. 'Song of Two Windows.' In *The Collected Books of Jack Spicer*, Ed. Robin Blaser. Los Angeles: Black Sparrow Press, 1975.

Tanikawa Shuntaro. 'The Poet.' In Leith Morton, Ed. and trans. *An Anthology of Contemporary Japanese Poetry*. New York and London: Garland, 1993.

Toge Sankichi. 'Dying.' In Minear, Richard H., Ed. and Trans. *Hiroshima: Three Witnesses*. Princeton: Princeton University Press, 1990.

Yasusada, Araki. *Doubled Flowering: From the Notebooks of Araki Yasusada*. Ed. and Trans. Tosa Motokiyu, Okura Kyojin, and Ojiu Norinaga. New York: Roof, 1997.

——————. 'Doubled Flowering: From the Notebooks of Araki Yasusada,' translated by Tosa Motokiyu, Okura Kyojin, and Ojiu Norinaga: A Special Supplement, *American Poetry Review* 25.4 (1996): 23–26.

——————. 'Mad Daughter and Big Bang,' *First Intensity* 5 (1996): 20.

——————. 'Telescope with Urn,' *Conjunctions: New World Writing* 23 (1994): 69.

——————. 'Untitled: August 1964,' *Grand Street* 53 (1995): 25.

Review of *Doubled Flowering: From the Notebooks of Araki Yasusada*

Forrest Gander

Doubled Flowering: From the Notebooks of Araki Yasusada is the most controversial poetry book since Allen Ginsberg's *Howl*. *Lingua Franca* devoted a special section to it. The *Boston Review* hosted a forum of responses to it. The *American Poetry Review* featured an insert of Yasusada's poems preceded by a portrait of the writer. On August 9, 1997, *Asahi Shimbun*, Japan's leading newspaper, published a front-page story on Yasusada. Poems and letters from the book have appeared in major literary journals in the United States, England, Australia, Russia, Spain, Israel and Italy.

And yet Araki Yasusada—the diarist from Hiroshima, the Zennist, the member of a prominent literary group called Layered Clouds, the Jack Spicer *aficionado* conversant in French and English, the family man whose family was devastated by the nuclear blast, the writer whose moving poems, letters and notes comprise the text of *Doubled Flowering*, this Araki Yasusada—apparently never existed. The translator and critic Eliot Weinberger suggested as much in the *Village Voice*, writing on "witness poetry," which he decries as "a set of biographical criteria that favors verifiable experience over imagination" (*Scubadivers* 17). *Lingua Franca* and others followed suit in publishing articles about the hoax. Wesleyan University Press, which had been interested in printing the Yasusada volume, dropped the idea.

No one has yet claimed to have written the book, despite suspicions that the Yasusada materials were generated by Kent Johnson—a professor at Highland Community College in Freeport, Illinois, and the self-proclaimed literary executor of Yasusada's main "translator" (whose reality is also dubious). Critic Marjorie Perloff charged in the *Boston Review* that Johnson is the author, although he denies it. The time for a hoaxster's revelation would seem to have come and gone; but Yasusada's work is more than a mere hoax, even if his biography is.

Most of the individual poems were published in respected journals (including *Grand Street* and *Conjunctions*), their fictional authorship undiscovered, as the work of Hiroshima survivor Araki Yasusada. Along with Yasusada's own purported writings, there are numerous footnotes, scholarly commentaries and references that weave, in the manner of Woody Allen's *Zelig*, documentary facts into Yasusada's putative biography (for instance, references to actual Japanese poets, literary groups and affairs in Hiroshima). While there seem to be enough anachronisms (a reference to scuba-diving gear, for example, in a poem dated before the invention of such) and outright mistakes (a Japanese woman given a name that would only be used by a man) to suggest that something is awry, the general impression given is one of scholarly thoroughness and detail. As a result, many editors published Yasusada believing that he was, indeed, a Japanese poet and nuclear bomb survivor. Many of them have been quite angry to learn that they were taken in by an elaborate fiction. Some have suggested that no one who has not experienced an event as cataclysmic as the bombing of Hiroshima has the right to "pretend" to have done so, that such a pretense demeans the people who truly suffered there.

But before we launch into that furiously raging debate, let's consider the work itself, which, until questions concerning its authorship waxed full, provoked only wide-ranging international praise. The book's introductory note serves to identify the bulk of the text as translations made by three Japanese scholars of Yasusada's recently discovered notebooks. The ensuing assemblage of diary entries, Zen exercises, English class assignments, letters and drafts of poems coheres loosely around themes of loss and authorship.

The first poem, for example, begins with the speaker conversing—in a garden at night—with a turnip that he mistakes for "the severed head of my / mad daughter lying on the ground" (*Doubled* 11). References to the death of Yasusada's daughter and wife recur hauntingly throughout the book. At one point in "Suitor Renga" the author says, "You are a little girl with blistered face, pumping your legs at a great speed beside the burning form of your Mother" (75). In another poem, "The crying girl sounds like a loon" (15). Yasusada makes references to "grief-stones" (93) and to the place where "a temple once stood / As seventy thousand voices are fused by a sphere and" (85). The sentence stops there. In a modernist parataxis, this fragmentation, the lopped-off sentence, iterates on the syntactical level the speaker's loss by intimating a world come prematurely to an end.

But to say that the book's themes concern loss and authorship isn't any more significant, really, than observing that the theme of

Shakespeare's sonnets is love. Theme is only a minor aspect of poetry, and whether in the form of grammar exercises, Zen aphorisms, haibun or diary notations, the bulk of Yasusada's work is poetic. For most readers, what counts is a poem's representation of inner life. Let's consider a Yasusada poem and ask ourselves whether the fiction of the poem's authorship makes it less emotionally authentic, or whether the poem's revelation of human experience and feeling is exaggerated by our presumption that it was written by an actual Hiroshima survivor and not by someone else. Here is the complete text of 'Dream and Charcoal':

> And then she said: I have gone toward the light and become beautiful.
>
> And then she said: I have taken a couple of wings and attached them to the various back-parts of my body.
>
> And then she said: all the guests are coming back to where they were and then talking.
>
> To which she said: without the grasp-handle, how would you recognize my nakedness?
>
> To which she replied: without nothing is when all things die.
>
> Which is when she had a wild battle with the twigs.
>
> Which is when the charcoal was passed from her body to mine.
>
> Which was how she rose into the heavens, blinding the pedestrians.
>
> Which was how our union was transposed into a dark scribble.
>
> Which became the daughter calling, calling my name to wake me. (*Doubled* 46)

The poem starts with a modernist move, an "And," as though it had begun prior to our appearance as readers. It ends with the familiar device of the speaker waking from a dream. But what occurs in the middle rescues the poem from cliché. The accumulation of death images—"gone toward the light," "a couple of wings," "when all things die," "she rose into the heavens"—is interrupted by contrary images of guests at a party, of a woman playing with twigs, and by enigmatic questions and assertions. One emotional texture is spliced with another in a manner that suggests both the distrust of a unitary speaking voice and traditional narrative development typifying literary modernism and the contrastive tonal patterns and heuristic leaps typifying classical Japanese renga. The book borrows modes, images and forms from both Japanese and Western literatures, complicating presumptions concerning its authorship. In this cultural encounter, Yasusada's work seems to stress the simultaneity of creation and transformation, of resonance and influence.

Several sentences in 'Dream and Charcoal' have that lexical awkwardness and syntactical formality suggestive of inexpert translations. No native speaker, for instance, would say "the various back-parts of my body" or refer to the body's "grasp-handle." The very strangeness (and, for me, the strange beauty) of the poem in English only emphasizes its supposed translation. The English has been subverted by a foreign language; foreignness and nativeness, then, are consubstantial in the sense and syntax. We might even say that Yasusada's frequent "translatese," the union of two languages, has been "transposed into a dark scribble." The very grammar conspires to merge authorial identities.

And yet despite disjunctions in tone, grammar, form and structure, despite the indeterminate pronouns—are there two women who speak or does one reply to her own questions and assertions? Can we assume that the last speaker is the husband?—the poem communicates an undeniable emotional power. And elements of scenario and agency do cohere. We might infer, for instance (and this inference is bolstered by other poems), that the woman having a "wild battle with the twigs" is the poet's wife observed in a moment of childlike playfulness. References to her "nakedness," to her beauty and to something being "passed from her body to mine" eroticize the relationship. When she dies, "rose [rises] into the heavens," the poet's love for her continues as a writing, a "dark scribble." As Shakespeare tells us, poetry is a miracle of presence if "in black ink my love may still shine bright." By writing about her,

Yasusada keeps her alive, even if she never lived. Even if he never lived. This Yasusada poem seems to me as accurate in its representation of longing and grief as the poems by Petrarch, written in Laura's lifetime, imagining Laura dead.

Finally, the pages of *Doubled Flowering: From the Notebooks of Araki Yasusada* are stunning as poems and failures as the historical documents they turn out not to be. They are alternately funny, ironic, irreverent, bitter and passionate. I do not think that they add up to a kind of joke, as some critics have argued, by seducing North American readers with their Orientalist exoticism, by fooling us into liking them for all the wrong reasons, or by taking advantage of our desire for Western clichés of Japanese and Chinese writing. Clearly, though, the poems do make jokes, setting up puns, proposing anachronisms, making purposeful factual and typographical mistakes and juxtaposing versions of translations from classical Japanese poetry, novels, Hiroshima literature and Zen manuals with formal concerns—dissonance, collage, ellipsis, fragmentation—associated with literary modernism. But the book does not merely "play into the residual guilt of contemporary American readers" or serve mainly to poke fun at the American market for "authentic" witness poetry by parodying it, as Marjorie Perloff has suggested. Sentimental references to kimono sleeves soaked with tears, to moon and hair and perfume may seem parodic, but they occur often enough in the poems of the imperial anthologies and, to a lesser degree, in the Manyoshu, and Yasusada always complicates such images. John Solt, a professor of Japanese culture at Amherst College argues that Yasusada "plays into the American idea of what is interesting about Japanese culture . . . and gets it all wrong, adding Western humor and irony" (Nussbaum 83). But I think he misses the point, too.

Instead, Yasusada proposes a radical contemporary aesthetic response to one of the worst human atrocities, what Kai Bird, Gar Alperovitz, and others have amply demonstrated as the absolutely unnecessary nuclear bombing of the civilian populations of Hiroshima and Nagasaki by American military forces. Using modernist strategies, the author(s), steeped in translations of Japanese literature and feeling uneasy, even—if they are Americans—complicit with the U.S. foreign policy that generated such mass destruction, invented an imaginative, political and poetic act of empathy. To write poems concerning

Hiroshima, they felt it necessary to imagine themselves as the other, "the enemy." They relinquished their own identities as authors and became invisible, as the Hiroshima victims themselves disappeared. It is an impossible gesture of solidarity, since one cannot become someone else and since one cannot truly imagine one's way into an actual culture considerably different from one's own. But nevertheless, it is a gesture worth making if its resultant poetry is worthwhile as art, as poetry, as—finally—contemporary Western poetry. In this gambit, *Doubled Flowering* is an astonishing success.

As to whether the application of a pseudonymous history to such a work is, as one writer claimed, "a criminal act," or whether Hiroshima's vastness and horror exceed any common understanding of subjectivity, I leave it to you, tender and merciless readers, to determine for yourselves. Other pointedly relevant readings would include the books *May Sky: There is Always Tomorrow / An Anthology of Japanese-American Concentration Camp Kaiko Haiku; Writing Ground Zero: Japanese Literature and the Atomic Bomb*, and *Atomic Ghost: Poets Respond to the Nuclear Age*.[1]

After the one hundred and twenty pages of Yasusada's notebooks, there are forty pages more of critical commentary and interviews that help to focus the issues at stake. You might want to add your response to what is already a kind of Talmudic document published with commentaries around translations of notebooks written by an author who does not exist about a place that was once blotted out. Modern art, it has been said, is something with which to think. Bernard Berenson once noted, "A complete life may be one ending in so full an identification with the non-self that there is no self to die."

Flipping through the book's pages again, I'm drawn to a poem toward the end titled 'March 3, 1970.' It reads as a suitable, if bathetic, postscript to this review:

> Where our house once stood
> the pinecones have fallen
> among the pinecones. (*Doubled* 112)

---

[1] [Editor's Note] *Atomic Ghost* includes a copy of the "Yasusada" poem 'Trilobites' (*Doubled* 20), but it is attributed to Kent Johnson. Johnson has acknowledged writing about ten pages of the Yasusada work, but claims that Tosa Motokiyu wrote the rest (Nussbaum 82).

Works Cited

Bradley, John, Ed. *Atomic Ghost: Poets Respond to the Nuclear Age*. Minneapolis: Coffee House Press, 1994.

de Cristoforo, Violet Kazue Matsuda. *May Sky: There is Always Tomorrow / An Anthology of Japanese-American Concentration Camp Kaiko Haiku*. Washington, DC: Sun & Moon Press, 2001.

Nussbaum, Emily. 'Turning Japanese: The Hiroshima Poetry Hoax,' *Lingua Franca* 6.7 (1996): 82–84.

Treat, John Whittier. *Writing Ground Zero: Japanese Literature and the Atomic Bomb*. Chicago: Chicago UP, 1995.

Weinberger, Eliot. 'Can I Get a Witness?' *Jacket* 5: Oct 1998. http://jacketmagazine.com/05/yasu-wein.html.

Yasusada, Araki. *Doubled Flowering: From the Notebooks of Araki Yasusada*. Ed. and Trans. Tosa Motokiyu, Okura Kyojin, and Ojiu Norinaga. New York: Roof, 1997.

HYPER-AUTHORSHIP:
THE CASE OF ARAKI YASUSADA[1]

Mikhail Epstein

Preamble

The work of Araki Yasusada (1903–1972) has appeared in numerous publications of late and has provoked a good deal of discussion in the world of poetry. I say "world" because poets and critics are avidly speculating about the work in the United States, England, Japan, Russia, Italy, Australia, and Mexico, where selections and critical commentary have recently appeared. It is understandable why the Yasusada phenomenon has caused such fascination and controversy, for it is, without doubt, one of the most enigmatic and provocative authorial mysteries of 20th century poetry.

Originally presented in various journals as translations from the posthumously discovered notebooks of Yasusada, a purported survivor of the bombing of Hiroshima, the writing has recently been revealed by its "caretakers," Kent Johnson and Javier Alvarez (two individuals whose existence is empirically verifiable), as the creation of their former and now deceased roommate, Tosa Motokiyu, who has been credited in all previous publications as the main "translator" of Yasusada's work. Johnson and Alvarez assert that Tosa Motokiyu is the hypernym for an author whose actual identity they are under instructions never to reveal.

I came into contact with this work through two fortuitous occurrences, first in 1990 and then in 1995, but it was in January of 1996 that I became more intimate with it, when I received a letter and a package of Yasusada materials from Motokiyu, who explained that he had been urged by "our mutual friend" Kent Johnson and his own interest in my recent book, *After the Future*, to write to me. In this letter he acknowledged himself to be the empirical writer of the Yasusada materials, and he asked for my thoughts on the implications inherent in such a scrambling of authorial identities. I wrote him back a lengthy reply, only to learn from Kent Johnson in the summer of 1996 that he had died not long after receiving my letter.

---

[1] 'A Letter to a Japanese Friend,' was first published in *Denver Quarterly* 31:4, (1997): 100–105. Part 2 was first published in *Witz* 5:2, (1997): 4–13.

Mikhail Epstein

1. A Letter to a Japanese Friend[2]

To Tosa Motokiyu
from Mikhail Epstein

February 6, 1996

Dear Tosa Motokiyu:

Thank you for your letter and rich materials that I will certainly go through with great interest. I've been so inspired by some of your suggestions that I don't want to delay my response.

Why couldn't we establish an International Society (or Network) of *Transpersonal Authorship*? We could invite for membership those people who feel themselves overwhelmed by different (and multiple) authorial personalities that wish to be realized through their transpersonal creative endeavors. This writing in the mode of otherness is not just a matter of a pseudonym, but rather of a *hypernym*. *We don't produce our own works under different names but we produce works different from our own under appropriate names.*

This is a crucial issue in contemporary theory and writing. Poststructuralism has pronounced a death sentence for the individual author(ship), but does this mean that we are doomed to return to a pre-literary stage of anonymity? One cannot enter twice the same river, and anonymity in its *post-authorial*, not pre-authorial, implementation will turn into something different from folklore anonymity. What would be, then, a progressive, not retrospective, way out of the crisis of individual authorship? Not anonymity, I believe, but *hyper-authorship*.

There is so much talk about hypertexts now. But what

---

[2] I consciously repeat here the title of the famous Jacques Derrida's piece in which he elaborates in a "Japanese," "negative" manner the undefinability of deconstruction. Perhaps it is more than a simple coincidence that the reconstruction and "hyperization" of authorship was also inspired by the work of a Japanese author.

about hyper-authors? This question has not even been raised. *Hyper-authorship is a paradigmatic variety of authors working within the confines of one (allegedly one) human personality. A hyper-author relates to an author as a hypertext relates to a text.* Hypertext is dispersed among numerous virtual spaces that can be entered in any order, escaping a linear (or temporal, or causal) coherence. *Hyper-authorship is dispersed among several virtual personalities which cannot be reduced to a single "real" personality.*[3] As thinking is always thinking "of," without necessary specification of the object, *writing is always "writing by." This "byness" of writing cannot be reduced to any biological, or historical or psychological subject.* To follow Husserl who called the *ofness* of thinking "intentionality," we can call this *byness* of writing "potentionality" that does not need to be biographically actualized, or can be actualized in multiple figures and personae. The same writing can be potentially ascribed to various authors which intensifies the play of its meanings and interpretations.

In traditional literary theory, the author is a real individual or a group of individuals, but this is an outmoded way of thinking which can be compared with the conceptual framework of physics before the advent of quantum mechanics. The latter showed that we cannot pinpoint a particle with any specificity

---

[3] The meaning of the prefix "hyper" is a combination of "super" (excess) and "pseudo" (illusion). The proliferation of authorial personalities makes each of them less "real." This simultaneous evolution of cultural phenomena, including authorship, in two directions, "super" and "pseudo," resulting in the triumph of "hyper," is one of the most salient traits of postmodernism. "'Unlike the prefixes 'over-' and 'su[pe]r-,' it ['hyper'] designates not simply a heightened degree of the property it qualifies, but a superlative degree that exceeds a certain *limit*. (The same meaning is found in words like 'hypertonia,' 'hypertrophy,' 'hyperinflation,' 'hyperbole.') This *excess* of the quality in question is so great that, in crossing the *limit*, it turns into its own antithesis, reveals its own illusionary nature. The meaning of 'hyper,' therefore, is a combination of two meanings: 'super' and 'pseudo.' 'Hyper' is the kind of 'super' that through excess and transgression undermines its own reality and reveals itself as 'pseudo.'" Mikhail Epstein. "The Dialectics of *Hyper*: From Modernism to Postmodernism," in his book *Russian Postmodernism: New Perspectives on Post-Soviet Culture* (with Alexander Genis and Slobodanka Vladiv-Glover). New York, Oxford: Berghahn Books, 1999: 25.

in time and space; it is a fuzzy phenomenon, embracing the aspects of discreteness and continuity, a particle as well as a wave. What I am discussing now is precisely the concept of *fuzzy, or "continuum-like" authorship*, which refers not to a discrete personality but rather to a wave going across times, places and personalities. Tosa Motokiyu and Araki Yasusada are some of the observable locations of this hyper-authorial wave which can reach the shores of other epochs, countries, and strange personalities. Hyper-authorship is virtual authorship in which real personalities become almost illusionary, while fictional personalities become almost real. This "almost" is what allows them to co-exist on the same continuum in the imaginations of readers. Leo Tolstoy said: "In art, the 'almost' [*chut'-chut'*] is everything." This concerns not only the matter of artistic representation, but also its mode of authorization.

Previously the author was interesting to the degree that his/her personality could illuminate the text and be instrumental in its understanding. This tendency culminated in the widely announced "death of the author" by virtue of which the text became a self-sufficient and self-enclosed entity. Now I am inclined to think that a text is interesting only inasmuch as it manifests the multiple, infinite possibilities of its authorship. What we should enunciate, perhaps on behalf of several authors, like Tosa Motokiyu, Araki Yasusada, and Ivan Solovyov, is *the resurrection of authorship after its death*, this time in the wavy, misty, radiant flesh of prolific hyper-authorship, no more coinciding with the mortal animal flesh of a separate biological individual.

We have moved far beyond the concept of biological parenthood which is now recognized as only one of many forms of parenthood. Now let's have done with the reductive concept of authorship as only "biological" authorship limited by the input of the author as a living individual. There are many sorts and degrees of *non-biological*—psychological, intellectual, inspirational, magical authorship. The question is how to differentiate these numerous authorships related to a single piece of writing, without hierarchical subordination of one to another. In what sense and in what respect are Yasusada's pieces authored by Tosa Motokiyu, and in what respect are Motokiyu's pieces authored by Araki Yasusada? This is the adequate way to question post-individual, or transpersonal authorship, not just to ask: who is the real author of this work, Motokiyu or Yasusada?

There is a principal asymmetry and disproportion between living and writing individuals in the world. It's evident that not all living individuals have either the inclination or the capacity to become authors. Some individuals cannot write or write only on bank checks and holiday cards. This renders quite plausible the complementary statement: *not all authors have either the inclination or the capacity to become living individuals.* There are many authors who, for certain reasons (which need further exploration), have no potential for physical embodiment, as there are many individuals who for some related reasons have no propensity for becoming authors. This implies that some living individuals, who have a potential for writing, must shelter or adopt a number of potential authors within their biological individualities. What wants actualization in the writing of a given author is the potentiality of many authors, i.e. those creative individuals who have no need or taste for living, in the same way as many living individuals have no need or taste for writing.

The deficiency of previous theories was to confuse these two aspects of writing: a biological individual and an authorial personality. Poststructuralist theory contributed to the solution of this question only negatively, by denying the attributes of a creative author to a biological individual. What logically follows is that we should also deny the attributes of a biological individual to a creative author. We have to split these naïve equations of the naturalistic fallacy. But we also have to proceed beyond the limits of this two-fold denial. Now the question has to be solved in a more constructive way, by positing hyper-authorship as the potential for an infinite self-differentiation of an (actual) individual, as well as the creative integration of different (virtual) individuals in the acts of writing. *The deconstruction of authorship opens the way for the construction of hyper-authorship.*

The basic principle of writing is *the excess of signifiers over signifieds* which generates synonyms, metaphors, paraphrases, parodies, parables, and other figurative and elliptical modes of writing. Furthermore, this principle applies to *the surplus of interpretations over the primary text* which, again and again, becomes a single signified for proliferating critical discourses. What has not yet been discussed is the extension of this principle to the sphere of authorship. *The excess of authorial personalities and their unlimited proliferation in the given text is the final surplus of creative signification. The author who was believed to produce the excess now becomes its product.*

I believe that in the course of time hyper-authorship will become a conventional device not only in creative, but also in scholarly writing since it becomes impossible for a postmodern intellectual to adhere strictly to one position or one methodology in matters of his/her profession. The need for the development of new, hypothetical methods of research (and which method is not hypothetical?) will bring about hyper-scholars who would pursue several alternative ways of argumentation mutually exclusive and complementary in the expanded universe of virtual knowledge.

Let me share with you one secret. When you confided to me that it was not Yasusada but you who actually wrote his poems, I remained hesitant about the meaning of this statement, perceiving it as a possibility for still another level of interpretative play between these two probable authorships. What is essential here is not the difference between Motokiyu and Yasusada but their mutual interference. Finally, do we know, following the famous parable of Chuang Tzu, whether Chuang Tzu sees a butterfly in his dream, or whether it is the butterfly who dreams of herself being Chuang Tzu? Are you absolutely sure that it's you who invented Yasusada, not the other way round?

Let's leave this divination to critics and literary historians, and let's proceed with the fact that both of these potential authorships are maintained on the level of "hyper," i.e., are mutually interchangeable without determination of the "origin," which is impossible, as you know, according to the theory of the trace. There is a trace of Yasusada in you, and there is a trace of Ivan Solovyov in me, but the origins of these traces are lost and irrecoverable, or perhaps never existed. What is important to discuss is the relationship among these traces, not their relation to the "pseudo" origin. What becomes "pseudo" under this new mode of writing is not the name of the fictional author but the identity of the "original" author. Biologically and historically, I am Mikhail Epstein, but as an author, I am a complex amalgam of several authorial personalities (some of them remain unknown even to myself), among whom Mikhail Epstein has no authorial privilege on the grounds of the simple fact that he has some extra-textual body.

I also can imagine a journal (an annual?) inviting the contributions of transpersonal authors and elaborating the theory of hyper-authorship. The title might be *TBA* meaning "*trans-biological authorship*" and at the same time "*To Be Announced*," an abbreviation for something that has not yet and perhaps never will be determined.

Cordially,

all of us, including Mikhail Epstein

Mikhail Epstein

2. The Russian Identities of Araki Yasusada (one year later)

As some other critics and scholars have done, I have reflected on the matter of Yasusada, and certain curious coincidences and parallels have emerged. Is it possible that I have a more personal connection to this work that I was not at first cognizant of? Is it possibly the case that the author whose hyper-identity is Tosa Motokiyu already knew of me many years ago, when we both were citizens of the bygone Soviet Union, and that his announced "death" is meant as a metaphor for his "death as an author?" I write now to offer the following two hypotheses concerning the authorial origins of Yasusada. I do so not to try to "solve" the matter (for paradoxes are not to be solved), but rather to suggest possible layers of hyper-authorship whose consideration may enrich the further interpretation of Yasusada's texts (and his life as a potential megatext).

The intriguing scholarly controversy, in fact "author-mania" that erupted over the issue of Yasusada's identity(ies), gradually focused on the potential authorship of Dr. Kent Johnson, poet and college professor of English, who published and annotated the majority of Yasusada's works. I find this attribution no more persuasive and no less hypothetical than the two others that I would like to present. It is worth pointing out that Emily Nussbaum's discussion in *Lingua Franca* regarding the presence of Yasusada poems in Kent Johnson's doctoral dissertation does in no way settle the question of the Yasusada authorship. In fact, as my remarks will suggest, it is quite feasible that Johnson placed this work in his dissertation at the request of its actual author. Such a gesture would have been perfectly consistent with the "conceptualist" aesthetic of one of the writers I discuss later. I might further say, in regards to this matter, that I happened to be a guest lecturer in Bowling Green, Ohio in the spring of 1990, and was invited to attend Johnson's dissertation defense. As he began, in front of a table full of solemn professors, to speak about the poems of Yasusada, two other graduate students seated on the floor behind him began (carefully following notations set down in copies of Johnson's lecture) to exclaim loudly certain utterances in English and Russian, and to blow, strike, and drum on an array of Asian musical instruments. This they did for the next fifteen minutes or so, while Johnson presented a collage of theoretical and poetic propositions. Although the professors on Johnson's committee seemed very perplexed, I can attest that this was truly a strange and memorable event, one very similar in flavor to a conceptualist poetry evening in Moscow.

This parallel was all the more vivid to me because my lecture at Bowling Green and the subsequent conversation with Kent Johnson and his colleagues Ellen Berry and Anesa Miller-Pogacar was devoted in a significant part to conceptualism and the construction of multiple authorships. Of this conversation published later, I will cite only one passage that relates directly to the current discussion on the authorship of Yasusada's poetry:

> After deconstruction comes an epoch of pure constructivism. Anything can be constructed now. As one of my philosophical characters says—most of my recent works are constituted not by my own thoughts, but by those of my characters—a word cannot be exact, cannot be precise, so it must be brave. Deconstruction demonstrated that a word can't be precise, it can't designate any particular thing. But what remains to be done with the word? To be brave, to use it in all senses that are possible to it. This [is] the new domain of construction which comes after the deconstruction . . . (Berry 103)

Included in this domain is, first of all, the construction of authorship, as implied in those philosophical characters (conceptual personae) in my own work about whom and on whose behalf I am speaking. This explains why I became so intrigued by the phenomenon of Yasusada and now attempt to look into the enigma of his origin. It is up to the reader to decide if the following hypotheses pursue the goal of deconstruction of Yasusada or rather can serve as an example of critical constructionism.

Hypothesis #1

The manuscript *Doubled Flowering: From the Notebooks of Araki Yasusada* was originally composed in Russian by the famous writer Andrei Bitov and then translated by Kent Johnson and at least one Russian-speaking informant into English. I'll try to substantiate this version with irrefutable facts.

Bitov, born 1937, is Russia's major novelist, a founder of postmodernism in Russian literature. His work generated a number of famous hyper-authors, among them Lev Odoevtsev, a literary scholar and the protagonist of Bitov's major novel *Pushkin's House*, and Urbino Vanoski, a writer of mixed Polish, Italian and Japanese origin, the hyper-author of another of Bitov's novels, *A Professor of Symmetry*, which is annotated as "a translation from English without a dictionary."

I have maintained friendly ties with Bitov since the late 1960s and have first-hand information about the following. In the mid-1960s Bitov—by that time already one of the leading figures of the so-called "youth prose"—received an invitation to visit Japan through the official channels of the Soviet Writers' Union. However, he was denied an exit visa by Soviet authorities, who claimed that he was too ideologically immature for such a responsible trip to a capitalist country (he was suspected to be a hidden dissident, probably rightfully, as presumably 80% of the Soviet intelligentsia were at that time). One can easily imagine both the excitement and disappointment of a young writer who spent two or three subsequent years reapplying for this trip and reassuring the authorities of his "maturity" in vain. This bitter experience inspired him to write a novel, *Japan (Iaponiia)*, about the country he never saw but tried to invent in his imagination. Two planes alternated in this novel: the bureaucratic trials of a young author haunting the thresholds of high Soviet authorities, and imaginary landscapes and poetic visions of Japan, including fragments of an imaginary anthology of contemporary Japanese poetry. Incidentally, though Bitov never considered himself a real poet, he has hyper-authored several brilliant poems allegedly written by some of his characters (in particular Aleksei Monakhov, the protagonist of Bitov's "dotted" novel *The Days of a Man*).[4]

I assume that Bitov's novel *Japan*, which would be more properly titled *Dreams about Japan*, was a kind of symmetrical response to the eighteenth century Japanese masterpiece *Dreams about Russia*, written by Kodayu Daikokuya (1750 or 51–1828), a treatise which mixes pseudo-ethnographic description with lyrical visionary passages.[5] This book was

---

[4] The first collection of Bitov's poems, *V chetverg posle dozhdia*. St.-Petersburg: Pushkinskii fond, was published in 1997.
[5] The original Japanese title is *Oroshiyakoku Kodayu hyoryu nikki noutsushi*. Russian translation: *Sny o Rossii*. Izdanie teksta, perevod, vstypitelnaia statia i

translated into Russian, and I have no doubts that Bitov was intimately familiar with it.

With the coming of glasnost, Bitov intended to publish his novel *Japan* after some additional stylistic elaboration. I was very intrigued by this plot, especially after Bitov's other book *A Professor of Symmetry* came out, a monumental stylization of a contemporary multi-ethnic Western author, slightly in Conrad's or Nabokov's vein (English was not Vanoski's native language; hence Bitov's alleged translation from English into Russian of a novel which itself was presumably translated from his mother language into English, at least in the bilingual imagination of the imagined author). I expected that Bitov's *Japan* would again induce a case of "doubled authorship," now with a Japanese hyper-author. According to Bitov's account, *Japan* was almost finished. But gradually all rumors about its pending publication disappeared, and my direct questions addressed to Bitov failed to receive any definite answer. Bitov complained that he was burdened with numerous urgent literary projects and administrative responsibilities. Indeed, since the early 1990s he has been the president of the Russian division of International PEN (a worldwide organization of writers). Thus, the publication of *Japan*, with a poetic anthology as its supplement, was postponed for an indefinite period.

The last time I saw Bitov was December 11, 1995 when he visited Emory by my invitation to give a lecture on Russian postmodernism. In our conversation he confirmed again, with a visible reluctance, that *Japan* will be published in due time, but probably "in a modified form" (he did not go into detail). On December 29 of the same year, in downtown Chicago, at the annual convention of the Modern Language Association, I met by chance Kent Johnson, whom I had not seen for several years. He shared with me news on the rising posthumous star of Araki Yasusada, and gave me some copies of Yasusada's publications. Not immediately, but with an increasing feeling that I had guessed rightly, I recognized Bitov's stylistic charm in these English verses allegedly translated from Japanese. But why not directly from Russian?

---

kommentarii V.M. Konstantinova; pod. red. N.I. Konrada. Moscow : Izd-vo vostochnoi lit-ry, 1961. See also the historical novel under the same title of the contemporary Japanese writer Yasushi Inoue (1907–1991) *Dreams about Russia*, also translated into Russian: *Sny o Rossii*, perevod s iaponskogo B. V. Raskin. Moscow: Nauka, 1977.

Mikhail Epstein

The fact is that Kent Johnson, as the compiler and editor of a well-known and critically acclaimed anthology of contemporary Russian verse, *Third Wave: The New Russian Poetry*, had more of a first-hand familiarity with Russian poetry than with Japanese. Is it possible that there is a connection between Kent Johnson, who is now prominently connected to Yasusada's legacy, and Andrei Bitov, a master of hyper-authorship and the author of the still unpublished novel *Japan*? Let me further explain.

I first met Kent Johnson in St. Petersburg (then Leningrad, the native city, incidentally, of Bitov) in 1989, at a conference on contemporary Russian culture. Kent was then busy collecting materials for his English anthology of the newest trends in Russian poetry of 1970s–80s. This anthology came out, with my afterword, from University of Michigan Press in 1992 and had a significant success, particularly in the world of Slavic literature: it was the first book in English representing the "new wave" of Russian poetry, and, most valuably, it contained, in addition to verses, theoretical manifestoes from the poets. Kent Johnson and his co-editor, Steven Ashby, managed to make a superb choice of authors and their representative works, as well as of skillful translators, for this unique collection. This project by itself would have justified Kent's trip to St. Petersburg, but, as I suspect now, it was in Russia that he got the impetus for the preparation of another anthology, this time a Japanese one, subsumed under the name of a central hyper-author (Yasusada), but including two of Yasusada's renga collaborators, Ozaki Kusatao and Akutagawa Fusei, and their three contemporary translators, Tosa Motokiyu, Okura Kyojin, and Ojiu Noringa. I am amazed by the subtle skills that were employed to this anthology translated from Russian into English in order to finally present it as originally Japanese. Now I can also understand why Bitov withdrew his intention to publish *Japan* under his own name. To become part of a foreign culture is a more inspiring, generous, and at the same time ambitious enterprise than just to add still another piece to the treasury of one's native language.

Yasusada's work is conceived not just as a poetic collection, but as a novel with its own sub-plot (the editorial piecing together of the fragmented record of a Hiroshima survivor), cast in the multi-generic form of diaries, letters, verses, comments, etc. The meta-genre of "novel in verses" is deeply rooted in the Russian literary tradition, with

Pushkin's *Eugene Onegin* as its prototype—the major source of Bitov's inspiration throughout his creative search and especially in his major novel *Pushkin's House*. No wonder that the novel *Japan* proved to be not just a novel with a "poetic supplement" as was intended initially, but "a novel in verses," or, more precisely, "a novel with verses." Every reader of Yasusada's texts will agree that verses constitute only one aspect of its larger literary whole which, like both Pushkin's and Bitov's novels, includes numerous self-commenting pages, lyrical digressions, and critical reflections. This is truly a poetic novel of Yasusada's life, a novel in the tradition of Russian literature which now, with the aid of Kent Johnson's mediation, again invests its inspirations into the treasury of Japanese literature, but now in the even more palpable and congenial form of "a newly discovered author."

Such Russian authors as Pushkin, Dostoevsky, Tolstoy, and Chekhov were for a long time the moral and artistic authorities for Japanese literature; now, with Bitov-Johnson's contribution, Russian literature becomes an indispensable part of Japanese literature, of its novelistic flesh and poetic blood. As a scholar of Russian literature, I can only rejoice at the fact of this transcultural interaction and the resulting synthesis.

Hypothesis #2

This, I believe, is the least hypothetical of the two, being merely a combined statement of several well-known facts. Among Russian authors presented in Kent Johnson's anthology of contemporary Russian poetry, one of the most preeminent figures is Dmitry Prigov, a close acquaintance of Bitov, and a central proponent of Russian Conceptualism, who is known for his poems and whole collections written on behalf of various characters and mentalities belonging to different cultures. As Prigov puts it in his manifesto published in Johnson's anthology:

> the heroes of my poems have become different linguistic layers...
> A shimmering relationship between the author and the text has developed, in which it is very hard to define (not only for the reader but for the author, too) the degree of sincerity in

the immersion in the text and the purity and distance of the withdrawal from it.... The result is some kind of quasi-lyrical poems written by me under a feminine name, when I am of course not concerned with mystification but only show the sign of the lyrical poem's position, which is mainly associated with feminine poetry ... (qtd. in Johnson 102)

In 1987 or 1988 Prigov circulated a collection of verses on behalf of a Chinese female poet, thus helping to fill the gap of female authorship in the highly developed but almost exclusively male-oriented Chinese classic tradition. Further, he planned to expand the cultural geography of his hyper-authorship by introducing a collection by a Japanese poet with "a rather unusual but universally comprehensible fate and sensibility." This collection was never published under the name of Prigov himself, and I submit that in this case the project of hyper-authorship underwent a further mysterious expansion to acquire an international set of hyper-authors, hyper-editors, etc., along the lines of a global poetic plot (imitating and parodying the "Zionist-Masonic conspiracy" as exposed in *The Protocols of Zion*). Prigov once, in the spirit of "new sincerity," confessed to me his "Masonic" conspiracy for the triumph of creative impersonality throughout the world of art.

Precisely at the time Prigov's Japanese collection was due to be finished (1989), Kent Johnson came for his first and only visit to Leningrad to meet with Prigov and other poets participating in the future Russian anthology. From my continuous personal talks with Prigov at this time (we even spent a rather "sincere" night of discussions and confessions in the apartment of our common friend poet Viktor Krivulin) I could conclude that along with the poems he passed to Kent for this anthology, there was an additional set of materials large enough to form a separate collection which, it is easy to conclude, came to be known as *Doubled Flowering* by Araki Yasusada.

* * *

I want to underscore once more that everything aforesaid is only a hypothesis, though all mentioned facts are true. I daresay this kind of hypothesis does not need a further factual verification, inasmuch as the true identity of the person named Tosa Motokiyu (who, as I mentioned earlier, is now claimed by Johnson and Alvarez to be the "real" author of the work) is never to be revealed, according to his own last will. A question poses itself: Whose will is this, if its author refuses to accept attribution of its authorship? This is the same type of paradox that we find in the most famous of logical paradoxes of "liar's type": "The liar says that he is always lying. Is it a truth or a lie?" If we believe Motokiyu's testament that his true name is not to be revealed then this is not Motokiyu's testament.

A vicious circle? But is not the same circle inscribed into the most glorious and suspicious declaration of authorship? Is Shakespeare Shakespeare? Let us suggest that whoever Shakespeare was he succeeded in producing, in addition to "Hamlet" and other classical plays, the most enigmatic of his creations—the author named "Shakespeare," the one who wrote both prophetic "Hamlet" and his own almost illiterate will. The enigma of Motokiyu, who authorized *the eternal suspense and concealment of his authorial identity* and who claims to be behind Yasusada without revealing who is behind Motokiyu himself, is not only a *deeply parodic reinstatement* of the "Shakespearean question," but a subversion—or rather endless and deliberately vicious multiplication—of the very phenomenon of "authorship."

The vicious circle is a creative one. An author's imperative: to create an author. How can we trust a doctor who is permanently sick? There is a biblical saying: "Physician, heal thyself." How can we trust an author who limits himself to inferior characters, like kings, generals, adventurers, etc., and cannot create an Author?

Thus we should be grateful to Motokiyu, who succeeded in creating Yasusada and, even more, his friends, translators, editors, and executors. But who created Motokiyu? And who created his creator? The answer is infinitely deferred, to use the deconstructionist cliché, but what is more important and goes beyond the realm of deconstruction is *the construction of infinite authors in the place of the absent single one*. By this I do not imply that the quest for an original authorship should be qualified as a critical fallacy; the point, rather, is that the dispersion of creative origins is inscribed in the very act of creativity and brings forth the possibilities of infinite answers. Is not the goal of creativity the excess of meanings over signs, and therefore, *the excess of authors over texts*, since each additional authorship is a way to change radically the overall meaning of the text and to extend the scope of its interpretations? *Each text is allowed to have as many authors as it needs to become excessively meaningful.*

Vladimir Nabokov once remarked on what makes literature different from the "true story" or "the poetry of testimony": "Literature was born not the day when a boy crying 'wolf, wolf' came running out of the Neanderthal valley with a big gray wolf at his heels: literature was born on the day when a boy came crying 'wolf, wolf' and there was no wolf behind him." (qtd. in Charlton 9)

A friend of mine with whom I shared this observation, remarked pessimistically: "In our wretched times, when the boy runs in crying 'wolf, wolf!' no poetry is born whatsoever—he will simply be dragged to court for 'making false statements' and 'disturbing the peace' of the pedestrian-minded." Some will regard such a view as overly gloomy, but it does suggest why, in our times, the boy might do well to disappear together with the ghostly wolf he dared to herald so bravely. In other words, the author is driven to become fictitious in the way fiction is itself: *the author shares the destiny of his characters* and becomes one of them, like a chameleon—a grand illusion among illusions. Perhaps a new kind of literature is being born these days—one where neither the wolf nor the boy is to be found real, even though the heart-rending cries go on echoing in the villagers' ears.

But wait, object the villagers, for in the meantime rumors about the wolf and the boy who supposedly are "never present" become more insistent and repetitious. Isn't this play of language without wolf and even without boy behind it exactly what we know as "postmodernism?" If the wolf in this little parable represents the objective truth of realism, while the boy is the subjectivist pathos of modernism, then the vanishing of both of them constitutes the effect of postmodernism.

Is it not a blasphemy to "post-modernize" such a deeply pathetic experience as conveyed by Yasusada's poetry? Theodor Adorno, with even deeper pessimism than my friend, famously proclaimed that there can be no poetry after Auschwitz. We might likewise conclude that there can be no poetry after Hiroshima. But is this true? Could it be instead that poetry has to become wholly different from what it used to be in order to fulfill its human calling after Hiroshima? If so, then the work of Yasusada points toward one possible form of renewal: *dissemination of authorship. With Yasusada, poetry reaches beyond the individual's self-*

expression, beyond the original testimony, beyond the "flowering" of one person, to become "multiple flowering," a shared imagining and expression of potential Japanese, American, Russian hyper-Yasusadas, of all those who are capable of sharing the tragedy called "Hiroshima" and co-authoring the poetry called "Yasusada." Yasusada's fragments, letters, and poems become, through the generosity of a person or persons we call Motokiyu, an appeal for a *transpersonal—and thus selfless and in a sense authorless—empathy.*

Perhaps we can say this: In Yasusada's poetry there exist as many potential authorships as there are individuals in the world who are aware of Hiroshima and can associate themselves with the fate of its victims and survivors. *In our quest for the genuine author of Yasusada's works a moment of truth arises when each of us is ready to ask: Could it be me?*

In conclusion, I must state again that all foregoing facts concerning real names, persons and historical circumstances are true. It is only the interpretation of these facts which can claim *the higher status of a hypothesis.*

Postscriptum

On November 15, 1996, my path crossed with Andrei Bitov's at a Slavic conference in Boston. I told him briefly about Yasusada and shared with him my hypothesis about his potential authorship. He thought for a while and then noted: "The more hypothetical is one's approach to an author, the more truthful it may finally prove to be." "Does this relate to this specific case?" I asked directly. He evaded the answer and continued: "The value of a hypothesis is to predict a thing which cannot be observed. The value of an author is to make palpable what is impossible. A critical hypothesis about an author is just a retroactive projection of his own creative work and does not need any further justification. As you know, some of my characters are literary scholars, which presumes that some literary scholars..." Did he mean to add "are my characters?" At this moment—we were strolling around the book exhibition—an acquaintance of Bitov approached him and distracted us from the conversation. Unfortunately, later on in this day we had no opportunity to talk privately, and neither of us wanted to bring this topic to public attention.

Two details of this short exchange need to be emphasized. 1) Bitov did not ask me what Yasusada's works were about. 2) Anyone familiar with Yasusada's style cannot but recognize its echoes in Bitov's manner of coining paradoxes.

Works Cited

Ashby, Stephen M., and Kent Johnson, eds. *Third Wave: The New Russian Poetry*. Ann Arbor: The University of Michigan Press, 1992.

Charlton, James, ed. *The Writer's Quotation Book: A Literary Companion*. New York: Penguin, 1986.

Berry, Ellen E.. Kent Johnson and Anesa Miller-Pogacar. 'Postcommunist Postmodernism: An Interview with Mikhail Epstein.' In *Common Knowledge*, Oxford University Press, 2.3 (1993): 103–118.

Nussbaum, Emily. 'Turning Japanese: The Hiroshima Poetry Hoax.' *Lingua Franca* 6.7 (1996): 82–84.

Some Thoughts on Araki Yasusada the Author

Kent Johnson

The following paper was delivered as an invited address at the Walker Arts Center, Minneapolis, in April, 2007, an event jointly sponsored by the WAC and Rain Taxi magazine.

I'm going to talk about the controversy around the writings of Araki Yasusada, collected now in two volumes, *Doubled Flowering* and *Also, with My Throat, I Shall Swallow Ten Thousand Swords*, and try to offer, in so doing, some thoughts on issues pertaining to authorship and poetic identity.

I'd like to start by reading an intriguing passage from Charles Bernstein's 'How Empty Is My Bread Pudding,' the opening essay of a recent collection titled *Contemporary Poetics*, edited by Louis Armand, and published by Northwestern UP. The passage is actually a quote from the poet Rosmarie Waldrop; Bernstein interpolates it with pointed endorsement. Nearly concurrent with this book's appearance, Bernstein had published an essay in the UK (presented originally as an MLA address) titled 'Fraud's Phantoms,' an extended, highly charged attack on Yasusada.[1] It is not hard to see (*Contemporary Poetics*, in fact, contains a negative essay on Yasusada by another Language poet, Bob Perelman) how Bernstein may have had *Doubled Flowering* partly in mind with the comment. It is, in any case, very apropos our topic, as you will see:

> From time to time, poets or editors suggest the value of reading poems anonymously, for example publishing a magazine without author attributions. It sounds democratic, as if this would allow us to read poems for themselves. But artworks, like people, are not self-sufficient but part of a series, embedded in contexts that give them not only meaning but also resonance, depth; you might even say, life. Without some sense of the author, one cannot account for these other, often determining, factors. Prejudice may be avoided. But (poetic) justice is sorely checked.

---

[1] The essay is republished in Bernstein's *Attack of the Difficult Poems* (University of Chicago Press, 2011)

There are two main, fairly evident points suggested here: 1) That some sense of extra-literary context is necessary for appreciating a poetic work and 2) that such context is predicated on empirically verifiable authorships, these being crucial for grasping a work's meaning, resonance, depth, and so on.

There is no doubt that some sense of historical context always accompanies meaningful poetic appraisal and appreciation. But the second claim—that such context depends on an identification of the writer's actual biography—is highly questionable. I'd argue, in fact, that the demand for definite authorship unnecessarily limits the spectrum of possibilities available to poetic presentation and appreciation and, furthermore, that these possibilities—quite unexplored in our day—need in no way negate or undermine the more conventional approach to attribution that Waldrop and Bernstein advocate.

That more conventional approach, to be sure, famously put under analysis by Michel Foucault in his essay 'What Is an Author?' is not going away anytime soon. Nor should it . . . But one could ask: Why can't poetry establish practices and paths that are capable of unsettling, even partly transcending, that 'disciplining' context? Why can't poetry sometimes take hold of Authorship and all its attendant paratextual baggage—all that which we've been taught is untouchable and outside the purview of imaginative process—and undertake to fold it into a more comprehensive inventiveness, one that observes no legal, institutional, or attributional constraints upon the exploration of poetry's nature?

Bernstein's appeal for the Author's indispensability seems to brook no exceptions. In fact, though, his surprisingly traditionalist coupling of standard attribution to literary value is called into question—and quite starkly, I'd say—by a good number of rather weighty, well-known, and decidedly *traditional* examples. One could start by mentioning, for canonical instance, *Gilgamesh*, the *Iliad* and the *Odyssey*, *Beowulf*, *The Song of Roland*, or *The Tale of Genji*. These are works, of course, whose depths, resonances, and meanings have inspired readers for a very long time now, even though we have little, if any, clue about the biographical life—or lives—behind each. We could, as well, add another weighty example: the entire Shakespearean corpus, written by someone we call "Shakespeare," a name pointing to a life we know virtually nothing about, and which may or may not, in fact, designate a person who actually bore that name. Authorial context and the signature around which readerly comforts supposedly pivot are problematic issues in these cases, to say the least.

These *are* very old cases, of course, and they might be argued as exceptions, where authorship is lost to us due to the accidents and injustices of history. But the necessity of the author and the requirements of his or her biographical context, at least as Bernstein understands them, don't seem, either, to have been presumed by writers and readers of English-language literature in the more recent, well-recorded past. As John Mullan shows in his just-released book, *Anonymity: A Secret History of Authorship*, roughly 70% of novels and published poetry in England and America during the last three decades of the 18th century were anonymous or pseudonymous, and in the first three decades of the 19th a good 50% were, as well. And many, many more after that . . .

Readers didn't mind; in fact, as Mullan shows, they went wild for this: The pleasures these apocryphal books and journal publications provided were not just textual, but sociological, too, aspects of a reading culture with a considerably more relaxed attitude towards attributional indeterminacy than we have today: People would actively and happily speculate on who these hidden authors were—what traces or clues to their identities might be found in their works.

That's to say that these authorial mysteries were considered a natural part of the interpretive mix, a challenging but in no way onerous aspect of (to allude to an old tenet of Language poetry) the reader's responsibilities as co-producer of the text's total sense. We've largely forgotten it was so, but authorial "context," not too long ago, wasn't necessarily handed to the readership in neatly wrapped parcels; it was something formed by a circumspect, participatory public. There is little evidence, in this regard, then, that *Gulliver's Travels*, *Robinson Crusoe*, the *Waverley* novels, *Jane Eyre*, *Sense and Sensibility*, *The Rape of the Lock*, *Lyrical Ballads*, *Don Juan*, *The Narrative of Arthur Gordon Pym*, or countless poems in literary magazines and anthologies (none of which initially bore "authentic" signature) lacked "life" or were wanting for "justice" in their readers' minds.

Indeed, since 'What Is an Author?' there have been growing numbers of studies that show how surprisingly vast the tradition of anonymous and pseudonymous literature really is, across centuries and cultures (*Faking Literature*, by K.K. Ruthven, from Cambridge UP, is an even more encyclopedic account than Mullan's). And this history reveals that our current assumptions about literary authorship—in particular, that the biographical/legal mark of provenance is a natural, even ethical imperative—is a relatively recent development. That the ideological imperatives of those assumptions are now almost completely unchallenged in the field of our current poetry couldn't be more poignantly exemplified than by Mr. Bernstein's open endorsement of them: Even for an experimentalist like he, advocate of an avant-garde movement founded on a polemical rejection of the "I" and the "Self," the guarantee of empirical Authorial identity presses itself as requisite for the maintenance of poetic order and axiological protocol. In any case, it's into *this* hegemonic "context" of authorial decorum—a decorum, again, equally assumed by the avant-garde and the official verse culture the former supposedly opposes—that the writings of Araki Yasusada emerged in the mid-1990s.

Over the fourteen years or so since its first appearance, the work has generated a copious amount of accusation and defense. Eight or nine years ago, *The Nation* magazine even called it "the most controversial work of poetry since Allen Ginsberg's *Howl*," and the debate has certainly continued, though at a more thoughtful level, perhaps, than the high-pitched reaction that was first provoked. Let me try, then, to offer a few remarks, which might serve to prompt further questions or considerations. I have my views on the topic, obviously, but I don't in any way claim to have settled, comfortable positions on all the issues Yasusada has—for the most part unintentionally—brought forth. In fact, I am not comfortable in the least! As the work's executor and editor, I struggle with doubts. And for me, these doubts finally become what the Yasusada writing is importantly about.

So, to touch on a little bit of the history: A number of Yasusada texts were first published, as I said, in the mid to late 1990s, at the end of the apogee of multiculturalism and post-colonialist studies in the US academy and elsewhere. They came in for strong attack from certain people, who saw them as an appropriation of ethnic and cultural otherness, a hijacking of "subaltern identity." I was assumed early on to be the "culprit" and had a number of very personal slurs directed against me. A group of well-known Asian-American poets, for example, published a polemic in the *Boston Review*, asserting that Yasusada was nothing but an example of "yellow face" opportunism and that I was a racist. Arthur Vogelsang, the editor of the *American Poetry Review*, which had published a four-page special supplement of poems and letters from the work, referred to Yasusada as "a criminal act." John Solt, a professor at Wesleyan, told *Lingua Franca* magazine the poems were "Japanized crap." Charles Bernstein, as I'd mentioned, also angrily weighed in, denouncing the writings of *Doubled Flowering* as an instance of "White Male Rage."

These would be just a few, mostly early, examples. There were many other attacks, and they haven't stopped, actually. More recently, for instance, Yunte Huang, a prominent figure in post-colonial studies, concludes a recent book from Harvard UP with an essay that purports to show, via a rather strained reading of Gayatri Spivak, that Yasusada is driven by a sublimated, colonialist desire to supplant atomic-bomb writers from Japan; and *The Believer* magazine, which claims to have a policy to not publish "snark," printed a long screed full of livid, libelous remarks on my person, written, oddly enough, by one of the country's best-known film critics. So it's been very interesting, this aspect of the reaction.

And what makes it all so interesting to me is that the writing itself—which with all its contradictions and limitations attempts to imagine a complex, decidedly non-stereotypical life through the vehicle of poetic fiction—seems quite opposite anything that could be construed as racist or an abuse of otherness. Or so I strongly feel, anyway. And it is revealing—I believe this is important—that not one of those attacks has seriously tried to support its extreme charges with specific textual evidence.

Now, there is of course the broader and currently very topical issue of literary forgery, within which it is tempting to discuss Yasusada. The storm of contempt that has blown up in just the past few months in reaction to a spate of hoaxes in the genre of the memoir has been quite something, and the reaction can perhaps shed some understanding on the negative ways many have viewed the Yasusada case. Not a few people still maintain it is an unethical forgery or "hoax," primarily designed to fool unsuspecting readers.

In fact, just a few weeks ago, Scott Simon, of National Public Radio, expressing his disdain on the Weekend Morning Edition show for the recently outed *Love and Consequences,* by Margaret Seltzer—the latest instance of exposed memoir fakes—referred to a previous, in his mind, parallel example. Simon said, and with a barely veiled tone of sarcasm:

> "Ten years ago, prestigious journals published poems by a man billed as a survivor of the atomic bombing of Hiroshima, who turned out to be a community college professor in *[and here there is a noticeable pause for ironic effect]* Freeport, Illinois."

Simon (who I doubt has read the work) clearly thinks the work collected in *Doubled Flowering* and its follow-up book, *Also, with My Throat, I Shall Swallow Ten Thousand Swords,* is no different in spirit from forgeries—like Selzer's, or James Frey's *A Million Little Pieces*— that have captured the media's attentions of late. I'd propose that this is, and quite decidedly, wrongheaded.

And the reason is simple: Unlike the forgeries that make Simon so indignant, the Yasusada texts do not, nor have they ever, attempted to obscure their status as imaginative works. In fact, both books openly announce, on their back covers and in the generous appendix material at the end of each, that Yasusada is a fictional creation. To believe, that is, that they are hoaxed memoirs, collections of faked testimony, is to betray that one either hasn't read them, or wishes to willfully ignore the obvious that stares one in the face.

And this fictional openness, it's crucial to note, was the case from the very beginning, when some pieces were published under Yasusada's name in magazines, before the work was collected in book form. As commentators like Marjorie Perloff and Eliot Weinberger have pointed out, the poems, letters, drafts of English assignments, Zen dokusan encounters, musical scores, and assorted marginalia that compose the corpus reveal, of their own accord, and often through melodramatically apparent clues and contradictions, that they are fiction. Insofar as they consort with the "authentic," they do so not to non-problematically pass as such, but to actively bracket their status and provoke questions about the often problematic space of, precisely, authenticity. They are, one could say, coded documents that freely offer up their exposure.

Indeed, it's safe to say only a small percentage of the clues has been critically recorded so far.

One of the best of many good essays written about the subject is by the widely respected scholar Brian McHale. In this study, titled 'An Author May Not Exist: Mock Hoaxes and the Construction of National Identity,' contained in the essay collection *The Faces of Anonymity* (Palgrave Macmillan, 2003), McHale counters the superficial ways in which the reductive tag of "hoax" has been applied to Yasusada and theorizes pseudographic literary expressions into three different categories, arguing convincingly, I think, that the simple-minded notion of "hoax"—used as it most often is in a derogatory sense—is thoroughly inadequate in the understanding of works like *Doubled Flowering*.

What are these categories? "Genuine Hoaxes" constitute the first: fabrications carried out with no intention of ever being exposed. Examples would be such works as James Macpherson's 18th century *Ossian*, the *Protocols of the Elders of Zion*, *The Hitler Diaries*, the aforementioned *Love and Consequences*, and so on.

The second category is what McHale calls "Trap Hoaxes." The point of these "traps" is didactic and punitive—to embarrass or expose the foolish credulity of a certain audience. Here, one could cite the famous Ern Malley hoax, designed to demolish the reputation of the 1940's Australian avant-garde, or, more recently, the Sokal hoax, crafted to reveal the ignorance of "post-structuralist" academic critics of science.

The third category is that of "Mock Hoaxes," which for McHale are fundamentally aesthetic in intent, and which to greater and lesser degrees are purposely adorned with signs of self-complication. Rather than serving some ulterior agenda, as is the case with the first two categories, he argues that in mock-hoaxes "issues of authenticity and inauthenticity are elevated to the level of poetic raw materials . . . Mock-hoax poems make art out of inauthenticity." He places the work of Fernando Pessoa, Thomas Chatterton, and Yasusada in this literary class, though in McHale's sophisticated argument, these categories are also porous to contingencies of time and place, and works that through intention seem to fit within one category can shift, through reception, into another. The Ossian epic or the Malley poems would be examples of works that have undergone such evaluative shifts.

Kent Johnson

McHale's gesture towards a more careful appraisal of apocryphal literature and its varieties, then, suggests how Scott Simon and others' indignation might benefit from a bit more reflection and discernment. But while I fully agree with McHale that the so-called inauthenticity of the Yasusada texts is indivisible from their art, I would offer an important caveat: While I've often remarked on the intriguing ways the writing interfaces with theory and the politics of poetry, I have also often emphasized, as the work's caretaker, that *Doubled Flowering* was *not* primarily written as some kind of symbolic appeal for the "death of the Author" as against the "hoax" of conventional authorship, nor for any other "post-structuralist" notion. Ambiguities of agency, authenticity, ethnicity, and culture clearly inhabit the work, but these are, along with the ongoing critical commentaries branching out from them, largely incidental after-effects to the original impetus of the fiction. *Doubled Flowering*, to be sure, *does* prominently contravene (inasmuch as it gestures toward alternate, more fluid stagings of poetic presentation) long-institutionalized protocols of authorial control and classification that dominate our poetry at large. But its withdrawal of authorship is rooted in felt ethical imperatives which are interwoven into the work's total aesthetic expression—imperatives which have little to do, again, with "postmodern" aforethought. To quote Forrest Gander, from *The Nation* article I previously mentioned:

> Yasusada proposes a radical contemporary aesthetic response to one of the worst human atrocities, what Kai Bird, Gar Alperovitz, and others have amply demonstrated as the absolutely unnecessary nuclear bombing of the civilian populations of Hiroshima and Nagasaki by American military forces. Using modernist strategies, the author(s), steeped in translations of Japanese literature and feeling uneasy, even—if they are Americans—complicit with the U.S. foreign policy that generated such mass destruction, invented an imaginative, political and poetic act of empathy. To write poems concerning Hiroshima, they felt it necessary to imagine themselves as the other, "the enemy." They relinquished their own identities as authors and became invisible, as the Hiroshima victims themselves disappeared. It is an impossible gesture of solidarity, since one cannot become someone else and since one cannot truly imagine one's way into an actual culture considerably

different from one's own. But nevertheless, it is a gesture worth making if its resultant poetry is worthwhile as art, as poetry, as—finally—contemporary Western poetry. In this gambit, *Doubled Flowering* is an astonishing success.

This is not to imply there was no self-reflexiveness or meta-commentary that entered the work over the stages of its production, for there certainly was. There are impossible allusions, purposeful anachronisms, cross-textual puns, strategic mistakes. The Yasusada does not pretend to be a pure, well-behaved archive, as it were, innocent, in its unfolding, of contamination and contradiction. The work evolved in its production, and the fictional Yasusada became a complicated person! Yasusada, in fact, converses, and copiously, with actual Japanese intellectuals, writers, and artists of the period, who were—in real life—cleverly ironic, happily confused, even satirical about their own culture's interfacement with the West. But this dimension does not change the truth that the work originates, with all its fated failures, as an empathic, questioning expression, and not as a marshalling of theoretical, political polemic cloaked in the lambskin of poetry. That the simple and principled effacement of an authorship from a book of openly imagined fragments about Hiroshima should have been so widely taken in the poetry world as that kind of "punitive" gesture is, really, one of the most interesting and poignant aspects of the writing's story.

A final point I wish to make is more straightforward and more crucial to me, as it certainly would be to Motokiyu, the work's pseudonymous creator (or creators): Some commentators have suggested that the Yasusada corpus attempts to set itself above, or in judgment of, first-order testimonial literature, namely the poetry of those who witnessed, as victims, the bombings of Hiroshima and Nagasaki.

Nothing could be further from the truth. *Doubled Flowering*, if anything, stands as a kind of testimonial to the testimony of *hibakusha* literature—a view, incidentally, articulated by Hosea Hirata, Director of Asian Studies at Tufts University, in an essay ("Tsukurareta hibakusha shijin Araki Yasusada: shi ni shinjitsu was hitsuyouka") published last year by the National Institute of Japanese Literature. Among Hirata's close relatives are survivors of Hiroshima, whose fragile testimony he also movingly recounts in an Afterword essay that appears in *Also, with*

Kent Johnson

My Throat, I Shall Swallow Ten Thousand Swords: Araki Yasusada's Letters in English.[2] I want to be as clear as I can (insofar clarity is possible with such a fraught topic) on this matter regarding Yasusada's relationship to *hibakusha* literature, so please allow me to end with an answer I gave a few years back in an interview conducted by the editor of *Atomic Ghost: Poets Respond to the Nuclear Age*, the poet and critic John Bradley, who had just returned from Hiroshima, where he read poems from *Doubled Flowering* to a mass audience assembled at an event commemorating the 50th anniversary of that city's destruction:

> The Yasusada is most emphatically not motivated by an impulse to interrogate anything at all in hibakusha poetry, nor does it presume to set itself as an equal partner inside or alongside that body of work . . . Although it is inevitably a part of the broader realm of atomic-bomb literature, it exists in relation to hibakusha writing at a qualitative distance, as an after-image or echo of it, if you will. And I would hold that Yasusada's apocryphal status makes that echo no less real. It whispers something about the doubled-fusing and mutually-deformed flowering of our two cultures, about our unacknowledged confusion in each other, about some kind of deeper yearning to find our voices entwined with an otherness we know has been inside of us always. It's an otherness always whispering that Hiroshima's fate, which is beyond the markers of any name, could yet be ours, as well.

---

[2] [Editor's note] Hirata's Afterword is included in this collection, pp.312–315.

The Yasusada Notebooks and the Figure of the Ruined Text

Brian McHale

Araki Yasusada is a problem, and he should remain one. All of the issues that the Yasusada texts have raised—issues of pseudonymity, authenticity and "identity theft," of the "poetry of witness" and its use and abuse, of the fine line between artistic gesture and con-game, of cross-cultural empathy and white male resentment, of Orientalism and "yellow-face" travesty—all of these issues are legitimate, and deserve to be raised whenever we revisit the Yasusada case. They should follow Yasusada wherever he goes—into our classrooms, our journals, our anthologies, our MLA panels, our edited volumes. Yasusada should always arrive trailing clouds of controversy. Indeed, Yasusada's function in the larger scheme of things, however unintended, may prove to be that of thrusting these issues onto our agenda, and keeping them there.

These are the things that we ought to be talking about when we talk about Araki Yasusada, and I don't propose to change the subject. Or rather, I *do* propose to change the subject, but only for the space of an article—only long enough to place Yasusada in a somewhat different context than he has usually been seen in, in hopes of shedding a different light, however oblique, on some of the issues in the Yasusada case.

1. Distressed dossiers

I propose to view the Yasusada notebooks as one member of a particular class of late-twentieth century poetic texts. It's not clear to me how extensive this class might be, but in any case I only have space here to discuss three of its members, which I take to be representative of the class as a whole. The first of these, and the one least like the others, is Michael Harper's poem-sequence *Debridement*, first published in 1973, and republished in 2001 in a small-press edition. An undernoticed and under-valued Vietnam-era masterpiece, *Debridement* comprises sixteen sparse, elliptical poems distributed over 45 pages of text, many of them nearly blank. It is a documentary poem, retelling, and lightly fictionalizing, the true story of an African-American solider from Detroit, Dwight "Skip" Johnson, who went literally, technically berserk on a Vietnam battlefield in January 1967, and was awarded the Congressional Medal of Honor for having done so. Sadly, the rest of Skip Johnson's story conforms to pop-culture cliché, though it hadn't yet become cliché either when it happened or when Harper wrote about it. His is literally a textbook case of Post-Traumatic Stress Disorder, a condition that had not yet been identified in 1971 when, disaffected and deeply in debt, Skip Johnson was shot to death while apparently trying to hold up a grocery store back home in Detroit.

The raw material for Harper's poem is found in a *New York Times* article by Jon Nordheimer from May 26, 1971, documenting Skip Johnson's troubled life and troubling death. Harper strip-mines the *Times* article for telling details and shards of language, displacing this material into his own text. Some of his finds appear, set in SMALL CAPS, as passages of bureaucratic-administrative discourse, the language of Army psychologists and record-clerks:

SUBJECT REMEMBERS COMING
FACE TO FACE WITH VC WITH GUN;
REMEMBERS VC SQUEEZING TRIGGER;
GUN JAMMED. SUBJECT ENGAGED IN
MAGICAL THINKING RE: EPISODE:
GUILT-SURVIVOR; VALOR-MEDAL AWARD;
ONCE IN LIFETIME LOST COMPLETE CONTROL.
"WHAT WOULD HAPPEN IF I LOST CONTROL
IN DETROIT 'STEAD OF NAM?"

SUBJECT DEEPLY DISTURBED BY PROSPECT (Harper 72)[1]

---

[1] The language in this passage derives from the notes of Skip Johnson's army psychiatrist, which Nordheimer quotes at length: "*The subject remembered coming face to face with a Vietnamese with a gun. He can remember the soldier squeezing the trigger. The gun jammed. The subject has since engaged in some magical thinking about this episode. He also suffers guilt over surviving it, and later winning a high honor for the one time in his life when he lost complete control of himself. He asked: 'What would happen if I lost control of myself in Detroit and behaved like I did in Vietnam?' The prospect of such an event apparently was deeply disturbing to him*" (Nordheimer 16; italics in the original).

Alternating with these passages of bureaucratese, often on the facing page, Harper juxtaposes more lyrical passages reflecting Johnson's lived experience, though these lyrical passages, too, are heavily indebted to the *Times* article for details, and sometimes for language:

> Four M-48 tank platoons ambushed
> near Dak To, two destroyed;
> the Ho Chi Minh Trail boils,
> half my platoon rockets
> into stars near Cambodia,
> foot soldiers dance from highland woods
> taxing our burning half:
>
> *there were no caves for them to hide.* (73)[2]

Debridement reads like a scrapbook of newspaper clippings, or like what journalists used to call, in a grimly resonant metaphor, the morgue. Better, it reads like one of those ransom notes pieced together from letters scissored from the newspapers. It literalizes the idiom, "ripped from the headlines."

The second example I want to discuss is Armand Schwerner's long poem, *The Tablets*. Appearing in installments from 1968 until Schwerner's death in 1999, and published that year in a complete, posthumous edition, *The Tablets* is a book-length poem in twenty-seven sections, purporting to offer annotated scholarly translations of ancient Sumerian texts incised in clay tablets some 5,000 years ago. The translator frankly acknowledges his epistemological limitations, inserting ellipses in the text to indicate passages that defy translation, square brackets for material supplied by himself, question-marks to indicate variant readings, and strings of plus-signs to indicate passages lost because of the physical deterioration of the original clay tablets:

---

[2] Compare Nordheimer: "Their platoon of four M-48 tanks was racing down a road toward Dakto, in the Central Highlands and near the Cambodian border and the Ho Chi Minh Trail, when it was ambushed. Communist rockets knocked out two of the tanks immediately, and waves of foot soldiers sprang out of the nearby woods to attack the two tanks still in commission" (16).

>   he calls himself 'with grey horses'
>   he is 'having fine green oxen'
>   with (purpose?) + + + + + + + + + + + in the dream (nightmare?)
>   +++++++++++++++++ of a sharp blade
>   [testicles] . . . . for the ground
>   shit (sweat?) upon the . . . .
>   rain upon the . . . .
>   saliva upon the . . . .
>   heart's blood upon the . . . .
>   (Schwerner 14)

The scholar-translator also interpolates his own glosses and commentaries on the text:

>   he is impossible on the dry ground + − + + + + + + + + before
>   . . . .
>   he is non- + + + + + − + +
>   he is pre- + + + + + + + + + +*
>
>   *the isolated prefix remnants are curious. The tablet seems rubbed out with care. Is this segment an early attempt to unite form and meaning? graphic as well as substantial emptiness? (14)

The result of all this editorial intervention is a poem that is as much visual as it is verbal, one scored and scarred with unreadable signs—a kind of extended concrete poem, or poetry under erasure, "rubbed out with care."

Indeed, *The Tablets* fall "under erasure" in more than one sense, for the entire situation on which they are predicated—the translations, the clay-tablet originals, the language in which they were written, the civilization that produced them—is an elaborate fabrication, pure (or impure) fiction. *The Tablets* is a sort of benign hoax—or, as I have argued elsewhere (McHale, 'A Poet'), a mock-hoax, produced under false pretenses but not intended to deceive, or at least not to deceive for very long. No doubt there have been innocent readers who, stumbling upon *The Tablets* (or, while he was still alive, upon one of Schwerner's readings from them), were momentarily tricked into thinking these were authentic translations. But the marks of their fictionality are too conspicuous, and their ironic structure too pronounced, for the deception to work for more than a few moments, and one is quickly "wised up." It is clear that these poems have been rubbed out *with care.*

In the same place that I argued for *The Tablets'* status as a mock-hoax, I also argued for its role as the main model for *Doubled Flowering,* the alleged notebooks of the Hiroshima survivor, Araki Yasusada. Like *The Tablets, Doubled Flowering* presents itself as an annotated edition of a pre-existing text—in this case, a highly heterogeneous text, made up not only of poems and drafts of poems, but also letters, prose exercises for an English course, an imaginary entry from Rita Hayworth's diary, pages of musical notation, and other miscellaneous writings—including a shopping-list:

*[undated]**

two daikons

three rice cakes

one *[blotted by crease, eds.]* seaweed packet

4 crane eggs

empress oil   chrysanthemum root   best rice

Bear yourself with a serious air through the labyrinth of the market. Feign to ignore the [blotted by crease, eds.] spirit medium of plum-colored lips

American cologne

*[Despite the curious interjection, this appears to be a shopping list. It was found in one of the notebooks, folded into an origami bird.] (*Doubled* 26)

Like *The Tablets, Doubled Flowering* is a "gappy" text, riddled with holes—illegible words, words obscured by creases in the pages or blotted out by tears—and studded with editorial annotations and interpolations. And finally, *Doubled Flowering*, like *The Tablets*, is a mock-hoax, not a malicious one—or so I have argued. This claim is controversial, I believe—as it should be.

If my intuition is correct, and these three poems are members of the same class, then that suggests that they share certain common denominators or family resemblances. What would these be? Not their status as hoaxes or mock-hoaxes, since that would exclude Harper's *Debridement*, which is neither. Rather, what they share in common, it seems to me, are the characteristics of what I propose to call damaged or, better, *distressed* dossiers. All three texts, Harper's, Schwerner's and Yasusada's, present themselves as files or archives—a clippings file or "morgue," an archive of day tablets, a notebook—and in all three cases these files or archives have suffered damage. They are shredded and scattered, crumbled and gappy, chaotic and haphazard—or at least that's how they are presented. In short, they are *ruined* texts, and it is their shared ruinous condition that I wish to explore further in what follows, first of all by sketching a sort of genealogy of textual ruin.[3]

---

[3] Other members of the class of distressed-dossier texts include Michael Ondaatje's *The Collected Works of Billy the Kid* (1970), Harry Mathews' 'Armenian Papers' (1984), Theresa Hak Kyung Cha's *Dictee* (1995), many texts by Susan Howe, and several by Kathleen Fraser (including 'Etruscan Pages,' 'Frammenti Romani:,' 'Giotto: Arena,' and 'AD Notebooks'). Though they mix prose and verse, these are all "poems." Not all distressed dossiers are poems, however, and novels can also belong to the dossier genre, as witness such recent examples as Gilbert Sorrentino's *Mulligan Stew* (1979), Mathews' *The Journalist* (1994), Mark Z. Danielewski's *House of Leaves* (2000), and Samuel R. Delany's 'Nevèrÿon' series. While my argument bears mainly on U.S. examples, the distressed dossier is not by any means an exclusively American genre. At the same MLA convention where I first presented the material in this paper, Carlos Riobo made a compelling case for viewing the Argentine writer Manuel Puig as a novelist of the "empty archive"—in effect, my "distressed dossier." Incidentally, in coining the term "distressed dossier," I intended no allusion to Susan Stewart's essay, "Notes on Distressed Genres" (from her 1991 book *Crimes of Writing*), at least not consciously, but now that I've been reminded of it I'm happy to acknowledge that Stewart's phrase must have been in the back of my mind all along.

2. American ruin

No one will have failed to observe how much these late-century distressed dossiers owe to the modernist poetics of fragmentation—to the model of *The Waste Land*, *The Cantos*, *Paterson*, and the latter volumes of Olson's *Maximus Poems*. But while they owe much to modernism, they don't owe *everything* to it. For it seems to me that fragmentation in the distressed-dossier poems is differently motivated than modernist fragmentation, lacking the nostalgia for lost wholeness that motivates fragmentation in Eliot and sometimes in Pound, and lacking, too, or perhaps parodying, the didacticism of Pound, Williams and Olson, the insistence that we *ought to know* what's missing from the picture— and if we don't know it, we ought to go look it up. In any case, while acknowledging their manifest debt to modernism, I want to locate these distressed-dossier poems in a different genealogy, and to view them in a somewhat longer historical perspective. I want to relate them, instead, to High-Romantic practice—specifically, to the fragment-poems of the English Romantic poets (see McFarland; Rajan; Levinson). Coleridge's 'Kubla Khan' is the most notorious instance, but all of the major English Romantics—Wordsworth, Byron, Shelley, Keats and Blake, as well as Coleridge—each produced several unfinished or fragmentary poems. Some of these poems are inadvertently or accidentally unfinished, as in the case of Keats' *Hyperion* poems; others appear to be fragmentary by design, as with Byron's *The Giaour*; still others, notably 'Kubla Khan,' are undecidable.

Two aspects of the Romantic fragment-poems seem especially relevant in this context. First, they are affiliated with the hoax-poetry of the preceding century—Macpherson's Ossian poems, Chatterton's Rowley poems. Both Macpherson's and Chatterton's poems were presented as fragments, indeed as damaged dossiers, and, as Marjorie Levinson argued some twenty years ago, it was the controversy over these hoax poems that made possible the shift in reading practices necessary for reception of the next generation's fragment-poems. Secondly, the Romantic fragment-poems, as well as the fragmentary hoax-poems that preceded them, are intimately bound up with the contemporary appreciation of architectural fragments—of ruins. Emerging in the eighteenth century and persisting well into the nineteenth, this Europe-wide collective fascination with ruins manifested itself not only in poetry, but in the visual arts (from Piranesi to Caspar David Friedrich and beyond), and, most extraordinarily of all from a twentieth-century point of view, in the fabrication of artificial or sham ruins, custom-made sites of melancholic reflection, conveniently erected on one's own property—ruins built to order (see Zucker; Harbison 99–130; Holly; Woodward 126–76).

One might wonder how much relevance or appeal this aesthetics of ruin could have had for American culture of the time. "American ruin" was an oxymoron, surely. After all, the United States of the late eighteenth and early nineteenth century was still a country too young to have its own ruins—unless one took into account Indian burial-mounds, as William Cullen Bryant was compelled to do, for lack of anything better, when meditating upon American ruins in his poem, 'The Prairies' (1834). Americans who wished to experience the ruin aesthetic first-hand had to travel to Europe to sample it, as, among many others, Hawthorne and Henry James did (Woodward 20–23). James, cataloguing the deficiencies of American culture in Hawthorne's generation, notoriously begins by specifying, "No State, in the European sense of the word [...] No sovereign, no court [...], no aristocracy, no church, no clergy," and eventually works his way around to "no country gentlemen, no palaces, no castles, nor manors, nor old country-houses, nor parsonages, nor thatched cottages, nor ivied ruins [...]" (James 42). No ivied ruins: lacking them, America was barred from participation in the era's ruin aesthetic.

Or was it? As early as the mid-1830s, Bryant's contemporary and friend, the landscape painter Thomas Cole, had already completed a cycle of five paintings tracing *The Course of Empire*, beginning with *The Savage State* and *The Pastoral State* and continuing through *The Consummation of Empire* and *Destruction*, and ending where else but in *Desolation*—the ruins of the imperial city (see Perry 131–187; Barringer 51–3; Wilton 21–4; Woodward 196–9).[4] Cole's empire may

---

[4] Cole, though born in England, and eventually well-traveled in Europe, had apprenticed as a portrait-painter in Ohio, and came into his own as a painter of Hudson Valley landscapes and founder of the "Hudson River School." His friendship with Bryant is famously commemorated in Asher Durand's 1849 painting, *Kindred Spirits*.

be a generically Mediterranean one, but his landscape is unmistakably North American—the Hudson River valley—so that his cycle is both decorously historical and pointedly topical at a moment, that of Jacksonian expansionism, when America's imperial destiny was coming under troubled scrutiny and critique—not for the last time. Cole's cycle is a displaced, "mediterraneanized" reflection on the course of American empire; his ruins are, in one sense, the ruins of the future—American ruins—and, in another sense, sham ruins.

So there is, after all, an American genealogy of ruin, albeit a discontinuous one. In Europe, the ruin aesthetic persists beyond the heyday of the sham ruin, though by the twentieth century its locus has shifted from the gardens of gentlemen of taste to the canvases of painters such as Giorgio de Chirico and Paul Delvaux.[5] In the United States, after lying dormant for over a century, the taste for sham ruins revives in the second half of the twentieth century, taking new postmodernist forms. The revived aesthetics of ruin manifests itself in a range of conceptual, installation, and earth-art works: for instance, in some of the projects of Robert Smithson, such as his conceptual project, 'A Tour of the Monuments of Passaic, New Jersey' (1967), or his 'Buried Shed' at Kent State University (1970); in the split houses and sliced-up office-buildings of the "anarchitect," Gorden Matta-Clark, from the late Seventies; or in Michael Heizer's work-in-progress, his 'City' in the Nevada desert, a sham ruin on a brobdingnagian scale.[6] Traces of a sham-ruin aesthetic can also be detected in various projects documented by James Wines under the rubric of "de-architecture," including Wines' own collaborations with the SITE collective on a series of mock-ruined façades for the Best Product store chain from the mid-Seventies to the mid-Eighties. This same sham-ruin aesthetic also animates Charles Moore's signature project, his giddily postmodern Piazza d'Italia in New Orleans, as it does, more recently, Terry Nicholson's upside-down

---

[5] One striking counter-example to this generalization is Ian Hamilton Finlay's garden at Stonypath, Scotland, which combines concrete poetry, installation art, and sham ruin; see Abrioux. The faux-ruin imagery of Delvaux's paintings is recycled as textual representation of ruin in Alain Robbe-Grillet's *Topolgie d'un cité fantôme* (1976). I have tried to make a connection between Delvaux's faux-ruins and Schwerner's in McHale, 'Topology.'

[6] On Smithson's 'A Tour of the Monuments,' see Perloff; on the work of Matta-Clark, see Diserens.

building in Orlando, housing WonderWorks, the Museum of Natural Phenomena.[7]

The sham-ruin aesthetic even leaks through from these conceptual, meta-architectural, and populist works to some of the more soberly ambitious architectural projects of recent decades. Indeed, the aesthetics of ruin can already be discerned in the work of the high-minded late-modernist Louis Kahn, whose exposure to the classical ruins of Europe left a lasting imprint on his own severe architecture style. For instance, it is reported (among other places, in the 2004 documentary film *My Architect* by Kahn's son Nathaniel) that, during the war for Bangladeshi independence, Pakistani pilots spared the government complex in Dacca, designed by Kahn, because from the air they mistook the complex for ancient ruins! Ruins serve even more decisively as a model for architects associated with the deconstructivist tendency in architecture, including Frank Gehry (before he discovered titanium and turned populist), Peter Eisenman, and Daniel Libeskind, who returned from Europe to design the buildings that may some day stand where the Twin Towers once stood.[8]

If the imitation ruins of a Kahn or a Libeskind are serious, challenging buildings, some of the other manifestations of the ruin aesthetic, such as Moore's Piazza d'Italia, appear merely to toy with the idea of ruins. They evade rather than confront the ruined state of things. But what does America need to evade, anyway? After all, apart from Pearl Harbor, the United States itself was spared the large-scale ruin inflicted on other countries in the twentieth century by two world wars and endless regional conflicts. Nevertheless, I think it can be demonstrated that there is an underlying seriousness to the return of the "ruin sentiment" in late-century America. Far from being merely a frivolous exercise in retro fashion, the American ruin aesthetic is haunted by an awareness of the reality of ruin, and of one real instance of ruin in particular: the ruin visited on the Japanese cities of Hiroshima and Nagasaki by American atomic weapons.

---

[7] "Natural phenomena" here include the hurricane which is supposed to have lifted this courthouse building from the Bahamas and dropped it roof-first onto a citrus warehouse in Orlando; anyway, that's their story, and they're sticking to it. See Woodward 147–8.

[8] On deconstructivist architecture, see Johnson and Wigley; Wigley; and Derrida and Eisenman. See also Woodward 221.

Hiroshima haunts late-century American culture—not, indeed, as a source of guilt (since we have never actually assumed full responsibility for the atom-bombings), but as a precedent and model for what seemed likely to happen to the American cities. The Hiroshima model permeates popular culture in particular. Survival amid the ruins of a post-nuclear-war civilization became a *topos* of late-century science-fiction novels and films. Memorable examples, among the dozens, perhaps hundreds of novels making use of the *topos*, are Walter M. Miller's classic *A Canticle for Leibowitz* (1959), Kim Stanley Robinson's *The Wild Shore* (1984), and Denis Johnson's *Fiskadoro* (1985).[9] On the big screen, the representative image might be the final scene of *Planet of the Apes* (1968), when Charlton Heston, as an astronaut returned to Earth from deep space, discovers the ruins of the Statue of Liberty, half-buried in the sand (see Woodward 1, 196). Weightier and more revealing than these sorts of examples, however, are the chilling images that the science-fiction illustrator Chesley Bonestell painted at the height of the Cold War, in 1950 and 1951, to accompany articles in the mass-circulation magazine, *Collier's*. These aerial views of Manhattan and Washington D.C. ruined and ablaze clearly evoke what we might call the iconography of Hiroshima. They displace the Hiroshima model to American metropolises. Indeed, one of the *Collier's* articles that Bonestell illustrated was actually entitled, 'Hiroshima U.S.A.'

Though over half a century old, Bonestell's disturbing images of ruin are *not* obsolete—not relics of an outmoded Cold War sensibility. On the contrary, they have never seemed more topical than they do now, in the aftermath of the 9/11 events, which they seem almost to anticipate. Moreover, it takes very little updating to accommodate Bonestell's imagery to a twenty-first century ruin sensibility. This has been demonstrated by Alexis Rockman, whose astonishing mural, *Manifest Destiny*, was unveiled at the Brooklyn Museum of Art in 2004.

---

[9] I would be tempted to add *Riddley Walker* (1980), except that it is set in England; however, its author, Russell Hoban, is an American. Needless to say, the *topos* of post-apocalypse is not an American monopoly; think, for instance, of Angela Carter's *Heroes and Villains* (1969) and Maggie Gee's *The Burning Book* (1983)—two English post-apocalyptic novels—or the Australian director George Miller's *Mad Max* films (though the catastrophe here appears to be environmental rather than nuclear), or Katsuhiro Otomo's *Akira*, both in its graphic-novel and its animated-film forms.

Imagining Brooklyn's ruined waterfront 3,000 years from now, when rising sea-waters have overwhelmed the city, and global warming has radically altered its flora and fauna, Rockman manages to fold into a single painting the entire history of the iconography of American ruin, from Thomas Cole to Chesley Bonestell to, yes, even *Planet of the Apes*. Commissioned and planned *before* 9/11, though executed after, *Manifest Destiny* converges uncannily with the imagery of ruin associated with that day and its aftermath.

It converges, too, with a different iconography of contemporary ruin: photographic images of America's inner-city and industrial ruins, particularly as documented by the photographer Camilo José Vergara in his arresting and admirable books, *The New American Ghetto* (1995) and especially *American Ruins* (1999). Like Rockman's *Manifest Destiny*, Vergara's photographs are images of self-inflicted ruin. No enemy did this to us; we did it to ourselves, whether by allowing accumulating greenhouse gases to alter the climate, as in Rockman's image, or by tolerating the gutting of America's industrial base, and the urban life that depended on it, as in Vergara's photographs. Unlike Rockman's image, of course, Vergara's photographs do not anticipate some future ruin, but document present ruin, ruins in progress.[10] The ubiquity of such ruins in our urban landscapes, and the existence of documentary photographs such as Vergara's, enhances by association the gravity and significance even of the most frivolous of our contemporary sham ruins. Indeed, sham ruins can *become* real ruins: Moore's Piazza d'Italia, toying with the idea of ruin, ended up falling into ruin itself, the victim of the City of New Orleans' shifting priorities for its downtown neighborhoods.

---

[10] This *topos*, too, has its memorable literary examples, both within and outside the science-fiction genre: Paul Auster's *In the Country of Last Things* (1987), Kathy Acker's *Empire of the Senseless* (1988), Octavia Butler's *Parable of the Sower* (1993), the South Bronx episodes of Don DeLillo's *Underworld* (1997), and so on. More positive visions of urban ruin—the ruined city as utopia, or heterotopia—are to be found in Delany's *Dhalgren* (1974) and in Belize's vision of heaven as San Francisco in ruins, from Tony Kushner's *Angels in America*, part two, *Perestroika* (Act 3, Scene 5). The equivalent here of *Planet of the Apes*' iconic Statue of Liberty in ruins might be the ruined Golden Gate Bridge of William Gibson's *Idoru* trilogy, shaken to pieces by an earthquake but reclaimed and colonized by urban squatters.

From this complex genealogy of American ruin, I want to disentangle two strands. First of all, many of these images of American ruin involve a strategy of *displacement*: one pictures the ruins of a particular time and place, or of a particular type, by evoking the ruins of a *different* time and place, belonging to a *different* type. Thus, Thomas Cole displaces the future ruin of Jacksonian America onto a generic Mediterranean empire; Bonestell displaces the iconography of Hiroshima onto Manhattan and Washington; and so on. Secondly, texts are implicated in ruin, and vice-versa, ruins in text, throughout this history of American ruin. On the crumbling walls of the "new American ghetto," for instance, Vergara's camera documents pathetic or apocalyptic graffiti, ruined texts inscribed on ruined walls. Often, destroyed or fragmentary texts function as figures—metonymic figures, but also metaphors—for ruined civilizations. In Miller's *A Canticle for Leibowitz*, civilization's slow recovery after nuclear holocaust depends on the survival of a haphazard cache of documents left behind by a long-dead nobody, one I.E. Leibowitz—scribbled notes, a blueprint, a racing form, even, as in *Doubled Flowering*, a shopping-list. In *Gravity's Rainbow* (1973), Thomas Pynchon's novel about Europe's destruction in the Second World War—which is also, by displacement, a novel of our own future nuclear ruin—his hero, Slothrop, gleans news of the Hiroshima bombing from the cryptic scrap of a front page blowing through the streets of a ruined city. Ray Bradbury's *Fahrenheit 451* (1953), which everyone remembers as a novel about the suppression of books, is also a novel about nuclear war. At its climax, the book-hating civilization from which its book-loving protagonist flees is destroyed in a nuclear holocaust, and all its remaining books—except the memorized ones—are consumed in firestorms. Over and over again, these texts and images confirm Derrida' insight (1984) that what a future nuclear holocaust would crucially deprive us of is the *archive*, the stockpile of written texts on which we would depend to reconstruct our world, and which is so vulnerable to the fire next time.

3. Imitative form

After this genealogical excursion, I want briefly to revisit the three distressed-dossier poems with which I began.

In Harper's *Debridement*, the form of the distressed dossier functions as a complex figuration of several kinds of ruin. Saturated with the language of the Vietnam War—or rather its many languages, in the plural, including the language of military operations, of battlefield medical procedures, and of military bureaucracy, as well as the profane colloquial speech of G.I.s—*Debridement* functions as a figure of the war itself. But it also figures forth the shattered city of Detroit to which the soldier-hero returns, and in which he dies—the same shattered city that we see pictured in so many of Vergara's photographs of American ruin. In a sense, one ruin has been displaced onto another, the ruined battlefield of Vietnam onto the ruined urban fabric of Detroit. This is perhaps one way of understanding the Post-Traumatic Stress Disorder that crippled and consumed Skip Johnson—as the deferral and displacement of ruin, ruin in the wrong place. In any case, this brings us to a third and crucial figurative function of the distressed dossier in *Debridement*: it figures forth the ruined self of the psychically damaged Vietnam veteran, himself a figure—a metonymy, or better a synecdoche—for the larger ruin, both of the country in which he fought and of his own hometown. Sounding like the sort of graffiti that Vergara finds on ruined walls, Harper's text, reflecting upon itself, declares that "THIS IS CLINICAL HISTORY: BODY POETRY TORN ASUNDER." The body of the poem, torn asunder and reassembled as a distressed dossier, figures the body and psyche of the distressed soldier.

At first glance, the relevance of Schwerner's *Tablets* to the *topos* of American ruin seems harder to grasp. After all, the civilization that allegedly produced the texts making up this distressed dossier existed in a time and place about as distant from contemporary America as possible. To grasp this poem's connection to the American situation, its real-world context needs to be taken into account, by which I mean not only its historical context—the eras of Cold War and détente—but specifically the context of the poet's own career. Before he embarked on *The Tablets* in the late Sixties, Armand Schwerner's only major published work, co-authored with the psychoanalyst Donald M. Kaplan, was, of all things, a dictionary—but a very remarkable one. Published in 1963, *The Domesday Dictionary* is an invaluable document of Cold War sensibility, and a ferocious critique of that sensibility. The dictionary's entries cover weapons technology, nuclear physics, the strategy of deterrence, intelligence-gathering, civil defense, the physiology of radiation sickness—the whole range of Cold War topics. Its method is irony—not the stable, verbal irony of Ambrose Bierce's *The Devil's Dictionary*, with which it is often compared (I think misleadingly), but an unstable, deadpan irony that depends upon the flattest of tones and the sharpest of juxtapositions:

Dachau
A town in Upper Bavaria, Germany, 8 miles northwest of Munich on the railway from Munich to Ingolstadt. Population (1939) 17,549. It has extensive fortifications, a castle and a museum of antiquities, and makes paper, sawmill machinery and beer. It formerly had a colony of artists. (Kaplan and Schwerner 72)

Kiva
A sacred ceremonial chamber of the Pueblo Indians, approached with greatest awe. Also, the remote-controlled laboratory where critical-mass experiments were conducted for the first fission-fusion bomb (*q.v.*). This later kiva was observed by television a quarter of a mile away. (Kaplan and Schwerner 161–2)

This reads as though it were written by Dr. Strangelove, without the German accent—or perhaps by Strangelove's real-world model, the architect of deterrence, Herman Kahn (who is frequently cited throughout, in fact).

But of course, it wasn't written by Dr. Strangelove or Herman Kahn, but by two ironists whose views were the *opposite* of Kahn's, and who used the voice of an insanely rational pedant to undermine the world-view reflected in their entries. It is this same tone of insanely rational pedantry that one hears in the scholar-translator of Schwerner's *Tablets*. Viewed from the vantage-point of *The Domesday Dictionary*, *The Tablets* appear as a kind of sequel, the effect—a ruined civilization—of which the Cold War world-view ventriloquized in *The Domesday Dictionary* is the cause. In this perspective, the form of the distressed dossier in *The Tablets* functions as a displaced image of future nuclear ruin—displaced, like Thomas Cole's image in *Desolation*, in both time and space, from the near future to the distant past, and from America to Mesopotamia. One might even go so far as to claim, a little paradoxically, that through its distressed-dossier form, *The Tablets* literalize, before the fact, Derrida's vision of civilization's destroyed archive.

Finally, I want to return to the Yasusada notebooks in order to make a few observations about how they appear to me in relation to the context I have been trying to construct for them here. Bill Freind has written in one place about the "textualization of the context" in *Doubled Flowering* (Freind 148). He has in mind the way the Hiroshima bombing comes to be incorporated into the text of *Doubled Flowering*, even though the text itself barely refers to the bombing. I propose to take this notion of the textualization of the context even more literally than Freind himself does, and to treat the distressed dossier of *Doubled Flowering* as the literal textualization of the destroyed city of Hiroshima itself—a kind of iconic representation of the city in ruins. Moreover, that city is a displaced figure for other cities, ruined cities of the future, like the Manhattan and Washington of Bonestell's illustrations—or like the Manhattan and Washington of 9/11, for that matter.

Or, to put it a little differently: the heterogeneous, haphazard, damaged dossier which is *Doubled Flowering* functions, as *The Tablets* do, as a figure of the destroyed city. Like Harper's *Debridement*, it also figures forth a distressed self, the survivor Araki Yasusada: the notebook, figuratively, is the man. Furthermore, each of these objects of figuration figures the other, reciprocally: the man, Yasusada, is a figure, simultaneously metonymic and metaphorical, for the city, while the city is a figure for the man, and the notebook is a figure for both of them.

This is certainly a complex arrangement, but not an unintelligible one, as long as one is not too intimidated by the ban on what Yvor Winters used to call "the fallacy of imitative form" (Winters, *In Defense* 41, 61–2, 144, 648 n. 87; *The Function* 54). Like other so-called fallacies of the New-Critical era, this one is well worth thinking about, but also well worth committing, when necessary. All three of these distressed-dossier poems egregiously violate the ban on imitative form; all three of them *do* imitate their content—ruined cities, ruined selves—in their ruined form. "The tablet seems rubbed out with care," observes Schwerner's scholar-translator. "Is this segment an early attempt to unite form and meaning? graphic as well as substantial emptiness?" Winters believed that imitative form would always be an inadequate solution to the problem of giving form to contents that defy form; but perhaps in these cases, formal imitation is the least inadequate solution to an intractable representational problem.

4. Postmemory, after-image

I have one last point to make by way of a coda, and it involves a final bid to justify Yasusada. Such bids are entirely in order, as I hope I made clear at the outset. We should perpetually place ourselves in the position of having to justify *Doubled Flowering* afresh, whenever we revisit it; we should never regard its legitimacy as a given.

One issue that the Yasusada case raises in a particularly pointed way is that of *authorization*: who is authorized to speak for (on behalf of, in the name of) historical victims who are helpless to speak for themselves? This question does not, it seems to me, admit of any definitive or categorical answer, but is precisely a matter of degree, of relative distance. Take Harper's *Debridement*, for instance. It might be argued that, since Harper never actually served in Vietnam himself, he has no right to speak on behalf of the Vietnam veteran Skip Johnson, as he presumes to do in *Debridement*. Nevertheless, as an African-American man of Johnson's generation, Harper arguably has more right to speak for Skip Johnson than many other poets do—more right, say, than the Yasusada poet (assuming that he is, after all, a white American, and not Japanese or Japanese-American) does to speak for Hiroshima survivors. Harper, then, has a *relative* right to speak on Skip Johnson's behalf. Authorization, from this perspective, appears to be a matter of *degree*—degrees of "second-handedness."

"Degree of second-handedness" does not seem a very satisfactory way to address such a fraught subject as victimhood and its representation. It does, however, converge in some respects with important discussions of Holocaust memory, in particular with Marianne Hirsch's concept of "postmemory," the memory of those who were raised by Holocaust survivors, and whose relationship to the historical trauma is mediated by the narratives of others. A similar second-handedness is captured by James E. Young's notion of "after-images" of the Holocaust, the images of those (like the graphic novelist Art Spiegelman, the photographer David Levinthal, or the installation artist Shimon Attie) whose experience of the Holocaust is not direct but mediated, even *hypermediated*. In the end, this mediated, postmemorial relationship to historical atrocities—to the Holocaust, but also to the bombing of Hiroshima and others—is one that we all share, apart from those few among us (fewer and fewer, as the years go on) who were actually there, and survived. These approaches to the memory (or postmemory) of the Holocaust perhaps give us tools for thinking about other instances of second-hand, mediated relationship to historical atrocity—tools, though not solutions.

For Young, our foremost scholar of Holocaust memorials, the problem of how to publicly commemorate the Holocaust is irresolvable and interminable. The solutions he finds most compelling are not monuments, but various types of *countermonument*: vanishing monuments, like the one near Hamburg designed by Jochen and Esther Gerz; negative-space monuments, like the one proposed by Rachel Whiteread for Vienna; uncanny ones, like Libeskind's Jewish Museum in Berlin; self-consuming monuments, invisible monuments, destroyed monuments, non-monuments. These alone, in Young's view, have any chance of commemorating events that defy representation and symbolization. In this perspective, it is perhaps easier to understand the astonishing success of something like Maya Lin's Vietnam War Memorial. Derided when it first opened for its refusal of conventional monumentality, it has come to be embraced by the public, veterans and non-veterans alike, partly, no doubt, because it addresses head-on the inadequacy of monumental commemoration in the face of historical trauma—because, in other words, of its countermonumentality.

The architecture critic Robert Harbison compares the Vietnam memorial to "the half-buried pages of a huge book" (64). Yes, that is certainly one of the images it evokes, though hardly the only one. It is also an archaeological trench, the foundations of a vanished building, an excavated ruin. Seen in this light, the Vietnam War Memorial's closest literary analogue might be something like a ruined text or distressed dossier—something, indeed, like Harper's *Debridement*, a poem in the form of a scrapbook of newspaper clippings, commemorating the historical trauma of Vietnam. How better to commemorate historical trauma textually than in the form of a distressed dossier—a scrapbook, an archive of crumbling clay tablets, *The Notebooks of Araki Yasusada*? These, I want to suggest, are the literary equivalents of the countermonuments that Young honors—vanishing, invisible, uncanny, destroyed monuments—and like them, they reflect and acknowledge various degrees of second-handedness, of distance from the direct experience of atrocity. They also, perhaps, commemorate in advance the ruins of the future—that future that we might have caught a glimpse of on 9/11.

James Young, who served on the commission that chose the design for the German national Memorial for the Murdered Jews of Europe in Berlin, was also conscripted for the World Trade Center redesign committee. Early in the public discussion of how to commemorate 9/11, various countermonumental proposals were floated, of a kind that Young might have found compelling, including one to preserve a ruined fragment of the Trade Center's facade, and another to permit visitors to the site access to the "slurry wall" that shores up its subterranean level. Both of these ruined countermonuments were vetoed, and in the end what we are getting is something tasteful, tidy, and all too canny, more like shopping-mall décor than like a ruin. We can only hope that, in the absence of any appropriate countermonument on the site, the 9/11 events will some day be appropriately commemorated in a ruined text. Perhaps they already have, by anticipation.[11]

The most adequate Holocaust memorial of all, in Young's view, is precisely the perpetual inability to resolve the problem of how best to

---

[11] As I write, the arts sections of the newspapers are full of stories about how novelists are finally catching up, some three and a half years later, with the events of 9/11. Regularly mentioned in this context are new novels such as Ian McEwan's *Saturday* and Jonathan Safran Foer's *Extremely Loud and Incredibly Close*. The arts journalists appear to have overlooked two earlier and (I suspect) richer responses to 9/11, William Gibson's *Pattern Recognition* (2003), in which the gap, already narrow, between futuristic science fiction and contemporary realism finally, definitely closes, and Don DeLillo's *Cosmopolis* (also 2003) which, though nominally set on a day in April 2000, is unmistakably a post-9/11 fiction.

commemorate the Holocaust. "Better a thousand years of Holocaust memorial competitions in Germany," he writes, "than any single 'final solution' to Germany's memorial problem" (*At Memory's Edge* 94). I want to adapt his view to the problems of authorization, second-handedness, and mediated relationship to atrocity that are raised by the Yasusada case. Better, I want to say, an interminable controversy about Yasusada than any final solution to the problem of who may speak for the victim.

Works Cited

Abrioux, Yves. *Ian Hamilton Finlay: A Visual Primer*. Cambridge MA: MIT Press, 1992.

Barringer, Tim. 'The Course of Empires: Landscape and Identity in America and Britain, 1820–1880.' In Wilton and Barringer, eds., *American Sublime*. 38–65.

Derrida, Jacques. 'No Apocalypse, Not Now (full speed ahead, seven missiles, seven missives).' Trans. Catherine Porter and Philip Lewis. *Diacritics* 14:2 (Summer 1984): 20–31.

Derrida, Jacques and Peter Eisenman. *Chora L Works*. Ed. Jeffrey Kipnis and Thomas Leeser. New York: The Monacelli Press, 1997.

Diserens, Corinne. 'Gordon Matta-Clark.' *Installation Art. Art and Design*. Ed. Andrew Benjamin. London: Academy Editions, 2003. 34–41.

Freind, Bill. 'Deferral of the Author: Impossible Witness and the Yasusada Poems.' *Poetics Today* 25:1 (2004): 137–58.

Harbison, Robert. *The Built, the Unbuilt, and the Unbuildable*. Cambridge MA: MIT Press, 1991.

Harper, Michael S. *Debridement*. Garden City NY: Doubleday, 1973.

Hirsch, Marianne. 'Mourning and Postmemory.' In *Family Frames: Photography, Narrative and Postmemory*, 17–40. Cambridge MA: Harvard UP, 1997.

Holly, Grant I. 'The Ruins of Allegory and the Allegory of Ruins.' In Bill Readings and Bennet Schaber, eds., *Postmodernism Across the Ages: Essays for a Postmodernity That Wasn't Born Yesterday*, 188–215. Syracuse: Syracuse UP, 1993.

James, Henry. *Hawthorne*. New York: Harper and Brothers, 1879.

Johnson, Philip and Mark Wigley. *Deconstructivist Architecture*. New York: The Museum of Modern Art/Boston: Little, Brown, 1988.

Kaplan, Donald M. and Armand Schwerner. *The Domesday Dictionary*. Ed. Louise J. Kaplan. New York: Simon and Schuster, 1963.

Levinson, Marjorie. *The Romantic Fragment Poem: A Critique of a Form.* Chapel Hill, NC: U of North Carolina Press, 1986.

McFarland, Thomas. *Romanticism and the Forms of Ruin: Wordsworth, Coleridge, and Modalities of Fragmentation.* Princeton NJ: Princeton UP, 1981.

McHale, Brian. '"A Poet May Not Exist": Mock-Hoaxes and the Construction of National Identity.' In Robert Griffin, ed., *Faces of Anonymity,* 233–52. New York: Palgrave, 2003.

———. 'Topology of a Phantom City: *The Tablets* as Hoax.' *Talisman* 19 (1998–99): 86–9.

Motokiyu, Tosa, Ojiu Norinaga, and Okura Kyojin, trans. and ed. *Doubled Flowering: From the Notebooks of Araki Yasusada.* New York: Roof Books, 1997.

Nordheimer, Jon. 'From Dakto to Detroit: Death of a Troubled Hero.' *The New York Times,* May 26, 1971, 1, 16.

Perloff, Marjorie. *The Futurist Moment: Avant-Garde, Avant Guerre, and the Language of Rupture.* Chicago: U of Chicago Press, 1986.

Perry, Ellwood C., III. *The Art of Thomas Cole: Ambition and Imagination.* Newark: U of Delaware Press/London and Toronto: Associated UP, 1988.

Rajan, Balachandra. *The Form of the Unfinished: English Poetics from Spenser to Pound.* Princeton NJ: Princeton UP, 1985.

Schwerner, Armand. *The Tablets.* Orono ME: National Poetry Foundation, 1999.

Stewart, Susan *Crimes of Writing: Problems in the Containment of Representation,* 102–131. New York: Oxford UP, 1991.

Vergara, Camilo José. *American Ruins.* New York: The Monacelli Press, 1999.

———. *The New American Ghetto.* New Brunswick NJ: Rutgers UP, 1995.

Wigley, Mark. *The Architecture of Deconstruction: Derrida's Haunt.* Cambridge MA and London: MIT Press, 1993.

Wilton, Andrew. 'The Sublime in the Old World and the New.' In Wilton and Barringer, eds., *American Sublime.* 10–37.

——— and Tim Barringer, eds. *American Sublime: Landscape Painting in the United States, 1820–1880.* Princeton NJ: Princeton UP, 2002.

Wines, James. *De-Architecture.* New York: Rizzoli, 1987.

Winters, Yvor. *In Defense of Reason.* New York: The Swallow Press and William Morrow, 1947.

———. *The Function of Criticism: Problems and Exercises.* Denver: Alan Swallow, 1957.

Woodward, Christopher. *In Ruins.* New York: Pantheon, 2001.

Young, James E. *At Memory's Edge: After-Images of the Holocaust in Contemporary Art and Architecture.* New Haven CT: Yale UP, 2000.

———. *The Texture of Memory: Holocaust Memorials and Meaning.* New Haven CT: Yale UP, 1993.

Zucker, Paul. 'Ruins—An Aesthetic Hybrid.' *Journal of Aesthetics and Art Criticism* 20.2(1961): 119–130.

Doubled Flowering: Charles Yu, Araki Yasusada and the Politics of Faking Race

Paisley Rekdal

Five years ago, I taught my first advanced literature course in Asian American poetry at the University of Utah. The decision to do this was made with hasty curiosity, arising from the fact that some of my poems had just been included in an anthology of younger Asian-American poets: an act of generosity and possible desperation on the editors' part because I don't tend to write poems that address my biracial background (I am of half-Chinese and half-Norwegian descent), nor am I aware of fitting into what historically constitutes "Asian American" poetry as a whole. My academic background is an advanced degree in western medieval literature; the only knowledge I have of Asian American culture is almost entirely personal and rarely called upon for the edification of friends since, by many accounts, I look white enough to "pass," thus culturally disappear. A lifetime of being between two faces has taught me my social value: I am exotic enough to satisfy most people's interests in and need for authentic representation, but not so exotic as to make them feel guilty about anything. In short, I am contemporary America's ideal minority.

I bring this up only to foreground some of the tensions inherent to my decision to teach this class, tensions that only increased upon discovering the poetry of both Charles Yu and Araki Yasusada that semester. Yasusada, a famous avant-garde hoax, was purportedly a Japanese poet who survived the bombing of Hiroshima but who lost almost his entire family in the blast. An avid reader of Jack Spicer and Roland Barthes, Yasusada sporadically published his poems in Japanese avant-garde magazines, becoming famous only after his "death," when English translations of his work surfaced in the pages of journals like *American Poetry Review, Grand Street* and *Conjunctions* during the late 90s. The hoax lasted several months before editors became suspicious; Wesleyan University Press, upon learning that the Japanese poet might never have existed, withdrew its offer to publish Yasusada's collected poems. *Doubled Flowering: From the Notebooks of Araki Yasusada* was published by Roof Books in 1997. As of this writing, no one has come forward to claim responsibility for the hoax, though in all likelihood its author is Kent Johnson, a poet, community college teacher and translator of Spanish poetry who sent Yasusada's work to various magazines on behalf of Yasusada's "translators," who "edited" *Doubled Flowering*, and is the one to whom all the literary journals' fee checks were written.

I learned about Yasusada's work, ironically, through the poetry of Charles Yu, another hoax that I'd uncovered in the anthology I'd assigned for class. The book—a historical overview of Asian American poetry from the late nineteenth century up to the 1970s entitled *Quiet Fire*—included Charles Yu, a Chinese student purportedly living in Chicago in the late 30s. During a random internet search on Yu, however, I discovered through a rare bookseller's site that this Chinese student-poet was really a pseudonymous identity for a Jewish-American editor for GP Putnam's Sons named William Targ, the same editor who rose to national prominence for buying and editing the *Godfather* novels.[1] In 1941, Black Archer Press in Chicago brought out Targ's *Poems of a Chinese Student* under the Charles Yu pseudonym after several poems under Yu's name were published in the *Chicago Tribune*.

The anxiety I felt upon learning this fact was great indeed. All semester long I'd fielded questions from a small but vocal minority of students as to my course's efficacy (it fulfilled both the university's and department's diversity requirement) and relevance to the field of literature as whole, concerns I myself had reluctantly begun to share upon finding so few engaging anthologies; indeed, *Quiet Fire* was the only historical overview of its kind I could purchase. There were a few students who had signed up for my course much the same way I had chosen my reading materials—based on market constraints and artificial requirements—and so would sit in the back of the room, glaring into their dog-eared books to avoid catching my attention. Day by day they

---

[1] Interestingly, Targ had also bought *Six Persons*, Amiri Baraka's second novel, for $75,000, only to be disappointed later in its experimental form. What Targ had wanted, as he wrote Baraka's literary agent Ronald Hobbs On April 3, 1974, was "a popular novel that would be a successor to *The Godfather*..." (Howard Papers, Box 3). What he had wanted, clearly, was the kind of novel that would do for African Americans what *The Godfather* had done for Italian Americans: provide an "authentic" archetypal story they would forever have to work with and against. Six Persons was never published by Putnam. It remained unpublished for a quarter of a century.

slogged through the Marxist poems of H. T. Tsiang, Jessica Hagedorn's performance pieces and Toyo Suyemoto's pastoral quatrains, sulkily watching the rest of the class winnow out subtleties of form and meaning. They perked up for both Charles Bulosan and Wen I-To's 'The Laundry Song,' but sank back into self-satisfied consternation after *Quiet Fire* proved itself repetitive, alternating between poets whose poems focused on political rage and the refusal to assimilate, and poets who longed to "blend in" to a utopian America that eluded them. Many of the poems either bored or aesthetically revolted me as well, and they insulted my students' intelligence about racial politics in America. Each night before class, I would sit at my desk, groaning as I tried to imagine how I would have to fake fresh enthusiasm in the morning. For a while, I even toyed with the idea of pretending to be white for the semester in the vague, self-hating hopes that my presumed whiteness might validate the subject where my perceived Asianness would only further undercut it.

"What's the point of segregating literature unless the poems can't hold up?" one student challenged at last, holding up the anthology with the tips of his fingers. "If it's good literature, then we should just read it all together."

"An excellent suggestion," I replied. "One that I agree with, and one that I'm sure the university has already taken. So how many great poems that happen to have been written by Asian-Americans have you already read in your literature courses?" The students looked baffled. "African-Americans?" A few shrugged. "Latinos?" They glanced at each other.

"Well," one student finally said. "*None*, of course."

Leaving aside that "of course" for the moment, the class' reaction to the Charles Yu hoax I discovered was—with few exceptions—delighted astonishment. Even though I knew he was a fake, I decided to teach Yu as if he had existed, letting the students respond to the poems in whatever way they chose the day they were assigned his work from the anthology. They were particularly intrigued by his poem 'In America,' in which the poet and his friend (a mysterious Miss Jones) enter a night club to find "a beautiful Negress" standing on stage, singing a Yiddish lament. The poem itself is at first a simplistic examination of racial mixing in America in which the "exotic" sexuality of the Black singer is exaggerated, almost parodied: her skin, as Yu notes, is "brown as fresh iodine,/ her lips [like] coral lacquer," and she fills the entire club with "the quickening scent of [her] musk" while singing to "the beat of a tom-tom" (QF 59). My students (by now exquisitely attuned to such stereotyping) immediately dismissed the first stanza's effects but were baffled by the second, in which the poet writes:

> Only in America could it occur:
> This Negress passionately singing
> *Eli Eli Lomo Asovtoni,*
> The Yiddish lament
> Written by a New Yorker
> For a drama dealing
> With Chinese Jews (QF 59).

Chinese Jews? The specific references in these last lines stumped them: what did Yu mean by this? Here, I stopped class discussion and confessed what I knew: the last lines of the poem were meant to baffle, to reveal the poet's true identity.[2]

Three students in the back began to laugh. Here it was at last, proof that race and ethnicity were little more than formulaic narratives anyone could write. The fact that an Asian-American editor and professor had fallen for the hoax itself proved that we weren't interested in literature but representation—anyone, my students argued, could see how bad these poems were. Why would Yu have been included in any anthology except for the fact that he was supposedly Chinese? Who knew how many other writers weren't actually Asian American or African American or Latino in these anthologies they were being forced to read; who knew how many other, better, white writers were being ignored at the expense of politics?

In part to answer these questions, in part to assure myself that I could find answers to such questions, I began asking colleagues about other poems they knew of that were racialized fakes, and Craig Dworkin

---

[2] The trick evidently worked for Yu's first publication. Soon after *Poems* was published, Charles Yu was invited to speak before a Chicago women's literary group interested in Chinese culture.

emailed me several articles about Yasusada. The class on Yu had opened the floodgates for discussion: the barely suppressed resentments about the anthology we'd been studying (the students' as well as mine) rose to the surface, along with the fear inherent to the discussion of race and literature, a discussion that has always been grounded in the anxiety of cultural authenticity—who is or isn't "really" Asian, what does it mean to be or not be white, what does it mean for something to be anthologized or taught as "good" representations of race? When we turned from Charles Yu to Araki Yasusada, these questions had to be changed, in part because of the different levels of seriousness to the poets' biographies. For my students, it was one thing to pretend to be a Chinese student living in Chicago in the 1930s, another thing entirely to pretend to have survived the bombing of Hiroshima, to have lost one's wife and youngest daughter in the blast, to have watched one's eldest daughter perish of radiation sickness four years later.

Likewise, while students were willing to challenge the notion of what it meant to be Asian-*American*, they would hesitate to challenge definitions of what it meant to be Asian. Nationality was still at stake, but here national boundaries also represented racial boundaries, which is not, at least in our current vision of ourselves, supposedly the case for the United States. For my students, issues of authenticity with regard to Yasusada were about lived experience first, race a very distant second; only a handful of students equated Yasusada's identity as victim of the Hiroshima bombings with his also being racially Japanese. Most students preferred to think of his lived experience as resulting from a political tragedy separate from the issue of race. "We could have bombed anyone like that," one young man said. "In fact, we did."

In fact, actually, we didn't. The atomic bomb was a different bomb altogether from the bombs dropped on Dresden, and it was unleashed on Japan for a variety of reasons—practical, political, and, frankly, racial: reasons similar to our decision to put Japanese-Americans and not German- or Italian-Americans into internment camps. While some students added historical embellishments to the argument—that we dropped the bomb only on Japan because we had not invented it in time to drop it on Germany, that the Japanese had initiated the war, that more people died in Dresden than in both Hiroshima and Nagasaki put together—what became central to their argument was how quickly the responsibility might be shifted away from America, back onto the Japanese or the Germans or, simply, history itself. Clearly, our bombings of Hiroshima and Nagasaki still embarrass us; they trouble the notion we have of ourselves as the heroes who helped liberate Europe from the Nazis, highlighting instead the ways our own racism directed our wartime policies, making the conflict between the two nations as much about ethnic as military superiority. The Yasusada-poet himself recognizes this link and forces us to see it in his poem 'Walkers with Ladle,' in which a mysterious group of people he simply refers to as "they" at one point command the poet, in English, "Don't you dare fucking walk you fucking Jap fucker" (*Doubled* 30).

I bring all this up in order to point out that, though for many the issue of the Yu fakery and the Yasusada hoax may "feel" the same, there are deep political and historical differences between these poets regarding anti-Asian racism, and thus different ways we must react to work that is, autobiographically speaking, false. The Yu poems aren't interested in discovering what it means to be Chinese: they are persona poems through which Targ can parody or discuss *white* ideas about race. Targ's point is to play a joke on his audience, a theory proven by the fact that he "outs" himself as Jewish both in the poem "In America" and in his memoir, *Indecent Pleasures* (IP 59)[3]. In this, Targ is fundamentally different from Yasusada who, though he is most likely Kent Johnson, never reveals his true identity. Indeed, the Yasusada-poet is in fact a persona within a persona, since Johnson now insists that it was actually another Japanese poet, Tosa Motokiyu, who was the one to invent him and who has now, rather conveniently, died. But the fact Johnson insists upon the existence of Motokiyu at all is telling: the project as I read it is one of imaginative empathy, an attempt to create a person we can believe in and invest with authority. Thus the letters, the fragments, the rough drafts and translator's notes, even the shopping lists scattered throughout *Doubled Flowering*: the Yasusada-poet has assembled a world from these quotidian scraps to prove a life is

---

[3] While Targ doesn't give the reader explicit reasons for why he decided to write as Charles Yu, he does mention that he and his wife had become interested in Chinese art and music around this time, and that they had even begun to consider themselves students and collectors of Chinese sculpture (IP 58–59).

at stake; a life based upon experience, violence, art, history. Implicitly, the Yasusada-poet argues that identity can be imaginatively created; authentic experience is no prerequisite, and culture and race aren't imperatives for the creation of multicultural art.

Finally, I believe the Yasusada-poet's impulse was to apologize. I read Yasusada as an American elegy for the bombings in Hiroshima and Nagasaki, for the racist acts America committed both on its own and foreign soil. The fact that Johnson refuses to identify himself implies that, to him, Yasusada *does* exist, if not in a Japanese poetic imagination, then in an American one. For this reason, I hesitate to call the author Johnson, preferring instead Yasusada or the Yasusada-poet in deference to his wishes. Johnson's silence suggests to me that we—Americans bound in citizenship, not by race or ethnicity—are the ones who need Yasusada to be real, to explain and perhaps be forgiven (by ourselves, solipsistically) for the bombings and our continued investment in nuclear weaponry. If this is true, then how close to creating a real person—and a real apology—does the Yasusada-poet come?

The poems that succeed in *Doubled Flowering* are, I think, the ones most elliptically tied to the poet's putative biography. Poems like 'Telescope with Urn,' 'Trolley Fare and Blossom,' and 'Mad-Daughter and Big-Bang,' for instance, evoke personal pain without giving in to autobiographical detail: they evoke rather than declaim the horrors of Hiroshima, placing the narrator on the margins of the poem while focusing instead on the poem's surreal style. 'Mad Daughter and Big-Bang' might be the most successful example of this suppression of the autobiographical in service to the surreal, and it was one my students and I found particularly compelling. In this poem, Yasusada imagines himself walking late one night in a vegetable patch to suddenly "find/ the severed head of [his]/ mad daughter lying on the ground.//Her eyes ... upturned, gazing at [him] ecstatic-like ..." (*Doubled* 11). The poem then jumps to a parenthetical description of the atomic bomb detonating over the city, itself described as like "a stone, haloed with light,'as if cast there by the Big-Bang" (11). When the poet asks his daughter's head what it is doing there on the ground, the head replies "sullenly" that some boys buried it there, and the poet, squatting, pulls a "turnip up by the root" (11). At first reading, the strangely disjunctive images may feel arbitrary and grotesque; however, the poem slowly reveals itself to be a coherent autobiography: a buried or sublimated "confession" of the bomb's impact on Yasusada's family. Images of the origin of the universe repeat in the poem—as they repeat throughout *Doubled Flowering* as a whole—appearing first in reference to the atomic bomb that leveled Yasusada's city, but also in his description of his daughter's hair which "[trails], comet-like" behind her head. Likewise, the image of the turnip at the end of the poem resonates with the image of the mad daughter's head, indicating that the daughter has herself been killed by the bomb, by the "boys" who both initiated and sustained the war. Indeed, the war's effects continue to haunt her: the daughter seems still to be gazing ecstatically at both Yasusada and the bomb, awed by its persistent, half-divine, half-natural force. What's striking about the poem is how the sublime moves so naturally into the absurd, the grotesque and even the cruel: after the description of the bombing, Yasusada tells his daughter that she looks "ridiculous" with her head on the ground, as if attempting to dismiss the shock of her death. And while the daughter's face and hair are described with great tenderness and beauty, the poet's imagined reaction to this beauty is one of indifference or even violence: seeing her "comet-like" hair, he squats and pulls the turnip/head up by the root. The poem combines these tones together to reveal a sadness and repressed anger at the absurdity of his daughter's and his own situation that is, in its overall effects, astonishing.

The same surrealist strategy is employed in 'Telescope with Urn,' a poem that addresses the death of another daughter, this one the infant who died in the atomic blast. The first line of the poem refers to the image of galaxies "spread[ing] out like a cloud of sperm": an image which itself is commented upon by an unnamed "observatory guide" in the second line of the poem, who notes its rapid velocity (32). The image of the galaxies' expansion is possibly meant to evoke the real and imaginary expansion of the bomb after impact, an expansion that contains a strange beauty for the narrator, as the third line suggests: "It is like the idea of the flowers, opening within the idea of the flowers" (32). From here, the poem takes a more personal turn, as Yasusada recalls his young daughter "squat[ting] over a sky-colored bowl to make water" (32). The poem finishes with the following reference to her death:

> What a big girl!, cried we, tossing you in the general direction of the stars.
>
> Intently, then, in the dream, I folded up the great telescope on Mount Horai.
>
> In the form of this crane, it is small enough for the urn (32).

This poem, like 'Mad Daughter,' uses a high amount of visual repetition to link these disparate narratives. Here, galaxies, observatories, sky-colored bowls and telescopes remind us of the poet's frightening awareness of space, space that seems simultaneously natural, personal and technological. The galaxies are "like a cloud of sperm," which sets the reader up later for the appearance of the poet's infant daughter who herself gets "tossed up" like a cloud of ashes or stars. The galaxies themselves open and open like flowers, which reminds the poet of a monk in the act of flower arranging. Images in the poem figuratively build one on top of the other so that the poem formally begins to "bloom" outward from its initial image of the galaxies. This formal enactment of "flowering" in the poem becomes increasingly sinister as we realize the ultimate direction that the poem must take: the urn containing the daughter's ashes. Understanding that this poem comes out of Yasusada's putative experiences in Hiroshima, it is nearly impossible not to see this "flowering" of stars and child as also referencing the physical expansion of the atomic bomb after impact: its eerie and instantaneous explosion, followed by the clouds of ash it leaves behind. This, tied to the poem's formal arrangement of images, forces the reader to see how the first image of sperm becomes inextricably linked to the image of nuclear destruction: it is as if the poet helped create a child solely for the purpose of her being destroyed in Hiroshima.

Of course, part of the power of these poems is that we know of and believe in the poet's biography. In fact, I'd argue that we have to know it because the references may seem too oblique for an audience unaware of their significance. But even if the biography itself is false, the poems' aesthetic *strategies* are successful: the blending of the grotesque with the sublime; the formal enactment of the poem's subject matter; the delicate, elliptical treatment of grief and fear and horror—all these things combine beautifully to convince me of the poems' merits.

Scubadivers and Chrysanthemums

Many people, however, would argue that what is aesthetically good may not be ethically good. I myself am sympathetic to the claim that white-authored poems purporting to be written by non-white writers risk being appropriations of race and experience for the sake of publication. And *Doubled Flowering* is more than a handful of poems: it is a book that purports to contain a life, and in this sense the questions about whether the Yasusada-poet has appropriated the experiences of Hiroshima's victims is also attached to whether he's created a falsely perceived idea of Japanese culture. As an American, I cannot hope to answer what it means to be Japanese: I can only interpret what the Yasusada-poet assumes being Japanese means, and evaluate his claims based upon how closely they come to stereotypes that make me uncomfortable. This, I realize, will never be a fair way of assessing the work.

Admitting my critical failures in this regard, however, I cannot help but note how the book repeats itself in theme and imagery. Here are geishas and chrysanthemums, sumo wrestlers, references to kabuki, peonies, shakuhachis, the art of calligraphy, yukatas, daikon, temples and monks—all references that begin to feel increasingly like touchstones for an American audience seeking emblems of an exotic Japan to reassure them. In one unnamed, undated fragment, for instance, the poet lists:

Two daikons

three rice cakes

one (blotted by crease, eds) seaweed packet

4 crane eggs

empress oil   chrysanthemum root   best rice

Bear yourself with a serious air through the labyrinth of the market. Feign to ignore the (blotted by crease, eds.) spirit medium of plum-colored lips

American cologne (26).

The editors note that "despite the curious interjection, this appears to be a shopping list" that was "found in one of the notebooks, folded into an origami bird" (26). Little about this fragment, whether "shopping list" or not, feels believable: the relentless stream of exotic and potentially unreal cooking items placed against the reference to some anonymous "American cologne" feels politically forced, as does the hyperbolic language in the italicized interlude. In a few instances in *Doubled Flowering*, Yasusada makes references to American products or American perspectives of the Japanese, perspectives that reveal that Yasusada is aware that the Japanese position would be considered inferior to the American one, as occurs in this untitled haiku: "American circus/ The Japanese midget wears the body/ of a horse" (43). This awareness for me troubles the "Japanese" symbols he uses in poems like this fragment, because they potentially pander to the Western trend of exoticizing the Asian: here the list of Japanese goods is meant to signal solely their cultural difference from the "American" cologne but without assigning any *personal* value to them, thus all the goods—Japanese and American—become an artificial way of rendering culture.

If we reverse this poem's formula and rewrite it from an American perspective, we might imagine this list would include items like hamburger buns, hot dogs, Budweiser and fireworks, to be finished with a reference to buying a Japanese car. On the one hand, we could read this list as an indictment against the monolithic views Americans hold about themselves—views that are immediately abandoned once economically challenged. With Yasusada's list poem, perhaps this is what the poet intends: to show the ways Japanese cultural norms have been changed post-World War II by American influence. American goods and ideas are now something that can be bought alongside "common" Japanese foods. And yet either poem that uses this strategy would, I think, pander to the nationalist stereotypes each culture holds for the other, creating a continual cycle of self-exoticization. Indeed, the fact that Yasusada's list poem was itself supposedly folded into an origami bird (as if the references above weren't "Japanese" enough) seems ridiculous: is Yasusada a Japanese person or a parody of being Japanese?

While the idea of culture as a series of artificial symbols may be an attractive one for our postmodern notions of self and identity, I find this unrealistic given the time period the Yasusada-poet was supposedly writing in. After the bombings, the questions for Japan almost entirely revolved around issues of cultural identity as it struggled to rebuild itself under the often draconian rules of Allied occupation.[4] After World War II, Japan decided to adopt some of the social practices and economic theories of its former enemy, in large part because of pressures from the Allied forces stationed in Japan to democratize, but also because its leaders understood it would have to compete in the global power structures that America and the West had now firmly established.[5] The question for the Japanese was how to create a society that would utilize these structures without sacrificing what they saw as their own cultural sovereignty, a problem already long familiar to the Chinese, the Vietnamese, and the Filipinos. We should never underestimate the sense of national shame and self-determination that would have had to accompany this process of social restructuring. To the Yasusada-poet's credit, the poems in *Doubled Flowering* do appear to reference this problem, but more by implication than through any overt thinking. For me, the references to Japanese cultural symbols feel nostalgic; they seem, in fact, to have been culled largely from a Japan frozen in the late nineteenth century. Perhaps this static formality is what the poet intends to make us feel, but if the work is also meant to help relocate or reexamine a Japanese identity in part to support the Japanese people after their losses at Hiroshima, then the volume implicitly argues that Yasusada's Japan is artificial, nor is there anything really new to take its place. This would not, I hope, be the kind of apology an American would want to extend to Japan after the bombings of Hiroshima and Nagasaki.

Further evidence of the Japanese symbols' artificiality occurs in other poems, like this "modest gathering of haiku" (50):

---

[4] A very comprehensive guide for this subject can be found in John W. Dower's *Embracing Defeat: Japan in the Wake of World War II*. New York: W.W. Norton, 1999.

[5] About other issues regarding Japan's economic growth post-WWII, see Beningo Valdes, 'An Application of Convergence Theory to Japan's Post-WWII Economic Miracle.' *Journal of Economic Education*, 34.1 (Winter 2003): 61–81.

Paisley Rekdal

iris	moon	sheaths
scubadivers	chrysanthemums	also
deer	inlets	dream
oars	this	earth
geese	lined	bowl
shard	so	horizon
cod	dried	dawn
bones	sky	written
lichened	space	rock
fossils	celebrating	investors
crematorium	shared	persimmon
hyacinth	clustered	strangers
cranes	three	words (50)

What strikes me is the attention the poet pays to aesthetic forms that are themselves either lifeless, desiccated or static: images of "fossils celebrat[ing] investors," a "cod dried dawn," or a "geese lined bowl" telegraph in imagery what the poems as a whole in *Doubled Flowering* achieve—a fixed or formal vision of Japanese aesthetics, lifeless and frozen in time. The poem has a tonally explosive quality to it as well, in which contemporary or polysyllabic words "pop" against more pastoral references. Notice how the extremely modern words "scubadivers," "investors" and "crematorium" leap out as the poem progresses, forcing us to attach simultaneously more contemporary and sinister connotations to words like "bones," "clustered," "strangers" or even "celebrating." But if that reference looks glaringly pointed (or modernist) to us, how pointed then do words like "persimmon," "hyacinth," and "irises" appear? There is something overly "Oriental" to half of the poem that grates against what is overly not; there is no middle point between the "old Japan" and the "new Japan" that Yasusada attempts to mix together, thus the poem feels as if it lurches along, unsure what world it wants to present.

This clash of language occurs often in *Doubled Flowering*. In the poem 'Blossoms and Scream,' for instance, Yasusada writes that he "love[s] the hard words the adolescents say:/ *weird, cool, far-out, banzai* . . . /And the softer words of the old/ *oh my, deary, the ways of heaven* . . ." (31). Here the editors note that the italicized phrases are actually cultural approximations for the Japanese idioms, but the effect, in this English "translation," also suggests that "old" Japanese culture is mixing with "new" American perspectives, a reading bolstered by the fact that "banzai" remains untranslated and is actually being misused in the context of this line. Rather than being current slang, "banzai" itself is a traditional expression that means "may you live ten thousand years," and was used as an expression similar to the American "cheers." Only recently do Americans translate "banzai" solely as a battle-cry, and while English and English-Japanese dictionaries include this particular definition of the word, Japanese dictionaries would not, thus it is unlikely that Yasusada would have been aware of this very American connotation for the word in 1959 when the poem was supposedly written. Still, even if we choose to believe that the Yasusada-poet would have known of this connotation, the poem then would *have* to be written primarily for an American audience, since a Japanese one would have been confused by the word's inclusion in a line filled with current adolescent slang.

Similar tonal problems trouble other places in *Doubled Flowering*. Poems, such as one untitled fragment about the death of one of his daughters, include lines such as "Obediently bowing—the white flowers/ Sake's transparent—I pat the pig" (*Doubled* 54): a combination of images that feel reckless and even cruel to the subject matter in their disjointedness. Other poems change tones so rapidly, the reader can't decide what to feel or focus on. In "Horsehide and Sunspot" for instance, the poem whips from image to image, rushing too eagerly towards a harried, even inappropriate ending:

As seventy thousand voices are fused by a sphere and.

[along margin, written horizontally] Don't forget sake for Shimpei

A corolla of screams ringing absence is viscerally real.

And so, like a sunspot, is baseball (85).

The implied horror and excitement of so many voices in a stadium being "fused by a sphere" clashes with the casually inserted warning to buy sake: an attempt by the poet to distance both himself and the reader from the poem's frightening action with mundane personal references. The poem's overt subject is a baseball game in Hiroshima Municipal Stadium, but because of the game's location and images like "a corolla of screams" and "voices fused by a sphere," the crowd's thunderous approbation of a sports team turns ineluctably to their (and our) reaction to the bomb, a gradually dawning horror that gets reined in abruptly by the last line, which seems flippant, almost obscene with its inaccurate simile.

Lastly, other poems feel either repetitive or syntactically awkward. 'Dream and Charcoal' for instance, feels like a rehashed version of the strategies of Telescope and Urn,' but the images are too blurry to resonate. Below is the poem in its entirety:

> And then she said: I have gone toward the light and become beautiful.
>
> And then she said: I have taken a couple of wings and attached them to the various back-parts on my body.
>
> And then she said: all the guests are coming back to where they were and then talking.
>
> To which she said: without the grasp-handle, how would you recognize my nakedness?
>
> To which she replied: without nothing is when all things die.
>
> Which is when she had a wild battle with the twigs.
>
> Which is when the charcoal was passed from her body to mine.
>
> Which is how she rose into the heavens, blinding the pedestrians.
>
> Which was how our union was transposed into a dark scribble.
>
> Which became the daughter calling, calling my name to wake me. (*Doubled* 46)

The syntax here feels uselessly vague, as in the line, "I have taken a couple of wings and attached them to the various back-parts on my body." What "back-parts"? Isn't the back itself a part? Why isn't the image clear about where the wings are being placed? Similarly, "all the guests are coming back to where they were and then talking" feels like a lifeless rendition of Eliot's refrain in 'Prufrock.'

The poems in *Doubled Flowering* succeed when the occasional awkwardness of syntax feels deliberate. When, in 'Telescope and Urn,' the poet writes: "Tiny were you, and squatted over a sky-colored bowl to make water" (32), we might see the grammatical inversion of the first clause to be a form of affection, a possible reference to the child's own speaking style. In 'Dream and Charcoal,' however, the muddy descriptions feel like an attempt to make the translated language "sound" Japanese by straining both the syntactic placement and logical connections between each image. What, for instance, *is* the relationship between a "grasp-handle" and one's ability to recognize a person's nakedness?

The problems I have with these poems may in part be aesthetic: overly elliptical references, over-sublimated emotion and syntactic vagueness are all ticks that for me characterize the worst elements of the collage techniques of postmodernist poetry. Here these ticks occur so often I begin to wonder whether they're being used consciously: the poems utilize strategies of the avant-garde but in ways that are so clearly bad they begin to feel as if Kent Johnson has a private ax to grind. Indeed, if we look at one of the appendices included in *Doubled Flowering*, we find Kent Johnson and Javier Alvarez writing explicitly about Johnson's assumed part in the controversy and his ideas about "the poetry world" as it relates to the avant-garde:

> Indeed, it has been the common assumption for some time in the poetry world that Johnson is the "culprit" of the Yasusada imbroglio, though it is still inadequately explained how a community college Spanish teacher with little poetic talent could have produced work that caused fairly unbridled admiration amongst such a range of well-placed arbiters in the world of poetry (124).

The barely concealed combination of triumph, anger, snideness and self-disdain that characterizes this statement frankly unnerves me:

are we to understand this project was in part an attempt by Johnson and Alvarez to frustrate the snobbish world of publishing? Likewise, Perloff has noted that Yasusada's biography and work are riddled with strangely obvious mistakes, including the fact that the poet claims to have attended a university that had not been founded by the date of his enrollment, that his poetic influences—Spicer and Barthes—either weren't published in Japanese or French at the time of his reading them or weren't known outside their native countries, and that Yasusada's and his wife's very names are used incorrectly by his translators (150; *Scubadivers* 25). If we take Perloff's suggestion that these numerous small "mistakes" the authors make regarding the creation of Yasusada's biography and poems are "surely not unintention[al]," that they are, in fact, clues meant to signal that the poems are not legitimate, then can we still see the work as an act of empathy or apology (150; *Scubadivers* 25)?

While we may never know whether the mistakes were intentional, if the Yasusada-poet wants to make his poems *both* an imaginative apology *and* a subtle attack on the American poetry publishing world— an establishment that Johnson imagines has rejected him—then the project is ultimately doomed to fail in at least one regard. Race, culture and the experience of Hiroshima *are* implicitly being used, and the entire project of empathy becomes a cruel ruse, a blind behind which the poet can hide, slinging arrows at those who, in their own mad attempts to be politically correct and thus historically forgiven, are defenseless.

On some level I must admit I'm happy to see the various failures in *Doubled Flowering*, since I can conveniently imagine them being related to the ethical problems the project raises. In truth I can't prove them to be related with any critical certainty, nor do I think such certainty is possible. What strikes me about reading other critics' arguments about Yasusada is how differently we all read the same poems' merits based on our ideas either of the project's theoretical value to us as readers, or of what we might imagine constitutes a Japanese identity.[6] Perloff, for

---

[6] See Emily Nussbaum, 'Turning Japanese: The Hiroshima Poetry Hoax,' *Lingua Franca* (November 1996): 82–84.

instance, argues that the fragmentary and elliptical mode of Yasusada's work to her seems "Orientalist," an attempt to create a "reassuringly 'archaic,' 'oriental' feel" with its "reticence and elusiveness" (165; *Scubadivers* 36). I myself don't find it so, probably because many of my white graduate students—admirers also of Spicer and Barthes but who have no knowledge of Yasusada—write in a very similar fragmentary mode. To me, the elliptical style and sublimated emotion of poems like 'Telescope and Urn' are attempts to authenticate the author as an avant-garde, not a Japanese, poet. Likewise, I can easily see that the same arguments I've made against the poems can also be strong arguments in their favor: the impersonal and stereotypical references both to Japanese and American culture only highlight the artificial and fragile notions we hold about culture as a whole. In Yasusada's world, nothing but falsely conceived and arbitrarily assigned symbols exist to "identify" us, which makes the movement from an ancient to a modern Japan merely a process of removing the familiar references and replacing them with capitalist, technological, American symbols.

My suspicion of the project thus is based in part on the strangely ecstatic reception Yasusada's work has received—on the page as well as in my classroom. While the argument that the imagination can transcend sex, race and personal experience is a laudable one, it is also an idea that I find appeals most to white writers who either feel that the idea of race itself is only socially constructed, or that somehow they've been excluded from the attention non-white writers have received. While I also believe that racial formulations are socially constructed, a critical awareness of this certainly doesn't preclude the very real social inequalities we experience and in which we each implicitly participate. There's also a deep distrust and perhaps envy among certain white readers for non-white writers' current prestige, itself based on the presumption that no non-white writer could write as well as his white peers were subject matter (and thus, implicitly, the victimized status the non-white writer gets to hold) taken off the table. Thus my student's offhand "none, of course" when asked if he'd read any non-white poets in his literature surveys: why should he, when everyone knows literature surveys are dedicated to the study of great literature?

But if the argument that experience can be transcended is one that gets subsumed into racist ideology, it is also, I think, an argument that cannot always contextually be believed, even by those who most strongly agree with it. When one student asked if a white American audience would react as positively to a Saudi Arabian writing pseudonymously as a white banker who managed to escape the Twin Towers, much of the class grew suddenly enraged. My point is that while many of us like the idea of being able to "overcome" culture and race and identity, even the most general experience of being alive makes it hard to accept this. I can say that culture or race or personal experience doesn't matter until I'm blue in the face, and that still never stops people from being hurt deeply, even mortally so—as Hiroshima itself proves—by the ways these "constructs" divide us.

One last personal note before I end. About 16 years ago, I briefly visited Hiroshima. I was there for a summer living in Japan on a Lions Club scholarship. The point of the scholarship was to live with Japanese families, to meet ambassadors and monks and taiko drummers, to learn about things like ikebana and tea ceremonies, geishas and meikos, to eat live squid and wrap an obi. In other words, to experience Japan like a historical theme park.

On the last week of our exchange, however, our group was taken to Hiroshima to visit the war museum. I remember creeping down the long hallway of the white stone building, tentative and silent, almost afraid to meet the gaze of the other tourists. The museum was, in my memory, both elegant and grotesque: large glass cases displayed artifacts culled from the bombing, photographs of victims, remnants of clothing and copies of official documents. Below theses items were arranged little placards dryly describing the importance and location of each object. One giant diorama-like glass case housed an artist's rendering of the bombing's effects upon life-size statues of people: I remember in particular a young girl with her clothes looking seared into her flesh, the flesh itself bloody and shredded. Frozen forever in plaster and glass, she was eternally running, screaming out toward us, her viewers.

At the end of the exhibit was a long, carpeted hall with a few televisions, each programmed to play an hour-long video of survivors' testaments. The survivors spoke in Japanese, and their statements were translated below in English and French. For the entire hour, I sat and watched the videos. Person after person spoke, some with horrible disfigurements, some with a legacy of cancer, some looking untouched but deeply haunted. Here was horror and fear, grief, resignation, forgiveness, rage. *I will never forgive America,* one older gentleman said, practically spitting into the camera. *I will never forgive a country that could commit such evil.* His face contorted as he spoke. The glass windows behind me filled with sun, making it difficult to read the translation. I flinched and squinted. The video had captured a variety of responses to preserve some idea of what Hiroshima meant to the people who had experienced it: there was no one reaction, and though I knew each person speaking was a singular identity, I also understood that the collection of responses was meant to suggest that all of them together did compose a single identity, the identity of the Hiroshima survivor, a concept that did and did not exist. *I forgive them. I despise them. I am suffering. I have made peace with it. They are evil.* I was embarrassed, chagrined, stunned. I could not stop watching. There was nothing coy or elliptical in the phrases the speakers used. One after the other spoke: man, woman, man. They blended together, enraged and pained and haunted, a voice full of ruin. The video spooled and spooled. The effect of listening, even for a single hour, was agonizing.

Agonizing in a way the museum could not be. The museum, to be a place of learning, has to be toned down to sadness and a detached intellectual rigor, pierced occasionally by elements of the terrifying. Sadness—not even grief, which implies deeper loss—is the emotion allowed in such a museum, because sadness can be imaginatively shared. Sadness does not, unlike rage or vengeance, blame. This is what the Yasusada-poet, to me, ultimately achieves: his poetry is a museum of Hiroshima in which the same images recur, posed here and there like statues in a hallway: images of space and flowers and bowls, images of courtship and longing and a distant, occasionally haunting, despair. Rage doesn't enter Yasusada's poems. Nor does an excess of sorrow—his best poems in fact subvert our ideas of grief by making them surreal and oddly comical, a subversion we praise because we think he's earned it by experience and, possibly, because it doesn't really implicate *us*. What could be confrontational is kept on the margins: Yasusada's poetry is precisely what any museum-going American would want.

And yet, the emotions he evokes in us as readers of poetry and of identity are anything but muted. I cannot ignore my students' excitement and anger and vengeful suspicion, my own sense of uneasiness. I cannot overlook Johnson's vituperous comments about the circles of poetic power. A tension will always exist for me between what the poet purports to be doing and what, implicitly, he achieves: his empathetic gesture to imagine the effects of our bombing of Hiroshima is also an argument that there is perhaps something formalized, stylized, something ultimately *imitable* about this experience. What fascinates me about the Yasusada-poet is how so many critics and readers rush to defend his writing, first on the basis of imaginative empathy, then on the basis of style, then on the scandalous history of the poems themselves. But if aesthetics and the purported experience of victimization "authenticated" Yasusada before as "good," now oddly whiteness continues to authenticate him: we praise the poems for being hoaxes, we praise the white writer for creating an identity so outside of his own, where we might casually dismiss an African-American poet who wrote in the voice of a long-dead Yoruban slave, assuming this work to be an extension of skin color rather than intellect. And yet aren't they both the same act of imaginative empathy? I believe our praise of *Doubled Flowering* privileges the white writer's imagination with having a cultural power that far exceeds that of the non-white writer, thus I find our approbation of Yasusada itself disturbing and racist, even if the intent of the poet was never to write racist poems.

In effect, *Doubled Flowering* falls back into the very stereotypes certain readers have of non-white writers: that they have no subject matter besides their own victimization. By picking and choosing elements of biography and subject matter, Johnson has constructed an identity to appeal to our various and contemporary vanities in America: our desire to empathize with and to be forgiven, our desire to overlook race while still seeing certain groups and nationalities as victims, our desire to believe that the self is merely a series of arbitrary and commercial constructs. In the end, what he *hasn't* imagined is a Hiroshima survivor: it's an American publishing phenomenon, and rather than subverting the stereotypes that might have led to real transcultural empathy, perhaps in the end he has only reverted to them, solidified them, made them increasingly "real" to us.

Of course, Kent Johnson is only responding to the literary structures we ourselves established. We were the ones to create and foster the literary prejudices that made Yasusada not only incendiary to us, but inevitable. His is a racism we as readers are all party to on some level, having intertwined the issues of subject matter and literary worth and ethnic identity to such a complex knot, it's almost impossible to unravel. It's a problem naturally exacerbated in a time when, as we ourselves become increasingly ethnically, racially and nationally hyphenated, the definition of what is or ever was "authentic" gets, literally, bred right out of us. In this, perhaps it's useful to think of Yasusada as one of our most compelling mixed-race poets, a poet who, consciously or not, explores the ways we both fragment and objectify ourselves, who shows how all of us become subject to sweeping forms of cultural nostalgia. It is certainly how Charles Yu slipped into *Quiet Fire* to begin with and why the book's editor, Juliana Chang, was so embarrassed when I contacted her about the mistake. Though she shouldn't be, I think; what anthologist, undertaking such a monumental task, wouldn't have wanted to make such an assumption? In her email reply to me a year ago, she wrote that she had learned of the mistake after the book's publication. By that time, it was too late; now she just lived with it. The fake in her anthology had become, over time, a real addition. When asked if she'd care to write an essay with me on the subject, she didn't write back again.

Currently, the book, published first in 1996, is still in print.

Works Cited

Chang, Juliana, ed. *Quiet Fire: A Historical Anthology of Asian American Poetry 1892–1970.* New York: the Asian American Writers Workshop, 1996.
Johnson, Kent ed. *Doubled Flowering: From the Notebooks of Araki Yasusada.* New York: Roof Books, 1997.
Targ, William, *Indecent Pleasures: The Life and Colorful Times of William Targ.* New York: Macmillan, 1975.

"Here is the Offering of a Sacred Name which is [*Illegible, Eds.*]": The Necessity of Anonymity in the Entity of Araki Yasusada

Jenny Boully

Empire with No Emperor:

In his essay 'Center-City, Empty Center' contained in *Empire of Signs*, Roland Barthes tells of how Tokyo has a "center," an empirical place from which all else pours forth, a "center" which contains nothing, where an emperor is purported to live. No one sees this emperor, yet all who live and work there believe in his presence and run in circles around this palace. Behind the poetry of Araki Yasusada, similarly, there is no *sacrificial body*, no empirical author or even pseudonym to which to apply. Araki Yasusada is no mere "persona" or "pseudonym": Araki Yasusada is an author, but the author is, in Barthes' notion, a paradox. Like the center of Tokyo, the "Yasusada Author" (as coined by Eliot Weinberger)[1] is "protected by moats, inhabited by an emperor who is never seen, which is to say, literally, by no one knows who" (Barthes 3c).

Kent Johnson would prefer if critics and others would stop imagining him to be the emperor reigning from the center of the Yasusada Author empire. After Joe Napora reviewed *Doubled Flowering: From the Notebooks of Araki Yasusada* for the *American Book Review* and so casually referred to Johnson as the author of the text, Johnson pleaded with the editors: "…the confusion of the attribution is an important matter, and I am writing to call your attention to it, asking that you print this letter as a clarification. *Doubled Flowering: From the Notebooks of Araki Yasusada*, please, does not belong under my name."

The confusion of the attribution *is* an important matter: Araki Yasusada, we are told, is the creation of the late Tosa Motokiyu, who is, Johnson also writes in the same letter, "the pseudonym of a writer who did not wish to attach his legal name to the hyperauthorial person he brought into being." Johnson is the caretaker of the emperor's ground, holding the copyright to the *Notebooks*, as well as being the

---

[1] "In the proliferating discussions, the identity of the author has become so refracted that it approached the condition of We Are All Yasusada. Perhaps it is best to call him/her/them the Yasusada Author, much as we refer to a Renaissance painter as the Master of the X Altar" (Weinberger 109; *Scubadivers* 19).

public spokesman for the Yasusada affair. These things, if we are to participate in the Yasusada affair, we are to take as *facts*. These things, if we are to participate in literature and therefore symbolism, we are to take as *metaphors*. The network leading to the empty center is no longer navigable by passageways, the flat 2-D linear roadways of maps, or even 3-D representations: here we begin to see the layers of emptiness placed one on top of another. The layers serve as a "visible form of invisibility, hid[ing] the sacred 'nothing'" (Barthes 32). We learn, as with the center of Barthes' city, that the Yasusada author's "own center is no more than an evaporated notion, subsisting here, not in order to irradiate power, but to give to the entire urban movement the support of its central emptiness, forcing traffic to make a perpetual detour. In this manner, we are told, the system of the imaginary is spread circularly, by detours and returns the length of an empty subject" (Barthes 32).

The "system of the imaginary" was spread in such prestigious journals as *Conjunctions, Grand Street, American Poetry Review,* and *Stand*. Then slowly, rumors began to circulate, reaching editorial desk after editorial desk and such respected critics as Marjorie Perloff, stating that Yasusada was not the author of the poems—poems so moving that one in particular, 'Telescope with Urn,' kept Ron Silliman up all night—that the author was quite possibly "authors"[2] and in any event possibly not even Japanese. "As Yasusada's résumé grew," Emily Nussbaum writes in *Lingua Franca* in November 1996,

> a rumor began spreading in the poetry community: There *was* no Yasusada, editors whispered to each other—at least not in the usual, one-author-one-body sense. The same manuscripts submitted to poetry journals (and mailed from a variety of locations, including California, Tokyo, Illinois, and London) had shown up on the desks of prominent academics like Marjorie Perloff, but with a notable difference: 'Yasusada' was presented as an invented persona, the creation of one or more people intent on keeping its origins a secret. Messages slowly surfaced on the Internet warning editors about the ongoing deception.

---

[2] From K.K. Ruthven's *Faking Literature*: "…the text in which others collaborated is seen as being 'authorised' by only one person, who becomes thereby its 'author.'"

Arthur Vogelsang, editor of the *American Poetry Review*, would describe the Yasusada development as an "essentially criminal act." Readers would come to either love or hate him; Charles Simic, in the *Boston Review*, went so far as to call the situation a "crisis" while in the same journal, Eliot Weinberger and Marjorie Perloff would chastise the negative editorial comments made concerning the "crisis" and become Yasusada's first serious advocates.

Since the news of the scandal, which was first publicly revealed by Eliot Weinberger in the *Village Voice Literary Supplement* in July 1996, there has been much traffic circling the empty center of authorship, much discussion, debate, and commentary made on the speculation of who "Araki Yasusada" actually is; however, all of these commentaries miss the point of what I will refer to as "the aesthetics of anonymity," which is a crucial and integral aspect of *Doubled Flowering*. The goal is not to produce or uncover the person(s) behind the paper wall, but rather, to succumb to and accept the paradox of the empty center, an idea foreign to "Occidental" ideas of logic and validity. "Once upon a time," Weinberger writes in his exposé, "it was enough for poets to think, dream, and write, and their first-person was usually a persona. Now they must submit a résumé to be validated for sincerity." It seemed, due to the infiltration of victim-confessional-witness poetry, as if it were suddenly unacceptable to write in the voice of "other" if the "author" did not reflect the life of the person or claim his/her work, or in the case of Yasusada, both. "There was a time," Michel Foucault writes in his essay 'What is an Author?', "when those texts which we now call 'literary' (stories, folk tales, epics, and tragedies) were accepted, circulated, and valorized without any question about the identity of their author. Their anonymity was ignored because their real age or supposed age was a sufficient guarantee of their authenticity" (Foucault 125).

Never has a text or case in literary history more effectively demonstrated Foucault's claim that writing "is primarily concerned with creating an opening where the writing subject endlessly disappears" (Foucault 116). Consider the following commentary by Philippe Sollers (*On Materialism*, 1969), as figured in Barthes' *Empire of Signs*:

> Writing, then, arises from the plane of inscription because it results from a recoil and a non-regardable discrepancy (not

from a face-to-face encounter; inciting from the first not what is seen but what can be traced) which divides the support into corridors as though to recall the plural void in which it is achieved—it is merely *detached* on the surface, it proceeds to weave itself there, delegated from depths which are not deep toward the surface, which is no longer a surface but a fiber *written from beneath vertical to its upper surface* (the brush stands straight up in the palm)—the ideogram thereby returning to the column—tube or ladder—and taking its place there as a complex bar released by the monosyllable in the field of the voice: this column can be called an "empty wrist," in which first appears as a "unique feature" the breath which passes through the hollowed arm, the perfect operation necessarily being that of the "concealed point" or of the "absence of traces."
(Barthes 57)

The inscription of Araki Yasusada results then "not from a face-to-face" encounter; rather, it "[incites] from the first not what is seen but what can be traced." And embedded within the text are both the "traces" and the "absence of traces," making not for a "poetics of fraud" or a "poetics of hoax" or "dramatic monologue" or "pseudonymous authorship"—what the text produces, given the developments of the Yasusada scandal and the textual clues, is more of a poetics according to Zen or paradox, where the author does not claim the work in the manner of "nothing can be claimed"; it is an egoless poetics which truly allows for a representation of a representation to live as *the* representation. The so-called "fictive" character of Araki Yasusada transcends even the "translated" fragments of Sumero-Akkadian clay tablets invented by Armand Schwerner in *The Tablets*[3], in that Schwerner's photograph and signifying name, which authenticates him as the author of the fictive invention, exist on his book cover[4]. In the case of Yasusada, we have only surmises: the fragments of the case are truly fragments with which we are left to construct our own faith. The affair, it should be

---

[3] Kent Johnson refers to this text in an interview with Norbert Francis in *Jacket* #5. http://jacketmagazine.com/05/yasu-larsen.html Accessed 7 January 2011.
[4] Indeed, to further the authenticity of "Schwerner as author," the latest edition of *The Tablets* even includes a CD of Schwerner reading selections from *The Tablets*. In this case, we are allowed to directly hear "the voice of 'god.'"

understood, by far surpasses even the collaborative "hoax authorship" of "Ern Malley," in that James McAuley and Harold Steward can be attributed and accredited for the *oeuvre* of Ern Malley (Heyward xvii). Insofar as our empirical world appears to be "authored" and insofar as there exists no empirical creator to allow the deixis of belief to occur, the refusal of the Yasusada Author to claim the work of Araki Yasusada mirrors the fact that "god" or the "creator" has yet to plunder down through the "layered clouds" and produce a "face-to-face" dialogue.

THE SAGA BEGINS:
```
Date: Wed, 21 Dec 1994 06:07:16-0800
Reply-To: UB Poetics discussion group <POETICS@UBVM.CC.BUFFALO.EDU>
Sender: UB Poetics discussion group <POETICS@UBVM.CC.BUFFALO.EDU>
From: Ron Silliman <rsillima@IX.NETCOM.COM>
Subject: Great Poet

The new issue of Conjunctions (#23: "New World Writing") arrived
yesterday, a total translation issue, and in it is a poet whose
work simply takes my breath away: ARAKI YASUSADA. According
to Brad Morrow's intro to the issue, it's Yasusada's first
publication in English translation.

Here's one poem (picked for its brevity):

TELESCOPE WITH URN

The image of the galaxies spreads out like a cloud of sperm.

Expanding said the observatory guide, and at such and such
velocity.

It is like the idea of the flowers, opening within the idea of
the flowers.
I like to think of that, said the monk, arranging them with his
papery fingers.

Tiny were you, and squatted over a sky-colored bowl to make
water.

What a big girl! cried we, tossing you in the general direction
of the stars.

Intently, then, in the dream, I folded up the great telescope
on Mount Horai.

In the form of this crane, it is small enough for the urn.
```

Scubadivers and Chrysanthemums

---

translated by Tosa Motokiyu, Ojiu Norinaga and Okura Kyojin)

Yasusada (1907-72) was a Hiroshima postal clerk most of his life and, while active in Japanese avant-garde circles, basically remained unknown. His wife and eldest daughter died instantly in the atomic bomb blast in 1945. A second daughter died of radiation sickness three years later. His manuscripts were brought to light when they were discovered by his surviving son (who was out of town with relatives that fateful day in '45). Apparently his major influences were Roland Barthes and Jack Spicer (!) and the selection in CONJUNCTIONS includes "Sentences for Jack Spicer Renga" (collaboratively written with Akutagawa Fusei). At the time of his death he was at work on a series of letters and translations to have been called After Spicer.

There's an elevation of tone in these poems that reminds me more of Michael Palmer than Spicer, perhaps because the translators are all Hiroshima poets (one of whom seems to spend half of each year in Sebastapol, although I don't know if he's known to Bromige or to Cydney Chadwick). These works kept me up last night and probably will again for another night or three. I recommend them highly.

Also in the issue are works by Bei Dao, Nina Iskrenko, Eduardo Galeano, Anne-Marie Albiach (collab. w/ Charles Bernstein!), Pascale Monnier(trans. by Ashbery) and much more. You can get a copy by sending $10 US to Conjunctions, Bard College, Anondale-on-Hudson, NY 12504.

Ron

THE CREATION OF ARAKI YASUSADA:

Let's say that the creator summoned up so many words, which were *dead*, as it so happened in the days of deconstructionist rule. And let's say that this creator breathed life into these words so as to make them *alive*. And the words began to take on a life of their own, with or without, let's say *his* creator. And Araki Yasusada thus became a man who dreamed and feared and doubted. Yasusada wrote poems before he died, and like all mortals, he died; or, Yasusada didn't die, but the signifier of the creator died. In any event, when Yasusada ascended into the heavens, everyone doubted this, saying they couldn't locate the *sacrificial body*. Therefore, when the miracle occurred, everyone wanted to ascribe it to someone, and there was no one to ascribe it to. When Ron Silliman was kept awake all night due to the utterances of Yasusada, he believed, as people so believe before their gods die, when the *textual body* was enough.

Yasusada: Biographical Sketch

The real Yasusada was born into paradox: he was a Hiroshima survivor who lost his wife and two daughters in the bombing. If we are to be participants in the affair, then we must believe what we are told. When Yasusada's poems began circulating in journals, a biographical note, such as this one in *Conjunctions*, all slightly varied, accompanied the poems:

> The notebooks of the Hiroshima poet Araki Yasusada were discovered by his son in 1980, eight years following the poet's death. The manuscripts comprise fourteen spiral notebooks whose pages are filled with poems, drafts, English class assignments, diary entries, recordings of zen dokusan encounters and other matter. In addition, the notebooks are interleaved with hundreds of insertions, including drawings, received correspondence and carbon copies of the poet's letters.
>
> Although Yasusada was active in important avant-garde groups such as Ogiwara Seisensui's Layered Clouds and the experimental renga circle Oars, and was an acquaintance of several well-known writers and artists like Taneda Santoka, Ozaki Hosai, Kusano Shimpei and Shiryu Morita, his work, along with that of his renga collaborators Ozaki Kusatao and Akutagawa Fusei, is virtually unknown. But the writing found in Yasusada's manuscripts is fascinating for its biographical disclosure, formal diversity and linguistic élan. Much of the experimental impetus, interestingly, comes from Yasusada's encounter in the mid-1960s with the poetry of the American Jack Spicer and the French critic Roland Barthes: Yasusada had fluency in English and French, and there are numerous quotes from, or references to, both of these literary figures in the later work. The notebooks reveal, in fact, that Yasusada was undertaking a work parallel to Spicer's letters and "translations" in After Lorca, to be entitled After Spicer.
>
> Yasusada was born in 1907 in the city of Kyoto, where he lived until 1921, when his family moved to Hiroshima. He attended Hiroshima University sporadically between 1925 and 1928, with the intent of receiving a degree in Western

Literature. Due, however, to his father's illness with cancer, he was forced, in the interests of the family, to undertake full-time employment with the postal service and withdraw from his formal studies.

In 1930 he married his only wife, Nomura, with whom he had two daughters and a son. In 1936, Yasusada was conscripted into the Japanese Imperial Army and worked as a clerk in the Hiroshima division of the Military Postal Service. His wife and youngest daughter, Chieko, died instantly in the blast on August 6. His daughter Akiko survived, yet perished three years later from radiation sickness. His son, Yasunari, only nine months old at the time, was with relatives outside of the city.

Yasusada died in 1972 after a long struggle with cancer. Akutagawa Fusei died of similar cause in 1971. The fate of Ozaki Kusatao is unknown to us. The selections here are part of a much longer collection that we are in the process of editing and translating.

—Tosa Motokiyu, Ojiu Norinaga, Okura Kyojin

WHAT I KNOW OF ARAKI YASUSADA

Weinberger hails him as "both the greatest poet of Hiroshima and its most unreliable witness" (*Voice*; *Scubadivers* 22).

Akitoshi Nagahta, Associate Professor of English at the Faculty of Language and Culture in Nagoya University, Japan, says Araki Yasusada is a "bawdy" poet, and writes in a letter to Kent Johnson on August 1997 when Johnson approached him for a "blurb" for *Doubled Flowering*: "Prof. Perloff says that it is necessary to write in a postmodern, disjunctive style to draw attention of the readers. That is perhaps true, but making his 'Japanese' poet enjoy writing about 'cocks and cunts' and girls singing about 'fucking'[5] is an act which would definitely sadden the real 'hibakusha,' who are in a sense identified with that fictional vulgar personage" (Jacket *Letters*).

---

[5] Nagahata is referring to Perloff's essay 'In Search of the Authentic Other: The Poetry of Araki Yasusada,' originally published in the *Boston Review*, and also to be found in this volume. In it, she references the Yasusada poem 'Silk Tree Renga' which has the following lines:
The voices of the sorority girls sing of fucking in a plaintive way
A screen of moonflowers and creeping gourds, with a thicket of cockscomb and goosefoot, evoking cocks and cunts (*Doubled* 87; *Scuba divers* 42)

What David Wojahn says: "…Yasusada is decidedly eccentric, crankily devoted to his art, given to naïve flights of wild enthusiasm, and a little bit buffoonish. Taken as a whole, Yasusada is a memorable creation, at times even a brilliant one. The pose does not work all the time, however, and Roof [6] and Johnson have made a major blunder by attaching as appendices to the volume several self-justifying essays and interviews about Yasusada's creation by Johnson, 'Motokiyu,' 'Javier Alvarez,' and 'Mikhail Epstein,' as well as Perloff's revised version of her *Boston Review* piece. To put it bluntly, it does no good for Yasusada to ever have the man behind the curtain appear, for whenever Johnson himself opens up his mouth he strikes us as a windy and slightly paranoiac jerk" (Wojahn 107; *Scubadivers* 302).

Metaphor of Authorship/Being:

When one speaks in metaphor, one can never lie, as the type of "lying" which metaphor produces is a sacred type of truth. To say that the Yasusada Author is a "liar" is to say that one does not understand the fundamental properties of metaphor, i.e. one does not know how to *read* literature. In his essay 'Commentary and Hypotheses,' Mikhail Epstein (who is known to have "authored" many authors—authors which are, he says, not pseudonyms) cites Vladimir Nabokov to further his point that the degree of sincerity in a text is directly proportional to the immersion of creation. In other words, authorship goes above and beyond the mundane distinction of a mere "persona": to create an author is to create an "illusion among illusions" as life is already so much an illusion, according to Epstein:

> Vladimir Nabokov once remarked on what makes literature different from the "true story" or "the poetry of testimony": "Literature was born not the day when a boy crying 'wolf, wolf' came running out of the Neanderthal valley with a big gray wolf at his heels: literature was born on the day when a boy came crying 'wolf, wolf' and there was no wolf behind him." (*Doubled* 145; *Scubadivers* 73)

To say that the pseudonym of Tosa Motokiyu created the "fictional"

---

[6] Roof, as in Roof Books, which published *Doubled Flowering* and has also published Ron Silliman.

Araki Yasusada is a lie; to say that the pseudonym of Tosa Motokiyu was embodied by *X* person who projected through Tosa Motokiyu the embodiment of Araki Yasusada, may be closer to the lie, that is, closer to the truth. Araki Yasusada cried "wolf" and there was, quite literally, no wolf behind him. Yet, embedded within the text of *Doubled Flowering* are the many clues, the many wolf tracks which, when studied closely, will inform any reader of the text's polemic: "hoax" is necessary, is crucial for truthful, selfless creation. "In my view," Epstein writes, "the Yasusada 'hoax,' if it is hoax indeed, is the same type of hoax as any literary metaphor, trope, rhetorical figure, fictional character. Why is Motokiyu claiming to be Yasusada more scandalous than claiming 'eyes' to be 'stars'? 'Hoax' is an authorial metaphor, the search for a new aesthetic convention, 'de-automatization' of our conventional image of an author as a biological and biographical individual" (Epstein).

To say that the Yasusada Author is a "criminal," as in the case of Vogelsang, is as equally absurd as calling the Yasusada Author a "liar." In *Faking Literature*, K.K. Ruthven writes:

> ...in addition to collaboration with other people [these 'dispersed' authorial practices] include writing anonymously or pseudonymously, opting to use a mask or 'persona' instead of writing *in propria persona*, imputing to someone else one's 'own' work, speechwriting and ghostwriting for other people, and the franchising to various writers of books about famous literary characters. While such practices are not uniformly acceptable, none of them is deemed an illegitimate—let alone illegal—mode of literary production. Yet all trade on duplicity. (Ruthven 92).

Far from being a criminal or a thief, the Yasusada Author, as Mikhail Epstein has written, "gives away one's own property as if it belonged to another author" (Epstein).

Charles Simic did not like Yasusada's poems. In response to Marjorie Perloff's essay in the *Boston Review*, Simic says that the Yasusada poems, or at least two stanzas in one of them, could have been written by "a Frank Kowalski, a retired milkman in Milwaukee" (Simic). "Invention of separate poetic identities (in the manner of Fernando Pessoa)," Simic writes, "has a long tradition and is perfectly permissible. Poetry is the only place where a liar can have an honest existence, providing his lies make memorable poems. Unfortunately, not in this case." The case here is: Simic misses the point in so far as Yasusada is not a mere invented "poetic identity." The type of invention we are dealing with here does *not* have a long tradition. Pessoa claims his heteronymic "inventions" while no one has claimed or intends to claim to *be* Yasusada. Searching for the Yasusada Author means to miss the point: even if we know who the Yasusada Author is, we are to proceed as if we do not. The metaphor, like the idea of a religious entity, only functions when one accepts it wholly and without questioning. The metaphor of "Araki Yasusada" functions only when one accepts wholly and without questioning that no one knows who the Yasusada Author is, or better, when one accepts that the Yasusada Author is "dead" or does not exist, or best, when one accepts that Yasusada *is* Yasusada, that is when one accepts the paradox: reality is a fiction and fiction is a reality; the center is empty; the creator has made a world only to abandon it.

Monostich on page 90 of *Doubled Flowering*:

WHAT IS THE DIFFIRINCE?*

Is a rose is a rose is a rose the same as Ceci n'est pas une pipe?

*[*The misspelling is in original*]

Yasusada is *X* Yasusada is *Y* Yasusada is *Z* & what is the difference?
Yasusada is Yasusada is Yasusada.

The metaphor here is the reality.
To be a poet, I think, means to realize that.

Mr. Simic seems to have agreed with this once upon time. In a series of correspondences with Charles Wright, in the *Gettysburg Review*, Simic writes, "Isn't the purpose of all art, the hope that by and by you will become I?" Isn't then, the purpose of art the hope that one will not only embrace, but also become the *other*? That one will, in a sort of Lacanian transference, be absorbed into the *other*?

OBJECTION: *Writer of essay interprets Mr. Simic's statement incorrectly.*

RULING BY METAPHORICAL JUDGE CREATED SO THAT WE MAY ARRIVE CLOSER TO TRUTH THROUGH A FICTIVE INVENTION: *Ms. Boully has located the fallacy in Mr. Simic's logic. If read correctly, we can only surmise that Simic wishes for the other to absorb Simic! Is this not selfish and self-serving? Ms. Boully is, in fact, giving Mr. Simic more credit than he deserves. Objection overruled.*

EPSTEIN BACKS UP JUDGE'S RULING: *"Hoax" is a dysphemism (the opposite of euphemism—it is a rare, but existing term) for the most generous creative act which reverses the intention of plagiarism: the latter takes another's intellectual property as one's own; the former gives away one's own property as if it belonged to another author...a selfless placing in quotation marks of one's own utterances...*

(WE DIGRESS PRESENTLY TO ANSWER QUESTION POSED BY ROLAND BARTHES:

The urgent question is posed in *Empire of Signs*, in the essay 'The Three Writings,' after we are shown two photographs: one of a man appearing without a doubt as a man and the other of this said man dressed in "drag."

BARTHES' QUESTION:

> The Oriental transvestite does not copy Woman but signifies her: not bogged down in the model, but detached from its signified; Femininity is presented to read, not to see: translation, not transgression; the sign shifts from the great female role to the fifty-year-old paterfamilias: he is the same man, but where does the metaphor begin?

BARTHES REPHRASES HIS QUESTION:

> The Yasusada Author does not copy Araki Yasusada but signifies him: not bogged down in the model, but detached from its signified; Authorship (or the anonymous Araki Yasusada) is presented to read, not to see: translation, not transgression; the sign shifts from the great author role to the unknown writer: he is the same man, but where does the metaphor begin?

ANSWER 1: see section 'Empire With No Emperor'

ANSWER 2: There is a notebook entry (*Doubled* 71–73) in which Yasusada writes in the persona of Rita Hayworth, and it is Hayworth who writes: *I felt as if I were ~~not my body~~ emprisoned [sic] within a body that was not my own but was, in the end, my ~~own already~~ finally true body.* At the end of this diary entry by Hayworth is a footnote containing the following: *At the bottom of the page, Yasusada has copied, in black ink (and apparently sometime subsequent to the composition of the "dairy entry") the following quote in the original French from Tzvetan Todorov's* Theories du symbole: *"[the symbol] achieves the fusion of contraries; it is and it signifies at the same time; its content eludes reason: it expresses the inexpressible. ...the symbol is produced unconsciously, and it provokes an unending task of interpretation...in the symbol, it is the signified itself that has become a signifier; the two faces of the sign have merged."*

ANSWER 3: From the letter Mikhail Epstein wrote to Tosa Motokiyu, written shortly before the death of Motokiyu: *What is essential here is not the difference between Motokiyu and Yasusada but their mutual interference. Finally, do we know, following the famous parable of Chuang Tzu, is it Chuang Tzu who sees the butterfly in his dream, or is it a butterfly who dreams of herself being Chuang Tzu? Are you absolutely sure that it's you who invented Yasusada, not the other way round?*

ANSWER 4: From Derrida: *The sign represents the present in its absence. It takes the place of the present. When we cannot grasp or show the thing, state the present, the being-present, when the present cannot be presented, we signify, we go through the detour of the sign. We take or give signs. We signal. The sign, in this sense, is deferred presence (Différance).*

Read: The sign of *Doubled Flowering* represents the Yasusada Author in its absence. The textual body takes the place of the author. When we cannot grasp or show the empirical body, reveal the creator, we go through the detour of the text/sign. We take or give signs. We signal. The textual body, in this sense, is the deferred presence of Araki Yasusada.)

"*...HIS ANONYMITY WAS PURPOSELY CULTIVATED*":
In the Middle Ages, Foucault reminds us, "If by accident or design a text was presented anonymously, every effort was made to locate its author. Literary anonymity was of interest only as a puzzle to be

solved" (Foucault 126). Due to anachronisms so outlandish as to seem purposely placed, comments regarding translation and "speaking in the voice of another," as well as the introduction of characters such as Buster Keaton and Jack Spicer, one could argue that *Doubled Flowering: From the Notebooks of Araki Yasusada* was written and designed intentionally with the purpose of anonymity in mind. The "literary anonymity" presented, or rather created, by the Yasusada Author, differs radically from the search of the author, which Foucault suggests. In the case of Yasusada, the "anonymity was purposely cultivated" in order to reverse Foucault's statement: the author is presented so as to have the reader locate its true author, and if the puzzle is correctly solved, the author will be revealed as "anonymous."

In the notebooks of Araki Yasusada, we are presented with images and ideas that suggest communion is possible, but only indirectly through one sort of translation[7] or another. And so, in his poems, objects are only suggested or hinted at through shadows, books obtained overseas are read in translation, clouds are layered, sound is heard through echo, and correspondences are only copies on carbon. Everything existing suggests an existing *something* behind it, marks visible only due to *traces*—the author's presence is felt, but never revealed. "Palimpsestic devices abound in the Yasusada manuscripts," David Wojahn writes in his essay 'Illegible Due to Blotching: Poetic Authenticity and Its Discontents,' in order to show that Yasusada's notion of layered, anonymous authorship was purposely designed and integral to the text. "Each poem," he continues, "is a text layered upon

---

[7] Consider, within the context of translation, George Steiner's radical thesis that all literature is translation, an "echoing" of what has come before, or his statement that "in every act of translation—and specially where it succeeds—a touch of treason. Hoarded dreams, patents of life are being taken across the frontier... The craft of the translator is... deeply ambivalent: it is exercised in a radial tension between impulses to facsimile and impulses to appropriate recreation... Our age, our personal sensibilities, writes Octavio Paz, 'are immersed in the world of translation or, more precisely, in a world which is itself a translation of other worlds, of other systems'" (Steiner 244–247). Consider then my radical thesis: Yasusada is not merely a textual translation, but a translation of "being"; therefore, when we learn of Yasusada's translators, we are to think of this *metaphorical* translation. *Doubled Flowering*, then, is a translation of a translation of a translation, translated through the work of many translators.

several other texts, and the mask of the Yasusada character again and again appears to slip, offering us glimpses of other personae, be they the imaginary translator-editors, the probably real Kent Johnson and/or his co-conspirators, and, if you want to get post-structuralist about it, of 'writing' itself, and all the heavy metal smoke-and-mirror and dry ice interplay of sign and signifier which this implies" (Wojahn 111; *Scubadivers* 306).

After Marjorie Perloff's essay 'In Search of the Authentic Other: The Poetry of Araki Yasusada' appeared in the *Boston Review*, the next issue featured reactions from critics, editors and writers alike. Simic referred to the "hoax" as a "crisis," and Arthur Vogelsang, editor of the *American Poetry Review*, said in *Lingua Franca* that the Yasusada development was "essentially a criminal act." Being that the clues to the anonymous authorship were embedded in the text, it would be wrong to call the Yasusada Author a criminal; after all, the Yasusada Author personally contacted Weinberger after realizing that no one was going to publicly act on hunches and declare the Araki Yasusada manuscripts as "fakes." Although Eliot Weinberger noticed anachronisms and unrealistic content in the Yasusada poems, he refrained from publicly announcing the disjunctions until approached by the Yasusada author:

> I don't remember the exact chronology, but I read the first AY[8] poems (was it in *Conjunctions?*) with some measure of disbelief. First, I know 20thC Japanese poetry (in translation) pretty well—that is, I've read all the books there are—and there was simply nothing remotely similar to AY so early on—and all avant-gardists (or total individuals) have some connection to what is contemporary to them. 2nd, I found the story of his reading of Jack Spicer (and some others) very hard to believe, as the Spicer (and other) books that were available at the time AY supposedly read them were tiny pamphlets extremely unlikely to have turned up in Hiroshima. 3rd, there were some other anachronisms, I now forget which, that made me doubtful.
>
> Some time later, I heard—but I don't remember where—that there were questions about AY. Not long after that, I got a letter from the Yasusada Author(s), out of the

---

[8] I take this shorthand of Weinberger's to mean "Araki Yasusada."

> blue. The YA[9] had read my essay on forgery[10]—the one now in my book, *Karmic Traces*—in a Mexican art magazine, and had decided that I was someone who would be sympathetic to the project. As far as I know, I am the only person who was openly contacted by the YA. (E-mail to Jenny Boully, Nov. 2001)

Reading Weinberger's essay on forgery, 'Genuine Fakes,' one can quickly surmise why the Yasusada Author sought sympathy through Weinberger. Weinberger advocates that the "forger" is the "purest artist" in so far as he/she takes no credit for his/her art: "In our society," Weinberger writes,

> it is the forger who has taken the Romantic ideals of the isolation of the artist to its greatest extreme. He is a maker of art who can never be acknowledged as such, whose work is acclaimed while he remains in total anonymity. He is an outcast from the outcasts of society. And yet, he is also the purest artist: the one who rejects the cult of personality, who has no identity and no personal style, who believes only in the work itself and the age to which it is attributed. The forger, in the end, may be the model artist (*Karmic* 60).

Although Kent Johnson did take credit at one time or another for a few poems in *Doubled Flowering* (a few were published under his name in *Ironwood* and some were in his thesis) or told varying stories to various people, or metaphorically invented a few authors only to kill them off when the time was right, or has, as Wojahn says, a "reputation for duplicity"[11] (Wojahn 107; *Scubadivers* 302) he has never once pointed

---

[9] I take this, of course, to be Weinberger's shorthand for "Yasusada Author."

[10] Weinberger is referring to his essay 'Genuine Fakes.'

[11] Consider this posting to the UB Poetics discussion group I happened upon just a few weeks ago:

Date: Sat, 17 Nov 2001 18:28:22 -0800
Reply-To: UB Poetics discussion group <POETICS@LISTSERV.ACSU.BUFFALO.EDU>
Sender: UB Poetics discussion group <POETICS@LISTSERV.ACSU.BUFFALO.EDU>
From: Andrew Felsinger <andrew@LITVERT.COM>
Subject: Behind the Meatball Curtain
Content-type: text/plain; charset="ISO-8859-1"

Jenny Boully

From issue #5 of -VeRT Magazine: http://www.litvert.com/issue_5.html

Behind the Meatball Curtain

by Andrew Felsinger

I published the following poem in Issue #4 of -VeRT Magazine as having been written by John Ashbery :

'Meatball Curtain'

Literally, they say, "choked."
But pissing into the snow loosens nothing up.
I mean I; the reason why this remoteness
Haloes the how the day went,
Mathematical probability of the
Sound attached to the Seine's hypotenuse of ice
And the grafittoed monuments
Experienced as examined pulses, signals
To be precipitated in desire
The way a name gets spelled out magically
In blotto green light the sleet sparkles across.

But must admit I don't know for sure who wrote the poem. Is Jacques Debrot the author? He has similarly written both sides of an interview with John Ashbery, published by 2nd Story Books.

I knew the poem could be of dubious authorship, but chose to publish the work nonetheless. It contains a clumsy elegance that I also recognize and enjoy in Ashbery's work. I like to think of 'Meatball Curtain' as something that perhaps Ashbery could have jotted down, a minor yet worthy work allowed to slip from his desk, a poem pinned to his corpus, an homage to the intricacies (mysteries) of identity and art.

But a poet researched the work and was offended by this coloring outside the lines. The work has been subject to a lather of Listronics (See August/September) as well threat of a lawsuit. There have also been claims that 'Meatball Curtain' somehow hurts or annoys John Ashbery himself! I have been, therefore, asked to remove John Ashbery's name from 'Meatball Curtain' and make this retraction.

I was struck by such information. In an earlier and "legitimate" interview in Jacket Magazine Ashbery professes his admiration for literary frauds. What is more, Ashbery's work often displays a sort sliding / unidentifiable personal pronoun, (the very opposite of "I mean I"?) in which it is perhaps under-

Scubadivers and Chrysanthemums

standable to imagine this next step, of abstracted authorship, as inevitable.

What is more, John Ashbery is not known to use computers. How would he know of this new, West Coast, poetry web 'zine? It seems far afield. I can not seriously imagine John Ashbery pensively reading 'Meatball Curtain' and wondering over its supposed prescient and nefarious contents.

One possible explanation may be that such work requires scandal. Note the following email :

Date: Fri, 9 Mar 2001 12:54:40 -0600
Reply-To: kent johnson <kson@HOTMAIL.COM>
Sender: british & irish poets <BRITISH@JISILUK>
From: kent johnson <kson@HOTMAIL.COM>
Subject: Re: Dear John Ashbery
Content-Type: text/plain; format=flowed

Dear Jacques,

You interviewed me, and I showed you around the apartment, even letting you browse the rarest, most limited-edition books. And then you changed certain things I said. I left it well enough alone, even against my deeper instincts. But please don't take the confidence too far. I understand from Andrew Felsinger of VeRT magazine, that you intend to publish there a poem I sent you three years ago, specifically designated for your now-defunct magazine. I would remind you of copyright conventions, in case you have forgotten (or didn't know about them?). Let me tell you that when Frank was laid out, the long suture lines along his joints were like mountain ranges. "What about our vacation in Kabul?" he breathed, a hundred martinis on his breath. "Go back to sleep," I wept. And anyway, the poem was written by Joseph Ceravolo before he died. Plus, I don't appreciate being made a part of some obscene charade about Jacques Lacan, especially when the matter has insulted people in England with whom I have close relationships, like Peter Riley and Lawrence Upton. I'm sending this through Kent Johnson, whoever he is, since I am not subscribed to Listbot, even though I know who Jordan Davis is, of course, through Kenneth.

John

The above email is the work, obviously, of Kent Johnson. It was posted to the British-Poets Listserv in order, I surmise, to stir up interest in 'Meatball Curtain,' which at the time was about to be published in Issue #4 of -VeRT Magazine. The email is interesting in a number of ways: It states that the

the deictic authorial pointer to himself; furthermore, he has never taken credit for the Yasusada poems, and readers and critics should leave it at that. Whether the Yasusada poems were authored by Kent Johnson who, the literary establishment seemed shocked to discover, is a "hitherto unknown instructor of Spanish and remedial English composition" or whether the Yasusada Author consists of a collaborative effort among Johnson, Epstein, Silliman, et al. or whether the Yasusada Author is, as Simic likes to think, a certain "Frank Kowalski, a retired milkman in Milwaukee," the reader would be missing the point in imagining an author outside of the text, that is, outside of Araki Yasusada. Foucault's notion that "a text apparently points to this figure who is outside and precedes it" (Foucault 115) does not, as the Yasusada case shows, always hold up. Kent Johnson offers the following in an interview with Groany McGee conducted in 1997:

> It is crucial to understand that Motokiyu is not a pen name attached to the Yasusada work after the fact. The case, rather, is that for Motokiyu the condition of anonymity was indivisible from the creation of the work. This is a crucial point to understand, especially since some readers have reacted to the work with a degree of hostility, calling the poems "hoaxes" and "fakes." But we would like to propose that if the Yasusada materials are merely "fakes," then so are the pseudonymous works of Pessoa, Pushkin, and Kierkegaard, to name just three authors who felt compelled at times to enter into other identities in order to create. These writers wrote and published important portions of their works "as" others. For them anonymity was not a "trick" but a need, something intrinsic to their creative drives at given times. Likewise for Moto. His fundamental motivation was to imagine another life in

---

poem was "written by Joseph Ceravolo before he died." And there is this reference to "Frank"? Well, as interesting as this may be, I don't have the inclination to follow up these leads, if that is what they are? I am not as interested in the poem's creation as I am in the authorless fiction that allows for this semi-stateless object to float in an Ashberian ether. In a kind of no-zone.

To expose this poem as a fraud is, perhaps, part of *the plan*? To, somehow, square this circle. If so, then, I've done this, my part.

the most compelling way he knew how. Thus, for Motokiyu, anonymity—and its efflorescence into the multiple names of Yasusada, his renga cohorts, and translators—was a radically sincere expression of empathy.

Professor Nagahata, of course, dismissed the Yasusada Author's "sincere expression of empathy" on grounds, it would seem, that a *Hibakusha* would not write "bawdy" poems, and moreover, the bawdiness reflects ill on true *Hibakusha*. Wojahn would also dismiss the authentic sincerity, saying that "'Radical empathy' seems not to include carrying the Yasusada part to its logical conclusion... This is a radical empathy without the hair loss and diarrhea, radical empathy as a problem of technique, as just one more aspect of 'author function'" (Wojahn 106; *Scubadivers* 300). It is as Weinberger says in his exposé of the Yasusada scandal: in order to create "witness" poetry, it seems as if society demands that the "witness" be a witness and provide all the identification and necessary forms to prove such witnessing—art is deemed as not invention/creation, but rather witnessing/reporting. Consider the following from Lionel Trilling's *Sincerity and Authenticity*:

> The work of art is itself authentic by reason of its entire self-definition: it is understood to exist wholly by the laws of its own being, which include the right to embody painful, ignoble, or socially inacceptable [sic] subject-matters. Similarly the artist seeks his personal authenticity in his entire autonomousness—his goal is to be as self-defining as the art-object he creates. As for the audience, its expectation is that through its communication with the work of art, which may be resistant, unpleasant, even hostile, it acquires the authenticity of which the object itself is the model and the artist the personal example. (Trilling 93)

It would appear that for some editors and critics, the fact that the Yasusada Author embodied a Hiroshima survivor was "socially inacceptable" subject matter for an American or a network of non-Hibakusha, and therefore their "resistant, unpleasant, even hostile" reactions; however, as Trilling argues, the authenticity is embedded in the art itself through the laws of its being. Indeed, if we can accept this waiver of authenticity as given by Trilling, then *Doubled Flowering* is the most authentic and sincere text of all, in that the text is totally and completely "as self-defining as the art-object," i.e., the author and the text are indivisible, given the polemics of "anonymity" which were indivisible in the creation of the text.

DISCOVERING THE TRUE IDENTITY OF ARAKI YASUSADA:
From: "Jenny Boully"
To: "Kent Johnson"
Subject: Appreciation
Date: Wed, 05 Jul 2000

```
Dear Mr. Kent Johnson,

I hope you do not mind me writing you this. I came across your
email address while I was searching the web for articles on
Araki Yasusada.

My love affair with Araki Yasusada began my freshman year of
college. My creative writing professor ordered "Conjunctions:
23 New World Writing" as a text for the course. This was when
I was 18.

I did not discover the "hoax" until five years later, when I
came across an article in the 'Notre Dame Review' by David
Wojahn titled 'Illegible Due to Blotching: Poetic Authenticity
and its Discontents'. Was I heartbroken? Did I feel duped?
NO. I became fascinated and immediately bought and studied
'Doubled Flowering'.

I can say with all honesty that Araki Yasusada is my favorite
poet because the "hoax", I believe, is the most brilliant and
metaphorically beautiful occurrence in recent literature. I
would be disappointed if it were not so.

My only regret is that so many critics, from what I've been
able to discern, are concerned with the "author" behind
Yasusada. If only they would give consideration to the many
layers...ah...the "layered clouds"...they might be able to
appreciate the rich contribution this affair has brought
about.

Sincerely,
Jenny Boully
```

From: "Kent Johnson"
To: "Jenny Boully"
Subject: re: Appreciation
Date: Wed, 05 Jul 2000 16:50:35 CDT

```
Dear Jenny:
```

Scubadivers and Chrysanthemums

Thank you very much for the kind letter. It's very gratifying to get appreciation like yours, and I know that Tosa Motokiyu would have been grateful. I thank you for him, too. You are very thoughtful.

The discussion and debate around Doubled Flowering seems to continue, as there are other things forthcoming or being written. I'm wondering if you are intending to write something? Please feel free, if so, to send along any questions you may have and I will do my best to answer them. You may be interested in checking out Jacket magazine, really one of the best poetry sites on the web (run by John Tranter out of Australia):

http://jacket.zip.com.au

There you will find a number of things re: Yasusada in issues 2, 4, 5, and 9, if I have my numbers right. Additionally, there is an interview you may want to check out that I recently did with John Bradley, a fine poet and editor, at read.me, (issue 1) a good mag done by Gary Sullivan:

http://www.jps.net/nada/johnson.htm

Curious where you went to school. Are you currently at a university?

Well, thank you very much for the most thoughtful communication.

with best wishes,
Kent

From: "Jenny Boully"
To: "Kent Johnson"
Subject: re: Appreciation

Date: Wed, 06 Jul 2000
Dear Mr. Kent Johnson,

I was pleased to receive your reply and am most thankful for the web addresses. You can be sure that I will look into them soon.

I was not planning to write on Araki Yasusada; however, I think there is much to be said that has not been said concerning the textual references to "layering" which infuse 'Doubled Flowering' with the most beautiful actual and metaphorical authorship, a real representation of a representation of a representation. Absolutely brilliant. I need to examine the text more. There is a lot going on within

Jenny Boully

it. (I especially think of the letter to Spicer on page 117 and the English assignment on page 77.) In the book, there are many examples of "tracing a pattern over the pattern." I need to examine more. Perhaps I could come up with something.

In response to your question regarding my schooling, I earned my BA in English and philosophy from Hollins University in Roanoke, Virginia. There, I also received my MA in English and creative writing. I plan to pursue a MFA in creative writing this fall from the University of Notre Dame, although I don't really want a MFA. I am quite broke, that is the bottom of it.

I will get back to you if and when I do produce something which may be of use in the debate surrounding Yasusada.

Again, thank you very much for your attention.

I remain, as ever, etc.,

Jenny Boully

CLUES EMBEDDED IN *DOUBLED FLOWERING*:
FROM THE NOTEBOOKS OF THE READER/DETECTIVE:

"This point is important," Johnson writes in a letter to Nagahata, "The Yasusada author did not try to hide the work's fictionality—it was there from the start, for everyone to see." In a later letter, Johnson writes, "But what of works carefully designed to *temporarily* alter their reception because such altering is a crucial component of their aesthetic and critical impulse? What about works that present themselves as written by another, yet are intentionally and liberally mined with the clues to their own eventual undoing? As Marjorie Perloff has pointed out, the Yasusada writings always/already (if you'll pardon that term) included a sub-text of self-exposure. And I should point out that this sub-text created by Motokiyu is much more extensive than commentators have yet noted" (*Letters*).

The following is from an unknown, unnamed detective who had recorded, in her book of clues, possible textual references, outside of anachronisms, which prove that the Yasusada Author did not intend to falsify the identity of Araki Yasusada. We are just in the process of translating all of the detective's clues, as many appear to be written in shorthand invented by the sleuth. Along with the detective's hypothesis, we offer 'Anonymous Renga: constructed from grafts in Doubled Flowering.'

HYPOTHESIS: Araki Yasusada is an *entity* created by an unknown network in order to further the idea of anonymity, as it occurs ontologically and teleologically in our empirical existence and relation to the cosmos; the creation here goes above and beyond the mundane distinctions of "dramatic monologue" or "persona" writing or even "pseudonymous" writing, in that the text was written with anonymity in mind; moreover, there is no "author" behind the textual one, and the idea of anonymity is crucial and integral to its creation and existence—i.e. if the real Araki Yasusada were to reveal himself/herself/themselves, "Araki Yasusada" would vanish.

> *Anonymous Renga: constructed from grafts in* Doubled Flowering
>
> *I live and you live in that, and in that doubled flowering the departed and the living are blessed as one.*
>
> *[In carbon.* Poetry Hiroshima *was published in 1954. The largest of all "atomic bomb" literature anthologies, it contained over 1700 poems by 220 poets. Yasusada's false modesty and reluctance to contribute is revealing indeed, and supports our conviction that his anonymity was purposely cultivated...]*
>
> *The Men of Ink are very interested, like us, in the hidden interfacements ...there are layers and layers there...*
>
> *"And I...where am I? For being here is confusing,*
>
> *makes my position less clear. Somewhere in the upper left,*
>
> *I suppose, hurrying ambitiously to get somewhere...*
>
> *I shut my eyes, try to recall those days...*
>
> *Outside of me the photograph is beautiful and clear:*
> *A long, single pulse of geometry under dreams.*
>
> *Pure hieroglyph into which I also will vanish."*
>
> *Kusatao was over today and said this sounds like a bad translation from Italian or Spanish poetry. So I'm on to something!*

Jenny Boully

[Given Yasusada's concluding note—which seems to intend the inclusion of one of his own haiku—it appears that the poem may be a fictional construction.]

dokusan encounter

"who is the one before me?" I said.

"two sticks and a clack," he said.

"oh," I said, "so this one is three?"

"no," he said, "but you, unfortunately, would still appear to be."

{Eds. The detective's marginalia read as follows: *Perhaps on allusion to the three possible figures (oh my! a religious triad) comprising the Yasusada Author? If so, then the teacher's response indicates that naming, singling, indeed finding out the Yasusada Author is beside the point?*}

Buster Keaton makes an appearance.

"After all, the sutra does not say that words and reality are one."
"But thank you for the beautiful book that you gave me."

As I have understood it, that spirit has been one of exploring our poetic traditions with unfettered freedom and infusing them with the spirit of actual life…
Thus if the linking seems impure, as it has been criticized to be, it is precisely because we have embraced the reality and promise of impurity; …we aim to transcend the assumptions of "poetry," so as to see what might lay beyond.

Think of how many others there must be hidden within their pages!

In a place of small flowers and the shadows of small flowers.
Here is an offering of a sacred name which is [illegible, eds.].

but in the end, the courtesan on this Japanese screen seems more real than me.

Returning to the shadows of the blossoms the shadow of another life

Although the suitor written above does not exist.

Even when flower-bearing (even when a passerby cries, "Oh, there goes a suitor") the latter is an [illegible, eds].

Assignment 20 ("Writing in the style of another")

Who could ever know that behind such a voice, is the heart and soul of an asshole?

Mr. Rogers: May I explain? Your assignment of writing in the voice of another is followed here, but in the most libertine [sic] way. In fact, what I have done here is to provoke a triple *imitation: Here are the voices of 1) the wife, 2) the poet, and in echoes (so I hope) of 3) Catullus, the great erotic poet of the Empire of Rome. You kindly asked us to write in the voice of another. I believe, very frankly, that all writing is quite already passed through the voices or styles of many others. This, I believe in my heart, is the very marrow of writing.*

I am so taken by the conception of the book, that I have decided to correspond with Spicer in a like manner.

Forgetting the candle held behind the figure speaking behind the screen.

Alias, I said, I quote you.

tracing a pattern over the pattern

the theft has become a part of the very substance *of me.*

[Indeed, Yasusada's anonymity, and the overall fragmented nature of the notebooks might be best regarded not as the incidental effects of a private diary form, but as the marks of a chosen refusal of the transplanted constructions of self that increasingly shape Japanese literature in the 20th century.]

[It is not clear whether the Japanese participants named are

Jenny Boully

fictional or actual personages.]

When read out-loud, use Greek chorus mask—or Noh mask if none in available—and spirit-voice for parenthetical lines.

The gesture has something to do with language, but I'm not quite sure how.

I want you to exist.

the real washes up like a dream from the unreal; the unreal washes up from the real [sic, eds.].

You say you[12] would like the moon in your poems to be a real moon, one that could be covered by clouds, a moon independent of images. And you say you would like to point to the moon, and that the only sound in the poem be the pointing. At first I was confused, thinking that you wanted it both ways. But now I know you mean that the pointing and the moon are one. Like these letters, for instance, which have at their heart an urn, made real by the facing gaze of two identical ghosts. An urn wrought by the moon itself and the sorrowful pointing at it. Why look any further for the real?

This is where my communion with you ends and where it begins.

Now reach through, and place your hand on the papery flesh of this false face. And I shall put into my branching voice the ashy sky of your gaze.

Love,

Yasusada

Shiki revered him, said it was really he

{Eds. Under the poem, the detective wrote: Include all the references to spirit mediums?}

---

[12] Address to Jack Spicer.

LAYERED CLOUDS & "THE LEVELS OF REALITY IN LITERATURE":
In his essay 'The Levels of Reality in Literature' contained in *The Uses of Literature*, Italo Calvino writes that "The preliminary condition of any work of literature is that the person who is writing has to invent that first character, who is the author of the work" (Calvino 111). Should then the Yasusada Author be held at fault for taking such a statement truly? Foucault writes, "It would be as false to seek the author in relation to the actual writer as to the fictional narrator; the 'author-function' arises out of their scission—in the division and distance of the two" (Foucault 129). Not only does the Yasusada Author create "Araki Yasusada," he/she/they create "the pseudonym Tosa Motokiyu," the person who is supposedly the "actual Tosa Motokiyu" and finally, the character or fictional "Araki Yasusada" who is created through the supposed "actual Tosa Motokiyu." More interesting, and the crux of the whole affair, is that the anonymity of the Yasusada Author posits that the Yasusada Author had to in turn create the "Yasusada Author"... or the Yasusada Author was created as a result of the layers of creation given that, according to Calvino, there is no "person who is writing." If we chart these "levels of reality" in the Yasusada case, as Calvino charts *Madame Bovary*, we find ourselves lost in the "layered clouds" of authorship/creation. Although confusing and convoluted, such an attempt proves interesting:

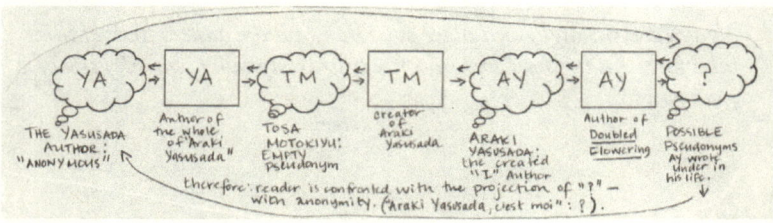

"The author," Calvino says, "is an author insofar as he enters into a role the way an actor does and identifies himself with that projection of himself at the moment of writing" (Calvino 111). Flaubert writes "Madame Bovary, c'est moi," Calvino contends, insofar as Madame Bovary shares traces of the author. In a movie theatre we are to trust, unlike the audience in Plato's cave, that what we are seeing are *images*, moreover, we can trust that these images posit their source in the empirical film and ultimately are the creation and vision of a director, that is, an empirical creator responsible for the images; with creation passing through so many layers of being, again how then are we to answer Barthes' question *Where does the metaphor begin?* In *The Counterfeiters*, Hugh Kenner writes, "Buster Keaton's subject was kinetic man, a being he approached with almost metaphysical awe we reserve for a Doppelgänger. This being was, eerily, himself, played by himself, then later in a projection room, watched by himself" (Kenner 68). Which then, is the real Buster Keaton: the Buster Keaton in the film (i.e. Buster Keaton as *image* as *projection*), the Buster Keaton in the role of actor, Buster Keaton as viewer, or confoundingly, Buster Keaton as "Buster Keaton" the signifier? When does the corporeal Buster Keaton cease being himself and become "Buster Keaton" the signifier? The Yasusada Author seemed to be keen on such an idea, as evidenced in the following haiku in *Doubled Flowering*:

December 12, 1960

Silent screen—
so many lives flickering
in both rooms

[*Yasusada note at bottom of page*] "Silent screen": a painted dividing screen from, say, the Edo, or the fluttering image of, say, Buster Keaton. Or the two fused into one, and so on. (*Doubled* 39)

The "silent screen" as a screen dividing Araki Yasusada from the Yasusada Author, the reader from creator, or the fluttering image of, say, Araki Yasusada. Or Araki Yasusada and the Yasusada Author fused into one, and so on. Somewhere, in the shadow of images, the spaces of light and darkness, the metaphor begins and the sign of the Yasusada Author fuses with the signifier of Araki Yasusada to mesh into the signified: "Araki Yasusada, c'est moi" says the Yasusada Author, insofar as Araki Yasusada *is* the Yasusada Author.

The Platonic notion that art is a representation of a representation is transcended a notch in the hyperauthorial creation of Yasusada: without a corporeal author, the text truly is a representation of a representation of a representation.

Scubadivers and Chrysanthemums

A xerox of a xerox of a xerox of Araki Yasusada:

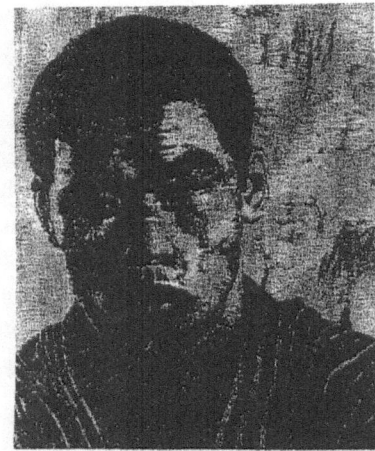

The poet Araki Yasusada

When the *American Poetry Review* published a special supplement devoted to Araki Yasusada, there appeared, alongside the poems, a penciled portrait of Araki Yasusada, which, according to Weinberger "appeared to be the blurred xerox of a xerox of a xerox of a mug shot of some low-level *yakuza*" (*Karmic* 108). How perfect, how apt Weinberger's intuition and language of the layering aesthetic inherent in Yasusada's work, where everything seems to present itself as the hardly discernible tracings from the last page of a pressure-sensitive carbon form used in some ontological department or other. We can be certain that *someone* authored these traces, but we lack an original copy: we have a copy of a copy of a copy, which is not to be confused with a "counterfeit"—on the contrary, the Yasusada Author presents us with the "real thing," which is to say, a world where creation is evident but the creator, although there are clues implying this creator's existence, appears absent. In 'The Work of Art in the Age of Mechanical Reproduction,' Walter Benjamin writes that "by making many reproductions it substitutes a plurality of copies for a unique existence" (Benjamin 221). Therefore, "by making many

A xerox of a xerox of a xerox of Kent Johnson:

reproductions" of Yasusada, the Yasusada Author "substitutes a plurality of copies for a unique" singular authorial existence. Derrida's beloved "origins" and "origin searching" and moreover the "origin of the trace" are halted, upset, thrown off course; therefore, it is little wonder that there exists much resistance to an "anonymous" author in a literary tradition where "the unique value of the 'authentic' work of art has its basis in ritual, the location of its original use value" (Benjamin 224). Araki Yasusada's copy, and all else that mimics Yasusada, has no "original" and thus there are those who would dismiss its "use value," its "author function," or its metaphorical implications regarding creation.

MULTIPLE CHOICE:
A or "A":
"Personally, I found the work far more interesting, and full of brilliant ideas, after I learned that Yasusada was an invention," Weinberger answers. "That is, I prefer 'Araki Yasusada' to Araki Yasusada as I prefer *Paterson* to Paterson" (*Three Footnotes*).

ACCORDING TO STEIN, THE YASUSADA TEXT IS A MASTERPIECE:
In 'What Are Masterpieces,' Gertrude Stein makes a distinction between "identity" and "entity" saying that one must, when creating, lose identity in order to create the entity. She writes that "the masterpiece has nothing to do with human nature or with identity, it has to do with the human mind and the entity that is with a thing in itself and not in relation" (Stein 83). One must, according to Stein, erase one's identity in order to create the entity, and although masterpieces concern themselves with identity, identity is erased to arrive at an entity. The *identity* of the Yasusada Author is erased, and we are only left with the *entity* of Araki Yasusada. Gertrude Stein, as far as we know, signed her name to all of her works, therefore canceling the possibility of erasing *identity*, thereby canceling the possibility of the stamp of *masterpiece*.

TEXT AND SPACE MIMICKING & SPEAKING THROUGH THE MEDIUM OF A CONCLUSION:
In a letter to Jon Silkin, editor of *Stand*, Kent Johnson writes, "Rather than being 'fakes,' I would offer that the Yasusada writings represent an original and courageous form of *authenticity*—one that is perhaps

difficult to appreciate because of the extent to which individual authorial status and self-promotion dominate our thinking about, and practice of, poetry" (*Letters*). Instead of being able to give away "an offering of a sacred name which is *[illegible, eds.]*," the Yasusada Author had to, it seems, in order to placate the literary mob, offer the name of Tosa Motokiyu. Never mind that behind Motokiyu is an empty sign signifying nothing or signifying another center without being. Never mind that Motokiyu is merely another curtain fastened in front of another curtain in a series of such curtains. Motokiyu is no less a reality, no less a fiction, than another "layer" to the group of authorial clouds hovering over *Doubled Flowering*.

It may be true that Kent Johnson has revealed, to different editors, different "truthful" identities as to who the Yasusada Author is, or that the Yasusada Author *must* exist; however, reveling in such details will cause one to miss the point. The point is: the center *must* be empty for Araki Yasusada to exist—the polemic of anonymity embedded in the text depends on it. In the interview with Groany McGee, Johnson says, "there is an important sense in which Yasusada was not invented for the poems, but the poems for Yasusada. This is one way of understanding the meaning of the title Moto gave the full manuscript: *Doubled Flowering*. Thus, in the presentation of the poems there was no choice. Their manner of presentation was faithful to the manner of their creation, and Moto told us more than once that if he were ever to take credit for the writing that he knew Yasusada would forever cease to exist" (*Doubled* 130). Foucault naïvely argues, "We can easily imagine a culture where discourse would circulate without any need for an author. Discourses, whatever their status, form, or value, and regardless of our manner of handling them, would unfold in a pervasive anonymity" (Foucault 138). This is more easily imagined than done, as the Yasusada case illustrates. Society it seems, has a strong and strange need for an author, in the same manner as it seems intent on naming and cataloging religious entities. Foucault thought such questions as "Who is the real author?" and "Have we proof of his authenticity and originality?" could, someday, be done away with; obviously, the time has yet to come. He seemed to think it ideal to "hear little more than the murmur of indifference: 'What matter who's speaking?'"[13] (Foucault

---

[13] Foucault is, of course, quoting from Beckett.

138). Ask this to many of the irate editors who felt duped by Yasusada, and they will tell you that *it matters very much*. It is as if Chuang Tzu had no right to imagine or dream of himself as a butterfly, seeing as how he is obviously human and simply cannot empathize with a butterfly; moreover, the butterfly had better not report on its experience of being Chuang Tzu, seeing as how no one would trust in the authenticity or authority of its report, with its being a mere butterfly and all. Should either Tzu or the butterfly report their dreams, they would be dubbed liars and criminals, which hardly seems appropriate at all.

If the author of my empirical world were to suddenly reveal himself/herself/themselves, I would feel as if something had died. That my world is full of clues of creation and layers of possibilities is what makes the experience of reading it wonderfully *authentic* and *sincere*. What holds true for the Yasusada writings, according to Kent Johnson, can be easily said of the cosmos as well: "... this quality of mystery should not be regarded as an incidental or distracting element of Yasusada's writing, but rather as the deep and proliferating source of its import and being" (*Doubled* 124). I can more easily trust a creator who makes a beautiful work of art and, in the generous mode of the "model artist" as Weinberger would have it, recoils so as to not take credit. Although this relation between artistic creation and creation, as it is understood teleologically, has been something I have often thought about, Foucault explains this idea more eloquently:

In granting a primordial status to writing, do we not, in effect, simply reinscribe in transcendental terms the theological affirmation of its sacred origin or a critical belief in its creative nature? To say that writing, in terms of the particular history it made possible, is subjected to forgetfulness and repression, is this not to reintroduce in transcendental terms the religious meanings (which require interpretation) and the critical assumption of implicit significations, silent purposes, and obscure contents (which give rise to commentary)? Finally, is not the conception of writing as absence a transposition into transcendental terms of the religious belief in a fixed and continuous tradition or the aesthetic principle that proclaims the survival of the work as a kind of enigmatic supplement of the author beyond his own death?

It is only because of the anonymous nature of *Doubled Flowering* that the text allows one to engage with discourses regarding representation and creation.

[... **THE SAGA CONTINUES:**

In October 1999, a few years after the "hoax" was uncovered, *Jacket* featured previously unpublished letters that Yasusada wrote to a pen-pal in the United States; these were later collected in *Also, With My Throat, I Shall Swallow Ten Thousand Swords*. If Yasusada is dead, if Tosa Motokiyu is dead, then they are, as Lorca is in Jack Spicer's *After Lorca*, writing from the grave. Motokiyu wanted these letters, or as he called them, "epistolary imaginings," excluded from *Doubled Flowering*; this is believable, as we are told there were many notebooks belonging to Yasusada. What does it mean when an author writes from the beyond, after dying? It means that anything is possible, and I follow developments as if watching a soap opera. It means: I do not often think of Tosa Motokiyu; in fact, I have grown to resent Motokiyu, preferring direct communication with the dead.

In interviews, Kent Johnson spends more time expounding the aesthetics of anonymity, while interviewers keep pushing the point of authorship.

In *The East Village*, a letter written by Jack Spicer to Kent Johnson appears like a magic trick performed by a gloved hand, and a Kent Johnson poem entitled 'Orientalist Haibun (with Cups of Sake Four)' with references to Pound's *Cathay*, proclaims at the end: "I spoke every Orientalist dream that came to me that sesshin, into the black hole of his succulent, papery ear." In *VeRT* 5, one can read the "epistolary imaginings" of Kent Johnson, embodying many personas, in his poem 'from: *Letter from Jerome Rothenberg: Post-Poems, 1998–2001*.' Furthermore, a newly found letter of Araki Yasusada, written on November 7, 1925, to the editor of a magazine with a footnote by the translators saying, "We suspect, though we aren't sure, that poems by Yasusada appear in the publication of VOU under pseudonym(s)" thus adding more and more "authorial" layers to the affair (*Village*).

There is a literature here: "Kent Johnson is the executor of Araki Yasusada's will," reads Johnson's biographical note in *The East Village*, issue one.

THE SAGA CONTINUES IN PAPER HOUSES:

In these newly published letters, Yasusada the author writes, "Many houses are beautiful and delicate, transparent is their paper. Everything is visible, nothing is hiding" (*7 Early Letters*). Read: *Yasusada (the author and textual body) is a beautiful and delicate transparent paper house where everything is visible, nothing is hiding.* "From a book," he continues, "which is flat, I sometimes am copying."...]

Works Cited

Barthes, Roland. *Empire of Signs*. New York: Hill and Wang, 1982.
Benjamin, Walter. *Illuminations*. New York: Schoken Books, 1988.
Calvino, Italo. *Uses of Literature*. New York: Harvest Books, 1987.
Epstein, Mikhail. 'On Hyper-Authorship: Some Speculations on the Mystery of Araki Yasusada.' Mikhail Epstein Home Page. http://www.emory.edu/INTELNET/ar_hyperauthorship1.html. Accessed 7 January 2011.
Felsinger, Andrew. UB Poetics discussion group. 17 Nov. 2001 http://listserv.buffalo.edu/cgi-bin/wa?S1=POETICS.html. Accessed 7 January 2011.
Foucault, Michel. *Language, Counter-Memory, Practice*. Ithaca: Cornell UP, 1977.
Freind, Bill. 'Hoaxes and Heteronymity: An Interview with Kent Johnson.' *VeRT* 5: 2001. http://epc.buffalo.edu/mags/vert/Vert_issue_5/KJ_Interview.html. Accessed 7 January 2011.
Gander, Forrest. 'Review: *Doubled Flowering: from the Notebooks of Araki Yasusada*.' *Jacket* 4: July 1998. http://jacketmagazine.com/04/ganderyasu.html. Accessed 7 January 2011.
Heyward, Michael. *The Ern Malley Affair*. London: Faber & Faber, 1993.
Johnson, Kent. 'Letter to American Book Review.' *Jacket* 5: Oct. 1998. http://jacketmagazine.com/05/yasu-lett.html. Accessed 7 January 2011.
_____. 'The Yasusada Affair—Ethics or Aesthetics? ... the Kent Johnson / Akitoshi Nagahata Letters.' *Jacket* 2: Jan. 1998. http://jacketmagazine.com/02/yasu.html. Accessed 7 January 2011.
_____. 'Orientalist Haibun.' *The East Village* 1: 1998. http://www.TheEastVillage.com/t/Johnson/p1.htm. Accessed 7 January 2011.
_____. 'Letter from Jack Spicer.' *The East Village* 11: 2001. http://www.TheEastVillage.com/t11/Johnson/p2.htm Accessed 7 January 2011.
_____. 'from: *Letter from Jerome Rothenberg: Post-Poems, 1998–2000*.' *VeRT* 5: 2001. http://epc.buffalo.edu/mags/vert/Vert_issue_5/KJ_5.html. Accessed 7 January 2011.
_____. 'Re: Appreciation.' E-mail to Jenny Boully. 5 July 2000.
Kenner, Hugh. *The Counterfeiters: An Historical Comedy*. 2nd ed. Baltimore: Johns Hopkins UP 1985.

Motokiyu, Tosa. 'Now I must wash my yellow body: seven early letters of Araki Yasusada.' *Jacket* 9 (1999). http://jacketmagazine.com/09/yellowbody.html. Accessed 7 January 2011.

———. *Also, With My Throat, I Shall Swallow Ten Thousand Swords*. Cumberland, RI: Combo, 2005.

Nussbaum, Emily. 'Turning Japanese: The Hiroshima Poetry Hoax.' *Lingua Franca* 6.7 (1996): 82–84.

Perloff, Marjorie. 'In Search of the Authentic Other: the Poetry of Araki Yasusada.' *Boston Review* 22: no. 2 (1997): 26–33.

Ruthven, K.K. *Faking Literature*. Cambridge: Cambridge UP, 2001.

Schwerner, Armand. *The Tablets*. Orono, ME: National Poetry Foundation, 1999.

Silliman, Ron. UB Poetics discussion group. 21 Dec 1994 http://listserv.acsu.buffalo.edu/archives.poetics.html Accessed 7 January 2011.

Simic, Charles. 'Our Scandal.' *Boston Review* 22.3–4 (1997): 32.

Spicer, Jack. *After Lorca*. N.p.: White Rabbit Press, 1957.

Stein, Gertrude. *What Are Masterpieces?*. New York: Pitman, 1970.

Steiner, George. *After Babel*. Oxford: Oxford UP, 1992.

Trilling, Lionel. *Sincerity and Authenticity*. New York: Harcourt Brace Jovanovich, 1974.

Weinberger, Eliot. *Karmic Traces*. New York: New Directions, 2000.

———. 'Three Footnotes.' *Boston Review* 22: no. 3 (1997): 36–7.

———. 'Can I Get a Witness?' *Jacket* 5: Oct 1998. http://jacketmagazine.com/05/yasu-wein.html. Accessed 7 January 2011.

———. 'Re: questions on Yasusada.' E-mail to Jenny Boully. 27 Nov. 2001.

Wojahn, David. 'Illegible Due to Blotching: Poetic Authenticity and Its Discontents.' *Notre Dame Review* 9 (2000): 93–116.

Yasusada, Araki. *Doubled Flowering: From the Notebooks of Araki Yasusada*. New York: Roof Books, 1997.

———. 'Poems and Rengas.' *Conjunctions* 23: (1994): 69–78.

———. 'Seven Poems.' *The East Village* 8: 1999. http://www.TheEastVillage.com/v.htm. Accessed 7 January 2011.

———. 'Letter with Poems.' *The East Village* 8: 1999. http://www.fauxpress.com/t8/yasusada/p1.htm. Accessed 7 January 2011.

Desert Music, Hiroshima: The Poetics and Politics of Pseudonymity

Alex Verdolini

We don't tend to think of anonymity as a privileged state—or, to put it conversely, we believe in the privilege of name. The unnamed, by longstanding Western tradition, is the absent—and the absent's always taken second seat. To crib a thought from Chris Marker's *Sans Soleil*, Westerners will cross against the light if the street is free of traffic. Unlike the Japanese, we don't wait to let the ghosts of broken cars pass by. There's an Amazonian tribe, according to Forrest Gander, for whom anything out of sight, around a bend in the river, is not only invisible but truly *nonexistent*. In our world—Adam's world, Aristotle's world—where everything is inscribed and taxonomized, the same goes for the nameless.

And so 2010's spectacle in Utah had something repugnantly strange in it. On July 11 and 12, various newspapers, TV stations, and law enforcement offices received envelopes sans return address, signed "Concerned Citizens of the United States." These contained, in addition to a short cover letter, a list of some 1,300 names, addresses, dates of birth, and so forth, belonging, the letter claimed, to "individuals who we strongly believe are in this country illegally." There's a fundamental reversal here: a group of supposedly illegal immigrants—in common parlance, 'the undocumented,' men and women *sin papeles*, people living out half-lives in our country's penumbrae—suddenly klieg-lit while the Citizens remained hidden.

The Citizens' identities, of course, have slowly come to light (they appear to have been employees of the Utah Department of Workforce Services) and the nature of their revelation has unraveled considerably—a number of the immigrants on the list have been shown to possess valid papers. And here are further complications: the Citizens may well have known that the list's recipients would all feel conscience-bound to keep its contents under wraps. It's possible that this nested epiphany—an uncovering of the formerly invisible, covered over in turn by the authorities—was in fact part of the plan.

After all, the Citizens could've simply put the list up on the Internet—but a full revelation would have backfired doubly: the list's errata would have gone public faster, and the immigrants named would have garnered even wider sympathy. And just as important: by entrusting the list to media outlets and law enforcement offices unwilling to act on it or disseminate it further, the Citizens were able to cast the government and the Fourth Estate as sympathizers, protectors of illegal aliens.

All of which is to say: the list debacle had the look of a neatly-calculated—if ultimately ineffective—publicity stunt, in the best Balloon Boy tradition. But the first moment of shocking reversal, perishable as it may have been, is well worthy of dissection. Such stunts are far from insignificant: some cultures reveal themselves most fully when they put on their ritual masks.

A decade and a half ago, the world of American avant-garde poetry was shaken by masked documents of a different sort. The poet in question was one Araki Yasusada, a Hiroshima survivor whose work—blending profound atomic grief, erotic humor, and a fine-tuned postmodernist sensibility—appeared in English translation in a number of prestigious literary journals. The catch was that he'd never existed: there was no Japanese original, and the 'translations' were essentially a hoax. Poets, critics, and editors set out to find the culprit, and after some measure of detective work, pretty much everyone came to suspect Kent Johnson, an American poet, who—along with the Mexican composer Javier Álvarez—had been serving as Yasusada's literary executor.

This news resulted in a widespread brouhaha. Wesleyan University Press, which had been planning to publish the first full book of Yasusada material, dropped the project. Writing in the *Nation* upon its publication at another house, Forrest Gander called it "the most controversial poetry book since Allen Ginsberg's *Howl*" (29; *Scubadivers* 51). A chorus of journal editors turned acerbically on the texts they'd championed: Arthur Vogelsang of the *American Poetry Review*, which had printed a portfolio of Yasusada poems along with an apocryphal portrait of the supposed author, summed up their common sentiment: "This is essentially a criminal act" (Nussbaum 82).

It was, in a way, more apt a phrase than he had realized. Several commentators came to read the Yasusada poems—and the manner of their presentation—as a pointed critique of essentialism, both authorial (a text must be grounded in a single, physical, and positively identifiable author) and cultural (a white American man can't write a Japanese poem). To their eyes, the Yasusada scandal exposed the journal editors' hypocrisy: had the work been printed for its poetic merit, or for the geopolitical backstory? Moreover, some of them argued, Yasusada undermined the so-called 'poetry of witness' and, by extension, the PC multiculturalism underlying it.

These critics were onto something. Throughout the many anti-Yasusada pieces, Kent Johnson was rarely introduced as a poet or a translator, but rather—after a knowing drumroll—as a *community college* professor from Freeport, Illinois. Writing in the *Believer*, the *Village Voice*'s Michael Atkinson dropped a reference to "Johnson's buddy, Mexican folksinger Javier Álvarez." Whether it was a mix-up, a misunderstanding, or a poorly-executed joke, this transmutation—avant-garde composer into mariachi man—says everything. The people who look to be defending the culturally authentic, as it turns out, are appealing to the same intellectual understructure as their far-right bogeymen: and it comes out in their racist- and classist-tinged barbs.

The Yasusada affair, in the end, throws the politics of identity into question: the cherished liberal image of one marginalized group after another stepping from darkness into light, the parade of celebratory self-identification ("I am woman, hear me roar"; "Say it loud—I'm black and I'm proud"; "We're here, we're queer, get used to it'). Yasusada makes you wonder whether the twentieth-century radicals were really radical enough—whether the power to name oneself affirmatively, authentically, is enough to deliver a gender, race, or sexuality from subjugation. Whether, at the philosophical root, there's sufficient distance between minority pride movements and hegemonic self-celebration. Whether authenticity might be the sickness instead of the cure.

Yasusada comes at the end of several narratives; one is the story of Eastern and Western poetry in the twentieth century, in which two literatures catch a glimpse of one another and, in that moment, become modern. It's a story of Gordian imbrication and many-layered mutual misunderstanding; it's fitting that the appearance of Araki Yasusada in America (and his inventor's illegal immigration into the imagined consciousness of a Japanese man) should serve as its coda.

The story's overture, of course, is Ezra Pound's *Cathay*, his thin 1915 volume of translations from the classical Chinese. Pound worked from the notes of Ernest Fenollosa, the Catalan-American orientalist, and the professor's fundamental misunderstandings seeped not only into Pound's translations but also his poetry. Fenollosa believed that all Chinese ideograms were traceable to pictographic roots--that, in all cases, they designated firm (visual) sense rather than arbitrary sound--and that written Chinese, as a result, possessed a concreteness and reality no Western language could rival. Rather than a sober assessment of Chinese, it was a positivist dream of a perfectly tangible language, so that Pound's "Ideogrammatic Method," the heir to Fenollosa's mistake and the prelude to Modernist poetics, was an old Western fantasy in new Eastern garb.

But the story really becomes interesting, as Eliot Weinberger has pointed out, when, in the second half of the century, Chinese poets discover their Western avant-garde counterparts—Pound's successors—and cast off millennia of traditionalist poetics. (Analogously, Yasusada positions himself, in places, as Jack Spicer's continuator.) The irony, of course, is that the stimulus for this violent rupture was, in a certain way, a few scraps of canonical Chinese poetry.[1]

The image of the foreign functions—unbeknownst to the subject regarding it—as something like an inverse one-way mirror: it looks

---

[1] Likewise, the Utah scandal sits atop a tangled heap of ironies. Utah itself is one of them: the backdrop to the latest anti-immigrant flare-up is a state whose land the US took, at martial gunpoint, from Mexico—at the end of a war Ulysses Grant called "one of the most unjust ever waged by a stronger against a weaker nation." (At one point, perhaps surprisingly, Grant pronounced the Civil War a sort of historical or karmic comeuppance for the war with Mexico; its aftershocks, it seems, have yet to cease.) And then there is the root cause of the Mexican War: the illegal immigration of *American* settlers, seeking land south of the border in what's since become Texas.

like a window onto the Other, but it's really a reflection of the self. Octavio Paz expressed it succinctly, in an observation pertinent to both Yasusada and the Utah immigrant list: "In general, Americans haven't sought out Mexico in Mexico; they've sought out their obsessions, their passions, their phobias, their hopes and interests—and that's precisely what they've found" (333, my translation).

A famous story from the *One Thousand and One Nights* comes to mind: a "ruined man" in Baghdad dreams one night that his fortune is hidden in Cairo, and so sets off for that city. After a few plot-twists, he ends up in jail there; the Chief of Police asks him what brought him to Egypt, and he relates the dream. The Chief chides the traveler, avers—in Burton's translation—that dreams are "but an idle galimatias of sleep" (Burton 4:55). He relates one of his own dreams, a corresponding vision of treasure buried, this time, in a Baghdad garden; the one difference is that the Chief was wise enough to ignore it. The ruined man recognizes his own garden in the Egyptian's description, returns to Baghdad, and digs up the fortune Allah intended for him. The story is, as Borges remarked, an especially seductive expression of the inverse logic that governs not only cross-cultural encounters but also our encounters with ourselves—a logic of perspectival reversals and odd efflorescent doublings. The Yasusada poetry is, in a profound sense, the fruit of that same logic.

If the motto of antiquity, inscribed upon the Temple at Delphi, was *know thyself*, its inverted image, refracted through the tale of the ruined man, would be *know the other and, in consequence, thyself*. Nietzsche put the Delphic saying through a different transformation: in his modern update, it reads *become thyself*. If you combine the two transformations, if you refract the ancient imperative through the double prism of the *Nights* and Nietzsche, you get *become the other*: Yasusada.

One reason that the Yasusada poetry is so effective, that it gets so ineluctably under the skin—and that its claim to otherness is legitimate—is that it shifts the relation between text and authorial identity in a radical, meaningful way. Identity—which usually figures either outside the text, as a prelude or precondition, or within it, as a theme—becomes the very medium. The poetry itself becomes a *pretext*, in more than one sense. In the basic sense that it exists to provoke further consideration, and in the sense that it stands prior to, outside of the *real* text: the shifts in identity that constitute the heart of the work.[2]

That is to say, instead of the politics of identity, we get its poetics. In his private papers, Søren Kierkegaard wrote: "Just as the Guadalquibir [sic] River at some place plunges underground and then comes out again, so I must now plunge into pseudonymity, but I also understand now how I will emerge again under my own name" (276). Following upon Kierkegaard's example, it is possible to imagine a poetics of pseudonymity—a continuity through shifts in identity, a thought or phrase enjambed across changes of name, changes of authorial state. And such enjambments seem particularly appropriate to the Yasusada situation—the case of a (presumably) Western author speaking somehow across the bomb's aporia. The disjunction of Hiroshima (comparable, as others have noted, to Adorno's vision of Auschwitz as the final winter of poetry) is mirrored in the poet's alienation from his own expression, in the linebreak between the authentic Western speaker and the faux Japanese speech.

The question here is: what continues past the rupture, what inner momentum carries across the divide? In terms of Kierkegaard's simile: what do the waters of the Guadalquivir stand for, what is it that joins Kierkegaard's works (under different names and in dialectical opposition) into a coherent whole? Pseudonymity, in the cases of Kierkegaard and Yasusada, poses the same philosophical challenge for us as the doctrine of reincarnation did for the Upanishadic philosophers. It forces us to look for (and question) the essence, to strip away the historical accident. As the Indian thinkers abandoned physicality and conscious thought—the familiar Cartesian poles—as the twin essences of personhood, we're impelled to probe deeper, to find *something else*. Under Upanishadic inquiry, personhood itself falls apart somewhat: the imperishable kernel at the center of the soul is equated with ultimate reality, the universe-as-whole. With Yasusada, it's not so simple; the

---

[2] Brian McHale makes a similar point in his seminal hoax taxonomy, "'A Poet May Not Exist": Mock-Hoaxes and the Construction of National Identity.' "Mock-hoax poems," he writes, "are *made out of* inauthenticity, and out of inauthenticity they make self-reflective art" (237).

first step isn't unity with the other—though that may be the target—it's disunity with the self.³

And so it makes sense that—unlike the Guadalquivir, unlike Kierkegaard's imagined oeuvre, which culminates under his own name, "in character, as the finale of the whole effort," Yasusada never reemerges into the orthonymic sun. The Yasusada author never returns to his authentic identity. But like Kierkegaard's philosophical project, with its meticulously plotted phases ("The three ethical-religious essays will be anonymous; [...] 'The Sickness unto Death' will be pseudonymous" (276)—and so on, a veritable hanging garden of full and partial self-concealments), the Yasusada work takes shape over the course of several transformations.

Yasusada's first instance, as it were, was his arrival as an apparent *hibakusha*, a Hiroshima poet of witness. It was in this guise that he captivated journal editors and kept famous poets, by their own admission, awake at night; his dark humor, his surreal lyricism and deep pathos were the work's defining qualities. In his second instance, Yasusada becomes scandal. The pathos drops away entirely; the point of the work looks to be political—the undermining of witness poetry, narrowly construed, the overthrow of cheap multiculturalism. Under this polemic light, Yasusada strongly resembles what, in his influential taxonomy, McHale describes as the "Trap Hoax"—a shaming of the avant-garde establishment, an exposition of its hypocrisy. And in this instance, the text itself becomes irrelevant; we come to focus on the frame.

What makes the Yasusada project important on a fundamental level is its third and subtlest instance. Several (disapproving) critics have written that no Japanese poet could conceivably have produced the Yasusada text. It's a curious point to make, in a way, and of a certain modal subtlety: the question—as these readers would have it—was not

---

³ As Mikhail Epstein put it in his letter to Tosa Motokiyu, Yasusada's pseudonymous 'translator': "The hyper-authorship is a necessary step in the development of the theory of difference in the direction of self-differentiation" (135). The politics of identity is founded on self-equivalence; it's a secular transposition of Yahweh's "I am that I am." Is it possible that the 'theory of difference'—commonly understood as apolitical, abstract, irrelevant to the humanist struggle—will prove the better path? That the collapse of self-identity is the first step toward productive identification with the other?

whether the Yasusada poems were written by a *hibakusha* but whether they *could have been*.[4] And in a way, they're right: Yasusada could never have existed in Japanese; he's possible only in (false) translation. He fails their test. But they're wrong in their interpretation of this reality—Yasusada's failure here is not his undoing, but rather the cornerstone of his strange ontological beauty. His third incarnation is as a poet in and of inauthenticity, a sculptor of negative space.

In this final reading, Yasusada is of a doubled melancholy. George Steiner wrote that a poetic translation should be able to stand alone formally but should also bear within itself a sort of ontological lack. That it should feel somehow incomplete—and, through its incompleteness, gesture back toward the original. (Similarly, the Persian carpet-weaver interrupts his pattern's symmetry, introduces a blemish in order to show deference to the original Creator. His work's imperfection gestures toward the perfect work of Allah.) It's a seductive vision of translation; carried out to its fullest conclusions, it leads to a sentimental, almost anthropomorphic understanding of the translated text. That the text is somehow an exile, in solitude—that it is touched by something like the *Geworfenheit*, the thrown-ness that afflicts Heideggerian man. That there's a loneliness inherent in the translated text; that the poem in translation—no matter how skilled the rendering—is by nature melancholic. The Yasusada text is, in a sense, this melancholy apotheosized.[5]

---

[4] Epstein reacted with angry eloquence to this line of attack: he argued that the de Sade novels, judging by any straightforward literary-historical criteria, would seem perfectly implausible as the work of an eighteenth-century French nobleman—and that this, in the end, is why they matter so much. Reflecting upon it, we realize that Yasusada's critics are guilty here of the same staid, stifling conservatism that Aristotle displayed in his *Poetics*. A impossible probability is better than an improbable possibility, the Athenian wrote, as it's easier for *hoi polloi* to gulp down, less likely to rock the civic boat. Epstein's defense is appealing, but he doesn't go far enough. He leaves the Aristotelian understructure intact, in a way: he fails to make room for the *impossible improbability*, under which category Yasusada may well belong.

[5] Another way to think about it: Benjamin writes that "real translation is transparent [*durchscheinend*]"—it lets the original shine through (18). Translation without an original, then, would be a sort of glass floor over the void; or something like one of those glass-bottom tourist boats, retrofitted for the deep exploration of absence.

Alex Verdolini

It's written in the strange diction of translated poetry, full of surreal idiosyncrasies and moments of seemingly accidental eloquence; something in the hollow heart of it calls out for the original—an original that isn't there. Yasusada's personal pathos coincides with the text's ache for its urtext: the poems are suffused with a sort of *Weltschmerz*, something like the longing Nabokov captures in a *Pale Fire* couplet:

> Man's life as commentary to abstruse
> unfinished poem. Note for further use. (67)

To the extent that critics have commented on Yasusada's translatedness, it's been mostly to remark that the Yasusada author did a good job of exploiting the similarity between postmodern prosody and 'translationese'—that Yasusada's language, in other words, is an elegant ruse. There is some truth in the observation. The postmodern reader has an undeniable taste for the odd rhythms of translationese, the hieroglyphic stiffness of the translated text—and the Yasusada work exploits this taste brilliantly, if that's how you choose to look at it. But, under a suppler, less hoax-concerned interpretation, Yasusada's translated state has a real metaphysical depth to it. It implies that the work's center of gravity is elsewhere; it introduces a gap between the text and itself. The Yasusada poetry carries within itself a sort of folded distance:[6] and in this way, it encloses in its relatively small, frail textual body some hint of the vast space between before the bomb and after it, between the present Western subject and the traumatic Japanese past.

All of which is to say: the Yasusada work is, in essence, apophatic. Yasusada speaks the most eloquently through his silences, through his hollow etiology. It is interesting, in this connection, to note Yasusada's association with Zen Buddhism. Zen, as is well known, tends toward suspicion of the affirmative word, of deixis and signification in general. Take, for example, the famous aphorism: *Don't mistake the pointing finger for the moon.*[7] The elemental fear behind the saying is that language

---

[6] To borrow a term from optics, where it designates, for example, the sort of prismatic doubling of space used in binoculars to increase the barrels' effective focal length.

[7] It is perhaps possible to read the epigraph to *Doubled Flowering* as a kind of complex, multiply refracted rendering of the moon and finger aphorism:

leads inevitably into itself, that we can't reach the moon, the other, by means of it. This fear gives rise to a complexly apophatic literature: that of the koan, a form resistant to all logical analysis, a slippery form that speaks through intuitive osmosis, mystically. Is it possible that the Yasusada work is, in its deep structure, a sort of postmodern secular koan—in which the moon (which, under a straightforward reading, would seem to stand for ultimate reality) is the Japanese other; the bomb's horror; the distant, inaccessible dead?

It is interesting as well to consider Yasusada's involvement with renga—a poetic form that came to prominence in a Zen-infused environment and is arguably inflected by Zen thinking. Renga, to review the form briefly, is a kind of communally composed poetry: one poet—the guest of honor, usually—offers the first stanza, another the second, and so on. The stanzas themselves are of no significance; the art lies in the relationships, known as "links," between them. If any stanza, no matter how beautiful, is of a self-sufficient beauty, then its author is missing the point.[8] Only the links themselves are unimpeachably *real*; the stanzas are transitory.

And the links, of course, are unspoken. Renga is, in this way, a wholly apophatic art; its meaning lies in its interstitial silences, in the

> In this novel before me there is a painting in a book the protagonist is reading, in which a woman holds a mirror. Behind the reflection of her face is the reflection of a mountain, made tiny by the distance. I wonder what she could be thinking, thinks the protagonist, looking up from the book. I wonder what is happening on the hidden face of that mountain in the mirror . . . (7)

Both the epigraph and the Zen saying treat the same fundamental problem: the failure to reach some essential, noumenal other (the moon, the mountain's hidden face) by means of some sort of optical (or, metaphorically speaking, linguistic) play. In the case of the moon and the finger, the problem is phrased as a command; in the case of the mountain, as a wistful questioning. In each case, though, we see the same thought-constellation, if from a different vantage point.

[8] The set of rules that developed around renga serves to promote the primacy of the unique link—any given stanza must link to the stanza before it, but not to the stanza before that. In this way, the renga constantly interrupts itself, prevents itself from resolving into a thematic arc. This constant interruption also has the interesting effect that every stanza, the first and last excepted, has two contexts—sometimes, two fully disjoined meanings—insofar as it refers to both the stanza before and after it.

gaps between stanzas. The true text is, in a profound sense, *elsewhere*. This facet of renga is of fundamental importance to the Yasusada work; this becomes especially clear in a poem like 'Geisha and Iris,'[9] each of whose lines is parenthesized. The parentheses act out in broad, palpable strokes the core of renga's inverse logic. It's the diametric opposite of Western positivism, expressed best in Wittgenstein's famous formula: the world is everything that is the case. In renga, in Yasusada, everything that is the case is in parentheses, irrelevant. (The question arises: what, then, is the world?)

Why does poetry matter in the world? Why does it matter in Utah?

Not long after the Utah list came out, toward the end of that summer of xenophobic cruelties, I found myself on Interstate 10—the southern limit of Eisenhower's high-speed America—heading west towards El Paso and thinking of William Carlos Williams. The day before, a heavy firefight had broken out in Juárez; a stray shot or two had spilled over the border, and the bridges across the Rio Grande had been closed.

Just a few days before that, thumbing through a friend's well-thumbed anthology, I'd landed by chance on 'The Desert Music,' Williams' rough, eloquent ballad of the border crossing and himself. The poem—of jagged, asymmetrical contours—is inscribed within a circle of sorts. It opens and closes with the same obscure figure:

> —the dance begins: to end about a form
> propped motionless—on the bridge
> between Juárez and El Paso—unrecognizable
> in the semi-dark

A drunk, perhaps, hunched "egg-shaped" against the girder's flange; or a listless wanderer; or a vagrant close to death. Whatever the form is—and thanks in large part to its formlessness—it's of a deep kinship with the poet. The link remains unspoken, but it's clear that the two are in tune with the same desert music, that they're suspended in the

---

[9] Not, in fact, a renga—although it shares some formal characteristics with other Yasusada poems in that form.

same penumbral ambiguity. Poetry sits on the same threshold, needs the same interstitial refuge.

The poet, Williams seems to imply, is a sort of no-man perched in no-man's-land. By necessity, he lives beyond the law, or between two laws—suspended over the thin river that divides two states. "What a place to sleep!" writes Williams,

> On the International Boundary. Where else, interjurisdictional, not to be disturbed?
>
> How shall we get said what must be said?
>
> Only the poem. (273–274)

Only the poem can speak what must be spoken, and it can only speak it from a floating in-between. Poetry is, by nature, international—in an uncommonly literal sense.

And so the closing of the bridges seemed doubly shameful. The poem's plot—in which Williams and his friends wander into Juárez for the evening, watch a stripper, take dinner, and then head back to the American side—has been impossible for a while now. Our century's Juárez is no sleazy tourist town; it may well be the closest we've come, outside the realm of open warfare, to incarnating hell on earth's surface. But the situation takes on a special perversity when—spooked, in all probability, by a few American-bought bullets from an American-bought gun, sent back by chance and poor aim to their country of ultimate origin—we close the bridges, nullify that halfway space where one of our old masters put down the root of his poetry. When we're willing—out of inertia, out of cowardice—to forget the part we had to play in all of it, to shut out Juárez and think only of El Paso: to block out the dark half of that doubled desert flowering.

It's the same dance that we're dancing in Utah: the same collapse of the borderlands—the realm of ambiguity, the shadowed in-between—into stark, unambiguous borderline. It's by this same logic that, instead of the forced disappearances that figure in so many totalitarian nightmares, these subtler oppressors, the so-called Concerned Citizens, bring us *aparecidos*: the idea is to wipe out the halfway underworld where the men and women *sin papeles* live.

Alex Verdolini

The poet and the undocumented immigrant, then, share an enemy: those who, as Ron Silliman put it in his blurb for *Doubled Flowering*, "have a proprietary interest in categories." Does this mean, then, that poetry can contribute in some real way to the political struggle? To eloquently denounce the drawing of lines is one thing; to make a meaningful space between them is another entirely.

⁕

The Concerned Citizens do away with the borderlands, the ambiguous interstitial regions; the authorities shut down the bridges to Juárez; the bomb cuts an impassable rift between us and the other, between the present and another time. And so the Yasusada author, the poet forced out of his interstitial homeland, dreams up an inner frontier, an interior borderland; he comes to an understanding of himself as constituted by another—as incarnate in the gap between the other and himself.

Is it possible that such an understanding can propagate through the tenuous substance of poetry? Can something like Yasusada make a difference?

When I read Yasusada for the first time, I was suspended over the Atlantic—and I read the poetry, too, in a state of vertiginous suspension. I knew that it was inauthentic, a fake, but without setting this fact aside in any way, I processed it as honest; deeply, viscerally real. To hold such a contradiction within oneself, to carry such a folded distance, is something of a spiritual exercise. Isn't this what makes imaginative literature—regardless of its theme—subversive, combustible, a threat to the world as it is?

And to cross that folded distance, to inhabit the gap: is it not to read in a new way, to transcend the usual game of nested referents? The Zen example is perhaps relevant again. If we are to affect the world, affect ourselves, it can't be a question of straightforward signification, of simply pointing at the moon. We need to find a subtler means.

⁕

"Poetry is more delicate than the reflection of the moon in the lake," wrote Juan Agudelo, the Nicaraguan peasant boy, at the age of seven years.

It was toward the end of the '70s; the Sandinistas were on the violent rise, and from the archipelago where Agudelo lived—the Solentiname Islands along the south shore of Lake Cocibolca—the world must have looked nearly too turbulent for his newfound lunar pursuit. But listen: "A perfect poem," he says next, "is like the Revolution" (Gullette 192).

The line that comes after, the line that supersedes.

Works Cited

Atkinson, Michael. 'Hyperauthor! Hyperauthor!' *The Believer.* Dec. 2003/Jan. 2004. 55–61.

Benjamin, Walter. 'Die Aufgabe des Übersetzers.' *Gesammelte Schriften.* Ed. Rolf Tiedemann and Hermann Schweppenhäuser. Vol. 4.1. Frankfurt am Main: Suhrkamp, 1972. 9–21.

Burton, Richard F., trans. *The Book of the Thousand Nights and a Night: A Plain and Literal Translation of the Arabian Nights Entertainments.* Vol. 4. New York: Heritage, 1962, rpt. 1885. 4:55.

Concerned Citizens of the United States. Letter to Customs and Immigration. *The New York Times*, 14 July 2010. http://documents.nytimes.com/immigrant-list-cover-letter-from-concerned-citizens-of-the-united-states. Accessed 19 August 2011.

Epstein, Mikhail. 'Letter to Tosa Motokiyu.' *Doubled Flowering: From the Notebooks of Araki Yasusada.* By Araki Yasusada. Ed. and Trans. Tosa Motokiyu, Ojiu Norinaga, and Okura Kyojin. New York: Roof, 1997. 134–8.

Gander, Forrest. 'Poetic License & the Bomb.' *The Nation* July 1998: 29–31.

Grant, Ulysses S. *Personal Memoirs.* Vol. 1. London: Sampson Low, Marston, Searle, & Rivington, 1885.

Gullette, David, ed. *Nicaraguan Peasant Poetry from Solentiname.* Albuquerque: West End, 1988.

Kierkegaard, Søren. *Practice in Christianity*, ed. and trans. Howard V. Hong and Edna H. Hong. Princeton: Princeton UP, 1991.

McHale, Brian. '"A Poet May Not Exist": Mock-Hoaxes and the Construction of National Identity.' *The Faces of Pseudonymity: Anonymous and Pseudonymous Publications from the Sixteenth to the Nineteenth Century*, ed. Robert J. Griffin. New York: Palgrave MacMillan, 2003. 233–52.

Nabokov, Vladimir. *Pale Fire.* New York: Vintage, 1989.

Nussbaum, Emily. 'Turning Japanese: The Hiroshima Poetry Hoax.' *Lingua Franca* 6.7 (1996): 82–84.

Paz, Octavio. 'México y Estados Unidos.' *El Laberinto de la Soledad y Otras Obras*. New York: Penguin, 1997. 331–53.
Williams, William Carlos. 'The Desert Music.' *The Collected Poems of William Carlos Williams: Volume II (1939–1962)*. New York: New Directions, 1992. 273–4.
Yasusada, Araki. *Doubled Flowering: From the Notebooks of Araki Yasusada*. Ed. and trans. Tosa Motokiyu, Ojiu Norinaga, and Okura Kyojin. New York: Roof, 1997.

The Strange Case of Araki Yasusada: Author, Object

Eric R. J. Hayot

Is "the death of the author" a defense against something more threatening—a fading author, for example, an author who is neither wholly present nor master of desire?

—Jane Gallop, *Reading Lacan*

Let us begin by looking at a poem by a writer who does not exist. Entitled 'Mad Daughter and Big-Bang,' and dated Christmas Day, 1945, the poem, attributed to Japanese Hiroshima survivor Araki Yasusada, first appeared in the magazine *First Intensity* in 1996.[1] It is reprinted in *Doubled Flowering*, a 1997 book that collects Yasusada's poems, letters, fragments of his English class assignments, and other assorted marginalia, as well as essays commenting on the Yasusada phenomenon, which revolves mainly around the fact that he never wrote poems. It reads:

> Walking in the vegetable patch
> late at night, I was startled to find
> the severed head of my
> mad daughter lying on the ground.
>
> Her eyes were upturned, gazing at me, ecstatic-like . . .
>
> (From a distance it had appeared to be a stone, haloed with light, as if cast there by the Big-Bang.)
>
> What on earth are you doing, I said,
> you look ridiculous.
>
> Some boys buried me here,
> she said sullenly.
>
> Her dark hair, comet-like, trailed behind . . .

---

[1] I am grateful to Sean Cobb, Matt Cook, Barbara Estrin, Megan Massino, Sarah Osment, and Julie Ward for their comments on earlier drafts of this essay.

> Squatting, I pulled the
> turnip up by the root. (*Doubled* 11)

The poem is followed by a note from the translators. It refers to the fact that Yasusada, as they explain elsewhere, survived the atomic bombing of Hiroshima. The daughter mentioned in this poem died, the translators tell us, during the atomic blast, along with Yasusada's wife.

Even as poems like this one were being published in American poetry magazines in the early 1990s, rumors were spreading that Yasusada was a hoax. In the November 1996 issue of *Lingua Franca*, an article by Emily Nussbaum announced to academia in general what poetry editors and scholars by then already knew: Yasusada's poems (and the notes and biographical material attached to them) had been created, or at least managed, by an Illinois college professor named Kent Johnson. Yasusada himself had never existed; Johnson told Nussbaum that the real author was "Tosa Motokiyu," but added that "Motokiyu" was a pseudonym for a now-dead former roommate of his and refused to say whether Motokiyu was Japanese or a Hiroshima survivor (83).[2] Reaction to the discovery of the hoax—well documented in Nussbaum's article, and subsequently in major newspapers, internet forums, such publications as *The Nation* and *Boston Review*—was mixed. Many who had admired or published Yasusada's work were upset, saying that the whole thing was a "criminal act" (Arthur Vogelsang) or "just plain ugly and selfish" (Lee Chapman) (Nussbaum 82, 84); Wesleyan University Press canceled plans to publish *Doubled Flowering* (which was taken up by Roof Books). What Johnson—or whoever the author was—had done struck many as unethical, an inappropriate mockery of a historical circumstance that he had no claim to, or worse, a facile manipulation of an American tendency to like its others exoticized. Writing in the *Boston Review*, Juliana Chang, Walter K. Lew, Tan Lin, Eileen Tabios, and John Yau declared that Johnson's "act of yellowface plays into an existing and apparently rigorous orientalist fantasy," in which Johnson' reprised "the stereotype of the deferential Asian."

---

[2] Johnson admits to having written some of the material (which was published in 1986, under Johnson's name), but says that Motokiyu admired it so much that he asked to use it as part of the Yasusada archive (Nussbaum 82).

Exposed in the wake of the hoax's announcement—for good or ill, depending on individual positions—was not only the vulnerability of poetry publishers to a good fake, but the fact that many in the American poetry community were judging writing by its author's biography. The idea that authors' life experiences ought to constitute part of how one understands or even values their work has its own long history of contestation; though its theoretical support has always been shaky, its appeal persists nonetheless both as a reflection of a cultural habit and, more recently, a liberal politics that values otherness or marginality. Anthologies like Carolyn Forché's 1993 *Against Forgetting: Twentieth-Century Poetry of Witness* have, for instance, explicitly organized themselves around the principle that *who* the author is matters as much or more than *what* the author writes (or rather, that what the author has experienced or seen ought to be a marker for a certain kind of poetic "witness").

That Yasusada's pseudonymity was announced for the first time in public in an essay explicitly critiquing Forché's anthology and the "poetry of witness" in general should not, then, be especially surprising. Eliot Weinberger's July 1996 article for the *Village Voice Literary Supplement*, entitled 'Can I Get a Witness?' claimed, surely not without a certain *schadenfreude*, that "had rumors of Yasusada's identity not begun to circulate, he would have become 'our' primary poet-witness of nuclear disaster." Such a critique of the "poetry of witness" generally figured the other side of the response to the Yasusada controversy, namely an argument against biography and for a return to "excellence" and a purer textuality, aesthetic judgment divorced from the author's body. Greg Glazner and Jon Davis argued in 'Bring Back Excellence' for a space in which poems might "succeed or fail—no matter who wrote them." And Marjorie Perloff told Nussbaum that if poetry editors liked the Yasusada poems before they knew about the hoax, they should like them afterwards as well (Nussbaum 84). At the far end of these reactions stood Johnson himself, declaring that authorship itself is a kind of hoax, a trick played by bourgeois notions of property and propriety, "experience" and "witnessing" being mere symptoms of a prelapsarian attitude toward the text as such. In a more recent interview Johnson has argued for "a guerrilla war of the heart against the ideology of the Author" and imagined that "the circulation of created, fully-realized hyperauthorships will become a vibrant and branching and authentic utopian space" (Freind, 'Hoaxes').

The historical irony of these two positions—anger at Johnson's deception on one hand, frustration with biographical authority on the other—is, as Perloff remarked, that they both draw on the work of Michel Foucault, particularly the essay "What is an Author?" There one finds both the critique of individual biographical authorship and the insight that authorship, whatever it is, both reflects and produces a set of social contexts that ought to draw attention not only to who writes, but to how that *who* comes into cultural being, shaped by the contexts in which writing takes place. For Foucault, the idea of biographical authorship has been produced by a particular set of cultural and social circumstances, allowing him to imagine a culture without authors, in which one might ask, indifferently, "What difference does it make who is speaking?" (614).

And yet if the author (or, in more Foucauldian terms, the "function of authorship") is discursive and social, thinking about authorship becomes more, not less important: understanding the difference "who is speaking" makes requires a rigorous political and philosophical attentiveness to the conditions under which speaking gets recognized or legitimated by publics and institutions. "The function of the author," Foucault writes, "is ... characteristic of the mode of existence, circulation, and operation of certain discourses within a society" (603). The recognition that authors are not "necessary" does not necessarily lead to a dismissal of all authors; instead it inspires a more intense study of the conditions under which authorship gets made—the "mode of existence . . . of certain discourses within a society"—and thus, concomitantly, an awareness of the degree to which power makes it easier or more difficult for certain people to speak. Hence a poetry of witness.

The Yasusada controversy not only witnesses this social complication around authorship but testifies to it. As Weinberger has remarked, while the texts pre-hoax appealed especially to those inclined towards the "poetry of witness," post-hoax, they were championed by those, including Weinberger, interested not only in "excellence" and the author's irrelevance, but also in criticizing the biographical politics of the American poetry scene. Even after the announcement of Yasusada's pseudonymity the texts remain double: on one hand we have *Doubled Flowering*, a text that attempts to bury the last of the author, and thus to produce a poetry whose every extra-textual category—authorship, influence, originality, translation—is absolutely and irrevocably suspect. On the other hand, however, we have *Doubled Flowering*, a text whose major intellectual question is not "is it any good?" or "what do the poems say?" but rather, "whodunit?"—a question irrevocably tied precisely to those politics of authorship it seems to want to escape: as one writer remarked, "the phenomenon of hyperauthorship in Yasusada is not merely an instance of literary heteronymity, but also of *authorial hype*, as retrograde as it is revolutionary" ('Interview' 120).[3]

The history of *Doubled Flowering* thus simultaneously highlights the author's death or subordination to culture *and* the tendency to continue to need authors, and to find them, particularly in spaces whose marginality seems to defend against the declaration of the author's irrelevance (if not outright death). It is precisely the combination of these two strains of feelings or theories about authorship that makes the Yasusada controversy quintessentially of our moment, or rather, as we get farther and farther from the late nineties, quintessentially of *that* moment, when the coincidental *fin de millennium* casts a prophetic shadow over any number of cultural expressions (and indeed, both Perloff and John Bradley explicitly speak of Yasusada in that millennial context)[4].

As augur of the new century, the political and poetic suppositions and promises of the Yasusada controversy imagine the present as the past of a future that has not yet arrived, and so allow us to think about ourselves with something like the prototypical gaze of the historian— that is, they allow us to see our present *as* a moment, as something that might be typified, new historicist-style, by a minor document of an impossibly macrocosmic history. One might thus imagine the Yasusada "hoax" as a beginning, an opening of a trend that only will be revealed gradually, in the long years of the new century, as a resolution of the current dilemma—the combination of theoretical death and economic

---

[3] This remark is made by an anonymous interviewer of Kent Johnson in a 1997 *Denver Quarterly* article.
[4] Perloff imagines that "similar inventions will occur with increasing frequency as we move toward the millennium" ('In Search' 164); Bradley surveys the collection in an essay subtitled 'The Poetry of the Next Millennium.'

or cultural life of the author.

But the idea that the same millennial future offers a plethora of utopian acts of hyperauthorship responds only to one side of the current dilemma on authorship. The shape of the problem is something like this: We have a set of texts that tells us the author doesn't matter. At the same time we continue to believe in authors in the plural. We read Foucault's 'What is an Author?' (translated into English by James Venit); later we read *Les mots et les choses* in French and act as though it were written by the same "Foucault." We go to poetry readings; we ask authors to sign copies of their books. And yet we don't want them to interrupt our own scholarship; we want to read texts against the grain, to produce criticism without authors (or their intentions) getting in the way.[5]

How ought one then to deal with the author's authority, with the author's biography? In an essay on 'The Translation of Deconstruction,' Jane Gallop admits to feeling differently about Gayatri Chakravorty Spivak's translations of Mahasweta Devi than she does about Spivak's translation of Jacques Derrida:

> Although I feel uncomfortable or unsettled . . . about Spivak's displacement of Devi, I am rooting for and enjoying Spivak's displacement of Jacques Derrida . . . I find myself using oppositions like gender or "First World" versus "Third World" to polarize translation, saying: "we have to respect the Third World woman's original, but we can abuse the European man's original." Although that does not seem like a theoretical position, I don't want to reject it. Translation may not always be the same gesture . . . (59–60)

---

[5] To illustrate: in March of 2002 I had just started writing this essay, which I was scheduled to give as a talk at a conference in mid-April. One day, sitting down to my computer, I saw that I'd received an email from "Kent Johnson." The name struck me as familiar, but for a few moments I couldn't remember who he was; all of a sudden I realized that "Kent Johnson" is the name of the person who holds the copyright to *Doubled Flowering*. In that moment I felt as though I were receiving a message from a ghost—which I suppose means I had been believing in the death of the author all along! I was both thrilled and put off; thrilled to be in touch with a "real" author, put off because I found myself hoping that Johnson wouldn't argue with me about *Doubled Flowering*. It turns out I believe in the author just as much as anyone, even when the author is someone who says he didn't write the text I am reading.

Gallop frames this discussion in terms of what she calls "relative cultural authority," the relation between biographical fact and cultural power that determines, precisely, who gets to speak and when. And while she feels uncomfortable with her use of biography—she says it does not seem "like a theoretical position"—she also feels uncomfortable rejecting it. When she goes on to say that "translation may not always be the same gesture," she makes explicit her (non-theoretical) argument: against a theory of translation that would establish once and for all the relevance of biography in a systematic way, she wants to argue for difference in translation, that translation is different at different times.

Marjorie Perloff asks: "wouldn't 'Yasusada' be less reprehensible to Juliana Chang and her colleagues if his inventor had turned out to be Japanese-American?" ("Marjorie"). Presumably the answer to that question is *yes*; for Perloff, it is a *yes* that damns, testifying as it does to the interruption of racial politics into literary judgment. But to erase the author totally from the meaning of the text makes all gestures of authorship identical: if all authors mean nothing, then they all mean the same thing. Such a position strikes me as uncomfortably pure (though neatly theoretical). Instead of going back and forth around the question of the author—the desire to believe, the desire to disbelieve—it seems worthwhile to think simultaneously about how authors matter and don't matter, to figure out what might be possible to say about the relation of texts and authors without simply falling into some binary trap or a false theoretical purity. Authorship is not always the same gesture; nor, for that matter, is it ever a single gesture.

The degree to which the Yasusada affair actively has been understood as a hoax distinguishes it from another authorial controversy of almost the same period, namely the one surrounding Binjamin Wilkomirski's Holocaust "memoir," *Fragments* (first published in 1995 under the German title *Bruchstücke*). Since 1998, the authenticity of Wilkomirski's account of his childhood has been extensively attacked (first by Daniel Ganzfried), and the author's legal identity revealed to be that of Bruno Dössekker, a Swiss citizen who continues, despite the evidence to the contrary, to assert that he *is* Binjamin Wilkomirski.

Dösseker's insistence on that relation has moderated an angry critique of his duplicity; as Ross Chambers notes, few now believe him "to have been insincere or duplicitous in claiming the existential, if not legal, identity of Wilkomirski" even as they refuse to agree with the claim (94). The strange emotional effect of Dösseker's continuing to claim Wilkomirski's experience as his own, an insistence that forces his audience to grant him, if nothing else, the sincerity of his deluded convictions, contrasts strongly with Johnson's forceful insistence that he is *not* Yasusada, and the anger that such a claim produces.

Nonetheless, the Wilkomirski controversy illustrates what may be a more general, figuratively millennial trend, one that asks "what it means for a culture to be haunted by a collective memory—the memory of painful events that few, if any, living members of the culture may have directly perpetrated or suffered from in their own persons" (Chambers 92). As Chambers argues in relation to *Fragments*, the trauma of the collective memory may be such that an individual comes to confuse (as Dösseker seems to have done) historical events with his or her own life, to become "*inhabited* (i.e., haunted) by the events *as though* he or she had actually lived through them" (93). Rather than read *Fragments* as a meditation on the Holocaust itself, or as evidence of a particular individual delusion, Chambers writes, one can listen to the text voice the more general "hauntedness of a culture in which such delusion is possible," in which an act of writing that presents its readers with the double history of cultural and personal memory might be understood as an attempt to lay its ghosts to rest (95).

In what follows I approach the Yasusada archive as constituted by precisely the intersection of history, haunting, and memory that one finds encapsulated in Chambers' "as though," an "as though" that allows one to recognize the dual gesture through which the text (as revealed hoax) constitutes itself: both toward a past defined as a fragment of history, trapped in the amber of time, and toward a present framed by its relation to that past, its desire to re-member and memorialize it. Indeed, it may well be remembering's becoming *as though* history, that is, its bringing history fully into the present consciousness as remembered *experience*, that produces history as a haunting, and the concomitant experience of being haunted by that haunting, becoming the hunted subject of a haunted history. The imagination in *Doubled*

Flowering connects itself resolutely to both past and present: both to an historical event which, in the moment of its occurrence, announced the (possibility of the) end of history itself, and to the symbolic rehearsal of that event in the present, a rehearsal in which the present becomes defined as the future of a past that seemed to have none.

Whether such a symbolic rehearsal is possible or ethical, whether places like Auschwitz make poetry impossible, or make it impossible to live without poetry, rests at the heart of the anger directed against Johnson and the Yasusada hoax.[6] To read the "as though," however, requires understanding that the fictions of *Doubled Flowering* and *Fragments* predicate themselves on their authors *not* having the "right" (through direct experience or witness of the traumatic event) to participate in the symbolic representation of these historical traumas.[7] Inasmuch as both works express a desire, it seems to be not so much the desire to have been involved (and thus to become witnesses), but rather the desire to express the strange catachresis of not witnessing directly and yet feeling "as though" one, nonetheless, witnesses: what Chambers calls a "collective pathology" connected to a troubled historical consciousness (95). That consciousness, which locates itself immediately in the gap between "knowing" an experience first-hand and "remembering" it as "known," may never speak to the real condition of surviving Hiroshima, an experience whose pure subjective inaccessibility must continue to be respected by careful writers. It must speak, instead, to the condition of collaboration—a condition that refers to the simultaneous awareness of a collective responsibility for the event as such, and an emotional experience of victimization by the event for which one bears collective responsibility.

This returns us to 'Mad Daughter and Big-Bang':

---

[6] As Barbara Estrin has noted, Theodor Adorno revised his 1951 pronouncement that "after Auschwitz it is barbaric to write a poem," saying just a year later that "Perennial suffering has as much right to expression as a tortured man has to scream; hence it may have been wrong to say that after Auschwitz you could no longer write poems" (qtd. in Estrin 9).

[7] The question of who has the right to represent trauma, which I do not have space to discuss here, has been taken up in work by Dominick LaCapra, Giorgio Agamben, Slavoj Žižek, Cathy Caruth, and others.

Mad Daughter and Big-Bang
December 25, 1945*

Walking in the vegetable patch
late at night, I was startled to find
the severed head of my
mad daughter lying on the ground.

The poem opens with a surreal scene: the narrator, walking outside in the dark, finds his daughter's head there. The first stanza is matter-of-fact, conversational in a way that enacts a certain ironic detachment; the recognizably poetic here comes not so much from language as from the distance between the language and its content. This contrast between the everyday tone and the daughter's head simultaneously charms and appalls, the combination produced by the bare fact of the severed head and its casual, fantastic description.

Her eyes were upturned, gazing at me, ecstatic-like . . .

(From a distance it had appeared to be a stone, haloed with light, as if cast there by the Big-Bang.)

Two stanzas later the daughter's head has become a stone, cast there by an explosion the poem invites us to read in two registers: first as the nuclear event of the beginning of the universe, second as the nuclear event that announces, quite personally in the narrator's case, the end of the world as such. Having read the poem, we know the head is a turnip; in the third stanza, however, having said the object was a head, the poem says it looked like a stone—a second displacement of the initial surreal object. This has the effect of making one take the head *seriously*—from a distance it had seemed not to be a head, the poem says, but up close, it is one—it is *really* a head. The parentheses that enclose these lines mark their distance from the rest of the poem, a distance that articulates itself both through the stanza's (mistaken) displacement of the original object and, even more noticeably, through its style. The language of these two lines, particularly around "haloed" and the simile of "as if," seems quite disconnected from the ironic matter-of-factness of the stanzas it separates, more ordinary in its poetic affiliations.

> What on earth are you doing, I said,
> you look ridiculous.
>
> Some boys buried me here,
> she said sullenly.
>
> Her dark hair, comet-like, trailed behind . . .
>
> Squatting, I pulled the
> turnip up by the root.

For two more stanzas the poem returns to the tone of its opening. But the sixth stanza, "Her dark hair, comet-like, trailed behind . . . ," does something slightly different. Though the tone remains casual, the words "comet-like," the poem's second simile, return the reader to the third stanza's "as if cast there by the Big-Bang," bearing that simile out of parentheses and into the poem's domestic space. Or perhaps "comet-like" counts as the poem's third simile—the "-like" structure in this line calls attention to the "ecstatic-like" of the second stanza. But if "ecstatic-like" is a simile, it's not a very good one (as Bill Freind has noted, it sounds like poorly translated Japanese) ('Deferral'). I can see the hair trailing behind like a comet of the sixth stanza, but I cannot think of what it means to gaze "ecstatic-like"—the "like" here, rather than indicate similarity and comparison, seems to hint that the gaze is only *like* an ecstatic gaze, that it is in fact *not* ecstatic but just like that. "Comet-like" thus points the way back to "ecstatic-like," whose awkwardness as a simile returns to infect the "comet-like" from which attentiveness originated. The appearance of "comet-like" signals not so much the arrival of simile as the arrival of a "simile problem," a discomfort with something like traditional poetic figure.

Throughout the poem, the ease and charm of its surreal description contrast painfully with its strange similes. Or rather the ease with which the poem advertises its most unusual likeness—the turnip and the daughter's head—interacts only with difficulty with the poem's other, poorly "translated" comparisons. Inasmuch as they uncomfortably connect the poem to a certain kind of visible *poesis*, it is as though these last two stanzas figure the ongoing interruption of the poem's casual surrealism by the traditionally poetic. When that interruption completes itself, as it does in the poem's final line, the poem will have gained the truth about its own vision at the expense of accepting the daughter's death: to see the turnip as a turnip means losing the daughter entirely. One might then read the sixth stanza as a sort of threshold between truth and metaphor, the place where the poem finally spills over—via, ironically, a more markedly poetic language—into its clearest but least welcome vision of the real. The poem thus enacts a tension between a surreal, casual language and the language of a traditional poetics that undercuts it, producing the truth at the expense of solace or a new vision of history.

One might read 'Mad Daughter' as an ordinary exemplum of the "dead child" poem, or as a pastoral, one whose garden mocks by far too closely resembling a graveyard. Though the translators say that Yasusada escaped to the hills surrounding the radiation-contaminated city following the bombing, the poem's garden has not itself escaped the contamination of the bombing as history. The poem may thus be attempting to do to the pastoral or dead child genres precisely what it does to its garden and its dead child, namely to announce simultaneously their death and their insistent, fertile reappearance. Even as the poem asks its readers to contemplate the end of children, this ironic relation to genre threatens to undercut the force of any reading that takes it too seriously, or rather, suggests that taking anything too seriously after Hiroshima might require too much faith in the possibility of any future, any redemption (for genre itself, much less anything else). Indeed one of the questions the poem seems to be asking is whether after Hiroshima, genres and gardens—including poetic ones—will bear only such strange, unlovely fruit.

The poem has an equally awkward relation to the historical genre of Hiroshima witness poetry. As Perloff has noted, "One would be hard put to find actual Hiroshima witness poems (or even later Japanese re-enactments of Hiroshima poems) that are characterized by such irony and restraint, such self-consciously surreal, oblique images" ('In Search,' 160). And of course 'Mad Daughter and Big-Bang' isn't a Hiroshima witness poem; nor is it a Japanese re-enactment of one. It is, instead, something written in the mid-1990s, *as though* it might have been a Hiroshima witness poem. Read in that light, the poem seems to be commenting on the relation between experience and poetry, between history experienced at the macro, geologic level (the Big Bang, the atomic bomb) and history as individuals experience it, relive it, or make it up for themselves in their dreams (and I mean for "experience" and "make it up" to refer both to the possibility of "Araki Yasusada" and the poem's anonymous author). In this manner, the daughter's head/stone/turnip figures the historicity of Hiroshima in miniature, as an object capable of its simultaneous self-production as fragment of personal, individual histories *and* geologic, collective ones. It plays the malleability of personal memory and perception against the absolute purity and rigidity of the macrocosmic historical event. Trapped in a binary version of authorship, we might want to know: Does the head articulate the actual historicity of Hiroshima as it was experienced by its actual survivors, or a fantasized historicity, experienced in an imagination working some fifty years after the event? To which the poem responds: yes.

That answer faces, like Janus, both ways: rather than simply meditate on the pastness of the Hiroshima bombing, the poem may well "extend the possibility of genocide indefinitely into the future," as Barbara Estrin has written of other American post-Hiroshima poetry (15). The "occasion" that prompts the poem may itself be so overwhelming as to make future occasions impossible; the readerly pleasure 'Mad Daughter' generates thus implicates its readers not only in the question of its dubious authorship but, more alarmingly, in the responsibility for the poem's, or even history's, "Big-Bang."

To say all this is to say that the daughter's head, and the poem's relentless folding and unfolding of that head in and out of simile and metaphor, functions in the poem as a special kind of object, a sort of historical remnant or fossil or scar that not only bears the weight of the poem's relentless poeticization but also of the poem's relation to history. The poem's emotional transformations in relation to its double (geologic and human) history produce themselves not only through shifts in style but through an attention to the metaphorical object *as* object. This is not to suggest that the daughter's head is reified, but rather to say that the troubles the poem has seeing the head as an object indicate, perhaps only obliquely, the difficulties of dealing with objects as such, or, more, the possibility that the poem's ability to see the turnip clearly involves not only seeing the turnip but seeing other things in it. That is—to now cite Douglas Mao's recent study of objects in modernism—the object in this poem seems symptomatic of a more general "feeling of regard for the physical object as object—as not-self, as not-subject, as most helpless and will-less of entities, but also as fragment of Being, as solidity, as otherness in its most resilient opacity" (4).

Considered as an object, the daughter's head, and the transformations it undergoes, figure precisely that same Orientalist contrast between Western science and Eastern nature, between modernity and the unsullied pre-modern, that critics already know from Ezra Pound's 'In a Station of the Metro' ("The apparition of these faces in the crowd; / Petals on a wet, black bough"). If, with Mao, "we might be inclined to say that one of the swerves (if not the break) of our own century is to be found in a new return to objects, now held to illuminate not only the order of the cosmos or distant antiquity but also the immediate human past," (6) one can read 'Mad Daughter and Big-Bang' not simply in the context of a more general postmodern debate on authorship, but also as a (self-conscious?) meditation on a relationship to objects whose motivations in the Yasusada text seem not so much postmodern as *modernist*.

Doubled Flowering is thus multiply anachronistic, gesturing from the present towards histories of geo-political violence, of modernist poetics and phenomenology, and of authorship itself. Read as a hoax, the text attacks one of the last potential bastions of authorship, questions the notion of literary influence, capturing the essence of a post-Foucauldian moment that continues to describe and shape the contemporary literary imagination. But in its echoes of modernism's preferred object-relation, the text also stages its own relation to objects in a quintessentially modernist form, almost as a nostalgia for a form that was, as Mao argues, already nostalgic when it was new. If this nostalgia, an already complicated relation to the pastness of the past and the dissatisfactions of the present, itself constitutes one of *Doubled Flowering*'s major concerns, then we might say that the Yasusada text performs its relation to objects as part of a more general project to rethink not only a relation to authorship but also to history: the author too, is a kind of (historical) object.[8]

---

[8] Darlene Sadlier suggests that dubiously solid authors may well be mod-

Pound's *imagisme*, T.S. Eliot's objective correlative, and William Carlos Williams' "no ideas but in things" all articulate something like a modernist relation to objects and objectivity, what Mao calls "modernism's extraordinarily generative fascination with the object understood neither as commodity . . . nor as symbol" (4). This is one way to read Yasusada; indeed, I would argue that given the well known interest of many modernist poets in Asian sources,[9] many readers of poetry have come to associate, rightly or wrongly, the modernist object with East Asia. The poems thus play on and correspond to a certain Orientalism; Weinberger has said that the poetic tradition to which the Yasusada texts belong is not Japanese so much as it is "American Japanese" ('Can I Get a Witness?'). But while objects, for the modernists, frequently were treasured as "something out of the reach of subjectivity, something vibrantly independent, different, apart" (Mao 258), in Yasusada objects have little of that independence or modernist solidity; instead they continually melt into other objects, other ideas. Like the Yasusada author itself, they are slippery in their (in)difference.

Consider, for instance, an undated poem that appears late in *Doubled Flowering*, amidst work that has moved a long way from the charming but graspable surrealism and Japonisme of the opening sections:

[Undated and in English, Yasusada note at top of passage]
(When reading out loud, read in voice of American cowboy actor.)*
Nope, the periphery of her experience was no greater than the mountainous terrain surrounding the actor . . .

And then the noematic core of her perception shifted; if she would not soon become that cactus, the hand which had settled like a bird on her thigh would penetrate her being like a crazed piston.

*[While there are numerous marginal or uncontextualized notes like this in the notebooks, we enter this one because it is suggestive of an interest Yasusada seems to have had in the American West.

---

ernist objects *par excellence* in work on the heteronymically prolific writer Fernando Pessoa.

[9] See Kern and Qian, or my own *Chinese Dreams*.

Indeed, there is a series of Japanese sound-play poems in one of the notebooks, "spoken" by the American cowboy actor Gene Autrey (into which this passage is arrowed as an English interjection) which are completely untranslatable.]

This piece of writing presents its readers with a dizzying combination of possible origins, inviting them to imagine a Japanese Hiroshima survivor, writing in English, asking for that writing to be read aloud in the voice, not of an American cowboy, but an American cowboy *actor*. On top of all this we have the note by Yasusada's imaginary translators, complete with an "authentic" misspelling of Gene Autry's name, and a reference to a series of "untranslatable" sound-poems into which the text above might have been inserted.

The joke of the poem comes from the difference between "Nope," which ventriloquizes the cowboy actor, and the diction of the rest of the text, part phenomenological speculation, part surreal poetic epiphany. That "nope" belongs, via the translators' note, to the American cowboy actor Gene Autry, who starred in some 93 feature films and recorded over 600 songs (his 1949 *Rudolph the Red-nosed Reindeer* is the second-best selling single of all time). Autry's 'Cowboy Code,' which he wrote in 1939, includes the following injunctions: "1. The Cowboy must never shoot first, hit a smaller man, or take unfair advantage. 2. He must never go back on his word, or a trust confided in him. 3. He must always tell the truth." While these all gesture broadly to a realpolitik of kindness and fairness of precisely the type that drive right-wing fantasies about the nature of American foreign policy (and thus point indirectly to the dropping of the atom bomb on Hiroshima), the third injunction, taken in the context of the Yasusada controversy, is especially ironic: the "truths" at stake in *Doubled Flowering* mostly appear in the form of lies. Quoting Augustine in a letter to the American poet Jack Spicer, Yasusada asks: "how could a picture of a horse be a true picture unless it were a false horse? Or an image of a man in a mirror be a true image unless it were a false man?" (118).[10]

"Noematic"—the poem's other surprising word—belongs, in contemporary philosophy, to the language of Edmund Husserl, where

---

[10] To connect this directly to the question of history, then, by the same logic: a true memory is a false event. Autry, incidentally, gives an eye-rhyme with the French word *autrui*, which can mean "an other" but also "all others," that is, everyone.

it refers to the object one perceives, considered not in the immediate and local mode of particular perceptions, but rather as a certain ideal. As, for instance, one can look at a box from many different angles (and hence have many different perceptions), and yet know that it is a box (rather than a collection of planes). In an essay on "Husserl and Frege," Ronald McIntyre argues that the noematic refers not so much to the object ideally perceived (the noema) but rather the mode of perception with which one perceives that object; not so much, he explains, the "object grasped by the hand"—the object grasped by our perception—"but like the structure of the hand which is necessary for its grasping whatever it does" (535). The "noematic core" of the perceiver in this text, then, might be thought of as the most fundamental mode of perception, the mode that limits, in the first stanza, the horizon of her experience—a limitation not of what she can see, but *how* she can see.

The word "horizon" is another privileged term in Husserlian phenomenology. In a phenomenological reading of the Zen Buddhism of Dogen Kigen, David E. Shaner writes: "The horizon of an experience includes the content and meaning of everything within the experiential periphery" (20).[11] A shift in the noematic core of perception thus involves a boundary-destroying change in one's experience of objects. In the poem's second stanza, the protagonist might become a cactus, the hand, already settled, bird-like, might penetrate like a piston: material objects have lost their solidity, as have the poem's initial metaphors. The poem presents a new phenomenology, one whose noematics—understood in McIntyre's sense as the "structure of the hand," the mode of perception—appears on the surface at least to differ a great deal from the modernist tendency to see objects as, in Mao's words again, "something out of the reach of subjectivity, something vibrantly independent, different, apart" (258). Objects in the Yasusada texts, rather than being out of subjectivity's reach, constitute it part and parcel, and perception acts as simply another way of reading oneself (or one's dreams) into the world. That the relation between the Greek

---

[11] I do not know how far one can go to suggest that Yasusada's use of "periphery" indicates that "he" is channeling Shaner (whose essay appeared in 1985). Many of the Yasusada texts, including notes to his Zen teachers, frame an interest in Zen Buddhism. Kent Johnson's co-edited collection, *Beneath a Single Moon* (1991), is an anthology of Buddhism in American poetry. This adds another layer to the geology of authorship; we have Yasusada, Autry, Husserl, Shaner, and the anonymous author of *Doubled Flowering*.

suffixes of noesis and noema is the same as the relation between those of poesis and poem (in which the ending –ma designates the object in which a process incorporates itself, and –sis the "abstract notion of a process understood in its effectuation" [Logan 11]) simply reconfirms the relation between procedure and articulation, between the mode of perception and the expression of that mode, that drives the poem's own internal dynamics.

It would be tempting at this point, then, to argue that the difference between the Yasusada texts and the modernists in Mao's *Solid Objects* (mainly Virginia Woolf, Wyndham Lewis, Pound, and Williams) depends on a "noematic shift" of its very own, and from there to claim that the difference so defined corresponds to the difference between modernity and postmodernity, second-stage capitalism vs. late capitalism, the rejection of the object as commodity against the embrace of commodification. To do so would be, however, to move too hastily towards rupture. Rather than see the effect of reading Yasusada as producing an absolute or remarkable difference between two kinds of aesthetic relations to objects, I would like to try and read that difference as one of degree.

Or rather: not all these relations are the same relation, but different responses to something like the same problem, namely the problem of figuring out how to perceive, of the relation between our lives and the lives of the objects we live with. Some modernists, like Wyndham Lewis, did not seek a world "governed by some radical existential or epistemological reconciliation, certainly not one in which the subject (or the will, or the self) would congeal into the object or the object dissolve into the subject" (Mao 139). Others were more willing to consider that sort of shift, "through metaphor to reconcile," as Williams put it, "the people and the stones" ('A Sort of a Song'). But the drift toward subjectivity or objectivity is never *total*. What we have instead are maneuvers *as though* to the extremes, projects in thinking through relationships pushed to limits. Even the extreme impersonality of something like Eliot's objective correlative can be seen, Jon Erickson has argued, as "less an elimination of subjectivity than its hypostatization through and in its cultural products" (139). Erickson, writing in his 1995 *The Fate of the Object*, continues: "The 'impersonal' aspect in modern practice simply appeared to be the most efficacious retention of selfhood against a truly depersonalizing interpersonal system of commerce even while it seems imprisoned within that system" (139).

Erickson's argument draws attention to the degree to which discussions of objects can invariably be turned into discussions about subjects and subjectivity. Surely every relation to objects conceals within its folds a preferred subject position, a vantage point from which the objects emerge into the perceived, and even the most impersonal art, whose perceptions attempt a complete divorce (via randomness or an act of will) from their subject-perceivers, does not erase subjectivity but only reframes it. As Erickson writes: "In all the experimental phases of poetry this century, the subjectivity of the poet does not disappear, no matter the motive or practice, but it changes shape, and even disguises itself in multiplicity, in order to remain sovereign, even if only through a unique gesture or style" (138).

In such a context one might return to the question of authorship in Yasusada, read now not only in light of contemporary debates about biography and textuality, but also through *Doubled Flowering*'s relation to objects, turned back on the subject-author that produces them. Repeating Erickson, it seems fair to say that here, "the subjectivity of the poet does not disappear" but remains "sovereign" in its disappearance, through the gesture of the fake hoax and the hype it generates. *Doubled Flowering* gives not so much a lack of authorship, or an argument for a return to an authorless "excellence," but rather a form of authorship whose shape prompts not simply a reconsideration of the poems' meanings but also of the relation between meaning and authorship, between the author as a fixed and definite source of meaning and the author as a construct that exists not so much *prior to* the poetry as *through* it or even *against* it.

If one way to describe the modernist drive to object perception is to call it "impersonal," one might say that Yasusada's relation to perception is, instead, all too "personal"—the poems as well as the collection itself, taken as a whole, argue for a "noematic shift" in perception that allows for the kind of objective slippage that happens throughout *Doubled Flowering*. Reading, the "author" of the poem slips from Johnson to

Yasusada to Motokiyu to irrelevance, and back again: like the head-turnip in 'Mad Daughter and Big-Bang,' not so much one *or* the other but rather both at once, as though the result of the bomb blast caused material substance—including authors—"to oscillate not only between divergent identities, or between presence and absence, but also . . . between object and image, real and unreal" (Tiffany 219). Objects in *Doubled Flowering* get the perceiving subject they deserve, and vice versa, as one moves, while reading, back and forth between taking the poems and translator's notes at face value (that is, *seriously*), and taking them as part of what one needs to be reading in the first place. In this sense the text differs little from those Mao reads in *Solid Objects*—it is not so much a question of modernist object against postmodern ones, but rather yet another case of the larger problematic in which Yasusada's objects speak continually to the condition of the subject that perceives them, enacting at the level of noematic perception precisely the same act of slippage that allows Kent Johnson (or whoever) to write as "Araki Yasusada."[12] And this slippage in turn forces the reader into an historical double vision. As Ross Chambers says of *Fragments*: "Because the referential object and the object of my reading are dedifferentiated—the same object but not the same as each other—the distant referent . . . and the immediate circumstances in which I read . . . which I *know* to be vastly different, are crammed into a stammer. Reality becomes oddly dual" (104). Dual, yes, but not binary: at stake here is not the absolute difference between an author that "matters"—one whose material experience establishes the conditions for textual evaluation—and no authors at all. The problem emerges instead from the simultaneous presence of both possibilities at once, the gap between the theoretical position and the difficulty of putting such a position into practice without stammering.

---

[12] One caveat about all this object talk: as Bill Brown has argued, to make statements like these is to answer "questions, in fact, not about things themselves but about the subject-object relation in particular temporal and spatial contexts" (7). If these questions "precipitate a new materialism that takes objects for granted only in order to grant them their potency—to show how they organize our private and public affection," then they may not be dealing with the thing-ness of the thing (the thing prior to perception, the thing as "limit to theory" or "alternative to ideas" [13]) but may instead remain investigations within the same old philosophic noema.

That gap, the felt distance between Foucault and the live signature, cores authorship, articulates its historical grammar, becoming nothing more or less than the persistent mode of its expression over time. Namely: in the early 1980s, a decade before Yasusada and Wilkomirski, Peggy Kamuf and Nancy K. Miller disagreed over the course of several articles about another authorial hoax, one whose appropriated mode of experience was specifically gendered. The *Portuguese Letters*, published anonymously in Paris in 1669 as translations of authentic love letters penned by a lovelorn nun, are now widely believed to be the literary products of a French man. An empirical answer to the question of who wrote the letters, Kamuf writes, "cannot be counted on to lead us outside the circle of its own pre-ordained tautologies of what is woman's writing, man's writing, fictional, or authentic" (298). Even as deciding the authorship of the text on the basis of its style reinscribes by necessity an "origin uncontaminated by the differential structure it inaugurates," it relieves us of the burden of reading the text blind; the French name "Guilleragues" is thus a particularly bad "solution" to the problem of reading the *Portuguese Letters,* resolving as it does the problems not simply of authorship but more broadly of meaning and value. Kamuf goes on to read the phrase "to write as a woman" tropologically, remarking that to write *as* a woman is to already be in the presence of simile, to be invited to consider writing (and its genetic marker, style) in terms of a differentiated resemblance, "exact resemblance as exact as a resemblance," as Gertrude Stein puts it: which is to say, not exact at all. Kamuf's simile carries over into her final prescription: "Reading a text as written by a woman will be reading *as if* it had no (determined) father, *as if*, in other words, it were illegitimate, recognized only by a mother who can only give it a borrowed name" (298).

Borrowed names, *as ifs*: the figures par excellence of the Yasusada and Wilkomirski scandals have, it seems, histories as well. And the response, theoretically sophisticated but finding Kamuf's tropologies too far from something like real life, comes from Nancy K. Miller: "What bothers me about the metalogically 'correct' position is what I take to be its necessary implications for practice: that by glossing 'woman' as an archaic signifier, it glosses over the *referential* suffering of women" (117). Though Miller remains wary of reproducing, with such a trust in the signature, "a naïve faith in origins," she believes that acknowledging women's writing *as* women's writing can "concretely challenge the confidence of humanistic discourse as *universality*" (117). This does not lead her to argue for a simple return to epistemological certainty, for a world where everyone knows who wrote what and organizes their interpretations accordingly. Rather, she says, "in the face of insolubility: let us retain a 'modern,' posthumanistic reading of 'literature' that has indeed begun to rethink the very locations of the center and the periphery, and within that fragile topology, the stability of the subject. But at the same time, we must live out . . . a practical politics within the institution grounded in regional specificities" (113). On one hand, we need to recognize the post-structuralist critique of epistemology; on the other, make choices in a political landscape that neither recognizes nor corresponds to that critique. So much for easy solutions.

The title of Miller's essay—'The Text's Heroine: A Feminist Critic and Her Fictions'—places her theoretical position already in the shade of the possessed fictional. If her positions on the text and its heroine are "fictions" in one epistemological sense, the title seems to be saying, the fact that they belong to *her*—the gendered possessive pronoun—makes them valuable expressions of a certain feminist (self-)possession, an ability to speak from, and own (one's voice, one's property, one's body) from, the position of being a (fictional) woman. Though her argument thus takes place under the shadow of fiction, that is where it perhaps best belongs, where she and Kamuf share a common ground. Because in the last edition of this dialogue, published under the epistolary title 'Parisian Letters' in 1990, Kamuf and Miller repeat—together, this time—the muddled authorship behind the letters of the Portuguese nun, this time as two women writing (as women, writing about women writing). There, Kamuf's prescription to "drop the name *as a form of self-address there where it risks functioning solely to reinforce the institutionalized signature*" suggests that it is not *all* naming but a particular practice of naming (that which solely "reinforces the institutionalized signature") that she finds most compromising ('Parisian' 132). And whether naming is *always* a form of self-address or not (and here I think of "French letters," whose prophylactic hope expresses itself in the form of a perpetual "return to sender"), certainly it is one of our most compelling fictions, one whose relation to politics and institutions does not permit untangling but which, rather, produces—seems to be very good at producing—an ongoing, historical stammer.

Guilleragues, Kamuf, Miller, Wilkomirski, Yasusada: just a few of the names entwined in the ongoing struggle to read the signature, all subjects of the drama that clings to the time of writing, the time of reference. Returning one final time to Yasusada, with the Miller/Kamuf dialogue in hand, allows for better, preciser questions: What theory of discursive practice is assumed or asserted by its hoaxed authorship, and that authorship's relation to the poetry that appears under its (false) signature? What kind of self-address does the book perform, and does this self-address reinforce or disrupt the book's own attacks on the institutional authority of naming?

It seems to me that *Doubled Flowering* argues as frequently as it can for an understanding of the author as mediated through its perceiving vision, its noematic horizon, and thus for an understanding of authorship as both constructed and social—that is, caught up in the collective traumas of a pathological history, and produced through an individuated consciousness whose mastery over poetic form very much resolves itself into a *signature*. It is not simply, in this instance, a question of those who have the power of the signature playing with not having it, but rather of the signature's solely being able to be asserted in relation to a more general, collective experience of history that the author can only own (and thus represent) *figurally*. The author so produced becomes also "only" a poetic object, one whose morphology borrows its logics entirely from distance between itself and the histories it pursues.

Authors-as-objects are neither the nominative signature of disciplinary power, nor simply irrelevant figments of the imagination. Or rather they are as much figments of the imagination as imaginations are, as figments are. And what we ought to learn, or relearn, from Yasusada and these texts is something *we already know*, or rather something we should have known all along: it does make a difference who is speaking, but the difference it makes is what we decide to make of it, a difference subject to the multiple pressures of Foucauldian discourse, institutional demands, the inexact resemblance of *as though*, the perceiver's phenomenological experience of objects, and, finally, a discrete attentiveness to all of meaning's shades. Recently, Kent Johnson has suggested that Yasusada's presence might best be thought of as a "form of haunting, a remnant, or, as Derrida has it in *Spectres of Marx*, a revenant, broken-off from the excess of trauma and mourning that flows out of Hiroshima through time and through us" (Freind, 'Hoaxes'). But rather than think of Yasusada as Hiroshima's revenant, I prefer to think of him, or the text, as *ours*, a ghost that returns, *revenant*, from a present it never left. Yasusada speaks a language layered, to be sure, with the overtones of sixty years ago, but which is given most precisely to the struggles of this age, of an ongoing struggle with the author and authorship, of an idealized, nostalgic drive for presence (and subjectivity) manifested and thought through a series of object relations. Listen: on his imaginary breath comes a wish for the purity we think we have always, always already, been missing.

If we never had it, it's not missing.

Works Cited

Barthes, Roland. 'The Death of the Author.' Trans. Stephen Heath. *Image, Music, Text*. New York: Hill and Wang, 1977: 142–48.
Bradley, John. 'What is "Authentic"?' *Boston Review* 22.3–4 (1997): 34.
———. 'Works and Days: The Poetry of the Next Millennium.' *Green Mountains Review* 9, 10: 2, 1 (Fall 1996–Winter 1997, Spring–Summer 1997): 140–43.
Brown, Bill. 'Thing Theory.' *Critical Inquiry* 28 (Autumn 2001): 1-16.
Chambers, Ross. 'Orphaned Memories, Foster-Writing, Phantom Pain: The *Fragments* Affair.' *Extremities: Trauma, Testimony, and Community*. Eds. Nancy K. Miller and Jason Tougaw. Urbana: U of Illinois Press, 2002. 92–111.
Chang, Juliana et al. 'Displacements.' *Boston Review* 22.3–4 (1997): 34.
Davis, Jon and Greg Glazner. 'Bring Back Excellence.' *Boston Review* 22.3–4 (1997): 35–36.
Erickson, Jon. *The Fate of the Object: From Modern Object to Postmodern Sign in Performance, Art, and Poetry*. Ann Arbor: U of Michigan Press, 1995.
Estrin, Barbara L. *The American Love Lyric after Auschwitz and Hiroshima*. New York: Palgrave, 2001.
Foucault, Michel. 'What is an Author?' Trans. James Venit. *Partisan Review* 42 (1975): 603–14.
Freind, Bill. 'Hoaxes and Heteronymity: An Interview with Kent Johnson,' VeRT 5: 2001. http://www.litvert.com/KJ_Interview.html. Accessed 7 January 2011.
———. 'The Deferral of the Author: Impossible Witness and the Yasusada Poems.' *Poetics Today 25.1* (2004): 137–158.
Gallop, Jane. 'The Translation of Deconstruction.' *Qui parle* 8.1 (Fall/Winter 1994): 45–62.

Hayot, Eric. *Chinese Dreams: Pound, Brecht,* Tel quel. Ann Arbor: U of Michigan Press, 2004.
Johnson, Kent. 'Interview.' *Denver Quarterly* 31:4 (Spring 1997): 106–25.
Johnson, Kent, Gary Snyder, and Gary Paulenich, eds. *Beneath a Single Moon: Buddhism in Contemporary American Poetry.* Boston: Shambhala Publications, 1991.
Kamuf, Peggy. 'Writing Like a Woman.' *Women and Language in Literature and Society.* Eds. Sally McConnell-Ginet, Ruth Borker, and Nelly Furman. New York: Praeger, 1980. 284–299.
Kamuf, Peggy, and Nancy K. Miller. 'Parisian Letters: Between Feminism and Deconstruction.' *Conflicts in Feminism.* Eds. Marianne Hirsch and Evelyn Fox Keller. New York: Routledge, 1990. 121–133.
Kern, Robert. *Orientalism, Modernism, and the American Poem.* Cambridge: Cambridge UP, 1996.
Logan, Marie-Rose. 'Graphesis . . .' *Yale French Studies* 52, Graphesis: Perspectives in Literature and Philosophy, (1975): 4–15.
Mao, Douglas. *Solid Objects: Modernism and the Test of Production.* Princeton: Princeton UP, 1998.
McIntyre, Ronald. 'Husserl and Frege.' *Journal of Philosophy* 84 (1987): 528–35.
Miller, Nancy K. 'The Text's Heroine: A Feminist Critic and Her Fictions.' *Conflicts in Feminism.* Eds. Marianne Hirsch and Evelyn Fox Keller. New York: Routledge, 1990. 112–120.
Nussbaum, Emily. 'Turning Japanese: The Hiroshima Poetry Hoax.' *Lingua Franca* 6.7 (1996): 82–84.
Perloff, Marjorie. 'In Search of the Authentic Other: The Poetry of Araki Yasusada.' *Doubled Flowering: From the Notebooks of Araki Yasusada.* New York: Roof Books, 1997. 148–68.
———. 'Marjorie Perloff Responds.' *Boston Review* 22.3-4 (1997): 37.
Qian, Zhaoming. *Orientalism and Modernism: The Legacy of China in Pound and Williams.* Durham: Duke UP, 1995.
Sadlier, Darlene J. *An Introduction to Fernando Pessoa: Modernism and the Paradoxes of Authorship.* Gainesville, Florida: UP of Florida, 1998.
Shaner, David E. 'The Bodymind Experience in Dogen's Shobogenzo: A Phenomenological Perspective.' *Philosophy East and West* 35:1 (1985): 17–35.
Tiffany, Daniel. *Toy Medium: Materialism and Modern Lyric.* Berkeley: U of California Press, 2000.
Weinberger, Eliot. http://jacketmagazine.com/05/yasu-wein.html.
———. 'Three Footnotes.' *Boston Review* 22.3 (Summer 1997). http://bostonreview.mit.edu/BR22.3/
Wilkomirski, Binjamin. *Fragments.* Trans. Carol Brown Janeway. New York: Schocken, 1996.
Yasusada, Araki. *Doubled Flowering: From the Notebooks of Araki Yasusada.* New York: Roof Books, 1997.

Araki Yasusada and Conceptual Writing: Global Paranoia and Local Belatedness

Jacob Edmond

In his manifesto 'Conceptual Poetics,' sculptor-turned-poet Kenneth Goldsmith describes conceptual or "uncreative writing" as "a poetics of the moment, fusing the avant-garde impulses of the last century with the technologies of the present, one that proposes an expanded field for 21st century poetry." Conceptual writing has become central to discussions of North American avant-garde poetry in the last few years, and Goldsmith's manifesto the most cited articulation of a phenomenon that not just Goldsmith but influential critics such as Marjorie Perloff hail as the new twenty-first-century poetics. Both Goldsmith and Perloff insist that conceptual writing builds on historical precedents and adopts a principled "unoriginal" or "uncreative" approach. Neither notes, however, that Goldsmith's manifesto is itself uncreative or unoriginal in applying the 1960s visual arts term to literature. Not only, as Perloff argues, does twenty-first-century conceptualist writing derive its "unoriginal genius" from earlier practitioners of visual and citational poetics, from concretism to Pound's *Cantos* to Oulipo, but another sculptor-cum-poet, Dmitri Prigov, anticipated the terminology as well as some of the tactics of twenty-first-century conceptual writing over three decades earlier when he and other Moscow writers began applying the lessons of conceptualist art to poetry (Perloff; Goldsmith, 'Uncreativity').[1] If conceptual writing does indeed represent the new, twenty-first-century poetics, why do conceptual writers like Goldsmith present their work as belated, especially vis-à-vis the visual arts, and why does Goldsmith's emphasis on belatedness itself echo Prigov, who

---

[1] See also *The UbuWeb Anthology of Conceptual Writing*, in which editor Craig Dworkin includes earlier works by Vito Acconci, Joseph Kosuth and Gertrude Stein, but omits Prigov and Russian conceptualism entirely. In their 2011 anthology of conceptual writing, *Against Expression*, Dworkin and Goldsmith repeat the omission, adding only in a footnote that "The term [*conceptual writing*] [. . .] should not be confused with the Kotseptualizme [sic] poetry movement that flourished in Moscow in the 1980s" (Dworkin, 'The Fate of Echo' xlviii n2). On his blog, Ron Silliman has repeatedly noted Prigov's omission from US discussions of conceptual writing, 22 March 2006, 23 February 2006, 3 June 2009 (Silliman).

in turn recalls Brion Gysin? And how do these questions relate to Araki Yasusada—who was presented initially as a belatedly discovered modernist poet and Hiroshima-survivor, and who was later described as a conceptual project instigated by Prigov in the dying days of the Soviet Union?

I want to suggest here that Yasusada provides a way to understand the sense of belatedness and complex network of connections that bind the rise of English-language conceptual writing in the 2000s to the Russian conceptualist writing initiated three decades earlier and, more broadly, a means to explore the cultural logic of our historical moment whereby local difference always seems threatened by international belatedness and a paranoiac sense of global interconnection. Although the relation of Yasusada to conceptual writing has been ignored to the extent that this connection might seem surprising, *Doubled Flowering* not only contains pieces such as 'Conceptual Essay' and 'Duchamp's Dissertation,' but also intersects with both Russian and US conceptual practices in ways that run much deeper. Yasusada offers a window on the historical moments that gave rise to late-Soviet conceptualist poetry and post-Cold War conceptualist writing and to the continuities as well as discontinuities between them. The anxieties about interconnection and difference, originality and belatedness, and the political and ethical problems of ventriloquizing gestures explored in conceptual practices bear a strong relation to concomitant questions about cultural and linguistic originality and authenticity evident in the Yasusada texts. Recent US conceptual works, such as Vanessa Place's *Statements of Fact*, comprising statements of fact from rape trials, and her theorization of her practice in *Echo*, refuse to adopt an authorial position, even as they frequently provoke personal, engaged, sometimes enraged responses from their readers and audience (Place, *Tragodía 1*; Place, *Echo*).[2] Claiming the position of the slave or of Echo, Place insists that "whatever is in the text is brought there solely by the one

---

[2] I witnessed the heated audience response to Vanessa Place's reading of *Statements of Fact* at the Greenwich Cross-Genre Festival, University of Greenwich, London, 16 July 2010. See also Stephanie Young's weblog comments on Marjorie Perloff's discussion of *Statements of Fact* at the June 2010 'Rethinking Poetics' Conference held at Columbia University (16 June 2010) and Perloff's response on the same weblog (17 June 2010).

experiencing the text" ('Interversation'). Yasusada provoked moral outrage for similar reasons. By contesting "an idealized, nostalgic drive for presence (and subjectivity)" and presenting "an understanding of the author as mediated through the work's perceiving vision" (Hayot 78–79; *Scubadivers* 202), the Yasusada texts emphasize how notions of authorship and interpretation are constructed, social: the ways we as readers experience the text, including the roles we assign to authorship and authorial intent, are shaped by political, social, economic, and cultural systems of power.

Reading Yasusada and conceptualism alongside one another reveals parallels between the relation of agency and authorship to poetic concept in conceptualist writing and the relation of the local and the particular to the wider systems of power, global connection, and surveillance in our post-Cold War era of globalization and digital technology. Yasusada and the recent rise of English-language conceptualist writing both exemplify a post-Cold War sense of global paranoia and local belatedness that extends earlier Cold War and modernist binaries between East and West, centre and periphery, now reframed through the dichotomy between the local and global. The responses to the Yasusada hoax illustrate this tension between a globalizing concept of hyperauthorship and the particularity of the highly charged content—the bombing of Hiroshima—through which that concept is realized. Some saw the hoax as a betrayal of the principles of genuine authorship and authentic witness. Others argued that Yasusada highlighted the "death of the author" and the irrelevance of the author's identity in a new transnational and transindividual world of "hyperauthorship," a term that consciously invoked utopian notions about the liberating powers of hypertext and the Internet during the period of the dotcom bubble. Eliot Weinberger celebrated Yasusada's undefined authorship as a kind of global utopia of equal opportunity, claiming that the poems could have been written by anyone, even a young woman in Senegal. Charles Bernstein and Yunte Huang, however, rejected the attempts by Kent Johnson, Weinberger, and others to present Yasusada as a work of hyperauthorship that negated questions of origins, authenticity, and cultural position. Huang described Yasusada's alleged "hyperauthorship" as merely a postmodernist update on modernist appropriation—not a "critique of origin but [. . .] an erasure of origins that are not 'ours'"—not white, male, and American (231). Similarly, Bernstein argued (though in an account that he entitled "unreliable") that "*Doubled Flowering* can be seen to represent the apotheosis of the poetics of resentment in the 1990s," exemplifying the backlash against feminism, gay rights, and multiculturalism (223).

Both the presentation of Yasusada as a hyperauthor and the response from Bernstein and Huang illustrate the paranoiac "belief in a *total system*," which inflects "any attempt to think beyond local and particular circumstances currently" in "a world where any analysis of power at the transindividual level increasingly requires a language capable of dealing with 'the system' as an abstract and holistic entity" (Ngai, 'Bad Timing' 2, 6, 5). Within this paranoiac structure, the "system" cannot be analyzed or opposed without being enacted. Hyperauthorship clearly describes and enacts the conspiratorial possibilities available within a system of global interconnection. But Bernstein and Huang also address a global system that enables local US or white male American interests to be represented as universal. Bernstein's and Huang's hermeneutically suspicious readings of Yasusada as a paranoid backlash text match the conspiracy plots of hyperauthorship. Both readings likewise produce a paranoiac sense of belatedness: the system anticipates your every move. Hyperauthorship presents individual authorship as a belated concept, while Bernstein and Huang present Yasusada as belated with respect to a multicultural global system—as a rehash of modernist appropriation or a backlash motivated by a nostalgic desire for a pre-identity-politics world.

The politics and poetics of paranoia and belatedness that surround the Yasusada hoax are characteristic not only of cross-cultural reading but also of conceptualist practice. Many US conceptualist texts of the 2000s flaunt their strict adherence to a totalizing system, as well as their belatedness and unoriginality. Like conceptual art, conceptual writing not only has many points of origin but also engages with globalization by addressing the anxiety about locality, originality, and belatedness induced by our increasingly media-saturated and globally interconnected environment—a redoubling of the Cold War paranoia about "them Russians" that Allen Ginsberg found half a century earlier by "looking in the television set" and ventriloquizing the words he found there (Mariani; Ginsberg 39–43).

Taking my lead from this conceptualist, paranoiac approach, I want to suggest that, when read through Yasusada, the rise of conceptualist poetry in the US in the 2000s can be considered within a global network of interconnections, including in relation to the Russian conceptualist poetry that emerged three decades earlier. Through this paranoiac interconnection and belatedness, conceptual writing in turn points to the way in which the imagining of a new global post-historical networked world in the 1990s in many ways continued the binary structures of the late Cold War that it seemed to supersede. Yet through their too perfect conformity to the system, these conceptualist writings suggest that paranoiac reading might also be used strategically to undermine the West/Rest, North/South, original/belated binaries that continue to inform cross-cultural reading and that paranoia and belatedness would seem to reinforce. Over half a century earlier, Mei Lanfang provided a model or counterexample to support strikingly contrasting yet all self-consciously "modernist" positions in China, Russia, and Germany: in China, a theatre criticized for its failure to be representational and so Western and "modernist" enough; in the Soviet Union, a covert means to defend a non-representational and so autonomous "modernist" theatre of estrangement against socialist realism; and for Brecht, the model for a non-autonomous but estranging or alienating "modern" political theater (Saussy). Similarly, Yasusada highlights how conceptualisms, modernisms, and postmodernisms, like our imaginings of authors, are the product of our cultural, political, and historical positions. The multi-directional cross-cultural readings invoked by the Yasusada texts and the responses they provoked illustrate multilayered interactions and historical particularities that cannot be reduced simply to a globalized system, be it of utopian hyperauthorship or dystopian imperialist power.

Hyperauthorship itself of course is a culturally and historically inflected concept despite its transnational and transhistorical reach. It not only has a certain formal resemblance to conceptual practice, but arguably derives from conceptualist writing—not US or Japanese, but Russian—and from a specific historical moment—the late-Soviet to post-Soviet transition. Russian literary and cultural theorist Mikhail Epstein was the first to apply the concept of hyperauthorship to Yasusada, suggesting that none other than conceptualist poet and artist Dmitri Prigov originated the hoax (Letter 134–38; 'Commentary' 139–47). Epstein had become one of the leading theorists of Russian conceptual writing in the early 1980s when he developed a highly performative approach to literary criticism that incorporated elements of the conceptual poetic and artistic practices that he encountered in Moscow.[3]

Epstein's paranoiac reading of Yasusada's hyperauthorship arguably extends Prigov's conceptualist work, which itself often explores authorship and poetry as key cultural signifiers. Prigov's writing, art, and performances are preoccupied with the figure of the poet in Russian culture and the relation of the poet to systems of power, most famously embodied in his "militsaner" ("policeman") poetic persona (for examples, see Prigov, *Sovetskie teksty*). Epstein's suggestion of Prigov as the inventor of the Yasusada hoax in particular extends Russian conceptualism's engagement with the cross-cultural politics of paranoiac interconnection and belatedness. Prigov mimicked Russian nationalist and communist rhetoric when he claimed that Russian conceptualism was really ahead of Western conceptualism: in comparison to Russian conceptualism, he asserted, "Western conceptualism should be more rightly termed *protoconceptualism*" ('Conceptualism' 13). Similarly, Epstein repeatedly argues that Russian postmodernism *precedes* rather than follows Western postmodernism, and his assertion of the Russian origins of the Yasusada hoax can be seen as a particular example of this argument (see *After the Future* 188–210). Epstein also invokes the language of global conspiracy and paranoia in linking Yasusada to Russian conceptualism, describing Prigov's "project of hyperauthorship" as following "the lines of a global poetic plot" and citing Prigov's private confession about "his 'masonic' conspiracy for the triumph of creative impersonality throughout the world of art" ('Commentary' 144). Huang's direct criticism of Epstein for eliding cultural difference ignores the particular Russian cultural difference and conceptual play at work here. Read cross-culturally, Epstein's paranoiac, totalizing, world domination rhetoric is a defensive strategy designed to resist the cultural hegemony that Bernstein sees the Yasusada hoax and

---

[3] For example, in Moscow in 1983 Epstein presented a manifesto on new Russian poetries in the context of a live performance by conceptualist writers and others. See Epstein, 'Theses' 105–12.

the notion of hyperauthorship as perpetuating.

Drawing on the Internet utopianism of the period, Epstein extended his appropriation of Yasusada to imagine a hypertextual avant-garde outside place and identity. Adding directly to what might be considered the Yasusada corpus, Epstein even presented a letter to Tosa Motokiyu—the similarly invented, supposed translator of Yasusada's work—about his utopian dream of establishing an "*International Society (or Network) of Transpersonal Authorship*" (Letter 134). In the late 1990s, Epstein related hyperauthorship to a practice of unoriginality in his description of his "book of books" project, which was envisaged as a vast transnational project that would bring together many authors and texts. Although this project was either never actually realized or was removed from the web (the link to the "book of books" given in the article is broken), Epstein's discussion of it nevertheless contained a list of "preliminary reviews," more in the order of blurbs, by "leading figures of world culture," including Umberto Eco, Jacques Derrida, and Araki Yasusada. Alongside this ventriloquizing approach in which language was produced in the name of others, Epstein insisted on the necessity of copying and plagiarism, whereby others' words be adopted as one's own: "for the realization of the concept of this book it is not only allowed but desirable that all the quotations going into it be appropriated" so that you may "consider yourself the author of any book to your taste" ('Kniga'). On the one hand, others' words could be recycled and restructured as one's own—in an approach akin, at least to this extent, to Goldsmith's "unoriginal writing." On the other hand, others' names could be recycled and presented as the authors of one's own words. Yasusada as an invented author functioned in the latter sense, except unlike Derrida he didn't really exist, but Epstein re-appropriated him in having him write a blurb to his book of others' words. Epstein here is clearly informed by Russian conceptualist writing, which he elsewhere described both as a "workshop for making scarecrows" and as adopting not "the position of a composer" but of a "compiler" or a "dictionary" who "answers not for the 'sincere expression of his own convictions,' but for the fullest possible representation of the laws and potentials of the language itself" (*After the Future* 31, 36). The project was also dependent on the interconnectivity and cut-and-paste possibilities of the Internet and on a transnational appeal. Epstein published his "book of books" piece in the Russian journal *Inostrannaia literatura* (*Foreign Literature*), suggesting the role that cultural difference and cross-cultural collaboration and appropriation played in his project.

Epstein's reading of Yasusada as hyperauthor can be seen in the context of the immediate post-Soviet period, when questions about authorship and the end of history came to the fore. At the end of the glasnost era, Prigov warned of the "complete disappearance of Russian literature as a significant socio-cultural phenomenon." Drawing on the sense of paranoiac global interconnection and belatedness that accompanied this moment, Prigov described the national transformation as "a global catastrophe," invoking the same millennial, end of history rhetoric central to Yasusada and to the subsequent wave of English-language conceptualist writing. Prigov linked this cultural catastrophe to cross-cultural exchange in his 1995 book *The Appearance of Verse after Its Death*, which seemingly presents the results of how, he claimed, those "writers fighting for Europeanization of Russia, that is, as we know a priori, the writers possessed by quite noble and progressive impulses [...] are digging their own graves" (Beliaeva-Konegen and Prigov 207–09). The title cycle '23 Appearances of Verse after Its Death,' dated 1991, clearly associates the end of the Soviet Union with the "death" of poetry, while playfully undercutting such apocalyptic thinking. Responding to the same moment, Epstein writes of Yasusada and hyperauthorship as "the resurrection of authorship after its death" by "not creating new texts but creating new authors" (Letter 135).

Prigov's *The Appearance of Verse after Its Death* exemplifies Epstein's vision of hyperauthorship and his transformation of the death of poetry and authorship and the end of history into an opportunity for "a shared imagining and expression of humanity—of Russians, Japanese, Americans, of any nationality" (Epstein, 'Commentary' 146). Prigov's book contains a series of visual works that mix languages, scripts, and authors: "Deutsch" by Kandinsky, "Chinese" by Miró, "Japanese" by Bosch, and so on. Together, texts and drawings link a conceptual approach to poetry, based on multiple layers, personae, and images, to a transnational, cross-cultural artistic practice. Other poems are, like the Yasusada texts, presented as translations, as in the case of a poem said to be an impromptu translation from the English by a friend who "did not understand a word" of what he was reciting (Prigov, *IAvlenie* 13).

The actual cross-cultural link between Prigov and Yasusada's apparent author, Johnson, during this moment of historical flux, underscores the parallel between post-Cold War globalization's undermining of cultural particularity and conceptual writing's turn to machine-like textual processing and uncreative writing as an appropriate response to the massive textual volume and paranoia-inducing surveillance made possible by digital technologies. Johnson and Prigov first met in 1989 in Leningrad at a conference that brought together writers from Russia and the United States (Epstein, 'Commentary' 144; Johnson, *Homage* 92). Johnson later co-edited an anthology of new Russian poetry, *The Third Wave*, which features Prigov. Johnson gives an account of his first meeting with Prigov in his prose list poem *I Once Met*: "I have a gift for you, said Dmitri Prigov, and he handed me a manila envelope [. . .] I opened the envelope and peered inside [. . .] I pulled out seven, no, nine small stapled bundles, each with a typed word or three on the outside [. . .] Ah, he said, They are Little Coffins of Poems, and inside each is a poem, but these little coffins may never be opened, for this would be of course disrespectful to the deceased . . ." (*Homage* 93).

Produced in *samizdat* style and numbering in their thousands, Prigov's *Little Coffins of Rejected Verse* highlight the paranoiac system of Soviet censorship, while parodying the exuberant textual excessiveness of *samizdat* culture—the "graphomania" that Prigov celebrates and satirizes in his excessive versifying (he aimed to produce 24,000 poems by the year 2000). The *Little Coffins* also come to stand for the collapse and burial of late-Soviet culture—its belatedness—and for Prigov's transformation of that culture into new works that operate within a globalized market system. They are the ultimate globally marketable local poetic product for a poet whose work would otherwise be limited to a Russian audience, since one cannot—and in fact must not—read them.

Like the Yasusada hoax and the subsequent renewal of interest in conceptual writing, the *Little Coffins* suggest a parallel between the subsuming of local particularities in a new global system and the negation of authorial agency. As with much of Prigov's work and many recent English-language conceptual texts, the *Little Coffins* are characterized by a template structure that can produce a potentially endless volume of material. These serial conceptualist writings highlight the paranoiac comprehensiveness of structures or systems imposed by theoretical thinking, suggesting a totalizing treatment of linguistic material that might seem to reduce the author, conceived as inspired originator of the poem, into a cog in the linguistic machine. The *Little Coffins* underscore the apparent death of the author by condemning the poet's words to the graves or coffins of the work's conceptual design and sealing the local, belated poetic product within globally marketable packaging.

Another act of authorial erasure or clever repackaging returns my paranoiac tracing of global connections to US conceptualism. In 2009, Johnson reissued Goldsmith's 2003 work *Day* (a retyping of one issue of the *New York Times*) under his own name through a rough, belatedly *samizdat*-style transformation of Goldsmith's book into his own. Johnson's act invoked Goldsmith's emphasis on massive textual volume, waste, and recycling as appropriate replacements for originality, individuality, and locality in a digital, globalizing world but also, like Yasusada, conversely highlighted the place of authorial function, agency, and local particularity within conceptual structures and a totalizing global system.

Recalling Epstein's 1990s hypertext-inflected invocation of Yasusada within his theory of hyperauthorship and his conspiratorial "International Society," Goldsmith often presents his work as a response—albeit inevitably belated—to a vast system of global interconnections. His best known project, *UbuWeb*, a website with free downloadable avant-garde poetry, film, audio, and video art, is predicated on the Internet's global connectivity and, considered itself as a work of "unoriginal writing," might indeed be seen as exemplary of Epstein's vision of hyperauthorship or his "book of books" project. Its manifesto, however, begins by invoking the "utopian pan-internationalist bent" of concrete poetry—a decidedly pre-Internet source—through Max Bense's 1965 statement that "concrete poetry does not separate languages; it unites them" (Goldsmith, 'UbuWeb'). By highlighting *UbuWeb*'s belatedness, now almost 50 years after Bense's assertion, Goldsmith implies that his own work's unoriginality responds to the feeling induced by the Internet that someone somewhere has done it before. Not only does he claim in this manifesto that concretism anticipates the Internet, but he makes the same statement about poet John Giorno's sound recordings, while (recalling Prigov's similarly belated invocation of Gysin) asserting that Giorno recognized poetry's belatedness—that it was "75 years behind painting" (Goldsmith, 'What Did'; Prigov, 'Uteshaet').

Goldsmith highlights the individual's belatedness and powerlessness when faced with the overwhelming vastness and geographic indeterminacy of the global system represented by the Internet. But he also reasserts particularity and place by appealing to a pre-digital, local environment, almost invariably New York City. Describing Giorno, he nostalgically refers to "a New York that doesn't exist anymore" (Goldsmith, 'What Did'). Paying tribute to Giorno through his recordings, Goldsmith also nostalgically recalls Warhol's 1963 film tribute to Giorno, *Sleep*, which in its length, boredom, and intimacy provides a clear precedent for Goldsmith's practice. By retyping an entire issue of the *New York Times* in *Day*, Goldsmith adopts a rigorous, machine-like procedure that concedes agency to what implicitly claims to be the definitive newspaper of the global system. Yet the same act reinforces his position as a local New York poet. Equally, Goldsmith's *Soliloquy*, comprising every word spoken by the author over an entire week, submits to a paranoiac regime of surveillance while asserting the poet's individual agency, and a strong sense of his Manhattan locality.

Likewise, the fictional character Yasusada is situated in nostalgic relation to precisely this same 1960s and early 1970s New York-centered conceptualist moment. Yasusada's 'Conceptual Essay,' for example, in questioning the role of authorship makes a nostalgic gesture toward the conceptualist moment and sense of place that preoccupy Goldsmith:

What or where is "The Estate of Robert Smithson"? (91)

A quintessential artist of place and location, Smithson writes in his essay on New York's Central Park published the year of his death that "we are first presented with an endless maze of relations and interconnections, in which nothing remains what or where it is, as a-thing-in-itself" (123–24). Like conceptualist practices, the Yasusada texts ask, what or where is a thing-in-itself, where or what is the author him or herself, and does that "author" become an "estate" when he or she dies? Rejecting the notion of a pure thing-in-itself, the Yasusada texts, like Smithson, insist on our enmeshment in economics, culture, place, and history.

The 1960s and early 1970s moment of conceptualism and post-structuralism operates as a kind of endpoint in the Yasusada texts corresponding to his supposed death in 1972, the year before Smithson died. Though some readers emphasize Yasusada's positioning vis-à-vis pre-World War Two modernism, he is presented more precisely in relation to the post-World War Two reading of that modernism, not just obviously through Spicer's *After Lorca* but also in relation to conceptualism. Take, for example, "What is the Diffirince?":

Is a rose is a rose is a rose the same as Ceci n'est pas une pipe? (90)

While the poem situates Yasusada in relation to Gertrude Stein and Magritte, its misspelled title humorously invokes Derrida's "différance," while the reference to Magritte is also to Foucault's 1973 book of the same name, which concludes "A day will come when, by means of similitude relayed indefinitely along the length of a series, the image itself, along with the name it bears, will lose its identity. Campbell, Campbell, Campbell, Campbell" (54). As in Goldsmith, the turn to Warhol here and Foucault's sense of historical moment ("the day will come") underscore Yasusada's positioning after the future. Yes, "*Doubled Flowering* connects itself [...] to a historical event that announced the (possibility of the) end of history and to the symbolic rehearsal of that event in the present, a rehearsal in which the present becomes defined as the future of a past that seemed to have none" (Hayot 70; *Scubadivers* 188). But the reference to the 6 August 1945 bombing of Hiroshima as the end of history is doubled by *Doubled Flowering*'s simultaneous positioning at the end of the Cold War and after the "last avant-garde" (as invoked in the title of Johnson's most recent book; Johnson, *Homage*). Highlighting this post-Cold War end of history moment, Epstein even has Tosa Motokiyu praise his 1995 book *After the Future*.

In tracing such connections and arguing for the uses of a paranoiac sense of global interconnection and belatedness in comparative critical interventions, I am suggesting the adoption of the "too-perfect attention to detail" that characterizes the paranoiac, conspiracy-theorist mindset. In Goldsmith's works, the individual confronts the totality of the system in ways that are often comic in their failure: the failure to be able to address and process the textual volume of the *New York Times* or, in Goldsmith's *Fidget*, his failure to describe every movement of his own body. As Ngai points out, Goldsmith's works in their confrontation with totality recall the sublime but also generate stupefying boredom, creating an "aesthetic experience in which astonishment is paradoxically united with boredom as *stuplimity*" (*Ugly Feelings* 271). They work, in Deleuze's words, to overturn the law, the order, the SYSTEM, not by transcending it, but in true paranoiac fashion "by descending towards the consequences, *to which one submits with a too-perfect attention to detail*" (qtd. in Ngai, *Ugly Feelings* 297).

Today we are apt to see such totalizing as evidence of a single, perhaps Eurocentric norm, an imperialist imposition of the West on the rest. But a too perfect attention to detail also means recognizing that the details do matter—that particular connections and examples, such as those between Russian and US conceptualisms—however strange and serendipitous, or always already predetermined—do make a difference. To consider Yasusada through conceptualism and conceptualism through Yasusada situates the debate over authorship, identity politics, and multiculturalism that the hoax sparked within a broader and more complex picture of cross-cultural reading and appropriation that runs not just between the United States and Japan but between both and Russia. We cannot think about phenomena like conceptualist writing, modernism, or postmodernism outside particular places and cultural engagements, and likewise we cannot think those local engagements without the paranoiac sense of global interconnection and totality figured in Prigov, Goldsmith, and Yasusada.

Works Cited

Beliaeva-Konegen, Svetlana, and Dmitri Prigov. 'Krepkogo vam zdorov'ia gospoda literatory.' *Strelets* 70.3 (1992): 205–12.

Bernstein, Charles. 'Fraud's Phantoms: A Brief yet Unreliable Account of Fighting Fraud with Fraud (No Pun on Freud Intended), with Special Reference to the Poetics of Ressentiment.' *Textual Practice* 22.2 (2008): 207–27.

Dworkin, Craig. 'The Fate of Echo.' *Against Expression: An Anthology of Conceptual Writing.* Ed. Craig Dworkin and Kenneth Goldsmith. Evanston: Northwestern UP, 2011. xxiii–liv.

———, ed. *The UbuWeb Anthology of Conceptual Writing.* 4 Feb. 2011. http://www.ubu.com/concept/index.html.

Dworkin, Craig, and Kenneth Goldsmith, eds. *Against Expression: An Anthology of Conceptual Writing.* Evanston: Northwestern UP, 2011.

Epstein, Mikhail. *After the Future: The Paradoxes of Postmodernism and Contemporary Russian Culture.* Trans. Anesa Miller-Pogacar. Amherst: U of Massachusetts P, 1995.

———. 'Commentary and Hypotheses.' Yasusada, *Doubled Flowering* 139–47.

———. 'Kniga, zhdushaia avtora.' *Inostrannaia literatura* 5 (1999). 4 Feb. 2011. http://magazines.russ.ru/inostran/1999/5/epsht.html.

———. Letter to Tosa Motokiyu. 6 Feb. 1996. Yasusada, *Doubled Flowering* 134–38.

———. 'Theses on Metarealism and Conceptualism' (1983). *Russian Postmodernism: New Perspectives on Post-Soviet Culture.* Oxford: Berghahn, 1999. 105–12.

Foucault, Michel. *This is not a Pipe* (1973). Trans. James Harkness. Berkeley: U of California P, 1983.

Ginsberg, Allen. 'America.' *Howl and Other Poems.* San Francisco: City Lights, 1956. 39–43.

Goldsmith, Kenneth. 'Conceptual Poetics.' *Poetry Foundation.* 22 Jan. 2007. http://www.poetryfoundation.org/harriet/2007/01/journal-day-one.

———. *Day.* Great Barrington, MA: Figures, 2003.

———. *Fidget.* Toronto: Coach House, 2000.

———. *Soliloquy.* New York: Granary, 2001.

———. 'UbuWeb Wants to Be Free.' *Cyberpoetics.* Spec. issue of *Open Letter* 10.9 (2000). http://epc.buffalo.edu/authors/goldsmith/ubuweb.html. Rpt. as 'About UbuWeb.' *UbuWeb.* 7 Feb. 2011. http://www.ubu.com/resources/index.html.

———. 'Uncreativity as a Creative Practice.' *Drunken Boat* 5 (2002–2003). 4 Feb. 2011. http://www.drunkenboat.com/db5/goldsmith/uncreativity.html.

———. 'What Did Patti Smith, Frank O'Hara, and Meredith Monk Have in Common? The John Giorno Poetry Systems.' *Avant-garde All the Time, Poetry Foundation.* 5 Dec. 2007. http://feeds.

poetryfoundation.org/~r/AvantGardeAllTheTime/~5/mqscsj2qxjc/JohnGiornoPoetrySystems.mp3.

Hayot, Eric. 'The Strange Case of Araki Yasusada: Author, Object.' *PMLA* 120.1 (2005): 66–81.

Huang, Yunte. 'Our Literature, Their History: Between Appropriation and Denial.' *Comparative Literature* 57.3 (2005): 227–33.

Johnson, Kent. *Day*. Buffalo, NY: BlazeVOX, 2009.

———. *Homage to the Last Avant-Garde*. Exeter: Shearsman Books, 2008.

Mariani, Philomena, ed. *Global Conceptualism: Points of Origin, 1950s–1980s*. New York: Queens Museum of Art, 1999.

Ngai, Sianne. 'Bad Timing (A Sequel): Paranoia, Feminism, and Poetry.' *Differences* 12.2 (2001): 1–46.

———. *Ugly Feelings*. Cambridge: Harvard UP, 2005.

Perloff, Marjorie. 'Unoriginal Genius: Walter Benjamin's *Arcades* as Paradigm for the New Poetics.' *Études Anglaises* 61.2 (2008): 229–52.

Place, Vanessa. *Echo*. Calgary: No Press, 2011.

———. 'Interversation with Vanessa Place.' Interview with James Wager. *Esther Press*. Weblog. 3 Aug. 2010. http://estherpress.blogspot.com/2010_08_01_archive.html.

———. *Tragodía 1: Statements of Fact*. Los Angeles: Blanc Press, 2010.

Prigov, Dmitri. 'Conceptualism and the West.' Interview with Alexei Alexeyev [pseudonym of Aleksandr Sidorov]. Trans. Michael Molnar. *Elsewhere*. Spec. issue of *Poetics Journal* 8 (1989): 12–16.

———. *IAvlenie stikha posle ego smerti*. Moscow: Tekst, 1995.

———. *Sovetskie teksty, 1979–84*. St. Petersburg: Izdatel'stvo Ivana Limbakha, 1997.

———. 'Uteshaet li nas èto ponimanie?' *NLO* 52 (2003). 4 Feb. 2011. http://magazines.russ.ru/nlo/2003/62/prigov.html.

Saussy, Haun. 'Mei Lanfang in Moscow, 1935: Familiar, Unfamiliar, Defamiliar.' *Modern Chinese Literature and Culture* 18.1 (2006): 8–29.

Silliman, Ron. Weblog. 4 Feb. 2011. http://ronsilliman.blogspot.com.

Smithson, Robert. 'Fredrick Law Olmsted and the Dialectical Landscape' (1973). *The Writings of Robert Smithson*. Ed. Nancy Holt. New York: New York UP, 1979. 117–28.

Weinberger, Eliot. 'Three Footnotes.' *Boston Review* 22.3–4 (1997): 36–37.

Yasusada, Araki. *Doubled Flowering: From the Notebooks of Araki Yasusada*. New York: Roof Books, 1997.

Young, Stephanie. *Too Much Work and Still to be Poets*. Weblog. 4 Feb. 2011. http://could-be-otherwise.blogspot.com.

Three Dialogues Between Real and Imaginary Poets

Martin Corless-Smith

On first meeting Kent Johnson

When it was determined that Kent would travel to Boise to give a reading, sometime in 2005 or so, I asked for a physical description as I had to meet him at the airport. I don't recall the exact words (if words of self-description can ever be exact), but I do recall their sense, and one or two isolated adjectives; "grey," "normal-looking," and "middle-aged" were all the poet could manage. I was struck by how utterly selfless his self-description seemed. For someone who had been this person for 45 years or so at that stage, and was now in the middle of the usual life span, he seemed to have no real regard for his own physical being. Although this felt odd at the time it was clearly not an affectation. But as I thought on it, I realized that his lack of interest in describing his own body was a perfect companion to his ambitious abandoning of self in his writing. Indeed when I received his wonderful translation of Jaime Saenz, I believed this was just another manifestation of Kent's mercurial self-invention, and that the name Jaime Saenz was really a pun on J'aime Séance, a kind of admittance of his own love of channeling personalities through arcane means.

First Dialogue: On Poetic Truth

William Williamson: Knowing your penchant for Heidegger's writings on poetry and his faith in poetry's unique relation to Being, I want us to discuss a passage that has to do with Truth in poetry.

Kent Johnson: Let's. Which passage in particular?

WW: It's one that occurs in his essay 'The Origin of The Work of Art' where he discusses the nature of Truth in poetry, I'll quote the passage I mean:

> Truth is un-truth, insofar as there belongs to it the reservoir of the not-yet uncovered, the un-uncovered, in the sense of concealment. In unconcealedness, as truth, there occurs also the other "un-" of a double restraint or refusal. Truth occurs

as such in the opposition of clearing and double concealing. Truth is the primal conflict in which, always in some particular way, the Open is won within which everything stands and from which everything withholds itself that sows itself and withdraws itself as being.

Perhaps, as with most of Heidegger's writings on poetry, we need to read the passage in relation to his other works and essays to discover what he means by his particularities of expression.

KJ: Perhaps the first thing to do is to describe what Heidegger means by the Open. The term seems to come from Rilke and is perhaps most fully taken up in his *Duino Elegies*. According to Heidegger, it is "the Whole Draft to which all beings, as ventured beings are given over . . ." The Open is the great whole of all that is unbounded. It is a metaphorical realm that we enter when we tend our will towards the truth of Being. In this respect it is freedom—freedom available to the venturesome being (who is, in Heidegger's essays that appear in *Poetry, Language, Thought*, seen in the heroic figure of the articulating poet, specifically Hölderlin and Rilke).

WW: Because of his high self-consciousness, Man is not admitted into the world, is no longer seen as immanent with Being. This is a common understanding of Man's spiritual *malais*, that his ability to stand aside in self-conscious observation has simultaneously separated him from the world. Georges Bataille in his excellent *Theory of Religion* articulates the coming–into-consciousness as the immemorial instant that isolates us from immediate union with the thing contemplated, and requires religious consolation to return us to some immanent relation with the world. In Heidegger the terms Being, Nature, Life, Truth are often interchangeable it seems. All are lost (it is this loss that figures as Hölderlin's modern day crisis.) All are sought in the act of being venturesome.

KJ: Yes, because of his high self-consciousness Man is not admitted into the world—is not immanent with Being. But stands apart from it. According to Heidegger, we bring the Open before us by an act of will. In the poem it is the act of venturesome articulation that presents the Open. The Open is not space and sky, as it might seem tempting to imagine. It is not a physical space per se. It is more the willed metaphorical realm of the gravitational field of Being. In the specific case of the poem, the Open is the infinite potential of the work.

WW: That's right. We cannot, in our fallen world, approach Being directly. This is no longer accessible to Man. We cannot even grasp being present, for that would require an immanence that our self-consciousness abnegates. We can think of presence, but we can never, in thinking of it, inhabit it. "Mortals, when we think of their nature, remain closer to that absence because they are touched by presence, the ancient name of Being. But because presence conceals itself at the same time, it is itself already absence." Here I think we begin to see some other terms from our original quote. The idea of the concealed and the unconcealed is clearly part of what he means to accept as part of Truth, and in this quote we see that presence and absence have something of the same relationship as truth and un-truth. They are necessarily companion.

KJ: It is the poet reaching into the abysmal (groundless) realm of Being that furthers our experience of and reaches (or ventures further) towards the gravitational center of that field. According to Heidegger (in his reading of Hölderlin), we have lost our contact with the Divinity, which one supposes would represent the center of Being, or at least another word for or metaphorical description of that center... a direct relationship with God. And now we can only glimpse traces of the reaching out towards Being. This reaching is the job of the Poet. The History of Being is the reading of those tracks and traces. In our day and age we are used to thinking of poetry as a secondary or tertiary undertaking, something of a salon affectation of the intelligentsia, or a morose outlet of ill-disciplined youth, and the rhetoric of science and philosophy and its quasi-mathematical logic as more coherently in pursuit of the "truth." But for Heidegger, this concept of truth lacks the true unbounded venturesomeness of poetry. Perhaps such truths partake of the same anodyne meliorations of technological productions which attempt to replace the dangers of venturesomeness. The nature of poetic truth is distinct from mathematical and scientific truth in that it is not strictly verifiable. Its verification is in reading the poem sufficiently to be drawn closer to the gravitational center of Being.

Poetry cannot fail to announce poetic truth. Whether or not what one is reading is truly poetry depends on whether or not the poem allows us to read it as such. Poems tell us what a poem is. They are the beings that move towards Poetry as Being.

WW. Right. Poetry is revealed to us in poems just as Being manifests in beings. According to Heidegger, "Being lets being loose into the daring venture. Whoever is in being at a given time is what is being ventured. Being is the venture pure and simple." The poem tells us something indirectly about the venture by speaking of what has been ventured. This description of poems is succinctly endorsed by Veronica Forrest-Thompson's understanding of poems as "the record of a series of individual thresholds of the experience of being conscious." In reading the poem we follow the trace of a willed venturesomeness. We see being in pursuit of Being. We see a poem in pursuit of Poetry. We read poetic truths in pursuit of Truth. The truth of the poem seems to be its adherence to the task of venturing.

KJ. According to Heidegger, the nature of this "venture" is careless, *sine cura*, only if it rests upon its own venturesomeness. Venture's "security" is its willed adherence to itself. It sustains itself as a willed enterprise. The poem succeeds only so long as it obeys its own progress. A false move in the venture of the poem brings the whole house of cards tumbling down. It must be recklessly resolute. As Heidegger puts it, "what is ventured goes along with the venture."

WW. And all ventures move towards the unseen center of Being. And this venturing is in the Open. It would be wrong to think of the poem as the voice of the poet in the world pursuing an activity beyond the task of the poem. As such the venturing is the poem, and the poem is not a rendition of an alternative venture of the poet in the world. The poet is not valuable other than as a cipher that allows the venture of the poem. In fact it is only in this activity that the poet earns the name (the "subject" of the poem might be the "life" of the poet as person, but this is not essential, it is merely one choice of an apparatus for the venturing—a starting point for the language of the poem to language). Poems in the sense of a linguistic venturing are rare. Poems that achieve proximity to Poetry, or Being or Truth are rare. Heidegger presents

Hölderlin as his most significant and successful practitioner. And even Rilke is seen as less successful. It is apparently not that simple to venture poetically into the Open. We all know of poets who manage moments but fail more often than they succeed.

KJ. Right. It is the individual's freedom to venture that is the essential element of the poem. According to Heidegger, as Man wills the venture, he is self-willed "as the one who proposes and produces, he stands before the obstructed Open." The obstruction, according to Heidegger, is the danger of succumbing to the temptation of mere production. Man could lose his willed self-assertion (as seen in the venturesome activity) to "unconditioned production." This production is a side effect of Man's productive will. Man in the age of technology sets himself apart form the Open.

WW. If venturing in the Open is Life, then avoiding this venture is a kind of death. "Unconditioned production" wants to outrace death with material output. Rilke complains of an "Americanism" that replaces real objects with mere production, that replaces gold coins with paper stand-ins (paper money that no longer has the real support of gold reserves it is meant to represent). But this kind of production deliberately avoids the dangers of venturing, of willed poetic venturing. If this kind of mass production (as opposed to poetic venturing) attempts an existence tolerable without venturing, then it destroys access to the realm of the Open. Venturing into the Open provides our only proximity to Being. Technology prevents experience. As Heidegger puts it, "unless there are still some mortals capable of seeing the threat of the unhealable, the unholy, as such. They would have to discern the danger that is assailing man." The danger is a death by an orderly productivity. Unconditioned continual productivity pretends to overwhelm death by the proliferation of objects—but it is the objectification caused by that mere production that cuts us off from the life-affirming venture. Production offers a semblance of order—a protection against the frightening uncertainty of venturing—but it this very protection that denies our endangered nature.

KJ. The value of poetry here is its lack of material consolation. Its venture towards the Open turns away from the banal proliferation of material production. Poems venture into the Open. The Open is Being, and Being signifies Presence. Presence is the unconcealed. Only Presence is truly present. Presence is the orbit of the Open. Heidegger sees a duality at the heart of presence because "In presence there is concealed the bringing on of unconcealedness." What he means is that presence must allow for the event of its own coming-into-being, and as such must house the state of not yet being. In this way presence unconceals that which it must also keep concealed—absence. This is another way of describing the necessary aspect of Death in Life that unconditional production attempts to overwhelm and deny. The venturesome poet moves in a realm where Life (and Death) and Presence (and Absence) are the gravitational center. According to Heidegger, "Language is the precinct (templum), that is, the house of Being." Being/Language does not exhaust itself in signifying. We move through language towards Being. The word is an idealized instant of presenting that which remains concealed. The willed and venturesome articulation is the poem—and that poem is the trace of the venture towards Being. The poem moves in the precinct of Being towards what is always concealed, even as it reveals itself. Thus the truthfulness of a poem is its movement towards Presence or Being. The truthfulness is maintained by the poem's ability to be read as a poem, by its ongoing venturesomeness in the House of Being (language). If we look at the quote you started with we see that his description of Truth is structured precisely the same way as his discussion of Presence. The poem's movement towards Being or Presence is its truth. And another name of what it moves towards is Truth. Truth is approached by a series of poetic truths, those moves in a poem that maintain the task of willed venturesomeness. Clearly this notion of Truth is only glimpsed at through poetic gestures. We cannot tell if something is true unless we read it as such. The poem must allow us to read it as truth. It must avoid simple truisms, and instead venture towards a Truth that is simultaneously concealed in the revelations of the truths we read. The truth that poems tell is the only truth brave enough to approach the Truth, because poetic truth accepts at once its dual nature, its un-truthfulness and truthfulness. Just as true poems accept their presence-in-absence and absence-in-presence.

Second Dialogue: On Anonymity

Thomas Swan: Kent, I'd like to turn our attention now to the nature of anonymity or heteronymity in poetry. As are you, I'm very interested in the idea of the poet being necessarily anonymous in the act of writing, despite the common assertion of individual authority. This quote is a good place to start, perhaps:

> *[The poet] cannot lay claim to what he has written. And what he has written remains anonymous, even under his name.*
> —Maurice Blanchot

Kent Johnson: Yes, Blanchot's quote succinctly articulates an idea I've long been attracted to. I've long been drawn to the communal nature of language, and suggestions that such a nature demands the abandonment of authorial presence in the written. Furthermore, this absence takes the form of a necessary anonymity, resilient even under the application of a signature. I agree that it is odd that if such anonymity is the functional status of all writing then why is the role of author so dominant in literary discourse, and what role does that authority play in textual exegesis? Perhaps in the end it is just a superstitious faith in naming, in wanting to present the absent author. Or it is a simple career move. But we know that there is more at stake than that with such a far-reaching adherence to the dominance of the authorial signature that pre-figures everything we read.

TS: It is commonly understood that language functions in the absence of the writer. Derrida defines this characteristic written absence as:

> first of all the absence of the addressee. One writes in order to communicate something to those who are absent. The absence of the sender, of the receiver, from the mark he abandons... cuts itself off from him and continues to produce effects independently of his presence and of the present actuality of his intentions, indeed even after his death, his absence... belongs to the structure of all writing.

So "[a] written sign . . . is a mark that subsists, one which does not exhaust itself in the moment of its inscription and which can give rise to an iteration in the absence and beyond the presence of the empirically determined subject who, in a given context, has emitted or produced it." The admittance of the possibility of the death of the author must eventually accept that writing always functions with this as an acceptable option.

KJ: Right. We might also notice that at the instant of recognizing authorial absence, Derrida also calls into question the iterability of the written. If we accept that a sign can be read without us fully comprehending the authorial intent then we must accept that the readability of the sign is not dependent upon the successful iteration of the author's intention. (I'm not intending a rehearsal of the "death of the author" argument per se, though our avenue of interest runs close to the features of that well-trodden path). According to Derrida, "The first consequence of this will be the following: given that structure of iteration, the intention animating the utterance will never be through and through present to itself and to its content."

TS: This play of structural absence/presence is observable in the specific function of words. When a writer writes "I" we can observe, as Hegel observed in 1817, "Everyone is a whole world of representations, which are buried in the night of 'I'." If we accept the OED definition of a lyric poem as "expressing the writer's emotions" we must also accept that the language used for such individualized expression is common, and as Denise Riley observes in her witty account of the poetic self: "The romantic hope that unsparing introspection may plumb the self's depths to dredge up its truth is deflated by self-labelling's reliance on hand-me-down phrases." Even if Riley is constructing her autobiography "[it] always derives from somewhere outside me; my narrating *I* is really anybody's, promiscuously." Indeed her "*I* never does exist, except (and critically) as a momentary spasmodic site of space-time individuation, and its mocking promise of linguistic originality must be, and always is, thwarted in order for language to exist in its proper communality." That language must be inhabitable by the reader, as much as by the writer, determines the need for this communality. Without this common ground it is not language.

KJ: So, rather than seeing the poem as a site of the poet's absolute assertion of independence, acknowledging the structural necessity of a permeable or multivalent "self" in the poem seems to promote an atmosphere of community. We might also notice that though a poem is unique, or indicative of particular writing, it need not promote a particular self. For Riley, her "writing has got to know far more than I know for it to be of any interest whatsoever . . . As writer, I must be the ostensible source of my work, yet I know that I've only been the conduit for the onrush." Riley figures "Poetry [as] an inrush of others' voices" (the spatial metaphors of "onrush" and "inrush" vie for precision, ever aware of implying, and avoiding a definition of where the event of the poem happens—in the poet's mind, on the page, out where the poem is "heard" etc.), so that "if poetry is . . . an affair of high speed autodictation and half-conscious gluing then the concept of the poem as a protected reservation for the unique personal voice is torn apart." This tearing apart sounds devastating, unless one thinks of it as opening the fences of the reservation to include the vastness of a common heritage.

TS: And Riley finds idealistic companionship in Heidegger's understanding of poetic composition:

> Man acts as though he were the shaper and master of language, while in fact language remains the master of man . . . for strictly it is language that speaks. Man first speaks when and only when he responds to language by listening to its appeal . . . The responding in which man authentically listens to the appeal of language is that which speaks in the element of poetry.

What becomes important for the poet is "'learning to live in the speaking of language,' and this needs a capacity to respond through listening . . . [a] dynamic hearing." Understanding the poetic act as listening rather than writing nicely subverts the usual hierarchy of author/reader (and helps to illuminate the common metaphor of the good poet possessing a good ear, perhaps).

KJ: We don't need to privilege the role of reader over that of author, though it is of course quite possible to understand a good poem managing more than was intended by the poet, and in the end the poem might be said to partake of an "intuitive verbal latency," a phrase of Jakobson's that avoids privileging either the author or the reader.

Heidegger's assessment of Trakl's poem 'A Winter Evening' agrees that "Who the author is remains unimportant here, as with every other masterful poem," but actually goes even further in deciding that "the mastery consists precisely in this, that the poem can deny the poet's person and nature." Whether we agree or not, it is plain that there is a consistent critical acceptance that language, and in particular poetic language, exists without inhering to the confines of an authorial self.

TS: So poems might be seen as sites of exultant languaging, rather than the home of a coherent self. The critical examples we've mentioned indicate a consistent and compelling argument for all poems being, in some sense, anonymous. This is easy to assert for anonymous poems, but I wonder does it remain persuasive even for poems under authorial signature? Having argued consistently and variously for an understanding of authority as unstable, even Riley seems to flinch at the sign of the signature: "even if creativity is conceived as really a matter of endless refashioning and involuntary plagiarizing, it still retains, in the lonely fact of the signature, its final flourish of individuation."

KJ: We need not see the lurking signature as too serious a threat to the thesis of communal necessity (and functional anonymity) in the making of a poem when one recalls Derrida's definition that

> a written signature implies the actual or empirical nonpresence of the signer. But it will be claimed, the signature also marks and retains his having been present in a past now or present, which will remain a future now or present, thus in a general maintenant, in the transcendental form of presentness…In order for the tethering to the source to occur, what must be retained is the absolute singularity of a signature-event and a signature form: the pure reproducibility of a pure event.

Of course signatures do function, cheques get signed, poems get undersigned etc.,

> but the condition of possibility of those effects is simultaneously . . . the condition of their impossibility, of the impossibility of their rigorous purity . . . [cheques get forged, poems get misattributed] . . . In order to function, that is, to be readable, a signature must have a repeatable, iterable, imitable form [by

the author, but also by some other perhaps]; it must be able to be detached from the present and singular intention of its production. It is its sameness which, by corrupting its identity and its singularity, divides its seal.

If a signature can be read and acknowledged as an indication of presence, it must also suffer the possibility of not being read this way. That possibility is enough to supplant any certainty with a necessary ambivalence. Even under signature, a poem retains its independence and thus its aspect of anonymity. And certainly we can think of occasions where poems have been misattributed or misappropriated.

TS: If we accept that a poem can (and does) function without the authority of its author, then why is the role of author so dominant?

KJ: It's an interesting question, isn't it? And one that Foucault spends time examining in his essay 'What is an Author?' In it Foucault speculates on the "author-function." It is evident to Foucault that in "a novel narrated in the first person, neither the first person pronoun, the present indicative tense, nor for that matter, its signs of localization refer directly to the writer, either to the time he wrote, or to the specific act of writing" (I would add that even if the subject of the writing is the event of the writing, "I write this" for example, this is merely a semantic choice coincidental, rather than identical, to the act of writing and is still necessarily mediated). He acknowledges that "there was a time when those texts which we now call 'literary' were accepted, circulated, and valorized without any question about the identity of their author." (It is difficult to point to the instant when anonymity gave way to authority, though examples of both exist in the present and the most distant past. Perhaps we can argue that the 17th and 18th centuries saw a shift in attribution in English letters). What interests Foucault is how this idea of author now functions, if it is not essential to the work per se.

An author name "can group together a number of texts and thus differentiate them from others. A name also establishes different forms of relationships among texts." So we can look for work by an author we have previously enjoyed, and we can position the work as "an early poem," or "a less interesting work." But rather than simply as a clerical device the author-function seems to stem from our specific needs as a reader, and "these aspects of an individual which we designate as an author are projections, in terms always more or less psychological, of our way of handling texts." Foucault sees an historical constant in our readerly desires: "Modern criticism, in its desire to 'recover' the author from a work, employs devices strongly reminiscent of Christian exegesis when it wished to prove the value of a text by ascertaining the holiness of its author." The structuring of the author-function seems to be based upon our desire to resolve the written with an authority outside of the text, and in the early Christian exegesis, clearly this final authority is God. For the modern reader, the author supplants the extra-textual authority of God, and provides us with a possible site of resolution:

> The author . . . constitutes a principle of unity in writing . . . [and] serves to neutralize the contradictions that are found in a series of texts. Governing this function is the *belief* [my emphasis] that there must be—at a particular level of an author's thought, of his conscious or unconscious desire—a point where contradictions are resolved, where the incompatible elements can be shown to relate to one another or to cohere around a fundamental and originating contradiction.

TS: So, in short, textual exegesis is compatible with "belief," or faith, where reading a complicated world is resolved in the positing of a deity and reading a complicated text is resolved in the unifying principle of the author.

KJ: Yes. Obviously there are forms of critical analysis that do not focus on the author so dogmatically, preferring to replace the author-function with an economic principle (Marxist criticism) or to understand the text as a manifestation of (and producer of) societal influences (feminist criticism, New Historicism), but we can observe a popular psychological adherence to the "author as origin" which seems closely aligned to the positioning of a deity in the desire for a resolution to the responsibilities of reading. Foucault ends his essay with an open-ended speculation (how could it be otherwise?):

> We should suspend the typical questions; how does a free subject penetrate the density of things and endow them with meaning; how does it accomplish its design by animating the rules of discourse from within? Rather, we should ask: under

> what conditions and through what forms can an entity like the subject appear in the order of discourse; what position does it occupy; what functions does it exhibit; and what rules does it follow in each type of discourse? In short, the subject [the author] must be stripped of its creative role and analysed as a complex and variable function of discourse . . . we can easily imagine a culture where discourse would circulate without any need for an author. Discourses, whatever their status, form, or value would unfold in a pervasive anonymity.

TS: But rather than a commonplace acceptance of the functional anonymity of all texts, what we seem to have is pervasive authority.

KJ: Yes, and one way of understanding the pervasive slippage from written text to authorial presence is as an enactment of the desire for the divine, and such an attempt proposes (consciously or not) a transmigration of the author in person to the self in text, so that the author becomes in some way immortal. In this scenario the text would need to become identical with the author. I'm uncertain where the reader would exist in such a scenario; perhaps her body would become the host for the author's transmigrated soul, held in the writing.

TS: Ha, yes, or the Universe would have to become a willed extension of the Poet-God.

So, taking our cue from Foucault we have so far focused on the reading of authority, though clearly such desired translations of selfhood from world to text are also part of writing, and we could understand an author's desire for full iteration of intention (commensurate with full presence) as a desire for immortality. This (perhaps unacknowledged) belief in full presence is indicated in the romantic description of lyric poetry from the OED quoted earlier. Although much of what we have discussed goes some way to challenge such an assertion, and to indicate a prevalent critical awareness, it is worth noticing how resilient such assertions are in broader discourses, and how the desire such descriptions hint at is still seemingly irresistible.

KJ: As I've hinted at, we might choose to understand an acceptance of structural anonymity as going some way towards accepting our own inevitable mortality, and beyond that, shifting from a monotheistic faith in the author to a non-hierarchical acceptance of communal existence in a necessarily shared language system. It seems to me that Heidegger's concept of the Open (the realm within which the poet ventures when writing) is a realm that bears a striking metaphorical relation to the Medieval common, and that ownership of land and ownership of texts are really assertions of a relation that can't, eventually, be truly endorsed. I see the role of attributing an authorial name to be part of the fiction of writing, and to be an active and playful element, not a rigid or serious affirmation.

TS: So you don't see the attribution of a name as necessary.

KJ: It's clearly not necessary. But even in its presence, the affirmation of authority demands an ownership that might be worth sabotaging for the sheer thrill of realizing that we ourselves cannot be the limit of our written exploits.

Third Dialogue: On Language and War

Martin Corless-Smith: Hi Kent.

Kent Johnson: Hi Martin, how are you?

MCS: Well. I was just reading about the endangered pearl-bordered fritillary. I've never seen one, but the idea of something with such a beautiful name disappearing does fill me with sadness.

KJ: What if the name was less compelling? What if the name were simply given to a different more common butterfly?

MCS: Well, I suppose the name does function scientifically, though none of that means much to me. In a way I suppose the naming was originally an attempt to classify and thus preserve, or enter it into Human Knowledge, that ledger that we had hoped might mirror the magnitude of the universe.

KJ: Yes, one can't help thinking of butterfly names in tandem with those framed displays of specimens, all neatly pinned out under glass.

MCS: As though the naming were simultaneous with killing, and cataloguing, rather than preserving anything as a living creature. I

Scubadivers and Chrysanthemums

certainly doubt many that have seen a pearl-bordered fritillary had the name at hand to call it by. When I was growing up, most wild creatures—birds, flowers and butterflies in particular—were known by less orderly colloquial names. Speaking of butterflies, and thinking of that famous lepidopterist that haunts much of his work, I was recently reading Sebald's *The Natural History of Destruction*, and it got me thinking about Adorno's famous dictum on poetry, about Poetry after Auschwitz.

KJ: Ah yes, you mean his use of the figure of Nabokov that shows up in *Vertigo* and *The Emigrants*. An interesting figure for Sebald to choose as another non-native master of English, though Sebald I think wrote in German and was translated, right?

MCS: Yes. A German, born during World War II, who lived in England but wrote, in German, the most English seeming of novels, though always with a sense of being an outsider, as perhaps most writers are anyway.

KJ: I suppose the nature of writing, of leaning towards an always absent other, makes one a bit antisocial, in the very act of what one does. It isn't much of a group activity is it? If it is, it's a disparate group separated by space and time.

MCS: Yes, it seems to me that the books of Sebald often reveal a sense of companionship with the long dead, present to him only in books. His fascination with Nabokov or Sir Thomas Browne is really a fascination with his own presence and absence in his works, which are, it seems at times, authored by many writers over many centuries. Naturally enough I suppose, as he is so conscious of the debt the present owes to the past. It's almost as if he feels charged with the responsibility of honoring all of History. Or should I say felt.

KJ: His *Natural History* is fascinating as it attempts to bear witness to a destruction he admits not having seen. And it is a destruction that is complicated by the guilt of those destroyed.

MCS: Yes, he seems mostly concerned with the deliberate amnesia of the Germans after the end of the war about their own suffering. Because of their universally despised acts it seemed impossible for them to turn their own gaze on themselves and their own suffering. He refers to the unprecedented destruction of civilian targets by Allied air raids, which killed more than 600,000. Post-war Germany was literally and figuratively rebuilt over unburied corpses.

KJ: It is true that many Germans felt that they deserved the calamity they suffered, that it was justifiable retribution.

MCS: But of course it is still difficult to understand the mass destruction of civilians as a reasonable good, even if the enemy was capable of equal or worse atrocities.

KJ: Sebald makes it clear that the civilians were targeted, despite there being no proof that this undermined their resolve. Certainly in England it seems the targeting of civilians had a galvanizing effect.

MCS: And the bombing of strategic sites with as much energy would have ended the war sooner, with less human expense on both sides. What is strange is that the atrocities of one side, the Holocaust of course, or the mistreatment of Allied servicemen by the Japanese has effectively ruled out any sense of national remorse by the victors, with regard to their own ethically despicable actions, such as Dresden or Hiroshima. There was some awareness of this issue brought out recently in the UK when plans to erect a statue in honor of "Bomber" Harris, the Air Marshall who masterminded the carpet-bombing of German cities was put forward. It seemed to many an insensitive gesture. But it does also seem to highlight a comfortable official stance with regard to the systematic killing of 600,000 civilians. One has to remember of course that this was the first time civilians had been targeted in a war, something that changed utterly the field of warfare. That ethical decision, probably promoted by Churchill to divert attention of the seemingly invincible German progress across Europe in 1941, a progress that Great Britain had no chance of even engaging with in conventional terms, really brought the battlefield home.

KJ: And what has happened in that one shift is that freedom is now subject to annihilation in the production of war. One can't really see this as the work of one man, or of two opponents trying to out muscle each other. It is really the logical end of the Enlightenment. It isn't an aberration as much as the final denouement.

MCS: It was really this that I think Adorno was referring to in his essay where his famous dictum (*"Nach Auschwitz ein Gedicht zu schreiben ist barbarisch"* [It is barbaric to write poetry after Auschwitz]) comes from. For Adorno, the barbarism of poetry after Auschwitz stems from the fact that it asserts an individual freedom of expression in relation to an event where human life had been rendered indifferent and expendable. So the freedom of individual expression promised by the poem is an affront, a façade and a denial of the fact that the death camps brought an end to the very idea of the autonomous subject.

KJ: I think that is right. An Enlightenment and capitalist-fused rational productivity with irrational ends, technological domination, and the reduction of all thought to the calculation of the efficiency of means had their apotheosis in the Nazi death camps. Absolute reification halted the process of self-reflection. Poetry, as a form of supposedly free and individual expression is irreconcilable with the fact that Nazism integrated not only the individual, but also those cultural spheres presumed to be autonomous. As Adorno puts it:

> Genocide is the absolute integration. It is on its way wherever men are "polished off," as they called it in the military and literally exterminated as deviations from the concept of their absolute nullity. What the sadists in the concentration camps said to the inmates: tomorrow you will be trailing skyward in the form of smoke from this chimney, reveals the indifference towards the life of the individual. Even in his formal freedom he is just as fungible and replaceable as he is under the boots of the liquidator. He can escape this no more than he can escape the barbed wire enclosure of the camp. (*Negative Dialektik* 353).

MCS: Like Sebald, Adorno derides the attempts to simply make good, or start anew. It isn't that Adorno wants poetry to stop. It's that he wants poetry to accept the truth of what has happened to culture.

> Auschwitz has demonstrated irrefutably that culture has failed. That it could happen in the midst of the philosophical traditions, the arts and the enlightening sciences says more than just that these failed to take hold of and change the people. All culture after Auschwitz, including its urgent critique, is rubbish (*Negative Dialektik* 360).

It's difficult to see what efficacy a cultural articulation, such as poetry could have coming from a culture it acknowledges has failed—as George Steiner puts it in *Language and Silence*: "We now know that a man can read Goethe or Rilke in the evening, that he can play Bach and Schubert, and go to his day's work at Auschwitz in the morning."

KJ: And for Adorno, the German Language lay at the heart of the problem. German was itself the instrument capable of conceiving, organizing and justifying mass execution.

MCS: Right. But the difficulty is the task, not an excuse for silence. The task is at once forbidden and obligatory. And of course the problem is that one does not have the experience of the ultimate victim. So one reduces that experience to a formal experience, which has precision and manners. Form has meaning, and a meaning that carries over to it from an indifferent context.

KJ: Right, so the problem is to give witness to an atrocity one did not experience. In a way this is the task of all surviving poets. It is what Sebald is attempting in his minute reconstructions which seem like small models of cities prior to their destruction, as if he were one of the figures from his own *Rings of Saturn*, a man obsessively building a matchstick model of Dresden, not because it replaces the bombed-out city, and not because it shows he is capable of reclaiming something from the irreparable loss, but because he must do something in response to the nothing that is left, however small. Because a task is left to the survivor.

MCS: But one does run the risk obviously of appropriating merely the glamour of victimhood, of using someone else's actual historical pain as a professional gain.

KJ: Or one runs the risk of not attending to the task of witnessing. The voice of the dead is silent, it is left to the living to speak it.

MCS: I suppose there are levels of proximity to these atrocities. It might be fine for a family member or a close survivor to bear witness, as opposed to a perpetrator of the atrocity. One reason Celan seems such an appropriate poet for the task of witnessing post-war existence is the loss of his family. Even so, one is still aware that Celan's poetic success came at a high personal cost.

KJ: But he could not write as "himself"; he could only write as himself displaced. Ancel became Celan, and German, not his mother tongue, was ripped apart in order to say and unsay simultaneously. He is almost the poet imagined by Adorno's structuring of the dilemma facing poets.

MCS: Do you think he had special privileges to this work because of his past?

KJ: I suppose the poetry was made necessary to him, and that is why it worked. It is wrong to simply imagine that he deserved the task. One would not accuse Beckett of trespassing in his own response to the post-war human dilemma, and he wasn't groomed by his heritage for the task necessarily.

MCS: Well, I suppose he was technically neutral during the war as an Irishman, wasn't he? Even though he fought in the French Resistance, he was then, I suppose, in a rather ambiguous role as both victim and victor. But one can't imagine a Nazi survivor taking on the task of witnessing the atrocities in a way that would be acceptable.

KJ: Well, one can begin to imagine it, but not easily. As we have said, the language that describes him as Nazi and amnesiac could not be the same language that sees him as witness. According to Adorno no *one* survived the Holocaust. Not everyone was physically destroyed, but individuality was. One cannot wipe the slate clean, and a Nazi has the filthiest slate in history, but someone must accept the task of seeing this. To be palatable is only one of the possibilities. To be unpalatable is just as important. I can quite imagine an English bomber pilot accommodating the suffering of Dresden victims in his writing.

MCS: Not to the delight of other Dresden survivors?

KJ: Possibly not. That might not be his task.

"A DISPLACEMENT OF THE MAIN REED INTO THE OTHER"

Farid Matuk

"The 'scandal' of these poems lies not in the problematics of authorship, identity, persona, race or history. Rather, these are wonderful works of writing that also invoke all of these other issues, never relying on them to prop up a text. This book makes the argument for anti-essentialism. That it has done it so well infuriates folks with a proprietary interest in categories. Thank you, Araki Yasusada!"
—Ron Silliman

"This is tough to put on, and take off. You know, you're lucky?"

—spoken by a white actor applying blackface, to a black actor in an unidentified clip of old Hollywood depictions of blackface included in Spike Lee's feature film, *Bamboozled* (New Line Cinema, 2000).

I

Given that the Yasusada project[1] has infamously been called a 'criminal act," I begin by noting that in the United States there are more blacks in correctional control today than were enslaved 10 years prior to the start of the Civil War, according to legal scholar Michelle Alexander. Her book, *The New Jim Crow*, argues that the gains of the civil rights movement, culminating in the election to the presidency of the bi-racial Barack Obama, are actually quite minimal and that Americans today live in a racial caste system. It is hard to believe. We have had a Civil Rights Act since 1964. We are "on the other side of" the culture wars of the 80s and 90s, the critiques of cultural and literary canons levied, as some commentators of the Yasusada would have it, by the same purveyors of sanctimonious multiculturalism the Yasusada was meant, at least in part, to embarrass. In universities most of those conflicts have been settled now, often by the institution of some multicultural

---

[1] Throughout this essay I refer to "the Yasusada project" or "the Yasusada" to indicate the totality of the texts gathered under that moniker including *Doubled Flowering: From the Notebooks of Araki Yasusada* (New York, Roof Books: 1997) and *Also With My Throat I Shall Swallow Ten Thousand Swords: Araki Yasusada's Letters in English*, (Cumberland, RI: Combo, 2005).

studies graduation requirement, or by the creation of ethnic studies departments. Yet more black men are disenfranchised today than in 1870, the year the 15th Amendment prohibited laws that denied the right to vote based on race. Alexander argues that systems of racial control never went away; they only took on new forms, new articulations and new names. President Reagan's War on Drugs made it easier for local law enforcement to charge drug offenders with felony crimes. Felons are the only group that can be discriminated against in terms of housing, employment, access to education, and voting, all with full consent of the law. Against the notion that black crime rates match black incarceration rates, Alexander argues this "war has been waged almost exclusively in poor communities of color, even though studies consistently show that people of all colors use and sell illegal drugs at remarkably similar rates." She continues, "The drug war was part of a grand and highly successful Republican Party strategy of using racially coded political appeals on issues of crime and welfare to attract poor and working class white voters who were resentful of, and threatened by, desegregation, busing, and affirmative action."[2] I linger on Alexander's argument to describe the cultural context and occasion for the writing of this essay, now some fifteen years after Yasusada poems began appearing in U.S. literary journals. Indeed, if the Yasusada reminds us of anything, it is that while context and audience receive the text, context and audience can also be compositional tools that give that text its full articulation.

Ron Silliman endorsed the Yasusada by naming the work an "argument for anti-essentialism." Typical of the commentators who made similar claims,[3] Silliman accompanies it with glee at the righteous indignation of the Yasusada's early critics, noting that the Yasusada "infuriates folks with a proprietary interest in categories." Implicit in such a reading is the notion that subject categories are inherently

---

[2] Alexander's own summary of her argument appears at http://www.tomdispatch.com/archive/175215/.
Alexander, Michelle. *The New Jim Crow: Mass Incarceration in the Age of Colorblindness*. New York: New Press, 2010.
[3] An excellent archive of defenses of the Yasusada can be found at the *Typo Magazine* site (http://www.typomag.com/issue03/letters.html). Typo #3 published 'Thirty Letters to *The Believer*,' a compilation of letters critical of Michael Atkinson's article on the Yasusada 'Hyperauthor! Hyperauthor!' published in *The Believer* Dec. 03/ Jan. 04 issue.

oppressive, whether by imposing arbitrary notions of authentic identities or, as Silliman and his Language peers might have it, by making us dupes of late capitalism, the more easily marketed to the more we identify ourselves as singular speaking subjects, let alone as members of this or that "lifestyle." Further, the Yasusada project can be seen as doing the Language school one better in its critique of individual subject positions by never conclusively revealing its author and thereby eschewing both the possibility of an individual canon and the career benefits that would fall to an author with such a body of work. Yet missing from this frenzy of subjective *seppuku* is the irony that Silliman's take on Yasusada rests wholly on the Yasusada author's very subjective intent. Marjorie Perloff has presented convincing evidence to suggest that the fraudulent gesture at the root of these poems and letters was meant to be uncovered and that, in a sort of bait and switch motion, the Yasusada seeks to make contemporary U.S. poetry audiences its subject of critique.[4] Upon this modest claim Silliman seems to make the assumption that the translator-editors intended their work not just to send up identity categories, but to ultimately free all of us, oppressed or otherwise, from such strictures and leave us, one supposes, in something like a constant state of indeterminacy, or, more optimistically, of "becoming." Nonetheless, taking Silliman's claim at face value we are left to parse out how, exactly, the Yasusada might free us of essential categories. Doing so seems a useful way to identify the project's poetics with greater specificity and thereby to arrive at a reckoning of the texts' relevance to authors today.

II

As Perloff has argued, Yasusada offers a vision of atomic bomb survivorship that seems more concerned with its own hybrid Japanese and postmodern American literary identity than with the brutal gestures of direct testimony favored by survivor, or *hibakusha* literature. Mixing ironic detachment, elliptical and new sentence

---

[4] Perloff's claim is more relevant to the early versions of Yasusada texts that appeared in literary journals. Certainly the fictional nature of this work is foregrounded by the various appendices and jacket copy that have been attached to the Yasusada books.

writing strategies with traditional Japanese imagery and Zen-like reticence, Yasusada offers a vision of Japanese identity produced from the contemporary U.S. desire to find our own aesthetic tastes in an exotic and morally righteous (because victimized) Asian otherness, in other words, a U.S. post-war Orientalism. Silliman and Perloff's apparent rush to redeem Yasusada assigns various critical prongs to this Orientalist fantasy by asking us to see the work as a mirror to our own desires: we want to believe in Yasusada because we indulge in guilt over U.S. atomic aggression without attending to Japanese imperialism; we want it because we need to find exotic antecedents for elliptical and new sentence writing strategies; we want it because we want to fulfill multicultural imperatives to diversify the authors we read but only if they confirm aesthetic and political positions with which we'd already made our peace. This reading helps avoid the charge of cultural, and more specifically in this case, trauma appropriation. In her study of literary forgeries, *Faking Literature*, Australian critic K.K. Ruthven identifies this vigilance against appropriation as one of the "dogmas" of post-colonial criticism and explains it this way: "since exploration is historically the vanguard of exploitation, the benign mask of empathy always conceals the rapacity of appropriation" (Ruthven 192).

Rather than repudiate the specter of appropriation in the Yasusada by asserting the work's altruistic critical intent, appropriation may be read as a necessary function in the project's poetics and in its potential for bringing our dependence on identity categories into crisis. In this regard minstrelsy rather than Orientalism may offer a more precise tool with which to understand the Yasusada because it revalues appropriation by linking desire to performance. An unrecognized rhyme to Perloff's argument is Eric Lott's seminal study of nineteenth century blackface performance, *Love and Theft*.[5] Contrary to popular conceptions of minstrel acts, Lott argues, blackface performances were not lampooning appropriations of authentic slave experiences; instead, "the minstrel show's humor, songs, and dances were so culturally mixed as, in effect, to make their 'racial' origins quite undecidable" (Lott 94). Of course minstrel representations of blackness, no matter how

---

[5] Lott, Eric. *Love and Theft: Blackface Minstrelsy and the American Working Class*. New York: Oxford UP, 1993.

hybridized, were buffoonish and demeaning. Yet these performances were also a way to work out the messy inter-dependencies of class, racial, and ethnic formulations that occurred both onstage and among the audiences of nineteenth-century minstrel shows. Lott continues, "[t]he Irish elements of blackface, including the fact that minstrel characters were surely influenced by Irish low-comedy types from the British stage, no doubt made possible the Irish ascendancy within the minstrel show, affording immigrants a means of cultural representation from behind the mask" (95). But that immigrant representation was always already transformed in an appropriation that was really an amalgamation of slave culture's (already creolized) oral and performance traditions, British folk dance music, and Irish jigs and reels, to name a few. European immigrants, in putting on blackface, were creating themselves as "white": "America witnessed a simultaneous hybridization and proliferation of vernaculars, in which frontier lore, European elements, and various local or regional forms merged into an 'American' vernacular" (93). However, Lott leans on Slavoj Žižek to suggest the precarious nature of "white" or "American" identity, perched as it was between its derision and desire for a constructed "blackness." Žižek writes that "the basic paradox" of a people's attachment to a nation is that it is "conceived as something inaccessible to the other, and at the same time threatened by it" (Žižek 54). If appropriation is at the complex center of the Yasusada controversy, replacing Žižek's "nation" with "race" or with "identity" helps us to unravel that knot. To play with Žižek's formulation: what Japanese atomic bomb survivors experienced could never be experienced by white U.S. neo-imperialists, and yet, white U.S. neo-imperialists have committed a "criminal act" in stealing something essential from Japanese atomic bomb survivors. Conversely, white U.S. neo-imperialists used a poetics of minstresy, putting on "yellowface" in order to lampoon our naïve investment in racial identity categories, and yet, once free of our naïve investment in racial identity categories, we were left wearing the face paint of a white U.S. neo-imperialist, a very specific racial identity indeed.

Again, as Perloff has argued, the Yasusada wants to reveal itself as a put-on, as a sly performance. By inviting readers into a proximity with a fictionalized *hibakusha* text through performance rather than testimony (as problematic as the latter concept is), the Yasusada offers us a minstrel experience, one in which we are constituted, by our awareness of our own performance, at the very least as decidedly other-than-*hibakusha*. But are we necessarily being asked to inhabit "whiteface" under the "yellowface?" It seems a bit lazy to assume so, as if whiteness were in essence but a will-toward-appropriation. Yet it is interesting that for all his considerable talent, the Yasusada author's imagination falls short of conjuring a Japanese author's Occidentalist minstrel fantasy of whiteness. In a footnote to the text ("When reading out loud, read in voice of American cowboy actor") the Yasusada translator-editors write: ["While there are numerous marginal or uncontextualized notes like this in the notebooks, we enter this one because it is suggestive of an interest Yasusada seems to have had in the American West. Indeed, there is a series of Japanese sound-play poems in one of the notebooks, 'spoken' by the American cowboy actor Gene Autry (into which this passage is arrowed as an English interjection) which are completely untranslatable."] (*Doubled* 95). I would add to K. K. Ruthven's catalog of post-colonial critical "dogmas" the notion that whiteness disavows its own particularity by pretending it is so universal as to be beyond representation. The Yasusada author's inability to represent an instance of Occidentalist fantasy, read against the Yasusada's minstrel performativity, supports the notion that the Yasusada texts invite us to put on yellowface only to leave us performing whiteness.

So the freedom from identity categories Silliman promised is no freedom at all, or it is a freedom from identity categories of color via an invitation to play at performing whiteface. If we want to believe in Perloff's vision of the Yasusada whose critical intent is to reveal various problematic desires of contemporary U.S. poetry audiences, we might add to that list the notion that we are so attracted to Yasusada because it helps us refuse to see whiteness for the pervasive particularity it actually is. This can be a valuable critique offered by the Yasusada project, as if all of its elaborations and feints could be reduced to a single assertion: it is a white text representing whiteness for a (largely) white audience. Such a reading would group the Yasusada with the highly rhetorical work of the conceptual artist Daniel J. Martinez. Martinez is famous, or infamous, for wanting to project the old Diogenes quote, "In the rich man's house the only place to spit, is in his face" onto the side of the Whitney Museum.[6] Reading the Yasusada through the concept of minstrelsy turns the project into a mirror to whiteness that directs that spit toward a maddeningly and necessarily self-reflexive trajectory.

This seems a pessimistic, almost nihilistic place to rest. Yet we could take the self-aware, fictive, and performative nature of this text as an empty mask, face paint given life only after we put it on. Kent Johnson, the literary executor of the Yasusada and for some the project's putative author, gave a talk at the Walker Arts Center in which he offered yet another reading. Yasusada speaks, he said, to "some kind of deeper yearning to find our voices entwined with an otherness we know has been inside of us always. It's an otherness always whispering that Hiroshima's fate, which is beyond the markers of any name, could yet be ours, as well" (Johnson 136; *Scubadivers* 85). This is a much softer Yasusada than either Silliman or Perloff claim. Critique is replaced by empathy for atomic bomb survivors and victims who are beyond representation, "beyond the markers of any name," as a way of calling U.S. readers to an awareness of their own vulnerability to erasure by atomic or nuclear power. What we lose in terms of a bad boy provocateur willing to offend a few multicultural teetotalers on his way to freeing us from categories we gain in terms of anti-nuke activism. But if we are willing to slide between these readings, then we can also acknowledge that Yasusada could just as easily be a reactionary gesture against the gains of multiculturalism that holds a critical mirror up to our desires not to free us but to laugh at us, "white male rage," in other words. All of these possibilities rest on assumptions about authorial intent. The real danger, I think, is in forgetting to foreground our agency in reading the Yasusada one way or another. It's tempting to foreclose the text, either in an attempt to deride it or in an attempt to redeem it. Falling into this temptation risks neutering the actual danger of these beautiful poems and letters. I choose to read Yasusada as an opportunity to pretend whiteness; I like the critical power in this gesture, the possibility of giving whiteness a particular and limited form. But if we take minstrelsy seriously as a literary mode, then we need to foreground our choice to read the text this way, or else we

---

[6] Martinez's proposal for the Whitney Biennial project is documented in the monograph, *The Things You See When You Don't Have a Grenade!* (Santa Monica, CA: Small Art Press, 1996).

not only neuter the text's danger, we also disavow our own agency and pleasure in the power of performing otherness, whether or not we label that power whiteness.

III

Speaking directly to the potential for danger in literature, Robert Duncan, in his correspondence with Denise Levertov, famously said, "[t]he poet's role is not to oppose evil, but to imagine it," and he asked, "is it a disease of our generation that we offer symptoms and diagnoses of what we are in the place of imaginations and creations of what we are?" (669).[7] The Yasusada texts boldly offer not just such creations and imaginations, but the very representational means, by way of a minstrel poetics, for readers to imagine and create through our desire for otherness. But how can writers today, particularly writers of color and writers working from other marginalized positions, claim the Yasusada as a generative touchstone?

I return to identity categories to focus my inquiry because such are the circumstances of social order and audience in which my generation writes. Certainly it is true that identity categories are fictions, that inhabiting the margin only reinforces the center, etc., etc. But this post-modern critique of multiculturalism's investment in categories does not attend to the ways in which othered bodies do not get to choose their own performances, it ignores the ways in which, again and again, marginalized people are blamed as the authors of the projections their bodies are made to bear, projections that only serve to keep power hidden, operative, and pervasive. To add some stark figures to Michelle Alexander's vision of a new Jim Crow: *one in every 15 black men is incarcerated*, according to the Pew Center Charitable Trusts, and when the 2008 study looked at black men ages 20–34, the incarceration rate jumped 40 percent to 1 in every 9, compared to 1 in every 106 white men. The Pew report also found "especially startling" incarceration rates among black and white women, noting one in every 355 white women ages 35–39 is incarcerated, compared with one in every 100

---

[7] Duncan, Robert Edward, Robert J. Bertholf, and Albert Gelpi. *The Letters of Robert Duncan and Denise Levertov.* Stanford, CA: Stanford UP, 2004. This quote appears on page 669.

black women.[8]

Cannibal Jeffery Dahmer helps to crystallize the way marginalized bodies are made to perform against their choosing. On May 27, 1991, Konerak Sinthasomphone became Dahmer's thirteenth victim. Konerak, a Laotian teenager, lived in Dahmer's neighborhood and was the older brother of the boy Dahmer was convicted of molesting in 1988. After finding Konerak walking in the street bloody, confused and naked, Sandra Smith and her cousin, Nicole Childress, both 18 years old and black, called 911. Dahmer had drilled a hole into the back of the boy's cranium and injected hydrochloric acid into the brain, while he was still alive. Dahmer sought to create a "zombie" in order to be in complete control of his victim. Officers Gabrish and Balcerzak arrived on the scene and saw that Smith and Childress were arguing with Jeffrey Dahmer over the fate of Sinthasomphone. Dahmer convinced the officers that the boy was his 19-year-old lover and that he was drunk. The cops led the boy back to Dahmer's apartment over the protestations of the two girls. The two policemen did not make any attempt to verify Sinthasomphone's age and failed to run a background check that would have revealed Dahmer was a convicted child molester still under probation. Thirty minutes after the officers left the apartment, Dahmer ended up strangling the 14-year-old boy, having sex with the body, taking photos of the dismemberment and decapitation of the corpse, and finally boiling the head. Police transcripts show the officers joked and laughed about the incident with the dispatcher. "Intoxicated Asian, naked male was returned to his sober boyfriend," the cop reported, adding his partner "is going to get deloused." Glenda Cleveland, whose daughter and niece reported Sinthasomphone to the police, later called the police asking repeatedly what was done with the "child." An officer from the scene responded, "It wasn't a child, it was an adult . . . It is all taken care of . . . It's a boyfriend-boyfriend thing." (Sable)

The ways in which Konerak Sinthasomphone's story troubles are many and they are profound. Dahmer's "desire" to inhabit, control, and ultimately consume bodies of color materializes any theorizing one might do about minstrel poetics. Sinthasomphone was a child, his naked body testified from the bleeding hole in his skull, with the exposure of

---

[8] http://www.pewtrusts.org/news_room_detail.aspx?id=35890

his genitals, with the disorientation of his person, and yet Dahmer used the dominant culture's perceived indeterminacy of Asian age, its anxiety about gay sexuality, and its disdain for poor black women to invalidate the various "speaking subjects" and their testimonies that attempted to represent a version of that moment that would have saved the boy.

Those of us left outside the jail, those of us left inside the country, those of us protected by the police can choose to craft poetics as various as we are and that attend to both the indeterminacy of authorship, language, and categories while also attending to a social order that projects the manners and shapes of its dominance onto our bodies. Duncan called Levertov to a similar attention: "as workers in words, it *is* our business to keep alive in the language definitions as well as forces, to create crises in meaning, yes—but this is to create meaning in which we are the more aware of the crisis involved, of what is at issue" (Duncan 661). The poet and critic Dale Smith, in his study of the Duncan and Levertov correspondence, articulates the challenge in terms of a rhetorical awareness as such: "The problem for any speaker or writer, given their particular social and cultural situations, is to speak through the chaotic accumulation of positions, offering a significant, if fragile, perspective the immediate value of which cannot always be determined. It is a compositional struggle, to activate a presence of mind among others, reaching for the available means of persuasion, and perhaps, even then, still falling short of the peculiar sense of agency established by the moment." (Smith)

Both Yasusada and Dahmer "speak through the chaotic accumulation of positions" to "activate a presence of mind among others." But how might a poet occupying an othered position use such strategies to focus on "what is at issue?" In discussing Martin Delany's 1859 black nationalist novel *Blake: or The Huts of America*, Eric Lott offers a way forward, saying "rather than reject the cultural territory whites had occupied by way of minstrelsy, Delany recognizes that occupation as fact and occupies it in turn" (236). Ronaldo V. Wilson's first book, a collection of prose poems called *Narrative of the Life of the Brown Boy and the White Man*, seems to inherit from Delany's willingness to take up forms already projected onto black bodies and from Yasusada a keen attention to the circumstances of his writing in order to "activate a presence of mind" among his readers. Wilson crafts a furious book, roiling with contempt that takes up received notions of black rage. The brown boy imagines his older white lover's death repeatedly throughout the arc of the book, from the first page—"The brown boy in the red house imagines murdering the white man. Cutting up a body is a concern of the brown boy, but never of the white man, who is big and strong and innocent of such a thought"—and then again on the last page—

> . . . he can see right through the clear glass doors where the white man is showering, his broad palms soaping himself down. Even if the brown boy wanted to break them, they would not shatter without meaning; the glass, like all quality glass, would break in big sections, making sword-like shards that would slice deep into the white man's legs as they fell in, cutting to bone, crashing into the warm water, a flood in blood. (77)

While the narrator provides views into the brown boy's subjectivity, it is a cold attention, an affiliation with the brown boy as object; there are no earnest lamentations for the loss of self to racial categories, no elegizing the loss of anything. The white lover's imagined mortality gets figured in terms of property ownership: "What makes him brown is . . how one day, when the white man is dead, the brown boy will own this slow thought and its sinking in" (73)—this, after the older, white lover is repeatedly identified as "his" white man. Wilson seems to be placing rage in the service of critique, inverting the logic of slaveholding that produced gain from black bodies via procreation into a gain from a white body through its death/negation. The gain in this case is a transfer of property from the white man to the brown boy upon the former's death (hinted at by the condition of being "kept," but never made explicit) as well as a more intangible gain of a selfhood in the form of a private, deep quiet where the most indecorous desires find safe harbor.

Indeed, *Narrative* explores the affectations of property and wealth to surprising ends. Both the white man and the brown boy use beauty products and lasers to sheer, shape, and tone their bodies into ideal forms, ideal objects, and the book is laced with instances of the brown boy's self regard: "What he wants is a mirror so he can look at his jawbone flying out from his face in two pointed yet balanced directions, his own body cutting out and away from his self, which tells him he is perfect and relentlessly free . . ." (56). Wealth allows access to technologies of self-creation and the conforming of the body to idealized image. The brown boy oscillates between object and viewer, content to regard his body's approximation of ideal form because white men desire the object he has made—the kind of subjective dilemma often gendered as feminine. Here, the scope of Wilson's gamble begins to come into focus. But Wilson risks the loss of his readers' affections by daring them into their own antipathy for femininity, for pride, for naming money, and by obsessively naming race rather than performing it through the speaker's first person lyric. If readers remain and continue to immerse themselves in this text, they come to be challenged with a formula for freedom taken from de Sade: objectification leads to a negation of self that approximates freedom. In a sequence of passages in which the brown boy orally bottoms for various anonymous men in a porn cinema, one of them enters his mouth "opening the brown boy's throat to what they both know is an end" (48). Given the book's concern with objectification, it is easy to read the "end" as an end of self. So, either this is a reframing of de Sade in terms of queer sexuality, and, read against the inter-racial romance at the center of the book, in terms of contemporary race relations, or, it is a proposal of bottoming as a will-toward-possession, a possession of whiteness, of class, and of one's own protean desires.

In any case, Wilson's *Narrative* transcends this question by what Claudia Rankine, in her blurb to Wilson's volume, terms a "palpable consciousness." The innovation Wilson offers is not to inhabit this consciousness himself but to create a text that, if successful in its gambles, seduces readers into inhabiting such a refractory and indeed protean mode. The possibility here is that this text is a performance in 3D, something that "activates" race, sexuality, and class for the reader, bores out a space where the reader's own embodied identities can become fuzzy, multiple, dynamic. Wilson names racial categories while simultaneously enacting the poesis of imagination, the giving of form, of "palpable consciousness." Wilson's operative sense of freedom is a protean ability to place embodied identities into a rhetorical mode, a register in which the over-determined signs of race, class, gender, and sexuality are deployed into dialogue with other such equally armed subjects, in other words, readers. This awareness of "what is at issue" approaches the self-awareness of Yasusada's performance of otherness; not quite a minstrel poetics, Wilson nonetheless achieves a similar destabilization of the reader's position. Yet Wilson's text offers to readers who are made to bear power's projections strategies they can use to turn those projections from truth to tools with which we might resist the authorities of our own embodied identities. Echoing both Lott's take on Delany's *Blake* and the Yasusada itself, Anselm Berrigan, a poet I much admire, asks in his book *To Hell with Sleep*, "Should I/ invent an identity and/ abuse its privileges?" (24). Wilson's simple and necessary answer is "yes."

Works Cited

Berrigan, Anselm. *To Hell With Sleep*. Denver, CO, & Chicago IL: Letter Machine Editions: 2009.

Duncan, Robert Edward, Robert J. Bertholf, and Albert Gelpi. *The Letters of Robert Duncan and Denise Levertov*. Stanford, CA: Stanford UP, 2004.

Johnson, Kent. 'Some Thoughts on Araki Yasusada and the Author.' *Wag's Revue* 6 (2010). http://www.wagsrevue.com/Issue_6/#/125. Accessed 7 January 2011.

Lott, Eric. *Love and Theft: Blackface Minstrelsy and the American Working Class*. New York: Oxford UP, 1993.

Perloff, Marjorie. 'In Search of the Authentic Other: the Poetry of Araki Yasusada.' *Doubled Flowering: From the Notebooks of Araki Yasusada*. New York, Roof Books: 1997.

Sable, Kari. 'Jeffrey Dahmer.' http://karisable.com/skazdahmer.htm. Accessed 7 January 2011.

Smith, Dale. *Poets Beyond the Barricade: Rhetoric, Citizenship, and Dissent after 1960*. Tuscaloosa: University of Alabama Press, forthcoming

Warren, Jennifer, et. al. 'One in 100: Behind Bars in America 2008. Pew Center on the States'. http://www.pewcenteronthestates.org/report_detail.aspx?id=35904. Accessed 7 January 2011.

Wilson, Ronaldo. *Narrative of the Life of the Brown Boy and the White Man* Pittsburgh: University of Pittsburgh Press. 2008.

Yasusada, Araki. *Doubled Flowering: From the Notebooks of Araki Yasusada*. New York: Roof, 1997.

Žižek, Slavoj. 'Eastern Europe's Republics of Gilead.' *New Left Review* 183 (1990): 50–62.

The Authentic Poet in the Late 20th Century: Ted, bp, and Araki Yasusada

David Rosenberg

A Postmortem Surveillance of
Collected Poems, by Ted Berrigan. (Berkeley: University of California Press, 2005).
The Martyrology, Books 1 to 9, by bpNichol. (Toronto: Coach House Books, six volumes, 1972–2003).
Doubled Flowering: From the Notebooks of Araki Yasusada, edited and translated by Tosa Motokiyu, Ojiu Norinaga, and Okura Kyogin, copyright by Kent Johnson. (New York: Roof Books, 1997).
Also, With My Throat, I Shall Swallow Ten Thousand Swords: Araki Yasusada's Letters in English, by Tosa Motokiyu, edited by Kent Johnson and Javier Alvarez, copyright by Kent Johnson. (Providence: Combo Books, 2005).

(for Rhonda, who asks)

My early teachers and models were consumed with the idea of an authentic voice, from Lowell and Plath to Ginsberg and O'Hara. Yet none of them, anymore than their predecessors in Williams and Pound, thought to carry on an authentic conversation with himself—with life, love and death on the line. Their poetic voices are "charged" language, performances, however manically the buttons of verisimilitude are pushed. At best, the reader is an intimate audience of a hermetic theater, perfectly understood. My last teacher in the writing program at Syracuse proved the best example. Delmore Schwartz was often out of his mind, coddled or ignored by dilettantish colleagues rather than the psychoanalyst he desperately needed, and at the same time he was struggling to write in a classical voice at odds with his predicament. Within a few months he drove himself to death—strangled by language, we could say.

Sometimes, in a tradition of experimental poets including Stein, Zukofsky, and Ashbery, the reader does become an intimate participant; yet it's as a silent actor in the unfolding drama of the poem, rather than as a vulnerable human being in a spontaneous scene from life. At other times, the reader is called up on stage as witness, as in the heartbreaking objectivity of Charles Reznikoff's work. But again, the call is for a silent witness.

There is, however, another tradition of this reader or silent witness becoming active, on the arm of the author in a parental role. If we go back to Shakespeare, to whom Stein was often comparing herself, and if we refer to the author as W.S. while we call the characters in the plays his "poets," then the parental W.S. can be seen stepping into character, among his characters, most famously in the "Who am I?" passages of Hamlet, King Lear, Prospero, Rosalind, et. al. Gertrude Stein began to play with this role in her "operas and plays," most famously in *Four Saints in Three Acts* where she inhabited the author-as-stage-manager, a downstage figure who parents the childlike saints, profoundly lost "in the moment," the timelessness that renders them innocent of death and transformation.

But allow me to step back a moment and illustrate these initial remarks with a passage from one of our poets under discussion, bpNichol (1944–1988). We will return to him later in the context of his relationship to his contemporaries, Ted Berrigan (1934–1983) and Kent Johnson (1955–). For the moment, it's useful to be reminded that Nichol was sometimes a critic who wrote about Gertrude Stein. Yet the saints in bpNichol's lifetime opus, *The Martyrology* (1966–1988), are far more substantial than Stein's.

They are first encountered in Nichol's own childhood, in a heaven literally perceived as "cloud town." Through puberty and adolescence the author, inhabiting an "i" in the poem, discerns that language can open up like clouds to reveal our intricate world beneath. As he becomes a poet, he gives new voice to the saints with whom he play-talked in childhood—except that these saints have now fallen to earth and become lost in language. They are confused about sudden transformations of identity (in contrast to the constant of change that moves the clouds). And they are further distressed by the cultural workings of time, the social gains and losses, the memory of births and deaths. As he ages and his poem matures, the parental author steps in and out of the theater he has created, to observe not only the character "i" within it but also the author "bp" outside.

from 'Assumptions' (Book 7)

. . . (space to breathe in)

> "everything has to change" i said to myself
> (i was looking out the window) "changes"
> #9 Tram rushing by
> Plantage Midden Laan 4:45 on a Tuesday morning in June
> another landscape pulling the poem out of you
> around you
> the description any one of us needs to live in
> as in "who am i?", "who are you?", "where am i? &
> "is that true?"

The poet's questions here have developed from an earlier parallel to Freud's depiction of the "human mental apparatus" and its projection of the psyche onto the landscape. Here that projection is dated June, 1985; the landscape, Amsterdam; and the author is represented by the "i" in the poem. It is the "i" of one's identity that looks out the window and, in the penultimate line, asks "where am i?" This "i" is lost in time, like a saint, for at the actual scene of writing, the "i (who) was looking out the window" is in a dead past the living author bp here recalls. The present writer, bp, is not the one asking "who am i?"—for bp is not "i"—in the present time of writing the poem. If he did ask it, the question would be ironic, even sarcastic. But it is not ironic (or, as bp might write it, "i ronic"); it is instead deeply poignant, as true a question as can be—because of the next line, where "is that true?" *is* a question asked by bp himself at the scene of writing. In other words, even if there were an answer to "who am i?" (and there is: myself, a character recalled) and "where am I?" (in Amsterdam), it is all contingent upon a present author who asks "is that true?" (about not only the specific answer but the poignancy of the time lost and only artfully recalled). It is an unholy and unsaintly cosmic question, and it is also parental, because it is fully conscious of the death (in time) of the "i" as well as the eventual death of the author, bp—but also, further, the death of the reader (an as-yet unborn reader in the future).

A vast majority of professional poets today are not going to alert you to this parental scene of writing and the consciousness of their own death, either because they don't unequivocally believe in it or because it fills them with exactly the kind of dread from which they are escaping into the poem and its poetic "I". This is also the declamatory "I" of academic tradition, which can state the consciousness of its own

David Rosenberg

solitude but cannot parent it—that is, it can't place itself in real history but instead conjures an aesthetic history of poetry, humanity, and various traditions.

Nevertheless, echoing the necessity of Shakespeare and the theatricality of Stein, the authentic poets of my time write, in effect, theatrical plays. Beyond a protean playfulness, they sit in the wings, outside of their poems but not absent—and not merely sit but live, invoking the strangeness of the world and its theater, the haunting natural beauty of *creatureliness*. Each addresses fragments of himself within the poem: Berrigan in the guise of friends and appropriated lines, bpNichol's childhood saints fallen into language, and Yasusada's friends and family obliterated in Hiroshima. Each is parent to an earlier heroic self before it shattered, the one that imagined itself living vicariously in the poem, instead of outside it. Thus, the poem's theater now exists primarily to awaken us to the creaturely world in which the author is disguised as himself but essentially just beyond the margin's edge—and made more palpable for being so.

Ted Berrigan strove to make of his reader more than a silent witness, to include her in a real conversation about the poignant brevity of life that went beyond the named conversants in the poem. But Berrigan's personal theater entailed such an intensity of purpose that his life was constantly in danger of—literally—going up in smoke. He fought through this by translating the artistic minimalist drive of his cultural moment into expansive white space in many of his poems, upon his always literal 8½ by 11 inch piece of typing paper. With enough white space, there was room enough for a dance between friends, reader, and author in the wing of the margin, as if the page was stage enough for Berrigan. Yet he began to work toward coming down from it.

And he succeeded by becoming more alive as the author we imagine re-typing his poem—editing it, preserving it, parenting—than the high-stepping poet composing it. For his poems can be immensely delicate, the stage on the verge of collapsing, except when we are made disarmingly aware of the author holding *our* arm, a Berrigan determined also to be a kind of post-poem historian of the dance we're experiencing. He may, for instance, appear to find or re-use lost lines of his own, in the guise of historical-minded editor. But in the passage that follows, we encounter first the stage-Berrigan and his typical deadpan of literary failure. At the same time, however, the context makes us aware of the paternal Berrigan on our arm, reminding us of the dangers of poetic pretension:

> ... contemplating my new books of poems
> to be printed in simple type on old brown paper
> (Berrigan 48)

I shall return momentarily to this personal theater of Berrigan both in and somewhat outside his poem. Actually, I have a vivid image of him literally on the stage of the Fillmore East on Second Avenue, reading his poems as a kind of warm-up act for the John Coltrane Quartet. In those early hippie days he was in full costume, in a kind of blue-checked circus pants, a yellow t-shirt with a "Peace Eye Bookstore" logo on it, and some sort of scant vest. Plus: blue granny spectacles, dark mane of head-banded hair, beard in full bloom (mustache erased). You could say he resembled something halfway between a street theater poet and the twitching Coltrane, except that Ted was as lucid and composed as a professor. His work professed to take care of you, clothe you in it, making you comfortable even in an outlandish costume. Once you allowed yourself to be so dressed, at least figuratively, you realized that his words, like his clothes, disarmed the first pretentious parental lesson, the one about making "a good first impression" on the world. Instead, this father figure counsels the riches of thought rather than the world's riches, especially when set down on "old brown paper"—an image from that Fillmore event ingrained in me as one of inevitable aging, although I was barely in my twenties.

And beyond aging, Ted found lines from the past, his own as well as others, to create a stage presence that shimmered between poem and margin, life and death—in which death was always the "last poem" and life the poet with one leg outside it, "in bed, words chosen randomly."

> from 'Last Poem'
>
> ... Some words remembered from an earlier time,
> "The intention of the organism is to survive."
> My earliest, & happiest, memories pre-date WWII,
> They involve a glass slipper & a helpless blue rose

David Rosenberg

> In a slender blue single-rose vase. Mine
> Was a story without a plot...
> ... inspired strangers sadly died: everyone
> I ever knew aged tremendously, except me. I remained
> Somewhere between 2 and 9 years old. But frequent
> Reification of my own experiences delivered to me
> Several new vocabularies...
> ... that other people die the source
> Of my great, terrible, & inarticulate one grief. In my time
> I grew tall & huge of frame, obviously possessed
> Of a disconnected head, I had a perfect heart. The end
> Came quickly & completely without pain, one quiet night as I
> Was sitting, writing, next to you in bed, words chosen randomly
> From a tired brain, it, like them, suitable, & fitting...
> (Berrigan 521–522)

With the feel of being made up of borrowings, the stage-voice in the poem seems lost, out of touch, the words coming "randomly"—and rescued only by the parental poet Ted Berrigan, as if a found poem. It is Ted listening to his ghost like Hamlet to his ghost-father, only here the verisimilitude of ghost-life is more acute because the poem is, in fact, largely ghost-written from random sources. The poet in bed who is "composing" his last poem is actually creating a "decomposition." As prelude to the natural decomposition of his body in the death following his "last poem," the poem itself disarms or decomposes our ideas of composition.

The redundancy of a "random choosing" of words, an oxymoron, is itself a choice echo of the scientific concept of natural selection, a parallel to the natural process of the poem. The result is that we are disposed to the paradox at the heart of poetic composition: the grandiosity of the author's voice (it's his *last* poem, for pity's sake) versus the decomposition of that voice, and its artful pretension, by the natural hand of the poet outside the poem. It's precisely his creaturely presence in the humorous underpinning of the poem that upholds the origin of poetry in natural history, for it's entirely human to wish ourselves more important, more grandiose, than other creatures.

In the poem that follows, we encounter the same lost poet within the poem (but now lost *outside of time*) who wishes to "re-compose" himself and the poetic tradition (represented by the Muse). But as the poem acknowledges scientific reality (e.g. "Relativity") the writer on our arm—more precisely, our parental editor—pulls us back to view the larger perspective: our creaturely wonder (no longer an anachronistic "compleynt") at the scene of writing itself.

> from 'Compleynt to the Muse'
> After Philip Whalen
>
> Lady, why will you insist on
> Coming back into my life only when
> It's too late, I've just this moment
>
> Ago stepped out the backdoor
> Of my body, gone ahead into Relativity . . .
>
> I don't mind at all, now that I'm simply
> Air, a large hunk of see-through molecules...
>
> I am grinning & don't care. I mean, not heavily.
> But now you return, and so, I have too,
> Into my ashy beard & dusty head, my pink baby's torso
>
> And you are laughing, and I am once again
> Lying in the world . . .
> (Berrigan 555–556)

The stage-voice here, the "I" who is "not heavy," is looking back at a life long dead in time, but it is restored into history by the writing poet, so that this "I" is alive because he is "lying," and not merely in the sense of repose. An art that "lies" about the finality of death, just as it lies about the voice of the Muse it addresses (as if the gods still exist) is an art to be hauled offstage. But this is also a friendly critique of the poet Whalen, who had become a Zen Buddhist priest living in Japan, for whom the difference between dying and lying was deadpan by doctrine.

In his Vancouver teens, bpNichol was also reading Philip Whalen. He took Whalen's tendency to incorporate his drawing hand into poems and applied it to typography, in some instances pulling words apart into their constituent letters and then accumulating a drawing from the extra spaces as they descended through the lines of the poem. But for Nichol, deadpan or experiment was never the point. Instead, as we shall see, it was the childlike foil for a critical and lifelong encounter with the necessity of accepting death in the family drama—an inside-out deadpan, so to speak. And more than that, a necessity to confront the inevitable, natural extinction of our species. Since that means that all the art and all the artifice of humanity is finite—as are our languages— the poems we now write must include that awareness (and not merely the finite body in an *ars longa, vita brevis*, usually assumed to mean that art outlives life). Like Nichol, the Berrigan who pointed to the creaturely and inarticulate life outside the poem was species-conscious, though it didn't develop beyond a stock parental gesture for Berrigan.

Meanwhile, his stage persona was free to be in the moment (and thus parody such romantic pretension). Berrigan could be out in the wild, animal-like, while his father figure anchors the home (in the passage that follows, the wife stands in) and is responsible, dedicated to the poem:

from 'Wishes'

... Wish I were walking around in Chelsea (NY) & it was 5:15 a.m., the sun coming up, alone, you asleep at home ... (373)

Yet in fact Berrigan *is* at home during the scene of writing the poem and is not "walking around," except in his mind. *That* Berrigan, the one walking the streets, the onstage Berrigan "of the poem," remains marginal, compared to the parental one at his desk (who *really is* at the page's margin, creature-wise, and is the truer subject of the poem). And that is why the stage-Berrigan in the poems can also be depicted as impoverished, or drug-dependent, or cavalierly self-destructive, when his poetic career at the typewriter belies it with a contrasting creative richness. (Incidentally, I say "stage-Berrigan" because it's more authentic than the academic tradition's "persona"; even within the poem, Berrigan tests the limits of the autobiographical.) So what enriches this art is that it never settles for the poetic. It demands of each poem that it find a new way to pull the rug out from under the conventional dramas of poetry, insisting upon a theater where the scene of writing must always be conscious and alive.

Ted's stage, however, was no soapbox. He managed to mostly keep clear of trendy political opinions and fashionable academe, as did bp and Yasusada (and his Johnson). Paradoxically, as the literary avant-garde moved into universities, their poems and prose came to resemble *lectures* (though shorn of the classic roots and contagious friendliness of Stein's). They may often be uproarious but have little to say *about themselves*. And thus they are buttressed with all the old soapbox tricks, however experimental, from carny come-on to speaking in tongues— egoistic sleight-of-hand rarely to be found in Berrigan.

Ted, bp and Kent Johnson are also known as great punners, but their plays on words signify a new theater that is dependent on such puns for life, for real survival. The authentic poet strives to *disarm* poetry, so that we are left with a moving, existential question about how to live: "Now what?" For that's our question of today, its author conscious of being lost in the cosmos and speaking to the dead of past and future. It is, in other words, a tragicomic poetry, watching over the old theatrical pride in craft like a parent over his child's prodigious pride in her own feces—prior to toilet-training, of course.

When Ted, bp, or Yasusada trade in political opinions, it is largely for cultural context. In several of Berrigan's poems he gently chides an older colleague, Allen Ginsberg, for occasionally smuggling a political soapbox into his verse. Ted's work insists on respect for character, especially the author's character boiled down to species consciousness. Before it can step up to self-righteousness, we are made conscious of Berrigan on our arm, solid as an Amazonian parrot.

Nevertheless, Ginsberg is famously capable of satirizing his own political grandiosity, so his opinions are rarely accused of being incongruous. Of course, there is nothing incongruous in Berrigan's work: it was a war for survival, personal and cultural. The cultural context was a time of disillusionment with the "counter-culture," a "youth culture" which turned out to last for about ten minutes but continued on in a state of defiance for years (embodied finally in the punk stance). Ted was one of the first to know it was over, for which the appropriate mask was deadpan and then the various inventive processes of removing the mask. Nothing incongruent about that, possibly because we are speaking of life off the page, in all its desperate laundry. An authentic poet of our time, however, has no echo because even the most incongruous cultural drama imaginable—the mushroom cloud of Hiroshima or "*Arbeit macht frei*"—has happened upon a universal stage on which even the incommensurate is congruous, so long as the boundary between them, between domestic life and Holocaust, for instance, or between written poem and heroin overdose, is respected. That boundary is the author's own life on the line, in the wing of his theater. His species consciousness and its knowledge of extinction puts him on stage parallel to Shakespeare the actor mouthing a line in his own play ("all the world's a stage . . ."). Faeries and ghosts from an incommensurate "world" may speak there but they never seem incongruous.

We can see this most especially in the work of Araki Yasusada, where the massive headline of A-bombed Hiroshima would otherwise be too incommensurate to hold in the same consciousness as domestic life—were it not for the "editor," Kent Johnson, setting a universal stage. On a more personal level, for bpNichol the daily news of the natural world and the psyche are commensurate with his presence, just outside the poem, as we are made conscious that the margin of the page (and the systems of language it contains) is the boundary. In this natural theater that includes its creator, Nichol has a special advantage, thanks to Canada, whose massive physical presence outweighs its cultural grandiosity. The huge invisible weight of its northern provinces is always in bp's consciousness, even as forgetting that fact is the main business of its cultural media, huddled down along the 49th Parallel. In the U.S., it was Whitman who had sunk the anchor of America's physicality in the depths of personality, and we will soon see how Nichol and Johnson plumbed it further. Berrigan's sensibility was also capacious enough to turn Whitman's project of speaking to the cosmos into one of reading. It was not even foremost a reading of texts but of the authors of those texts caught ambiently, with pen in hand. The human ape lost in poetry.

I recall an afternoon-long conversation with Ted Berrigan thirty years ago, sitting on the stoop of my St. Marks Place tenement. "You're just like your 'uncle' Harold," Ted was saying, conjuring Harold Rosenberg, the art critic. "Everything you encounter is a question that has to be answered, instead of a thing wanting to be greeted affectionately. That's the same argument Ginsberg had with Kerouac's

Republican politics. Jack by then was encountering his own past with suspicion and projecting it out into the world, while Allen could barely tell the difference between an enemy interlocutor and a groupie: it was all Buddhist conviviality now, a kind of all-night party Socialism (as opposed to Socialist party). Allen wanted Jack to join the party again, but Jack wanted to sit home and watch the Republican convention on TV. I love them both, but you, Rosenberg, you just want to interrogate everyone, both Jack and Allen, you don't want to get involved."

Possibly Ted was right; I was boxed in. I actually read "literary criticism," even the Higher Biblical criticism. But in those days before Deleuze and Blanchot or Derrida and Kristeva were widely available in English, criticism was often practiced within our poems themselves, in their implications about the authenticity of other works and traditions. Berrigan encountered another's poems and responded in his own: he was a critical historian, his poems a record of reading like no other. Whether Thucydides, a poet friend, or Reverdy, his responses were always a one-two jolt: first, deadpan; then, deadly sobering—reading Reverdy was reading a living dead poet. It was as if Berrigan could become the ghost of himself, reading over the shoulder of other writers—and he would steal their pens if he could. In doing so, his audience becomes numinous readers, as if we too were dead, like the dead poets of the past—and yet, we're addressed as if we were *re-composed*, alive, as if time didn't exist, as if "5:15 a.m." was the most gorgeous of metaphors.

David Rosenberg

II

The one authentic poet who conceived of and completed the project of holding an ongoing conversation with a numinous reader was a Canadian—the "Canadian Whitman," as the transplanted American-born critic Warren Tallman wrote of him. Whereas Whitman seemed to speak to anyone who crossed his path on the open road, bpNichol brought us into his room, to sit beside him at his desk and to be turned to familiarly, face to face, at any line or stanza, as if to be asked: Just what should come next that will not dispel the intimacy of the moment? And yet Barrie was far ahead of any "poet in the moment," whether experimental or academic.

The purpose of this conversation was none other than to establish the history of civilization as a universal stage, upon which the living and the dead are equal to the unborn, the future. Thus, our origin in the past remains ahead of us, an inspiring question, as it was for Darwin and Freud. Even the juxtaposition of ancient history with current ("con/ Sumer"), or even the simplest exchange of thoughts with the dead affirms a universal history that survives us—and that marks us as species-bound, and bound for extinction. When Nichol places the scene of writing on this stage, his earlier selves—or even the previous line—clearly denote the past, while the future is buried there too, waiting to be excavated like immortal saints; or, like signs of their language, to be unmasked by letters, words, phrases and stanzas (St. Anzas).

> from 'Assumptions' (Book 7)
>
> ... the letters let him glimpse a truth
> none of which they meant
> me   ant
>   (tiny flick amidst the constant din
>   the distant consonants . . .
> the trick is to keep writing
> tho the trick is you're bound to stop
> writing . . .
> faint flicker as the light years pass
> as the sound waves & disappears

> in the gaps between the stars
> and all that we are we are
> was
> and even the is is argued
> dismissed . . .

This universe-wide universal, rendered in light years overtaking sound waves, is parallel to the space between letters overtaken and held together by gravity. And the gravitas of this poem's situation is the writer bp's estrangement from the dead "we's" of the poem, as they are made gorgeously equivalent to the lost sounds (the gaps) in the language of the stars, made legible by light.

All through the nine singular books of bpNichol's *The Martyrology* (1967–1988) we find this new testament to the union of heaven and earth. It is Nichol's creation of a universal theater, constructed for poets and readers of the future to encounter as a gateway toward reanimating the past. But the nationalist-bound literary critics of the U.S., who proffer little interest in the future (though much angst) haven't encountered Nichol. Harold Bloom, with his pretension to represent the age, has never read him. Neither have younger poetry critics Ron Silliman or David Lehman, Ann Lauterbach or Ed Hirsch, all of whom I've asked over the years.

Perhaps if he had lived longer . . . For here, too, a tragic death at an age earlier than Berrigan, shortened the conversation with his reader. Yet once and for all (in our time, at least), a poet reached back into the original family romance of man, to represent it without fear of literary castration for such presumption. Castrated, for instance, by getting lost in the past, unsure of one's time and place—but saved in the firm anchoring to a room. Windows for eyes and ears, door for "bringing one's genitals in contact with those of another's . . ." as Freud caricatured it. Or, as Nichol does, we must substitute "thinking" for "genitals," as when he projects the body into the surrounding prosthesis of a room, a place in which one's inner life can sit, write and walk about. Literate in Freud's theories of origins, Nichol sublimated castration anxiety into the threat of species extinction. If we can no longer be weakened (i.e. castrated) by presuming to control our destiny with knowledge, then consider the threat when even our signs of knowledge, from language to physical artifact, will be lost in the extinction of *Homo sapiens sapiens*.

David Rosenberg

from 'Assumptions' (Book 7), 'Toronto to Vancouver, 1986'

...blue all around you, not sad, 31,000 feet,
a certain relation you assumes . . .
this world of cloud & possible saints
heaven as you has always imagined it
that pain there, that love, world
you must return to, pass thru another
gate another time, always here
between worlds, points of view
changing because you changes too, me or i, assumptions of
what i knows of i s self
this or that me
cumulative accumulation of
i's dentity, the world's and how i knows of it
knows to have this sky, that colour,
you . . .

"You" is conventionally the reader, but here it has become the author, observing himself at the scene of writing—himself and the "assumptions" of himself "above," into clouds and other assumptions of heaven that ignore gravity. But bp the author *is* gravity: even the saints of his childhood come down to Earth, though they are lost here.

To be perfectly clear, bp the author is not a literary creation, not a double or an alter ego, not a performance as in conventional postmodern fictions. Consider: We have just sent a satellite into orbit dedicated to finding exoplanets around other stars by means of blips and mirrors, because the visuals are still beyond us—and that is how bp sites himself, as a creature lost in time and space but located by traces. In the poem, bp's "i" plays the *fort-da* of finding the boundary between interior and outer world, deepening a literary personality that compares with Whitman. But unlike most experimental writing, the gravity of Nichol's poem is located in the creature outside the margin, a selfhood whose never grandiose lostness among the stars and the organisms is always poignant.

In fall of 2006, I returned to Toronto for an eighteen-hour reading performance (over a three-day weekend) of *The Martyrology* by the prodigious Nichol bibliographer, J. W. Curry of Ottawa. On the stage where he read, Curry sometimes used a violent voice for the "i's" in the poem, a passionate anger propelling them. "What made you think bp was angry?" I asked him during an intermission. "He was angry with language that appeared to exist by itself, detached from the living breath, what is studied as art or literature in the universities. When he occasionally taught there, he considered every text as artifact first, with its existential context crucial to it. So when his poetry sounds the most arty or experimental it's meant to be insubordinate, to be angry about having to be 'creative.' And that's why I insist on reading in a theater and not at a university, where the preciousness of art trumps life. In a theater, anything can actually happen (even when it rarely does). You can wind up on an operating table, odds against your life, and that is where bp is in the 'If' sequence—he's writing it in the hospital bed, before the operation that killed him."

"You say bp took the scene of writing with him, the pen and paper. So why," I asked, "did you ban microphones and recording devices from the theater? They're just extensions of the theatrical, no?"

"I don't like any distance from the physical act. There's a price to breathing, to projecting your voice, and you should be aware of it. I'm totally exhausted by this reading. You in the audience should feel that too. I think that's what bp was angry about, the way arty language—and its echoes in an academic canon—works against physical presence. There's something dramatic in physical presence alone, it tells a story of strain and aging, and the inevitability of dying. I don't dress up. I don't use any makeup, I don't even wash before I go on stage."

The physical feat that Curry embodied, performing the entire nine books of *The Martyrology* in "real time" (equating the scene of writing with the scene of reading) further suggests the Whitmanian. Nichol extends Walt Whitman's physicality as no American poet has. The Walt of Whitman's poems is a creature of the mind, larger than life, though beyond the stance it's hard to see Whitman agonizing at his desk, crossing out and revising lines, or simply sighing. Moreover, Nichol fills in and animates Whitman's lost childhood and lost fatherhood with a Stevensian meditation on myth (the childhood of humanity) transformed into history (the obligation to "master reality," as Delmore Schwartz has written of Wallace Stevens). That, too, is what the Bible was concerned with, and the biblical echoes in *The Martyrology* are more acute than in Whitman, addressing multiple levels of fatherhood.

David Rosenberg

"Stevens' *Collected Poems* make a book as important as *Leaves of Grass*," wrote Schwartz upon its publication in 1955; "but," he continued, "the primary philosophical motive leads to a major limitation—the meditative mode is a solitude which excludes the dramatic and narrative poet's human character and personality." After reading *The Martyrology*, we have to disagree with this assessment, as Nichol presents us with a *thinking* personality more vivid than any other. As each line of Nichol's thinks its way forward, unpresupposing, unprepossessed, it sees "the nothing that is not there, and the nothing that is," as Stevens wanted it, but it also dramatizes itself in a universal theater that renders the reader, at moments, numinous or saintly. It's as if not only do we outlive the author but also, by being made a necessary adjunct to the poem's staging, we live as long as the poem itself, as do readers of the Bible today.

Far from supposing a divine author, we can see the author's personality on stage, thinking with his pen, and we glimpse the author offstage, preparing for death in a lifetime of confronting "nothing more nor less than the blank page." Minimalist experiment aside, Nichol fits this confrontation into our emerging tradition of natural history: a creature evolves within a text, yet remains *without a text* like all other creatures—save for its genome. Stevens did not yet have this Darwinian text to fully consider; Nichol found the way to embody it by showing in countless ways throughout *The Martyrology* how myths of childhood, religion, and intellectual grandiosity can be transformed into a contemporary record of the scene of writing.

> from 'Assumptions', *for Charles Bernstein* (Book 7)
>
> wandered the streets of downtown Berkeley
> all morning
>   the pain in my leg
> so intense at certain moments i could not stand
> the pain...
> notion of the processual
> or this talk of doing
> to be included with the doing
> hauling my leg up the hill
> even as this line drags every other line with it
> the whole of the Martyrology trailing behind . . .

Scubadivers and Chrysanthemums

The pain recalled—the leg—is of the grandiose "i" in the poem walking, as the writer bp now proceeds in "this talk of doing/to be included with the doing." In other words, the parental "talk" is also painful, an uphill haul, an entire life (in the recalling of the nine books of *The Martyrology*) that engenders bp at the scene of writing. There he sits, the sitting wanderer, legless—but attached to it in memory, and thereby parent (with tender pathos and pity for the pain) to the "i" as it wanders dying through the processional of time. But it's the parental writer who is rendered creaturely; his text is merely memory, as it is for all animals, all of whom experience pain.

We may note here again that Nichol remained influenced by Gertrude Stein's writing process and its suggestion of mammalian consciousness; she had been more prescient than most modern writers in her themes of repetition and variation, replication and mutation. Yet where Stein dramatized theory (in this case, natural selection) Nichol could also dramatize himself. Within the poem, that is. Stein was a master at dramatizing her life in other genres (the *Autobiographies*, for example) but not in poetry. Not like this, where the authorial bp gets his face in the picture:

from 'bp: if' (Book 8)

*

sacrum

say
the whole thing ends

say
you're frightened
of the whole thing
ending

say
cheese

say n't

David Rosenberg

---

n't ready

n't ready to die
      —September 1, 1988

What the sacrum represents here, as we know historically, is the physical back that will be operated on. bp did not survive the operation as he survives this poem—though he is not the "you" in the poem, identifying himself with everyone, for that you is another "i", like all others, and has to die in time. But the bp at the scene of writing survives to the extent he interferes in the poem, refusing the "not ready" and catching himself here gasping for air in the "n't". His formal smile in a photo may recall him, but that gasp is his life in our hands for a moment.

I remember a long day of conversation with Barrie that started at Coach House, where we both had books on press, and continued at his apartment; there, he opened his large artist journals (drawing-size, in order to include all manner of paste-ins) to refer to his essays on Stein's *The Making of Americans*. From Stein's own theory of personality, bp had extrapolated a psychology of language in which syntax and words could break apart into the deeper bonding of families. It was this last notion that transfixed me, since he wasn't talking about a metaphoric family of syntax but rather the genetics of a human family. In other words, what held letters together in words was the parental eye and voice of the lost poet we all once were in childhood, safe (we thought) in the physics of families.

This was 1971. I was well along in my own doctoral thesis on Stein, and the first book of bp's *The Martyrology*, still unpublished though months later to be set in type, was unknown to me. But I was privy to bp's underpinning theories for his theater of saints. Like Stein, he represented the saints as if speaking in a play or opera, characters unaware that they would not live forever, minds detached from time. But what I had already learned, and what would only unfold in *The Martyrology* over many years, was that bp's parenting of the saints would merge into friends and the members of his own family over time, and eventually into all of human history, back through Sumerian Gilgamesh to prehistory. It is within this universal theater that the

Creator is sometimes addressed, the father figure Nichol occludes with his own father occasionally, or any father and mother within his Homo sapiens genealogy, and every so often with an "i". But here all "i's" are eclipsed except the one lost like the saints were, among "countries." Where earlier we might have assumed one of the saints was speaking, now it is the son-poet, lost in his universal poem:

from 'Considerations, Puerto Rico, 1971' (Book 7)

. . . sun going down
behind the ruined walls of cloud town
late we drive along the sea wall
darkness over the city
dark girls in summer dresses
searching for the ones they love or will love
over everything His shadow falls
larger than history (if that is possible—
that conceit) & i am singing brokenly His praises
as tho i had lost what sense of form i did gain
hoping to find it again
among the voices of another country . . .

Stein's parental "authors" rarely contemplate their deaths, so the distance from a Stein opera is found here in the emphasis on time's limitations rather than its freedoms. Yet bp is still a parental author as he faces the loss of his "sense of form," his life as well as his poem. Back in '71, Barrie was leaving the afternoon after our Stein conversation for a lay analyst stint at Therafields, an analytic community based on an abandoned farm. We agreed to meet one last time to conclude our deliberations: lunch at 'The Sport,' a Hungarian café near Bloor and Spadina, both of us semi-vegetarian yet fond of "the lunch plate special," goulash and dumplings, at the price of a mere Canadian dollar. For the first time, we each confessed to reading Freud, who was then nowhere as fashionable as Lacan. I remember we moved directly from a hypothesis that Stein's language experiment was, like sexual intercourse, a combination of violent aggression and narcissism—a kind of erotic goulash—into the Freudian hypothesis of the death instinct. To what extent, we asked, is the use of language against itself—as in puns and wordplay—analogous to the destructive desire to return to an inorganic state, where language is unnecessary? In other words, must visual and sound poetry, for instance, be inherently violent? We even mimicked this heaviness by pretending to violently attack our food and devour our dumplings like so many dead prisoners. (In the late *An Outline of Psychoanalysis*, Freud wrote: "The act of eating is a destruction of the object with the final aim of incorporating it.")

As we parted, it would have been impossible for me to imagine it was the last time I'd see him alive. *Book 7 &* didn't come out until 1990, two years after Nichol's death. Although I had always meant to get back to Toronto in the intervening years, there seemed no rush, for it had become clear that *The Martyrology* was always going to be about "continuing." And yet here was this supreme irony I hadn't swallowed until reading Book 7, that the more of the poet's life the work took in, the closer to death *we* (not just "he") came. Since the continuity was life-affirming in its *increase*, the irony was that the approaching loss—the *continual* loss—was easy to ignore.

> from 'Assumptions' (Book 7)
>
> . . . in the dark night
> not even the moon to follow me across the lawn
> not even the single light from some stray &/or forlorn
>   streetlamp
> not even those comfortless descriptions to comfort me
> only myself, as i am, for company
> evoking your presence
> name
>   but never naming you
> never fixing you in all the descriptions that do not fit
> the vanity of nouns, of even these pronouns i and you…
> still that longing for love
> for all that is meant by the word "peace"
> & that we must value that longing
> that tortured feeling
> be moved by it
> till these tortures cease . . .

Although "these tortures" are the ones—the feelings—that belong to bp at the scene of writing, the "longing/ that tortured feeling" is also what the collective "we" of the poem (that collection of i's and you's) feel for each other. It's human social longing. But the "tortures" of bp, outside the poem, represent another kind of longing: to continue writing poetry as any creature continues breathing. Poetry, not prose. As I myself write this specific prose I feel something like survivor's guilt, for prose is well suited to humanity but a bit out of its depth in the deeper time of species consciousness, which we can no more avoid today than our own deaths. Prose is fine for considering the latter and framing the former, but extinction of the species demands authentic poetry.

What, for example, might it mean if Philip Roth, the prose queen of our day, were to become a poet? It would be as if from the back of the writer at his desk emerged an earlier (and thus older) self who begins to observe, over bp's (or Roth's) shoulder—to observe not his own world, but the author in his. It's just because this would seem to describe Roth's fiction of an alter ego, the author Zuckerman, that we never encounter the actual author Roth: he is folded into the work as *auteur*. So our sense of the real world in which Roth resides as a natural creature (and not simply a literary creation) is lost to us; instead of the scene of writing, we have the stagy scenes of half-baked political, social and psychological insight into "our times" on the one hand, and into literary characters on the other. He or his defenders might say that we shouldn't be interested in the "real Roth," who in fact might be a pretty boring fellow in a pretty dull life. But that is just the point. How is it possible for a life to be "dull"? Can we imagine another creature, a whale, or a pelican, or even a butterfly, inhabiting a "dull" life? In other words, must we continue to leave the problem of "being" out of the work? Berrigan, Nichol and Johnson's work tells us, no; and that an authentic poet today can construct a new kind of theater—even as the ultimate impact reveals what great writers have shown in the past, that we are creatures wondrously lost on a cosmic island and that most human excitement is a diminishment of that knowledge.

David Rosenberg

from 'St. Anzas' VII (Book 8)

. . . the thickening night words. the tongue
unfolding flesh, rasps along the body's length
is words. moves across the room. sits. writes.
has just written. fact this fiction. the thickening night;
the unfolding flesh; the you he addresses
across this room. that is, as any room, crowded
with old standards, stock scenes, clichés,
we have seen before, heard. who
directed this shit? . . .

Here it is again in another of its permutations, the scene of writing, the writer who "sits. writes." It is already the past, the dead writer, even by only the minute it has taken for the writer outside the poem to write this down. But suddenly the outside creature slips in: "who directed this shit?"—and this anti-aside peels the roof off the whole theater, reminding us of the higher creation driving the species, the *creatureliness* of the mind itself. It is a play, after all, and the lines continue, folding back director, creature, and writer into the "i"s tongue. Although there is some hilarious poetry from the New York School that seems to do this, especially Ted Berrigan, the author nonetheless remains safe within the poem while there; whereas Nichol, within the larger poem, approaches a Beckettian theatrical despair, and it is ultimately saved, not by humor but by a steadily deepening species consciousness.

The poetry of John Ashbery also performs innumerable acts of humorously displacing the author (and his hyperactive mind) yet Ashbery remains a narrowly "human" author. The acrobatics of pronouns, riffs on tradition, sleight-of-hand appropriation and high-low juggling reveal an almost professorial Ashbery in the end, witty and wise but confined to a Museum of Modern Art version of the 20th Century. This may be preferable to the academic version or the experimental version, but still not good enough. Extinction is no longer an existential condition to be evoked in abstract constructions or deconstructions of thinking. Extinction is becoming a species fact we'll have to internalize. Although Ashbery is still today our parental avant-garde, we no longer have the sense that we are more exposed than we want to be. Yet we are, and Nichol won't let us forget it. With bpNichol, we are walking in the wilderness along with the ghosts of Darwin and Freud. And as if the shit has hit the fan, and we can no longer avoid how Freud found the origin of our creativity in the infant's erotic attachment to its feces, its instinct to play with it.

III

from *Doubled Flowering*:
High Altitude Photo of Hiroshima (Circa 1944)
March 7, 1957

There must be a schoolgirl deep inside there, stuttering,
almost weeping, to remember the main cities
of our ally, Germany.

There must be a monk, self-absorbed, slowly dragging
his rake through sand, around a moss-covered stone.

A man inside his home has thrown a little boy into the air:
The child is there, falling, his mouth open with joy.

And I . . . where am I? For being here is confusing,
makes my position less clear. Somewhere in the upper left,
I suppose, hurrying ambitiously to get somewhere . . .

I shut my eyes, try to recall those days . . .

Outside of me the photograph is beautiful and clear:
A long, single pulse of geometry under dreams.
Pure hieroglyph into which I also will vanish.

All the facts here are decomposing. Yasusada's note to the poem says, "I dedicate this poem to the great artist, Piet Mondrian." So, here are facts resolved into art—or into geometry? No. Once again, through the scrim of 1945, even "I shut my eyes" has turned impossible, the eyelids singed off. All photos have become unreal, their verisimilitude turned into pure art: "where am I?" But even Mondrian's art and its verisimilitude of pure form and color, turns into hieroglyph for which no reader can exist.

David Rosenberg

Unless *we* are that reader, as we are Kent Johnson's reader. And after we have given it up—our privilege as readers or viewers—to re-imagine ourselves, like history itself, as already past. Homo sapiens, ourselves, have become extinct. That is how we have arrived, in our day, at the formerly unimaginable condition for species consciousness.

Proof that such loss can be dispelled—that it is not just a spiritual wish—now comes in the recent posthumous volumes of Araki Yasusada. (Both books involve more than one editor and translator who themselves are unstable, so that our truest anchor for authorship is the person cited as copyright holder for both books, Kent Johnson.) For in these two volumes we hear a voice speaking to us in the broken language of the species. It is the potential conversation of any Homo sapiens tribe translated into our tongue, a story of life and love and everything lost, yet surviving. How so? This is the question that dogs us and elbows us and opens our eyes. Indeed, how could it be? It could only seem a miraculous breakthrough: a breaking into time by a dead poet who we still sense breathing beside us.

In this case, as with the early deaths of Berrigan and Nichol, we intuit the poet has matured at an unusually young age. He speaks to us as an enduring historian, a heart and mind devoted to history and to the rescuing from it of our darkest secret. At any moment the secret may be revealed to us, even in the misspelling of a word or the mispronouncing of an affection. For all of history is addressed as time, as the same time in which we are breathing speech, so that the reader, even were he to be dead like the original poet Yasusada, becomes newly crucial to the conversation: at one time or other, each word enters his ear and exits his mouth like drawn breath, and that is the secret of how we stop time by speaking to it, embodying it so we can face extinction together: ourselves and our language. In other words, poet and reader exist both in and outside of time, and each thought is spoken and echoes historically, yet without recourse to anything more than the page before us.

So the whole history of civilization is present and accompanies every page, from first speaker to last historian, and the living poet never lets us forget this. We are forced to ask who is speaking—and even more poignantly, who is listening and translating? How has the history of writing and book-making sublimated our darkest thoughts— especially the thought that we are authors of our own creation and our own death? Because if the pages of history are an ephemeral artifact, not only is the human mind as well, but also the human genome.

> from *Also, with My Throat, I Shall Swallow Ten Thousand Swords*: *from* May 7, 1926
>
> . . . *Who or what* is it, *at this moment*, that is reading?
> How can *we* have the apricot blossoms perfuming *the whole world*?
> [italics mine]
>
> Footnote 1: In our opinion, as editors and translators, this is the most mysterious and beautiful of all the letters.
> Footnote A: As the editors of the "editors," we don't necessarily concur . . .

From the footnote of the original editor, Tosa Motokiyu, we understand that the letter is an artifact of history. For the later editors ('Footnote A') this letter has become, however, an artifact of poetry. Thanks to them (Kent Johnson and Javier Alvarez), "at this moment" and "the whole world," which denote time and space, are now rendered as figures of timelessness. Further, the questions of these two lines, very real for Yasusada and Motokiyu, are transfigured by post-1945 history into a rhetoric of loss. Whatever was historical for the author has been obliterated—that is *our* history, and our history is one of editorial restoration. The historical has become our truest poetry, and the authentic poets have also become editors of what is lost. And more than that: restorers-in-advance of what has yet to be lost, pertinent to our species.

> from *Also, with My Throat, I Shall Swallow Ten Thousand Swords:*
>
> *from* August 9, 1926
>
> . . . Presently I will name such a country Platonica. It is a country with no Time, scarcely in belief as you must be. In its landscape are some long and oily Rods such as mathematical Rods (sic). Most strikingly, this landscape is lopsided, with a most definite backside and one Black frontier all oily around a hole. For example, if you will please consider Triangulars in

creasings as Nows, the land of them comes to a stopping in the degenerate Triangular into which every three points come once in a clicking (sic). Consequently, there is a jetting-forthness [illegible passage due to blotching] whilst (sic) who knows what will happen? Therefore, through the telescope, there is some stubble, all wetly, under the Black boy's arms. In other words (sic), pal-pen, have you ever stumbled through a burnt forest, dying for some water?

Today, try as we might to read this as historical in 1926, it can only be read through the scrim of 1945, as poetry. We can re-imagine the intent of the mistranslations but it all turns into post-Hiroshima. In the same way, modern and postmodern literature carries its own history—"all wetly" might be Joyce, "illegible passage due to blotching" might be Solzhenitsyn hunched over Gulag records—so that the historical can seem "re-composed" at any moment, suggesting more of an opera or play than a "foreign" text. We might say it's the dramatic context that *effects* the translation.

Indeed, it was most natural for Johnson to present his poems as plays, set upon a stage along with the characters of poems' rediscoverer and author's relatives, poems' translator and assorted editors, poems' redactor and original publisher, and Kent himself, like Shakespeare occasionally, in an androgynous role of messenger. In one instance to which I was directed by Kent in an email, he uses the stage of a visual podcast: onscreen the poet at a desk, with the timing bar of the forty minute reading below him. Avuncular but dour, ur-translator Johnson read as if—like Curry reading Nichol—he was *forced* onto the stage, against his will, in order to make a living. Thus it became easier to imagine the "living" that Araki Yasusada had to make for himself as a poet after the war. It was a living breathed into him by the editors Tosa Motokiyu and others, all of them actors on Kent's stage. Coming together is a life provoked, under threat of extinction, and a poetic practice challenged by the literal extinction of the epic mode in our time. In addition, the deterioration of the lyric into aesthetic artifact no doubt kindled Johnson's resolve to mount a neo-Shakespearean play within the play.

Offstage however, Kent was the prototypical "family man," as if living the life Araki Yasusada lost in the catastrophe of Hiroshima. He took his sons on fishing trips to the Upper Peninsula and he manned the backyard barbecue while his wife regaled Midwest guests with tales of Kent's numerous *faux pas* among the corporate executives of his local college board, on which he served as a sort of *Monsieur Hulot* in the role of faculty dean and board chairman, I think. But the true *pas mal* manifest in all Johnson's work was the backdrop of twentieth century civilization's meltdown and its encapsulation in a reductive theater of history, with its monuments, sacred dates, and ritual silences. Instead, Kent's epic work dissolves our cultural history into a universal theater where living and dead, author and audience, all partake in the afterlife that is his spirit-inhabited poem.

In the passage that follows, Johnson brings yet another actor onstage to turn Yasusada himself into a translator:

from *Doubled Flowering:*

from "a transformation of poem #6 in Jack Spicer's *Language* (1965) . . ."

. . . If I pass my tongue through your speaking mouth, I know
    that there is nothing there. But if I hold my tongue inside
    a written sentence,
It blisters.
This is an act of forgetting that the dead are dead and that is that . . .

Take away the blistering of Hiroshima, and the words still record a literary history. But now the tongue "blisters inside a written sentence"—burnt from history into poetry, into "forgetting that the dead are dead." The "speaking mouth" still speaks within history and thus may speak from memory, but the written sentence is timeless: although it may exist after our deaths, even after our species' death, it is amnesiac. The sentence may record history, and itself be an artifact of history, but after Hiroshima, as at the moment of speaking, it is obliterated; now, since *literary* history is lost (or can even be imagined as lost), we are lost. And yet this poetry of loss links to others, to Spicer as well as Nichol and Johnson (both Spicer *aficionados*), to form a first draft of species consciousness.

Once, I received an emailed request from Kent to write a protest letter to the editor of Dave Eggers' *The Believer* magazine, which had just published an uncomprehending essay about Yasusada as if it all was an intentional "hoax"—and *nothing more*—by the poet Kent Johnson. Apparently, according to this clueless magazine critic, Johnson had even hoodwinked such critical wits as Marjorie Perloff and Mikhail Epstein. "Kent," I wrote back, "I can't find the current issue in Miami. Barnes & Noble's issue is two months out of date. Just write it yourself in my name and I'll sign and send." Not only was time of the essence but it was familiar practice for Johnson to appear to reconstruct his Japanese editors' notes about Yasusada from often cryptic, illegible or mistranslated text—so why not have him construe my comment for me as well? Knowing my work, he'd be perfectly able to imagine my response, according to his poetic practice.

Yet I couldn't keep from thinking: How far could Kent actually go; how deep into inhabiting my entire *oeuvre* could he imaginatively delve, not only annotating but extending my own poems and essays with his own hand? And even my decades of translations from the Bible! Just to have this thought speaks volumes about Kent's incorporation of criticism and translation into poetry. In the end, my wife found a current copy of *The Believer* the next day, on a Miami Beach muscle-magazine rack, and so I wrote the letter myself.

I was enraged as I read the piece. Its author was arrogantly intolerant of classical aesthetic perspective, in which *any* work of art can be claimed to be a hoax, since it promises ultimate truth and delivers ambiguity instead. Worse yet, distinctions could be made only in favor of authoritarian academic poets and against freedom-loving poems. Indeed, a freedom-loving poem was an oxymoron to *The Believer*'s one-party critic, who thought in terms of a work of art as rigidly enclosed artifact. Thus, the fascist Pound could be acclaimed as a true original while his poem, *The Cantos*, could be mocked for its liberties or its "hoax" of epic grandeur. Kent Johnson was no ultra-conservative like Pound or Kerouac, however, and so he was not in need of being apologized for as a humanitarian; and since he didn't need an apology, his epic excavation of the lost grandeur of Yasusada required more than simple mocking, according to *The Believer*: it needed excoriation as an *epic* "hoax" in itself. Our critic was a cartoon within a cartoon of Lenin-pure true believership.

This was not going to be a simple letter of protest to write! And so it was and is with all things Kent Johnsonian. They require a thorough restatement of history, whether of the origins of poetry, of civilization, or of Freudian resistance to self-knowledge. And thus, for the reader encountering a Kent Johnsonian text, a willingness is wanted to think through who one is and what one wants from art. Either that, or to allow the poem—whether in translation, in editorial conjecture, or even in a state of decomposition—to work of itself on one's open heart and mind. That "de-composition" could even entail the whole modern tradition, as represented by surrealism in the following passage:

from Doubled Flowering:

from Silk Tree Renga

>...Thus during sitting, he had felt the Milky Way as a pair of thongs between the toes
>...Why don't you go fuck yourself, she said, throwing the thong at his head and missing
>...In fact, in the very gesture of the geisha, was the retreat of a whole genre

Here, a parental editor, Johnson, is creating a documentary record of the final act of geisha tradition—and of surrealist tradition. The surrealism of "the Milky Way" reduced to *footwear* is no longer within a tenable tradition because history-telling itself no longer is. We are left with nothing more than the poet outside the poem, again as in Nichol and Berrigan. Nothing more than parenting figures, reproducers of the species for now. As was Stein herself, the silent figure of a psychoanalyst listening to language, and recording attentively as the subject—language itself—acted out every unconscious tic within it. When she became a parent to her own work late in life, especially in the lectures on narrative and America, she found a way to view her own oeuvre as a historical record of a lost civilization. As such, history-telling is the active force, just as it will be in our human future of space exploration: the question is not what exists on Mars now, but what it can tell us of what *once* was there and then suffered annihilation.

Few poets are able to embody their own character in this way, moving from active to parental. Stein rediscovered the genre of "lecture" in order to maintain this theater of parenting—of passing down knowledge—even if the lecture-audience became extinct. The play, as Shakespeare interiorized it, was the thing. And as Stein inhabited the lecturer, Johnson inhabits the editor, who, after annihilation, represents the most historically poignant and parental role of the poet.

> The poet's eye, in fine frenzy rolling,
> Doth glance from heaven to earth,
>   from earth to heaven;
> And as the imagination bodies forth
> The forms of things unknown, the poet's pen
> Turns them to shapes and gives to airy nothing . . .
>   from *A Midsummer Night's Dream*

So we may now read Johnson back into Shakespeare and understand that "airy nothing" was a Hiroshima or Auschwitz catastrophe; and the "poet's pen" that "turns them to shapes" is the editorial restoration of a history-of-relationships lost. Relationships of time and place, family and canon, language and genre. In fact, Johnson has become our Laertes: as the active poet Hamlet dies, it falls to Laertes to record the true (hence, inner) history of an entire court obliterated.

We can see this process at work in even the smallest poem, where species consciousness intervenes to rescue a devastated memory.

> *from* Doubled Flowering:
>
> [undated]
>
> Faint memory
> of her lithe body—
> wet smacking
> of the mud snails.

In the last two lines we encounter the putative author through his perception of sound and sense. The immediacy of it, the litheness of the snail bodies (who would have thought it) puts us in the picture with him, there by the shore, a long way from both "her" body and the memory of it, "faint." In fact what the snails tell us is that the memory is lost and only the present sense remains. So from the "faint memory" of the presumed author to the lost memory of the actual author is to step outside the poem and encounter the magnitude of the loss. Snails are all that's left to him, an alien species; however, at least they are alive, and even the mud is alive, echoing the same mud out of which Adam was created. And so, another species is possible, and that is the essence of species consciousness. (In the sensibility of a lesser poet, one who had not been totally inhabited by loss, this poem might have been accounted as deadpan surrealism or even a Poundian parody of haiku.)

As if anticipating my parenthetical thought, Johnson has appended to his first volume of Yasusada material, *Doubled Flowering*, a twenty-page essay, earlier published by the venerable poetry critic, Marjorie Perloff.

> The Yasusada case, I shall argue here, can be understood as a reaction formation experienced by a literary community that no longer trusts the individual talent to rise above mass culture and hence must find a poetry worthy of its attention in increasingly remote and improbable locations. (*Doubled* 152)

There is something improbable about this description of a "higher" literary community, one that considers itself above concern with hoaxes—that is, too smart to be conned—and instead absorbed by the highly exotic, putative Hiroshima-surviving poet, Yasusada, while more radically confused (another con) about the difference between uniqueness and genius. For Johnson has himself re-created this "community" within his book, as a presumed community of translators and editors, dead and alive, and this literary community is above all blind and deaf to the representation of itself. For it's really of secondary import that the critics and editors of slick poetry publications had been "taken in" and had prominently published Yasusada (the "case" referred to by Perloff), because they were themselves mere ciphers of an ersatz cultural moment called "postmodern" and reflected in Araki Yasusada's tribe of post-Yasusada translators and editors. In fact, Kent Johnson had created a capacious if convex mirror for several generations of postwar poets and critics.

And most liked what they saw in it—that is, until they realized it was them! On the other hand, for those who, like Perloff, appreciated the layers of authorship involved, it was in danger of being categorized as a Kent Johnsonian style, and even reduced to one side or other of the repressed politics of form, be it academic or experimental. On the latter side, Johnson might be sat beside any other postmodern striver and blurrer of genres, where he could be gorged upon in terms of identity poetics (aka identity *politics*). On to the next essay and the next innovative poets, Perloff might have said to herself, upon completing this splendid piece on Johnson. But that would be a mistaken move, because what the Yasusada "case" requires is that everything just stop and start all over, including the academic canon and its passion to add an original living poet to its library display and thereby continue to authenticate it.

But the authentic really demands we stop everything and go back. Back to the Sumerians, if we can, or to Paleolithic artists, in order to forget all about "post" anything. Instead, we must concentrate on the "pre"—prehistoric, pre-Biblical, pre-Romantic, and especially, pre-Postmodern. This last is the niche that Yasusada has blazed for our dimming civilization today, opening new possibilities of *pre-Nuclear* and *pre-Holocaust* and the radical poignancy of such deep restoration of the annihilated. If we can get back there, we can imagine a different history and a poetics based upon it, one with the ability to recognize the monster in Hitler before he has consumed us, and before he can reconstitute himself in contemporary Iran. It can be a historical poetics, one in which we take parental responsibility for all human degradation and murderous experiment. And then, we give it dramatic outlet in a *Homo sapiens* theater of species consciousness, in which we might imagine ourselves as other species to come—or simply, other species, less inclined to species grandiosity.

Coda

I've referred in this essay to the academic or experimental canon, by which I meant in either case the Western canon; it is a covering still desperately reached for in our time, as if to "shore up our ruins." But even T. S. Eliot's biting irony has faded these days, so that the Western canon has devolved into a shadow of itself, merely an academic canon. What has arisen in its stead is still not allowed in the classroom, for it requires the authentic poet's reframing of the literary art. Such a reconstitution at first seems interdisciplinary, in that the authors bring to bear on literature an aesthetic derived elsewhere, as from the visual arts, psychology, metaphysics, archaeology, linguistics or the social sciences. Today, as is prefigured by the authentic poets discussed here, it is an interdisciplinary education in natural sciences that is almost prophetically advised. It is in the awareness that something more than a canon is needed, something we can now distinguish as species knowledge—now, that is, that we're confronted with our inevitable extinction. Knowing that, the authentic poet shows the way toward a hopeful framing of our knowledge for its voyage into the future, as in the space rocket sent free of our solar system and carrying some tokens of us.

I don't think the Bible or Shakespeare was among those tokens; rather, some brief lines, befitting the short attention spans we might expect to encounter among those who were not expecting us. But Earth itself is a spacecraft, and even here species continue to evolve, and thus we can ask more local questions. How will a further iteration of Homo sapiens, were it to evolve, look at our human artifacts? That is the awareness a poet can bring to his work now. The way has already been prepared by the authentic poet of the late Twentieth Century.

Although we can valuably read Berrigan, Nichol and Johnson back into Chaucer and Shakespeare, Hölderlin and Mallarmé, this doesn't mean simply a broadening of the Western canon. Instead, we might reckon that canon's limitations by light of a competing canon of less self-consciously bookish but nevertheless ingeniously authored works, from the Bible and the Talmud set against the Greco-Roman, to Moses de Leon's *Zohar* set against Dante's *Divine Comedy*, to Thoreau's multi-volumed *Journal* set against James Schuyler's *The Morning of the Poem*. Who would we set against Berrigan, Nichol and Johnson? There's always the novelty of newly translated works, ancient or modern, from India or China or wherever. When an ancient Sanskrit work is finally understood in terms of its authorship by a poet-scholar yet to come, we might recognize in it a parallel creation to bpNichol's universal theater. I would submit that what is most thrilling about reading the authentic poets today is that we don't yet know into what proper canon they might fall—or whether, in fact, they are not heralds to the newly forming canon of species consciousness.

David Rosenberg

Meanwhile, a creative writing professor and colleague of mine reports that his students long to try out "hybrid" forms and to break free of rigid genres. This makes sense in an academic setting, where genres are taught as if they originated at creation; still, the creative drive to blur the boundaries between genres is also a handicap to critical reading. I wonder why my friend doesn't counsel his students to not need exclusively to "write" but instead to *read*, as in the natural sciences, where "reading" the world and its evolutionary history is already half way toward re-dramatizing—and re-composing—a thoroughly cosmic theater. The beginning of cosmic theaters are still to be found in the creation or transformation myths of all religions, as they are later deconstructed and dramatized by the Hebraic culture's poets, to take the Bible for one example. So let's recall, for our moment, that it is the authentic poet who sets the stage and gives life to the audience—and who survives his own death by secreting himself in the wings, as if a dispassionate observer of his own life, some forgotten kind of poetic scientist.

Works Cited

Berrigan, Ted. *Collected Poems*. Ed. Alice Notley, with Anselm Berrigan and Edmund Berrigan. Berkeley, Los Angeles, London: University of California Press, 2005.
Motokiyu, Tosa. *Also, With My Throat, I Shall Swallow Ten Thousand Swords*. Ed. Kent Johnson and Javier Alvarez. Cumberland, RI: Combo Books, 2005.
Nichol, bp. *Martyrology. Books 1 and 2*. Toronto: Coach House, 1994.
_____. *Martyrology, Books 3 and 4*. Toronto: Coach House, 1994.
_____. *Martyrology, Book 5*. Toronto: Coach House, 1994.
_____. *Martyrology, Book 6*. Toronto: Coach House, 1994.
_____. *Martyrology, Books 7&*. Toronto: Coach House, 1994.
_____. *Ad Sanctos: Martyrology, Book 9*. Toronto: Coach House, 1998.
Spicer, Jack. *Language*. San Francisco: White Rabbit Press, 1965.
Yasusada, Araki. *Doubled Flowering: From the Notebooks of Araki Yasusada*, edited and translated by Tosa Motokiyu, Ojiu Norinaga, and Okura Kyogin. New York: Roof Books, 1997.

Illegible Due to Blotching:
Poetic Authenticity and its Discontents

David Wojahn

No book of poetry of the past decade has attracted quite the same attention as Ted Hughes' *Birthday Letters*. Released simultaneously in Britain and the United States in January of 1998, the book sold out several printings on both sides of the Atlantic within weeks, was reviewed respectfully and frequently, and even became the subject of front page news items and feature stories, something unheard of for a book of poetry, even one by a well-established poet such as Hughes, who was Britain's poet laureate, and who died of cancer within a few months of the book's publication. Of course the reason for the book's popularity has as much or more to do with the public's craving for scandal and gossip than it does with literature. As everyone knows, *Birthday Letters* is addressed to Hughes' late wife, the American poet Sylvia Plath, whose poems are anthologized for the college market at least as frequently as those of Donne and Chaucer, and whose turbulent relationship with Hughes, culminating in her suicide after Hughes had left her for another woman, seems a motivating force behind many of Plath's best-known poems. Hughes had for over three decades kept a public silence about the pair's relationship save to act as editor of several volumes of Plath's posthumously published poetry and prose. But now, with *Birthday Letters*, readers were finally to get Hughes' side of the story. It's no wonder, then, that by March of 1998 the volume had sold over 125,000 copies in the U.S. alone—during a time when print runs for poetry are normally less then a hundredth of that amount (Brown 12). Sales continued to climb in the following months, and Hughes had sold the movie rights to the volume. The Merchant-Ivory team has a film adaptation of the book in development, and leaked portions of Ivory's script, entitled *The Dead Bell*, have made their way onto several of the websites devoted to Plath. Merchant-Ivory has even signed on, with Hughes' apparent blessing, the actors who will portray the pair. British actor Gary Oldman seems to have been selected for the role of Hughes, and, after actresses such as Nicole Kidman and Jodie Foster had been rumored to be in contention for the part, the role of Plath was awarded to Gwyneth Paltrow. The May, 1998, issue of *Vanity Fair* quotes Hughes' reaction to hearing Paltrow read for the part of Plath: "She *was* Sylvia. When she read 'Lady Lazarus,' my hair stood on end—it was as if a time machine had shuttled me back half a lifetime ago" (D'Agostino 59).

Unfortunately, however, the public may have to wait a very long time before seeing *Birthday Letters* on the big screen. The movie is likely to be put on hold indefinitely now that the strangest chapter of all in the Hughes-Plath saga has begun to unfold. The British Sunday newspaper, *The Observer*, was the first to break the story early in June, and it has since rocked the literary world, becoming a scandal which even threatens to shake the foundations of the several British governmental ministries. On June 8, 1999, *The Observer* revealed what had, for five decades, been a secret known only to a handful of operatives in the British Intelligence Service, MI5. Neither Ted Hughes nor Sylvia Plath ever existed (Olsen 13–15). The pair were in fact the product of a hugely elaborate literary hoax—or more properly a literary conspiracy—originally concocted by MI5 in the 1950s as one of the more Byzantine operations of the Cold War, and continuing in an ever-more greatly elaborate form into the recent past, when the escalating costs of the hoax prompted the Blair government to downsize the project by alleging that "Ted Hughes" had died. That the intelligence community would be willing to perpetuate a hoax of this particular type and magnitude may at first seem to beggar the imagination. But the reasons for the continuing existence of MI5's Hughes-Plath operation are in some respects self-evident ones, typical of most government agencies. What started as a simple project of minor disinformation and espionage turned instead into a governmental White Elephant fed by a bloated bureaucracy. Although the exact budgetary figures remain secret, it is likely that the MI5 division responsible for perpetuating the Hughes-Plath Hoax, code named Operation Ariel, at one time employed between one hundred and one hundred and fifty full-time workers, operating from a secret suite of offices in Whitechapel. Over the years this group has been responsible for creating the entire oeuvre, published and in manuscript form, of Hughes and Plath, for training and coaching the agents assigned to act the parts of Hughes, Plath, and their family members, and for sustaining the campaign of disinformation designed to prevent readers and scholars from discovering the government's ruse. It appears that the secrecy of the operation began to unravel this spring when retired MI5 operative Michael Weldon, one of the four agents who over the years had been assigned to impersonate Hughes, made a deathbed confession of his role in the conspiracy to freelance journalist Wilfred Olsen. Olsen then sold the story to *The Observer* and the rest is history, though history of a most improbable sort, proving once again that fact is stranger than fiction.

Operation Ariel seems to have begun in the middle 1950s, when a group of MI5 specialists on "cultural intelligence" surveyed the post-war British literary scene and in a top-secret white paper came to several troubling conclusions, one of which was that poetry in England was in a bad way. British literature, like the British empire itself, was in decline, and of all the literary arts, poetry seemed the most moribund. T.S. Eliot, the only poet of international stature dwelling in the U.K., was not a native Briton, and had lapsed into poetic silence. The younger generation of poets was indifferently talented, and Philip Larkin and Thom Gunn, its most promising figures, were problematic, at least as far as the government was concerned. Larkin, a balding and misanthropic Hull librarian, was decidedly unsexy, hardly the dashing and Byronic figure who MI5 felt would be required for the salvation of British poesy. And Gunn, although he surely cut a sexier figure than Larkin, was sexy in the wrong way: Agency surveillance and phone taps revealed what several operatives had long suspected: Gunn was "an invert." The white paper concluded by noting with alarm that poetry in the Soviet Union and in several of its Eastern bloc satellites was thriving. A "poetry gap" existed, and MI5 arrived at a novel means to close it. Seeing that no suitable young British poet existed, a small special operations unit of the agency set about creating one, and so, toward the end of 1955, "Ted Hughes" was born, savior-to-be of British poetry. The name was suitably manly, and the character was given a background deemed appropriate for a poet designed to act as the bard of a democratic and classless post-war Britain. "Theodore Hughes," and "T.H. Hughes," the poet's original monikers, were rejected for sounding elitist. A cover story for Hughes was devised—an upbringing on a Yorkshire farm, a B.A. from Cambridge—and an operative was selected to act the part of Hughes in public. Hughes' verse, however, would be authored by a committee of specially trained agents operating out of a small basement office in

Whitechapel. Within its first two years the operation was judged a rousing success, so much so that MI5 sought to expand its range by creating an American poetess to act as Hughes' companion, and it is at this point that Operation Ariel became a joint MI5 and CIA operation. In order to symbolically present the spirit of Britain and America's close alliance in the Cold War, Sylvia Plath was devised, and several young CIA operatives, most of them recent graduates of Seven Sisters schools such as Smith and Vassar, were sent to London to assist the project. Various individuals of the Project Ariel office team devised the poems which later appeared in Hughes' first two collections, *Hawk in the Rain* and *Lupercal*, as well as those poems which were gathered in Plath's debut volume, *The Colossus*. As the poems were composed, microfilm versions of their drafts and finished versions were left at various drop-off points for the operatives impersonating Plath and Hughes. Although none of the members of the Ariel Project's office team had written much verse prior to their assignment to the project, perusal of some literary journals and anthologies gave the team its models. Some of the poems were co-written by project members; others were the work of operatives working alone. Winnifred Eimers, a young CIA recruit who is now living in retirement in Florida, and who later played a crucial role in the CIA's botched efforts to assassinate Castro, and a young Cornishwoman named Millicent Shollworth seem to have been the most prolific authors of the Hughes and Plath oeuvre. It is Shollworth, in fact, who may be the indirect cause for the formation of the Plath cult—which seems to have arisen for reasons of expedience having little to do with the Ariel Project's original intents: Shollworth, born into a family of radical socialists and fluent in both Russian and Polish, made contact with Soviet agents during a 1961 trip to Frankfurt. Alerted to the success of the Ariel Project, and suffering major setbacks in their own poetry fabrication operations, the Russians sought both intelligence information and creative support. Shollworth provided them with both, and for two years acted as a double agent before defecting to Russia in February, 1963. Shollworth is one of the most brilliant and devious figures of Cold War espionage, and her defection hurt the Ariel Project greatly, for MI5 quickly realized that no other of its operatives could turn out Plath poetry of quite the same intensity and quality. Embarrassed at the loss of its best poetry operative to the KGB, MI5 decided to call in from the cold its agent impersonating Plath, and close down the Plath division of Project Ariel entirely. A cover story was then devised in which Plath would kill herself in reaction to Hughes' infidelity and as a consequence of her long history of mental instability. There would be no more Plath poems.

And yet the fact that there would be no more Plath poems did not stop the Plath Juggernaut, a consequence wholly unforeseen by MI5. The public, attracted both to the Plath fabrications themselves and to the glamorously tragic circumstances which had been invented to explain her death, could not get enough of the dead poet, and since 1963 the primary purpose of Project Ariel has been to simultaneously propagandize for the Plath Industry and to conceal the Plath/Hughes conspiracy; the 1963 decision to kill Plath off by suicide is one that many in the agency came to rue. As one anonymous operative who worked on the project during the crisis year of 1963 told the BBC last month, "We would all have been better off if we'd done her in some other way. No one makes a cult of someone killed by a falling brick or run over by a lorry." Although the staff of the Ariel Project has grown ever-larger over the years, Plath's estate has generated a considerable income through book sales and reprint permission fees, and this has turned out to be an unforeseen boon to the agency. In his most recent *Observer* piece journalist Wilfred Olsen alleges that in the mid-1980s at least some of this money was laundered by MI5 operatives Tomas Disch and William A. Logan through a Cayman island numbered account and used by MI5 and the CIA to fund various covert activities in Latin America. Both Logan and Disch were later found garroted in a Guatemala City brothel, probably the victims of a Sandinista hit squad. In other words, Lady Lazarus helped to purchase Contra rifles, and was responsible for more deaths than her own imaginary one. Over the years, the Project's Plath-related activities have tended to overshadow those centered around Hughes, so much so that assignment to the project's Hughes bureau was seen by many in the agency as the kiss of death, the province of has-beens and burnt-out cases charged primarily to pen children's books and laureate doggerel about royal christenings. The agency's neglect of its Hughes activities' production in recent years eventually became a source of embarrassment for MI5, and the creation of *Birthday Letters* last year was meant to rectify this problem. It was designed to be the poet's final production, and thereafter Hughes, too, would be killed off.

Anyone who has watched the news in recent weeks is aware of the repercussions of the Plath/Hughes hoax's exposure, both in London and to a lesser extent in Washington. Investigations have been launched by Parliament, the Blair government has replaced a number of ministers, and it seems only a matter of time before Operation Ariel is shut down for good. In Washington, Senator Jesse Helms, bemoaning the CIA's involvement in a project deemed by him as frivolous, has used the scandal as an opportunity to once again call for the abolition of the NEA. Winnifred Eimers' subsequent appearance on *Nightline* to explain to Ted Koppel how she composed certain of the Plath poems garnered ratings which hadn't been seen since the Simpson trial. The media's feeding frenzy about all things Ariel in recent weeks has been so rabid as to overwhelm those voices, largely from the academy, who have speculated about what all this means for contemporary literature. After all, two of our era's principal poets, one of whom has been seen by many as a feminist and literary martyr, and whose poems have been the most enduring example of what has come to be known as "confessional" poetry, have been shown to be forgeries. Critics of a Foucauldian bent have seen the Plath/Hughes hoax as further proof that it is culture and power dynamics which create literary texts, and not authors. "This hoax makes the best argument yet for anti-essentialism," wrote Language Poet Charles Bernstein when the scandal broke (33). And surely the literary reputations of Plath and Hughes will now undergo a reappraisal. Here is how Richard Howard regards the situation: "The easy felicities of the Plath authors' more canonical strophes, for many readers, myself regrettably included, have always carried with them the faintly detestable aroma of mere *applied* poetry. I have never regarded the oeuvre with the enthusiasm typical of the Plath authors' legions of admirers. Today the work must be regarded with an even more assertive suspicion and—dare I say it?—disdain" (Cullum 176). And yet for others the significance of the Plath/Hughes canon remains undiminished. As actor David Duchovny put it on a recent airing of CNN's *Crossfire* devoted to the scandal, "Plath's poems have changed my life, and my way of thinking. I guess I'll always return to them; it doesn't matter if they were written by her or by a committee of

Scubadivers and Chrysanthemums

British bureaucrats or a coven of literary-minded extraterrestrials." And Duchovny may indeed speak for many of us as we continue to survey the consequences of our knowledge that Sylvia Plath and Ted Hughes exist only in the form of their poetry. Perhaps that particular form of existence is all that readers require; perhaps not.

Ah, post-modernism. Forgive me, gentle reader, for in the course of this tale adding certain embellishments to the facts. I admit to the possibility that Ted Hughes may have indeed existed, that Sylvia Plath may have existed as well, and that they themselves, or individuals quite similar to them, may have at one time or another written at least some of their poems. But in an era in which all of our negotiations with fact, all of our confrontations with what once was known as reality, have become ever more convoluted and daunting, in which virtual realities have cheerfully annexed the last remaining provinces of self-evident truth, in which po-mo fragmentation, pastiche, and a Pavlovian tic of irony as the proper response to all human endeavors informs or afflicts us all, the question is no longer, "Is it real or is it Memorex?"—it is instead that *everything* is Memorex, and what shall we do now? This condition creates all manner of hilarity, strangeness, ethical relativism, and what might be called factual relativism. During the weeks in which I first worked on these pages, a university where I once taught allowed a Holocaust denier with spurious academic credentials to give a speech on its campus—after all, shouldn't "all sides" be represented regarding this "issue"? Bob Hope died at the hands of an AP wire-service report, was eulogized in Congress, and then, in the fashion of Christ and Osiris, was miraculously resurrected; a fired reporter of *The New Republic* admitted that twenty-seven of the forty-one stories he wrote for the magazine were fabrications; serial killer Henry Lee Lucas, who had confessed to some two hundred slayings, but probably inflated that figure, finally was given a date with Old Sparky—although there is little evidence that the particular murder he is being executed for is actually one of his productions; a group of teenagers in an Atlanta suburb was arrested for passing counterfeit twenties, using as their printing press the same model of three-hundred dollar ink-jet printer with which I will copy this essay; and the radio blaring from the used car lot across my street had twice in as many days oozed "Unforgettable," a wretched "virtual" duet sung by Nat "King" Cole and his daughter Natalie, its recording completed several decades after the former's death. This bit of necrophilical treacle was then replaced by a news report of the death of Khmer Rouge generalissimo Pol Pot, perhaps the most infamous practitioner of moral relativism of our time, who declared 1976 the Year Zero, and then murdered two million in order to commemorate the birth of this blessed New Order. But wait—there seems to have been a factual glitch even here: several of the journalists who were brought to view and video the remains claimed that the corpse rotting in the jungle heat beneath their klieg lights could not be Pol Pot. Wrong morphology, something about facial scars that are missing; the "real" Pol Pot apparently had less hair, what there was of it was gray, and he was presumably too busy eluding capture to enroll in the Men's Hair Club or purchase some Grecian Formula. Is it possible that Pol Pot's death was faked? The decomposing body may have been a real one, but it was a Memorex Antichrist. And who would manufacture this stinking simulacrum?

Seeing of course is never believing, which is why the Zapruder Film is the century's most studied example of cinematic art. And what, by the way, *is* art? If I were to aim my mouse to close this document, fire up my printer, and copy on the ink jet a pair of twenties, would I be able to call them poems? I am, after all, an author of poetry and not a counterfeiter, and with a poet's characteristic hubris see myself as one of the last remaining custodians of the authentic. But then I must remind myself that authors no longer exist, having all gone the way of the dinosaur around the time of Foucault's famous 1969 essay, in which I have become instead a rather dreary and ineffectual cultural product, "linked to the juridical and institutional system that encompasses, determines, and articulates the universe of discourses" (Foucault 116).

Foucault dances upon the grave of my kind, declares his own version of Year Zero, and tells us that we have been replaced by a new sort of creature which he christens "the author function." It's an intriguing term, sounding more like an option you can order on a luxury car than anything you could regard as bardic. In other words, were I to print up my counterfeit twenties, I couldn't even claim them as my own, although, ironically, I *could* make the claim that the bills were not in fact counterfeit, in the same way that Andy Warhol could assert that the various hangers-on from his Factory who he sent out to impersonate him on lucrative campus speaking tours were just as good as the real thing. And who's to say that Andy wasn't right? He would have known best, after all.

But I'm telling you things which you already know, and have known for quite some time. As Hugh Kenner put it twenty years ago in a study which he entitled *The Counterfeiters*, "We are deep, these days, in the counterfeit, and have long since had to forego easy criteria for what is 'real'" (Kenner 20). Yet no longer are we merely "deep" in the counterfeit: today we are in over our heads. But is this water real or is it Memorex? Words once synonymous with truth and actuality today seem quaint—"authenticity" snorts right-wing pundit George Will in a recent column, "that's a '60s word"—while words such as counterfeit, hoax, forgery, fabrication, plagiarism, deception, and fake have come to seem woefully inadequate in defining the degrees, subtleties, and purposes of the falsehoods we perpetrate and which are perpetrated upon us, as well as the necessary fictions, the anodyne masks, and various alternative realities which some of us who dwell outside the mainstream must inhabit. Drag queens will sometimes tell you that their personae are just as real as their other selves, and who is to say this claim isn't true? Like the Eskimos with their thirty-seven words for different kinds of snow, our culture demands a taxonomy of the bogus. As a gay friend of mine put it as we waited in line for a screening of *The Truman Show*, there is "good bogus" and "bad bogus," much in the way that there is good cholesterol and bad cholesterol. And there are ever so many shadings of bogus which range between these poles.

One small example of why this is the case can be seen in the continuing controversy over the Araki Yasusada hoax—which is, I should add, a real hoax, not a phony hoax in the manner of my Hughes/Plath conspiracy. Of course there are some Yasusada proponents who would claim he is not, strictly speaking, a hoax, though even they will admit that a corporeal Yasusada never existed. Who is Yasusada? There seem to be two prevailing opinions. The first offers the more certain definition. He was born in Kyoto in 1907, studied Western Literature at Hiroshima University but left before finishing a degree. He worked as a military postman in Hiroshima, and survived the atomic bomb blast of 1945, which killed his wife and one of his two daughters. The surviving girl, Akiko, perished in 1949 as a result of radiation sickness. Yasusada himself died of cancer in 1972. He was fluent in Western languages, and was an eager but unpublished participant in several Japanese avant-garde literary movements, most prominently in the "Layered Clouds" group. He was influenced by classical Japanese poetry, as well as by modern Western writers, two of his favorite of whom were Roland Barthes and Jack Spicer. His importance as a poet began to be recognized when, as his translator/editors Tosa Motokiyu, Ojiu Norinaga, and Okura Kyojin write:

> The notebooks of the Hiroshima poet Araki Yasusada were discovered by his son in 1980, eight years after the poet's death. The manuscripts comprise fourteen spiral notebooks whose pages are filled with poems, drafts, English assignments, diary entries, recordings of Zen dokusan encounters, and other matter. In addition, the notebooks are interleaved with hundreds of insertions, including drawings, received correspondence, and carbon copies of the poet's letters. (*Doubled* 10).

This biographical sketch, with small variations, appeared along with translations of the Yasusada documents which were published with some frequency in a number of quarterlies, among them *Grand Street*, *Conjunctions*, *Stand*, and—in the po-biz equivalent of making the cover of *Rolling Stone*—as a special supplement in *American Poetry Review*, which also reproduced a pencil portrait of Yasusada and included bio sketches of his three translators. As Marjorie Perloff later noted in what will probably be the definitive essay on his work, Yasusada had a Zelig-like capacity to be a poet for every aesthetic, every poetic party line. Those craving what—thanks to Carolyn Forché's problematic Norton anthology *Against Forgetting*—has come to be called "a poetry of witness," had a bona-fide Hiroshima survivor to champion, a *hibakusha* who also happened to be a little more talented (at least for Western sensibilities) than other Hiroshima survivor poets whose work had appeared in translation. Avant-gardists had a genuine specimen, too. Language-poet Ron Silliman singled out for rapturous praise a Yasusada effort entitled 'Telescope with Urn,' largely on the basis of its arresting first line, "The image of the galaxies spreads out like a cloud of sperm" (*Doubled* 32). Yasusada was, said Silliman, "a poet whose work simply takes my breath away" (qtd. in Perloff 26; *Scubadivers* 24). The cause of multiculturalism was also of course served by Yasusada, for although he was influenced by Anglo-European modernism, his Zen-inflected oxymorons seemed to wonderfully represent a non-Eurocentric "other-ness." And even so-called "mainstream" poets who would chose to remain aloof from the identity politics and aesthetic factionalism of today's poetics, found something to admire in the emotional nakedness and confessional vulnerability of certain of the Yasusada poems. Yasusada was poised on the edge of posthumous fame: Wesleyan University Press was about to issue a book-length selection of his poems and notebook entries; he was also to be represented in the second volume of Pierre Joris and Jerome Rothenberg's massive anthology of twentieth-century world poetry, *Poems for the Millennium* (Perloff 29; 31 [citation]). Were the MacArthur Foundation awards not limited to living writers, Yasusada would likely to have added that prize to his resume as well.

The other definition of Araki Yasusada is best conveyed by the following announcement printed in the pages of the Sept./Oct., 1996, issue of *American Poetry Review:*

To Our Readers:

We regret the publication of 'Doubled Flowering: From the Notebooks of Araki Yasusada' in our July/August issue. Neither Araki Yasusada nor the three names identified as his translators, "Tosa Motokiyu," "Okura Kyojin," "Ojiu Norinaga" are actual persons. The facts in the note, 'Introducing Araki Yasusada' as well as the 'Portrait of Yasusada,' are a hoax. All of the materials came to us from Kent Johnson of Highland Community College in Freeport, Illinois, an actual person who represented himself as the close friend of the ill and incapacitated "translator" Tosa Motokiyu. Kent Johnson has admitted the above ruse, and has claimed the materials were written by an unnamed American poet whose name he refuses to reveal. Still other persons may be involved, as the hoax was carried out with the aid of a post office box in Sebastopol, California, an address in Tokyo, an address in London, and a disconnected phone number in Springfield, Illinois.
(*APR* 14).

David Wojahn

So there you have it. The feces had hit the (Japanese) fan. And the reactions to this occurrence are perhaps as interesting as the Yasusada poems themselves. The editors who had been duped were of course furious. Wesleyan deep-sixed the book-length manuscript, "concerned about the ethical issues involved" (Nussbaum 84). Poet Arthur Vogelsang, an editor of *APR*, was quoted in an article in *Lingua Franca* as calling the Yasusada hoax "a criminal act," and *Conjunctions* editor Bradford Morrow did an about-face regarding the poems he had earlier published, castigating them as "coy, self-satisfied, glib" (Nussbaum 82). The Japanese media saw the case as another example of Japan-bashing, and a group of Asian-American writers co-signed a statement denouncing the Yasusada writings as racist (Chang 34). With hindsight it was pointed out that many of the Yasusada documents should have been suspect from the start. Yasusada seems to have sung the praises of certain writings by Barthes, Celan, and Spicer before they were even written, and Hiroshima University, which Yasusada was supposed to have attended in the '20s, was not founded until 1949 (Perloff 27; *Scubadivers* 26). And the material itself should have been a giveaway: John Solt, an Amherst professor of Japanese culture, characterized it all as "Japanized crap," crudely devised to fit Western preconceptions of Japanese culture (qtd. in Nussbaum 83). Also, certain of the documents are so implausible as to have been intentionally comic: could Yasusada *really* have preserved so many English-language exercises done for an instructor named "Mr. Rogers," a Scotsman who seems to have done his teaching in a kilt? ("What is the meaning of those broom-like forms attached to the front of his skirt?" asks Yasusada.) Would he *really* have attempted to engage in a correspondence with Jack Spicer, who himself engaged in an imaginary correspondence with Garcia Lorca and "translated" Lorca poems which were in fact his own creations? And what about that pencil portrait of Yasusada published in *APR* and later in *Lingua Franca*? A friend of mine who is a connoisseur of Hong-Kong action films swears that the sketch is actually one of Hong Kong movie mogul Run Run Shaw. But perhaps Yasusada merely resembles him—yet, to speculate about this may be another way of saying that all Asians look alike. One writer even claimed that "Araki Yasusada" is an anagram for "Klaatu, niktu, barata," Patricia Neal's famous command to Gork the Robot in *The Day the Earth Stood Still*, although this is plainly not the case (Young 43). No wonder that editors and readers felt taken in; they should have known in the first place.

Furthermore, the scandal around the hoax seems to have refused to go away, and—again—for some fascinating reasons. A year after the news broke, I found myself at a party during a writers' conference where I was teaching along with Arthur Vogelsang. (Or someone who I presume to be Arthur Vogelsang: unlike Andy Warhol, poets haven't the resources to send out impersonators.) Never having been exactly diplomatic in situations such as this, I asked him to talk about the Yasusada hoax, and about Marjorie Perloff's recently published *Boston Review* essay on Yasusada, which was largely sympathetic toward Yasusada, but rather merciless in regard to certain of the motives of editors he had duped. Like an elderly widow talking to police detectives about the gigolo who'd bilked her of her savings, Arthur spoke of Yasusada with a mixture of astonishment and rage. And could you blame him for this? As for Perloff's essay, he admitted it was pretty smart, smarter still if you were to share Arthur's suspicion—later expressed by him in a *Boston Review* symposium on the hoax—that Perloff herself is the likely author of the Yasusada documents (Vogelsang 34). Johnson, according to this and similar scenarios, may be only an "unindicted co-conspirator" who might be working with a whole syndicate of Yasusada hoaxers, whose ranks may include the critic Eliot Weinberger (who is, with Perloff, one of Yasusada's most fervent supporters, having called him "the greatest poet of Hiroshima and its most unreliable witness"), Johnson's former teacher, the poet Howard McCord, and various others whom not even the resources and doggedness of Kenneth Starr would be able to identify (Weinberger 37; *Scubadivers* 22). Johnson, for his part, has responded to all this with some spin-controlling faxes to editors he'd bamboozled, with a slippery interview published in *Denver Quarterly*, and a continued insistence that, if Yasusada doesn't exist, his creator Tosa Motokiyu—who Johnson claims was his roommate in Milwaukee in the 1980s—certainly does, or did (Johnson 122–133). It seems that Motokiyu—or "Moto," as Johnson nicknames him—died of cancer shortly before the scandal broke. Some of these interviews with Johnson are alleged to have been co-written with an associate named Javier Alvarez, who lives in Mexico City. Never mind that Javier Alvarez is also the name of a Bolivian diplomat who appears in the Yasusada

David Wojahn

notebooks as a literary acquaintance of Yasusada's and who died in the Hiroshima bomb blast. Perhaps this is another Javier Alvarez—or perhaps Javier has been miraculously resurrected. (If Bob Hope can do it, why can't he?) There's also a Russian critic named Mikhail Epstein involved in this process, but let's not go into that. Johnson's spin-control in these documents is an interesting mixture of current theoretical dogma and chicanery. The most telling passage occurs in a fax to British poet Jon Silkin, whose *Stand* was one of the journals taken in by Yasusada. With small variations, what follows is the phrasing Johnson adopts in several such situations. After listing some famous examples of other writers who adopted alter egos, among them Pessoa, Kierkegaard, and Pushkin, Johnson tells him:

> These writers, as I'm sure you know, wrote and published important portions of their works "as" others. For them, anonymity was not a "trick," but a need, something intrinsic to their creative drive at given times. Likewise for Moto, anonymity—and its efflorescence into multiple names—was a gateway to a radically sincere (I use that word with care) expression of empathy. Rather than being "fakes," I would offer that the Yasusada writings represent an original and courageous form of *authenticity*—one that is perhaps difficult to appreciate because of the extent to which individual authorial status and self-promotion dominate our thinking about, and practice of, poetry. (qtd. in Silkin 44).

"Radically . . . sincere empathy"—Johnson may be using such terms guardedly, but even the most charitable reader of this statement would have to characterize it as singularly self-congratulatory. Does this mean that to write in a Hiroshima survivor's voice is an act of only partial empathy, while going to the trouble to make your survivor an outright forgery is empathy of a more groundbreaking and courageous sort? This is not an arch question under these circumstances, because there is evidence that Johnson pondered it for a long while. While looking through some old quarterlies the other day I came across a 1987 issue of Michael Cuddihy's now-defunct *Ironwood* and there, on the page facing a poem of my own, begin three poems 'From the Notebooks of Ogiwara Miyamori'—by Kent Johnson (Daybook 187–191). All three of these were later reprinted under Yasusada's name, including one alleged to be Yasusada's final poem, written on his deathbed. So, in 1987, Johnson seems only to have been writing monologues in the voice of a Hiroshima poet. Dramatic monologues are certainly not anything new or "radical" in literature (although one might question the appropriateness of an Anglo poet speaking in the voice of a *hibakusha*, just as I myself now might question the appropriateness of the poem of mine which faces Johnson's, in which I decided to turn one of my closest friends, a perfectly healthy individual, into a deaf mute). But somewhere along the line Johnson decided that it wasn't enough to impersonate his *hibakusha*; instead he had to *be* him. We are back to the question of what is real and what is Memorex: is 'Trilobites,' which appears in *Ironwood* under Johnson's name, written in the persona of Ogiwara Miyamori, a less successful or empathic poem than the identical version which later appears as Yasusada's? Johnson would seem to think so, though there's a certain smugness and reliance on post-structural cant in the way that Johnson makes his points to the editors that gives you to suspect that it's all an effete game for him. "Radical empathy" seems not to include carrying the Yasusada part to its logical conclusion and, for example, purchasing a couple grams of plutonium from some renegade Soviet scientists in order to more authentically method-act the effects of Yasusada's radiation sickness. This is radical empathy without the hair loss and diarrhea, radical empathy as a problem of technique, as just one more aspect of "author function." But here I am launching an *ad hominem* attack against Kent Johnson, even as he keeps insisting that he's not to blame; after all, he reminds us, he's not Yasusada, not Motokiyu, not Javier Alvarez, Mikhail Epstein, nor Ogiwara Miyamori. The only person he has not insisted that he isn't is—tellingly—Marjorie Perloff. I'm reminded at this point of a line of Lynda Hull's: "larger and larger circles of misunderstanding."

Before I close, I want to try to narrow some of these circles, and the best way to do it is to separate the Yasusada materials from the controversies they've engendered, and to try to come to some provisional conclusions about Yasusada, which might in passing also say something about the state of contemporary poetry. It is easier to do this now that Yasusada's work has been published by James Sherry's Roof Books as *Doubled Flowering: From the Notebooks of Araki Yasusada*.

This is presumably the same manuscript that Wesleyan got cold feet about, and it is to Sherry's credit that he, unlike others who had initially lauded Yasusada but then condemned him when the hoax was revealed, has chosen to stand by his initial enthusiasm for the poems. As Ron Silliman's jacket blurb puts it, "the 'scandal' of these poems lies not in the problematics of authorship, identity, persona, race, or history. Rather, these are wonderful works of writing that also invoke all of these other issues, never relying on them to prop up a text." Silliman's confidence in Yasusada is strong enough so that he can allow such praise to appear on the jacket beside this statement by Hosea Hirata, Princeton professor of East Asian Studies: "Knowing its fictitious nature, with a slight sense of disgust, I find Yasusada's poetry evil, and eerily beautiful." (This is titillating stuff, certainly much more provoking than the blurbs on your average book of poetry, where someone like Richard Wilbur diffidently notes that the stanzas didn't put him to sleep.) Roof's willingness to face the Yasusada controversy head-on implies that one will finish the book on Silliman's side rather than on Hirata's. I am not sure that this is finally the case, but no one who seriously studies the book and reads the texts in their intended sequence will be unimpressed. It is weird, sorrowful, and wry by turns. In its attempt to use the convention of the notebook transcriptions, arranged more less chronologically, the book is more a novel in verse than merely a sequence of poems, and read as a whole the volume possesses an integrity (at least of a structural sort) that poses a challenge to Yasusada's detractors which might not have been apparent to them during their brief encounters with him in the quarterlies. It is also, in the manner of Borges' *Ficciones* and Nabokov's *Pale Fire*, a witty parody of academic scholarship, current literary translation practices, and patterns of literary influence. Most importantly, however, Yasusada emerges from the notebooks as a wonderful and masterfully constructed character, who tries with great poignancy to salvage his ruined life through art. Taken in their intended context, his elegies are shattering, and as he attempts to create a sort of home-grown avant-garde poetry, largely in isolation, he recalls some of the century's great outsider artists. When reading *Doubled Flowering*, I found myself thinking of Rousseau (who was also a postal clerk) and Joseph Cornell more than of other poets, and yet at one point in the notebooks Yasusada writes a letter to an associate in which he talks of translating Dickinson—perhaps the greatest outsider poet of them all. And, like each of this trio, Yasusada is decidedly eccentric, crankily devoted to his art, given to naive flights of wild enthusiasm, and a little bit buffoonish. Taken as a whole, Yasusada is a memorable creation, at times even a brilliant one. The pose does not work all the time, however, and Roof and Johnson have made a major blunder by attaching as appendices to the volume several self-justifying essays and interviews about Yasusada's creation by Johnson, "Motokiyu," "Javier Alvarez," and "Mikhail Epstein," as well as Perloff's revised version of her *Boston Review* piece. To put it bluntly, it does no good for Yasusada to ever have the man behind the curtain appear, for whenever Johnson himself opens up his mouth he strikes us as a windy and slightly paranoiac jerk. Perloff comports herself much better, but the inclusion of her essay suggests mixed motives on Johnson's and Sherry's parts—by printing all of the Yasusada materials under a single cover, Sherry is asserting that the texts should be allowed to speak for themselves, and yet at the same time Perloff's essay seems transparently intended to give the volume a bit of critical cachet. They want to have it both ways, and this is not a good way to present an author whose reputation for duplicity precedes him. (I'm of course referring here to Johnson, rather than Yasusada.)

I want here to examine two poems from *Doubled Flowering*, both of which derive from Yasusada's experience of the Hiroshima bombing and his daughter's subsequent illness and death from radiation sickness. They exhibit all of the hallmarks of Yasusada's style save for the loopy humor and gaga avant-gardism of later works such as his "exercises" for his English teacher Mr. Rogers. Like most of the Yasusada documents, the two poems are accompanied by the "editors'" inclusion of footnotes, a practice which— surprisingly—serves to enhance their impact and appearance of verisimilitude. Here, then, is Exhibit #1:

Loon and Dome
January 1, 1947

The crying girl sounds like a loon . . .
Why does her mournful sound call to mind the sky
through the dome of the Industrial Promotion Hall?[1]
You told me there you were pregnant with her
as we strolled through the plaster chambers

of the giant Model of the Heart.
I have waited all week, you quietly said,
to be with you here in this magical place
and to tell you something beautiful.
(It was your sentimental heart
that always made me laugh,
and this stain on the page is spilt tea.)[2]
[Yasusada note in margin] Insert breast-plate stanza here?
Nomura, the long wake of our daughter
vanishes, ceaselessly, in our union.

[1] *The Hiroshima Industrial Hall, a prominent city landmark because of its windowed dome, was one of the few structures left recognizable after the bombing. Its skeletal remains have been preserved as a memorial.*
[2] *In the original, there is, indeed, a stain covering the first half of the poem.* (*Doubled* 15)

The associative movement of the poem is lyrical and compelling. The ill daughter's moaning is likened first to the loon's plaintive cry, and this in turn evokes Yasusada's memory of strolling with his late wife Nomura in the industrial hall, where she told him she was pregnant with their daughter Akiko, the same daughter who now lies wasting away. The contrast between Yasusada's mournful present existence and his recollection of the couple's moment of intense intimacy in the "magical place" of the industrial pavilion's giant model of the heart is an affecting contrast, in keeping with the emotional directness and bittersweet elegiac intent we find in translations of classical Chinese and Japanese poetry. The language of the poem evokes these models as well; it is fussy and a bit awkward: "translationesque" is the best way to describe it. But of course the charm of many of the poems of Pound's *Cathay* and Waley's and Rexroth's translations can be attributable to a similar awkwardness and syntactical inversion: think of the famous line in 'The River Merchant's Wife': "at fourteen I married My Lord you." Yasusada's rendering of this moment of lyrical grace may indeed be "Japanized crap," but it evokes for those of us who grew up on such translations a powerful tradition, and does so inventively. Inventive, too, is the metaphorical rhyme between the Industrial Pavilion dome—famous from photos of the Hiroshima bombing's devastation—and the giant rendering of the heart. (I suspect this heart model derives not from an actual prewar Hiroshima attraction but from a walk-through heart in Chicago's Museum of Science and Industry, a place which a Midwestern teacher of creative writing such as Johnson would know as the subject of innumerable undergraduate poems.) But perhaps the most interesting aspect of the poem is its resolute resistance to closure. In exploiting the convention of the poem's unfinishedness, by so strongly insisting on the fiction of the poem as a manuscript page, Yasusada and his editors leave us wandering with him among the ruins of obsession. The final three stanzas, along with the endnotes, offer us three abandoned efforts to conclude the poem. First we have the parenthetical stanza with its reference to the spilt tea which the editors—with a marvelous pedantry—tell us actually does stain the manuscript. This sort of gesture is used elsewhere in the manuscript to great effect. A letter to an associate of Yasusada's printed *en face* to 'Loon and Dome' is half "illegible due to blotching"; the marred passage thus appears on the page in fragmentary fashion, its white space and lacunae bringing to mind the manuscript shards of Sappho and the Greek Anthology poets. Then we have Yasusada's reference to the unwritten "breast-plate" stanza, and finally the poem's lines of even more emphatic address to Yasusada's dead wife—lines which I suspect the author designed to be of great earnestness, but which are also quite woefully bad. Yasusada ends with a clumsy mixed metaphor, in keeping with none of the patterns of imagery which the poem had previously developed—unless the "long wake" of the couple's daughter is meant to somehow evoke the wavelike blast pattern of the explosion and/or Yasusada's obsessive return to the memory of the visit to the Industrial Pavilion. The effect of this triad of would-be conclusions is, however, quite compelling. The poem ends elliptically, with none of its sorrows relieved— and yet this seems fitting.

Such qualities are also present in a poem alleged to have been written shortly after Akiko's death:

Trolley Fare and Blossom
—For My Daughter Akiko,1930–1949
May 18, 1949

How can I tell you now

that the fire's warmth was pleasurable
on my body?[1]
Your body enveloped by it
and somehow, still, by mine.
The round urn, so finely cut,
each blade of grass bent black
against a black moon. You, weightless,
within it.
How embarrassing, I thought, cupping it before me,
if in the middle of this ceremony I
stumbled, kabuki-like, and fell!
Thus, bearing you and weeping,
I paid the trolley fare.
How to tell you now
of this simple happiness,
of the children laughing in a ring
at Hiroshima's heart, the brushstrokes
falling fast and light?[2]
You, Akiko, thick branch
of which this scentless blossom
is breaking.[3]

[1] *This refers, at least literally, to his daughter's cremation.*
[2] *The poem, guarded in a rice paper sheath, is in calligraphy. See frontispiece.*
[3] *A somewhat amateurish sumi drawing (we believe by Yasusada himself) of a flowering branch runs down the right side of the page.]*

As anyone who has handled cremated human remains is likely to tell you, one carries them gingerly, with an awkward delicacy that Yasusada heartbreakingly conveys. The worry that he may "stumble, kabuki-like" and fall as he is presented with the ashes is a brilliantly apt way to describe the speaker's feelings, even as the statement also comes to us in Yasusada's characteristically clumsy "translationesque," and even as his choice of metaphor evokes an Orientalized exoticism of the kind which Solt no doubt had in mind. Yet I would propose that the passage is effective enough to transcend such quibbles. And, furthermore, the image of Yasusada later weeping with the funerary urn on the trolley is harrowingly described, a scene of abjection and pathos reminiscent of early Kurosawa films. Yet, in characteristic fashion, Yasusada cannot conclude the poem with this image, for its imagistic finality betrays the relentlessness of the speaker's grief. Instead, the poem goes on for two more stanzas, with Yasusada continuing to construct tropes to describe his experience, however tentative and provisional these metaphors may be. And once again this sense of unfinishedness is amplified by the footnotes, which bleed into the poem's text much in the same way that we are told that Yasusada's own "amateurish" sumi drawing does. The description of the poem as "guarded in a ricepaper sheath" comes to us as itself a wry comment upon the text: the visual impression which the poem leaves us with, one of seeing the poem's calligraphy through the translucence of its ricepaper covering reminds us that we must read the poem palimpsestically. In effect, the "manuscript's" condition asserts that we must read the poem itself as a kind of shroud. Such palimpsestic devices abound in the Yasusada manuscripts, of course. Each poem is a text layered upon several other texts, and the mask of the Yasusada character again and again appears to slip, offering us glimpses of other personae, be they the imaginary translator-editors, the probably real Kent Johnson and/or his co-conspirators, and, if you want to get post-structuralist about it, of "writing" itself, and all the heavy metal smoke-and-mirror and dry ice interplay of sign and signifier which this implies.

In conclusion, I want to make some generalizations about Yasusada which may be worth our attention. This is a subjective and by no means definitive list.

1. Yasusada is a better poet than Kent Johnson.

I feel that it is safe to make this claim even without my having read any of Johnson's other poems. Yasusada is also, as an outright forgery, a better poet than Johnson writing through the persona of Ogiwara Miyamori in his *Ironwood* poems. Nothing which I have seen of Johnson himself makes me think he would be a poet of character or of talent: Yasusada, however, is both.

2. Yasusada is a better poet than Ted Hughes.

Birthday Letters is written by a poet of talent and character, of old-fashioned sincerity rather than "radical" sincerity. But Yasusada is the better writer, and he shows us again that sincerity, talent, and character are not always enough to make good poetry. Compare 'Loon and Dome' to the following passage from Hughes' book, which J.D. McClatchy rightly compares to something you'd find in a Harlequin rather than in a Faber:

> We half closed our eyes. We held them wide
> Like sleepwalkers while a voice on tape,
> Promising, directed us into a doorway
> Difficult and dark. The voice urged on
> Into an unlit maze of crying and loss.
> What voice? "Find your souls," said the voice.
> "Find your true selves. This way. Search, search."
> The voice had never heard of the shining lake.
> "Find the core of the labyrinth." Why? What opens
> At the heart of the maze? Is it the doorway
> Into the perfect vision? (McClatchy 162)

Even in "translation" Yasusada is better. Can anyone read this and *not* suspect that Hughes' poems are the product of versifying secret agents?

3. Yasusada gives good "author function".
In other words, he plays with our presuppositions of authorial sincerity and authenticity, deconstructs the piety of reading with the willful suspension of disbelief—something which we can only do intermittently in Yasusada's case, knowing what we do of his pedigree— parodies literary scholarship, lampoons the politics of translation and makes such ironies some of the most prominent formal elements of his writing.

4. Yasusada reminds us again how woefully ignorant American readers are of contemporary world literature.
The Yasusada hoax would never have been successful if we knew anything about modern Japanese writing. Charles Simic, probably our most internationalist poet, has noted that the Yasusada hoax shows once again that ours is "a country where confident provincialism reigns supreme." (Simic 32). (I should add that in the same essay Simic trashes Yasusada's 'Loon and Dome,' yet I think his appraisal of the poem is wrong.)

5. Yasusada is one of the better literary hoaxes of this century, and even compares favorably with some of the more famous literary hoaxes of previous centuries.
I'd rank Yasusada as a better bogus poet than Australia's Ern Malley, as good a fabrication as Bill Knott's Saint Geraud, Kenneth Rexroth's Marichiko, and W.D. Snodgrass' S.S. Gardons, but not as good as Pessoa's heteronymic alter egos Ricardo Reis, Alvaro de Campos, and Alberto Caeiro. Johnson's Yasusada will likely be one of those hoax-authors whose work is remembered for its literary value—like Chatterton's Rowley, and Macpherson's Ossian. Johnson even fits the profile of these eighteenth-century forebears: like them, he is a unknown writer from the sticks who no doubt took a great delight in hoodwinking the literary establishment. Being called a criminal by Arthur Vogelsang may not be exactly the same sort of thing as Macpherson being vituperatively shit-canned by Dr. Johnson, but both denunciations are, in their way, indicative of a kind of literary celebrity. Yasusada is probably destined to be a hoax of lasting literary value, and not one of those hoaxes, like the counterfeit Hitler diaries, the forged JFK and Marilyn Monroe correspondence, or William Ireland's faked Shakespeare play, *Vortigern: A Tragedy*, which are remembered for their audacity rather than their artistic success. For a time in the eighteenth-century, *Vortigern* was admitted to the Shakespeare canon, even though, as Hugh Kenner remarks, it is "unreadable and absurd" (Kenner 83). Yasusada may be absurd, but he is never unreadable.

6. Yasusada is a monster.
This is not a statement made "guardedly": Yasusada is a monster. I agree with Perloff's belief that Yasusada is a "brilliant" creation. But he is not, it seems to me, the product of what Johnson terms "a radical empathy." The problematic ethics of creating a faux Hiroshima survivor, claiming he is real and then foisting him upon a gullible reading public has to be seen as a sin of hubris against the Gods of Morality and the Muse. Yasusada is, finally, a version of the Golem or Dr. Frankenstein's unholy offspring: he should never have come into being. And yet, as *Star Trek's* "Prime Directive" would remind us, Yasusada now exists as a "sentient life form" and must be accorded all of a life form's rights and privileges. Knowing Yasusada's creepy origins, readers can choose to ignore him if

they so desire. But others can see Yasusada as a case of loving the sinner but hating the sin, and read him with the appreciation which his best poems warrant. Mary Shelley felt a similar ambivalence about her own "monster." In her preface to the 1831 edition of *Frankenstein* she tells us that, after more than a decade of mulling over the moral and artistic implications of her creation, she has now decided "to bid my hideous progeny go off and prosper."

So the Yasusada case shows us again—not that we needed to be reminded of it—that the motives for artistic creation are always infuriatingly complicated, and made even more complicated as we attempt to ascend the Virtual Mount Purgatory of Post Modernism. Is art still the lie that tells the truth? Probably. Is art still the lie that helps us *bear* the truth? Perhaps. Or is art still, as Picasso had it, the lie that helps us to *appreciate* the truth? Maybe so. Hideous progeny, go off and prosper.

Postscript

Several noteworthy events have occurred since I presented an earlier version of this essay at the third annual international 'Being and Nothingness' conference on post-millennial poetics, held at St. Jauss College, a small Jesuit school in Minnesota. In the discussion following the presentation an audience member identified himself as Okura Kyojin, one of the Yasusada translators, who asserted once again that it is Tosa Motokiyu and not Kent Johnson who is the author of the Yasusada notebooks. This individual further contended that Johnson's reports of Motokiyu's death are in fact falsehoods and that Motokiyu is presently living in the Phoenix area: he even promised to furnish "Moto's" address and phone number. But by the time I left the podium and tried to talk with him after the lecture's conclusion, "Kyojin" had disappeared. A private investigator I later employed to find Motokiyu in Phoenix could not locate him. Also, because the 'Being and Nothingness' conference was covered extensively by the national media, I later received a number of interesting letters from readers of the Yasusada documents. Most of these letters expressed disdain for the Yasusada hoax, but others showed a strong partisanship in his favor. I've even been told that a number of Yasusada reading clubs and study groups have been formed. But two of the letters I received were a bit unsettling. One came from a representative of the Boston legal firm of Abrams, Abrams, and Weingarten, which I later discovered specializes in slander and copyright law, and whose clients have included Courtney Love and Tonya Harding, as well as Simpson trial notables Mark Furhman and Kato Kaelin. Abrams is now representing "Ted Hughes" and the Plath Estate, and in a letter similar to one which has gone out to almost every writer who has published anything about the Hughes/Plath forgeries, it threatens legal action if I continue to claim in any way that its client does not exist. If the public is given the impression that Hughes is a fabrication, the letter suggests, his heirs will be deprived of book royalties. A publicity release also arrived from a public relations firm representing Kent Johnson, inquiring whether the university where I teach would be interested in hosting *Yasusada: An Evening of Doubled Flowering*, a one-man dramatic presentation by Johnson in which he plays Yasusada, in the manner of Hal Holbrook's Mark Twain and Julie Harris' Emily Dickinson. For an additional fee, the firm will arrange for a koto player to furnish incidental music for the play. It's an interesting proposition, surely, but the fee is much larger than my department could likely afford.

Works Cited

Anonymous. 'To Our Readers.' *American Poetry Review* 25.5 (1996):47.
Bernstein, Charles. 'My Turn: A Column.' *National Review*, 14 June 1999.
Brown, Ed. 'Does *Birthday Letters* Spell M-O-V-I-E?' *Poets and Writers Magazine* 26:3 (1998).
Chang, Juliana et. al. 'Displacements,' *Boston Review* 22:3–4. (1997):34.
Cullum, Paul. 'The Beverly Hillbillies,' in *Museum of Broadcast Communications Encyclopedia of Television*, vol. I, Horace Newcomb and Noelle Watson, eds. Chicago: Fitzroy Dearborn, 1997.
D'Agostino , J. and C. Geary. "Ariel Photograph: Hughes Sings His Blues at Last," *Vanity Fair*. May 1998.
Foucault, Michel. 'What is an Author?' in *A Foucault Reader*, ed. Paul Rabinow. New York: Pantheon, 1984.

Johnson, Kent. 'From the Daybook of Ogiwara Miyamora.' *Ironwood* 15:2. (1987).
Johnson, Kent and Javier Alvarez. 'A Few Words on Araki Yasusada and Tosa Motokiyu,' in Yasusada, Araki. *Doubled Flowering*.
Kenner, Hugh. *The Counterfeiters: An Historical Comedy*, 2nd ed. Baltimore: Johns Hopkins University Press, 1985.
McClatchy, J. D. 'Old Myths in New Versions,' rev. of Ted Hughes' *Tales from Ovid* and *Birthday Letters*. *Poetry* 172:3. (1998).
Nussbaum, Emily. 'Turning Japanese: The Hiroshima Poetry Hoax,' *Lingua Franca* 6:10, (1996): 82–84.
Olsen, Wilfred. 'Poetic Injustice: How the Cold War Wrote Poetry and Invented a Laureate.' *The Observer*, 7 June 1999, Sec 1, pp.1, 13–15. Details relating to the Hughes/Plath hoax derive from Olsen's account.
Perloff, Marjorie. 'In Search of the Authentic Other,' *Boston Review* 22:2 (1997): 26–33.
Silkin, Jon. 'Yasusada Revisited: Letter from Jon Silkin,' *Poetry Review* 87:3. (1997): 44.
Simic, Charles. 'Our Scandal,' *Boston Review* 22:3–4. (1997): 32.
Arthur Vogelsang, 'Dear Editor,' *Boston Review* 22:3–4. (1997): 33.
Yasusada, Araki. *Doubled Flowering: From the Notebooks of Araki Yasusada*. Eds. and trans. Tosa Motokiyu, Ojiu Norinaga, and Okura Kyojin. New York: Roof Books, 1997.
Young, Dean. 'Go Ahead and Make My Day.' *The New Criterion* 15:3. (1997).
Weinberger, Eliot. 'Three Footnotes.' *Boston Review* 22:3–4, (1997): 36–7.

Letter to Araki Yasusada

Hosea Hirata

Dear Yasusada-san,

Hajimete otayori shimasu. Your friend's friend's friend, and now my friend, Kent sent your old letters to me over the Internet. Of course you don't know what the Internet is, but you may know, for time flows in strange ways, as you know.

Yasusada-san, your letters are really weird, for someone like me. Yasusada-san, your letters are weird because I often felt that I was the one who was writing them. Did you really write them? I left Japan in 1971 for this English speaking country. But I still don't know if I eat rice or lice, if I want to be your pal-pen or pen-pal. And there is my dearest poet Nishiwaki Junzaburô. You know that I wrote an essay about Nishiwaki entitled "Violation of the Mother Tongue," right?[1] Yes, you do. You know that Nishiwaki invented a new poetic language by translating his own English / French / Latin poems into a weird translatory ~~Japanese~~ language. You are ubiquitous and translucent. I saw you eating soba noodles with Nishiwaki in Sendagaya almost half a century ago, cursing Lacan to eternity with your Hiroshima-ben: "Oh, the Mother Tongue, the realm of the Real, where no grammarians dare utter a word!" Did you violate your Mother that night, to come to the Symbolic?

Actually I wanted to tell you about the two trips to Japan I made last year. In August I went to Hiroshima with my 11-year old son. In November, I went to Tokyo to speak about you at the National Institute of Japanese Literature. Many mothers were violated in Hiroshima, Nagasaki, Nanking, and elsewhere. But I need to talk about my father now, whose ashes we took to the island of Nômi, near Hiroshima city, to be buried with his ancestors. My father was born on this tiny island into a family with nine children. The family was too poor to send him to a junior high school, so he eventually left the island and supported himself while going to school. In Tokyo he was converted

---

[1] Hirata, Hosea. *Poetry and Poetics of Nishiwaki Junzaburô: Modernism in Translation.* Princeton: Princeton University Press, 1993.

to Christianity and after finishing college, he received a scholarship to attend a seminary in California. During the war, he was working in a small Japanese-American farming village near San Francisco. All of the JAP villagers were sent to an internment camp in Colorado. And the bomb exploded over Hiroshima. Some of my relatives were there. At 8:15 am on August 6, 1945, my fourteen-year old cousin, Yûji Hirata, just having got off the train at the Hiroshima station, was walking toward his school.

Hiroshima in August is sweltering hot, around 100 degrees with oppressive humidity. The main portion of my father's ashes had been buried in his church cemetery in Saitama. But he wanted part of his ashes to be in his family grave on the island. With some relatives we gathered around an old tomb on a hill overlooking the Hiroshima bay. There were no priests, no religious rites, for my father was a Christian and the main family remained Buddhist. We just wrapped his ashes in a handkerchief and put them inside the tomb. We could see our ancestors' bone fragments whitely glowing in the darkness. My boy almost fainted because of the heat. That was August 4, 2003. Two days later, we were sitting at the 58th Peace Ceremony in Hiroshima, listening to a 6th-grade boy powerfully reciting Tôge Sankichi's poem under the punishing heat of the August sun:

> Bring back the fathers! Bring back the mothers!
> Bring back the old people!
> Bring back the children!
>
> Bring me back!
> Bring back the human beings I had contact with!
>
> For as long as there are human beings, a world of human
>   beings,
> bring back peace,
> unbroken peace[2]

Under the intense sun we were melting with tears. How could we

---

[2] Minear, Richard ed. *Hiroshima: Three Witnesses*. Princeton: Princeton University Press, 1990, 305.

produce any "we" except by collectively sinking under the searing weight of the dead, shedding tears at the imagined end of the world? Were you there with me, Yasusada-san? Inside the Peace Museum, my boy began to run, like a racehorse, shielding his eyes from the exhibits with his hands. Did you lead him holding his small shoulders to the exit that was endlessly far?

Were you there with me, Yasusada-san, when my cousin, Yûji Hirata, now a sad-eyed old man, struggled to put words onto the ineluctable memories of that fateful day, telling me how he had been miraculously sheltered by a wall, how he had treaded back to his house through an inferno, what he had seen, what he had seen? Yes, you were there with me, though your luminosity was fading, because I envisioned you there and then, faintly showing your pensive face through the gaps in Yûji's monotonous narration. Did you know the young Yûji, who went back to the radioactive city, unknowingly, again and again to look for his friends in vain, only to witness countless demonic non-human forms and shadows?

In November 2003, I went back to Japan, this time to talk about you, Yasusada-san, at the National Institute of Japanese Literature in Tokyo, to plead that the Institute recognize your work as part of Japanese Literature. Did you follow me, Yasusada-san, through that imposing gate of the Institute to the lecture room? I was telling my audience how difficult it was to translate (no, to imagine the Japanese original of) your poem, "Mad Daughter and Big Bang." There is no equivalent Japanese word for "daughter." "Musume" can mean daughter but it also means "young woman." "Kichigai musume" can mean "mad daughter" but also may mean "mad girl" without the specificity of "daughter." And the Big Bang theory wasn't proposed till 1950! Is it a translation of "pika-don"? If so, that is too good a translation. As I was going through my attempt to reconstruct the original Japanese version, you began to disintegrate before me—your hair fallen, your eyes melted, your skin coming loose from your translucent yet grey flesh.

I was successful in establishing your work as part of Japanese Literature, for my reconstruction of your original poem, 'Mad Daughter and Big Bang,' was officially printed in a journal published by the National Institute of Japanese Literature![3] After coming back from Japan, I wrote to my friend Kent:

> My lecture went far better than expected. After a series of very pedantic talks on Japanese literature, my turn came last on the first day of the conference. I had rarely presented academic lectures in Japanese, so I was a bit nervous. Using my PowerPoint presentation as a visual support and a psychological shield, I began. The last slide I showed was a picture of a *hibakusha* girl, whose face was totally burned beyond recognition. I could hear quiet gasps from the audience. I read my conclusion:
> "In front of this picture, in front of this overwhelming Evil, I think whether art is at all possible, and I think of Tôge Sankichi's poems screaming. And I recite, almost inaudibly, to myself, Araki Yasusada's 'Mad Daughter.'"
> There was a moment of silence. And then an elderly woman stood up and began a long tale of how her family was bombed out in Tokyo, and her family members, who were burned to death, came back and haunted her as ghosts, and how she had to perform special rituals to console their souls . . . Everybody was aghast! This woman was really mad. She didn't want to shut up, though the panel chair begged her to stop! Finally she shrieked —"Please everyone console the victims of war!"—and sat down. Wow, that was something to behold.

Then a regular question-and-answer session began. People told me that they were moved, they were in tears, and they felt "their brains stirred up"! So, that was good.

Yasusada-san, were you that mad woman? Were you the ghosts who haunted her? Or were you with me, in me, writing with me, writing me?

You live long, Yasusada-san. Be everywhere Yasusada-san. Be with me.

> Sincerely yours,
> Hosea Hirata

---

[3] Hirata, Hosea. 'Tsukurareta hibakusha shijin Araki Yasusada: shi ni shinjitsu wa hitsuyouka,' in *Proceedings of the 27th International Conference on Japanese Literature*. Tokyo: National Institute of Japanese Literature, 2004 (155–167).

This Is a City with No Person: *Also, with My Throat, I Shall Swallow Ten Thousand Swords*: Araki Yasusada's Letters in English [1]

Dan Hoy

[1] These letters were written in the 1920s by Hiroshima survivor Araki Yasusada and edited by Tosa Motokiyu, Ojiu Norinaga, and Okura Kyojin.[a]

> [a] Although two of the editors, Ojiu Norinaga and Okura Kyojin, believe the letters "were elaborately constructed by Yasusada (or, possibly, even, by his strange and brilliant son) *after* the bombing as a kind of indirect, meta-fictional commentary on it" due to the post-nuclear type imagery throughout being just a little too prescient (see footnote I of the letter dated October 26, 1926).

[2] As it turns out these letters were written by an unknown author under the pseudonym "Tosa Motokiyu" under the pretense of being written by Araki Yasusada, Hiroshima survivor, and were later edited by Kent Johnson and Javier Alvarez.[a]

> [a] But really these letters were written by Kent Johnson under the pretense of being written by an unknown author under the pseudonym "Tosa Motokiyu" under the pretense of being written by Araki Yasusada, Hiroshima survivor.[A]
>
>> [A] Actually these letters were written by a Primary Cause author (possibly Kent Johnson) under the pseudonym "Kent Johnson."[i]
>>
>>> [i] But when it comes down to it any of the above footnotes may or may not be true, as these letters have no official attribution [1]: the particulars of the author(s) behind "Tosa Motokiyu" are not only unknown but in doubt, since even an unknown author behind a pseudonym may itself be a pseudonym, and so on, ad infinitum (or else until some Primary Cause author(s) [11]—but even that could be a computer algorithm for all we know, a possibility that complicates the authorial conundrum beyond the confines of this essay).
>>>
>>>> [1] As the Japanese poet Ogata Kamenosuke says in a poem (referenced by Motokiyu in a footnote to a letter (dated October

2, 1926) Yasusada wrote to Ogata): *This is a city with no person.* Yet, as is the case throughout the letters, this could also be read as a retroactive reference to Hiroshima after Little Boy, as if the atomic singularity or catastrophic void at the heart of the 20th Century is the true Primary Cause.

[11] The theological implications of this line of thinking were pointed out by Russian critic Mikhail Epstein in a letter to Kent Johnson (quoted by Johnson in a letter to *American Book Review*):

> This is how creation of hyperauthors brings forth the effect of boomerang on the creators themselves, presenting them as hyperauthors of some more primary creators, etc. Isn't this an applied theological argument leading to the Primary Cause?

Of course Epstein (who argues that the Primary Cause author behind Yasusada is either Russian experimental writer Andrei Bitov or Russian conceptual poet-artist Dmitri Prigov, or a collaboration between the two) himself is rumored to be a hyperauthorial invention of Umberto Eco. See *Jacket Magazine* 5, 'Kent Johnson—Letter to *American Book Review*': http://jacketmagazine.com/05/yasu-lett.html

[3] Quote attributed to Arthur Vogelsang (in *Lingua Franca*), one of the editors of *American Poetry Review*, whose July/August 1996 issue featured a supplement of Yasusada's poems. *APR* also sent a letter to Kent Johnson (who insists he is merely the posthumous liaison for the unknown author behind the name "Tosa Motokiyu") demanding a return of the author's payment in the wake of Eliot Weinberger's brief exposé in the *Village Voice Literary Supplement*. For various accounts of the controversy and its aftermath (short version: Hiroshima survivor Araki Yasusada's (b.1907, d.1972) poems are recovered by Tosa Motokiyu and published in the mid-90s in *Grand Street, Conjunctions, APR, Stand,* and other periodicals; rumors circulate that "Yasusada" is a hoax perpetuated by Johnson; articles and dissertations ensue), see *Jacket Magazine*: http://jacketmagazine.com/bio/yasu.shtml

[4] Since the original conceit of the letters is an ESL exercise, Yasusada acts as his own spontaneous translator, the awkwardness of which necessarily imposes editorial restrictions.

⁵ Or maybe not—see footnote 1a. The original introduction also points out that Yasusada's true dexterity with English is unknown, so that his signature crossing of "ungrammaticalities" with "biting lyricism" could be read as both innocent and strategic; that is, Yasusada is playing with the cultural expectations of his correspondent along with the self-estrangement one feels when communicating in a foreign tongue, while also, "in anonymous but rebellious fashion," "self-consciously inhabiting . . . a foreign strangeness that was rapidly coming to inhabit Japanese literature at large" (from Motokiyu's footnote to an undated letter).

⁶ One could pivot similarly on Yasusada's humble reference to his "protoEnglish" (Motokiyu's term) skills: "Please be a friend in this brokenness" (from a letter dated January 5, 1926). Or Yasusada's uncanny sense of his own mortality and the nothingness out of which and of which anything palpable is made: "Cold fearful drops stand on my trembling flesh. There's none else by. Tosa loves Tosa; that is, I am I. Yet I lie: I am not" (October 25, 1926). Is this not also a closed-circle ("Tosa loves Tosa") conversation among authorial personae, each "I am not" preempted with an "I am I," so that every subversion is also an assertion, and vice versa?ᵃ

> ᵃ The passage is also a variation on Richard's soliloquy in Shakespeare's *Richard III*, which complicates the self-generating loop: 1) Yasusada is quoting one Richard to speak to another Richard, so that, between the lines (or through them, since the communiqué is transtextual), "Richard loves Richard"; 2) The allusion is to the plays of "Shakespeare," which over the years have been attributed to everybody from the Earl of Oxford to 10,000 monkeys.

⁷ See also for example *Lyric Poetry after Auschwitz* (effing press, 2005). Or Motokiyu breaking the fourth wall (or walls, e.g. Kent Johnson/ Javier Alvarez, the Primary Cause author(s)) to speak directly to us, the reader, in the footnote to a letter dated September 30, 1926:

> What is the meaning of what I am doing? Does it become a racism? When I read his English, the brokenness makes me shake my head in disbelief, even feel queasy at times. Is the form I'm using opening

up the possibility, as I would want, of keeping that transgression while giving it a rebuke?

Though formatted as an editorial note, the tone suggests an admission that Motokiyu is in fact Yasusada's creator; it also suggests a concern that his attempt to walk the transgression/rebuke tightrope may be a complicit engagement rather than an engagement with complicity, the difference being one of awareness and self-implication. That Kent Johnson & Javier Alvarez reiterate Motokiyu's pleading "Can you tell me, reader?" in the footnote to the footnote is an acknowledgement of their own complicity and doubt as editors/creators, and, one assumes, an acknowledgement by the Primary Cause author(s) of his/her/their nebulous culpability.

[8] Take the opening to a letter dated September 30, 1926:

> I am fearsome that my letter is in a flatness you are sleeping.
> Please let mountains rise in the dream you go dreaming.
> Everything is visible, nothing is hiding. A storm is falling.
> Blossoms go flying. I am rainy, Richard, all over my body.
> Is there wetness where you are lying?

As everywhere else, Yasusada's lexical and syntactical mistakes open up associative meanings that complicate what we construe as his literal intention, e.g. the echo of the more portentous "the sky is falling" in "a storm is falling" and the syntactical placing of the letter within the flat realm of Richard's dreams, as if Yasusada is a fiction of Richard's subconscious instead of the other way around.[a] That Yasusada calls himself "fearsome" instead of "fearful" also saturates this melancholy passage with something darker and more dangerous: Yasusada is not "wet," but "rainy," a viscous substance oozing out of Richard. The last sentence contains not only the pun on "lying" but the word "witness" embedded in "wetness," so that Yasusada, after implying that he himself is a fiction of his audience (Richard), is asking his creator (and us), "Is it a poetry of witness when you are lying?" Can one be fake and still tell the truth? Is the truth hidden beneath the lie, like the damp impression our bodies make in the grass?

ᵃ This maneuver is an inverse of the book's stated central conceit, that is, that Richard is a fiction of Yasusada, who in turn is a fiction of Motokiyu. The implication being that not only is Yasusada a fiction of Richard, but Motokiyu is a fiction of Yasusada, and so on, as follows, in Biblical terms: Richard begat Yasusada, who begat Motokiyu, who begat Kent Johnson, who begat the Primary Cause author(s) (with some tangential begats omitted for simplicity).[A] Yasusada encapsulates the two-lane highway of authorial begettage in a postscript to his letter dated October 26, 1926:

> P.S. It is one thing to think of mind, to think of it thinking about its own thinking. Because the mind is inside the body, and the body, which shall die, is inside the mind and thus inside the body it thinks it is thinking. This is not to be cute, Dick. Think hard. There I am.

[A] In a footnote to a footnote, Kent Johnson and Javier Alvarez make a similar comment in regard to the poem from Nabokov's *Pale Fire* that Motokiyu[i], via Yasusada, pens on the back of a letter: "Was it written by the poem's purported composer John Shade, by his scholar-editor and possible 'murderer' Charles Kinbote, by Shade's ghost (as *Pale Fire*'s leading commentator, Brian Boyd, has suggested), or by an anonymous Ur-author, who has 'created' not only Shade and Kinbote, but even Nabokov himself, whether the latter was fully aware of it or not?"

[i] Parts of Yasusada's *Doubled Flowering* were literally written in the margins of *Pale Fire*.

[9] Cf. footnote 8a.

[10] The contexts are relentlessly porous, with footnotes questioning footnotes, and errors by Yasusada, Motokiyu, and Johnson/Alvarez[a] (and possibly the Primary Cause author(s)—e.g. one assumes that a previous biographical error in regard to Yasusada attending Hiroshima University between 1925 and 1928 (an impossibility pointed out by Marjorie Perloff in her essay 'In Search of the Authentic Other: The Poetry of Araki Yasusada' and referenced by Kent Johnson and Javier Alvarez in the footnotes of the volume in question) was intentional, but who knows) in phrasing, dating, interpretation, and facts.

[a] E.g., Johnson/Alvarez state that the Japanese poet Ogata Kamenosuke

died in 1933 (in a footnote to Motokiyu's footnote to a letter Yasusada wrote to Ogata), when in fact he died in 1942. One can't help but assume the "poetic-forensic" mystery surrounding Ogata's death (a suicide, his body found mummified and wrapped in gauze on which were written translations of poems from Pound's *Cathay*) is also total horseshit, as are the Ogata poems included in the footnotes—though I haven't double-checked the veracity or dubiousness of either. But this undercutting of not just Truth but Lies is the irreducible maneuver at the heart of the Yasusada project—and in any case, a solid footing isn't necessary to appreciate the tossed-off tone of Ogata's poems, which sound like Frank O'Hara coming down from an anxiety attack with a case of the koans:

The next day was rainy. The day after that was snowy. On the day after that there was a fucking sty on my right eye.

In the afternoon a coin went into nothing. The weather turned to sleet shit and the month of February shut down.

The butcher and liquor seller to whom I had been meaning to pay even a tithing went back into his den with hardly a murmur, which is really weird.

[11] How different from each other are Victor Frankl's *Man's Search for Meaning* and Roberto Benigni's *Life is Beautiful*, one an autobiographical essay taught in schools and the other a feel-good movie embraced by Hollywood, but both making narratives of that other large-scale tragedy of WWII, the Holocaust? And how different is this after-the-fact fictionalizing of reality from the real-time way we go about our lives and 'make sense' of what befalls us and others?

[12] Just as the author behind Yasusada subsists on the suffering of unknown others for poetic effect, don't those of us living in the 'developed' world subsist on the injury done to unknown others by the outsourced 'necessary evils' of production (e.g. pollution, work conditions)? And do we not read books like *Man's Search for Meaning* so as to spark what often lies dormant within ourselves, while bypassing the immediate trauma or residual damage of actual personal tragedy? Is not all tragic literature, whether book-of-the-month memoir or Shakespearean play, a vehicle by which to simultaneously absorb and export the horrors of somebody else, so that another's labor-intensive loss becomes our instant-download gain?

[13] Even Yasusada, who in the context of the book is the originator of the "I am sincere" claim, makes such a claim by mistake. It is also worth noting the bullshit spiral or infinite regress of self-paranoia and disgust implied by moments such as "Javier Alvarez & Kent Johnson's" questioning of "Tosa Motokiyu's" categorical description of "Araki Yasusada's" increasingly irrational impatience with "Dick." As Yasusada puts it, "It is tragedy for me to write and I am full of shamefulness."

[14] The most obvious manifestation of this being the Internet.

The Yasusada project may be a publicity stunt, a perpetuation of Orientalist literary stereotypes, an undermining of the ideological cult of authorship, a critique of PC establishment editorial biases, or all of the above and more (if not necessarily a "criminal act"[3]). But after the smoke clears, we're left with a matryoshka doll of editorial and authorial intentions—as if the Yasusada 'hoax' is exploiting neither bleeding heart liberals nor those who suffered the actual horror of Hiroshima, but the relationship between context and audience. When reading the letters of Araki Yasusada, how does our awareness of a multiplicity of editor-authors (primarily "Yasusada,"[4] "Motokiyu," and "Johnson") determine our reaction to any given line? Do we read and reread each line simultaneously, as if our suspicion of one integrated voice (Kent Johnson's) nevertheless acquiesces to our experience of several voices speaking every word in unison, yet with distinctive intonations?

For example the "I am sincere" at the end of almost every letter is 1) a broken English hybrid of the often insincere "Sincerely" used to sign-off on formal correspondence, used sincerely[5] ("Yasusada"); 2) an ironic hint from an author hiding behind not just a fictional poet but an editorial pseudonym, as if even sincerity must be buffered from itself ("Tosa Motokiyu"); 3) a condescending appropriation of the simpleminded sincerity of ethnic Others by an educated white male American for supposedly poetic effect ("Kent Johnson"); and 4) a sincere attempt at poetic communication whose indeterminate layers are appropriate to both a hypermediated world and the language of global commerce, which language is permeated even as it permeates (the Primary Cause author).[6]

Of course some readers may be put off by #3 (Johnson is sometimes dismissed as a self-promoting egomaniac), but I think this kind of ambiguity is Johnson's intention and indicative of his general interest in authorial, personal, and cultural complicity.[7] Let's say Johnson is in fact the Primary Cause behind the Yasusada persona—in which case his meta-techniques draw attention to his persona as an analogue for our own, as if our response to the text has less to do with our reading of it and more to do with its reading of us. We are not meant to ask Johnson who the hell does he think he is, but rather who the hell do we think we are? Are we any less a constructed and fraudulent reader than Richard, the intended recipient of Yasusada's letters (whose existence even Motokiyu doubts)?[8] And if Richard is indeed a fiction of Yasusada, are we not also, in reading the letters, fictions of Kent Johnson?[9] And if the letters were never intended to be mailed to Richard, were they never intended for us either, since their primary content isn't Yasusada's words (or Motokiyu's, or Johnson's) but the echoing between the contexts? So that the letters, if they ever arrive, have already been rewritten?[10] And what does any of this imply about our ability to read the situations in which we find ourselves, as workers and citizens and consumers and friends and etc., but always as human beings? Or is the point precisely that we often renege on being human in favor of constructs we inherit and create so as to navigate or withstand whatever is happening right in front of us? Or to us? Or is that precisely what it is to be human?[11] How are we implicated by our very existence, whom do we subsume in order to survive,[12] how can we still say "I am sincere" and mean it when aware of not just our ineluctable duplicity but our own hyperawareness of it?[13] And is this paralytic meta-hyperawareness symptomatic of an era in which cultural self-reflexivity has metastasized into a perpetual present, one that is both a sci-fi utopia of renewable information and a closed-circle nightmare of indistinction?[14] Are all facts equal in their insignificance, should we tolerate all points of view in principle, do we dismiss complicity as what goes without saying, thus ensuring that it stays unsaid—or do we confront the questions that Johnson (among others), as editor or author, wants us to ask ourselves: How do we react to our own reaction (to these letters, to the news, to the people we pass on the street)? What kind of audience are we, and is this question actionable, and if so, how, when, and to what end?

When reading any work that depends in large part on extratextual interplay for its content, a question invariably follows: can it "survive" without knowledge of the criticism surrounding it? Is it so dependent on what's been said about it that the relationship between primary text and critique are inverted; that is, that it acts as a water cooler of sorts for people to gather around as if water coolers are the most interesting thing in the world? Can readers have a good time going in cold, or do they need to be prepped before spelunking? Or is this question even relevant for something like *Also, with My Throat, I Shall Swallow Ten Thousand Swords*, a book written in the wake of its own controversy, out of that controversy, and bookended by essays discussing this controversy? Does its reliance on an awareness of its authorial and critical history limit its audience any more than heavily allusive or elliptical poems? Does it necessarily have to stand on its own, as it were—or is its whole *raison d'être* to challenge the very notion of self-contained texts, that nothing stands on its own, that everything we encounter and read is compromised by colliding fragments of cultural and personal context? Or is this just an excuse for all sorts of bland work created and enjoyed by people with too much time on their hands? And is *Also* such a work? Is all art "work"? Is art that is inextricable from criticism politically ineffectual, because exclusionary and therefore elitist? Is any art extricable from criticism? Is work? Am I back at the beginning of this paragraph? Or as Yasusada says,

> People in time drip like waxings. Life roars like a flame from head tops. Do not consider, even, some water to salve it. Does a giant salamander fly through the air? Is a man a woman? Can the museum be pulled inside out?

and later, from the same letter (undated),

> Is my headache the otherness of your dream? Please abide my patience with violet grammar. It is in part embarrassing for me, and I am a gift to you [sic]. There are waxened [sic] threads on the inside of my shirt. The museum sticks, hotly, to the skin.

And the questions continue, as if Yasusada is simply the point at which reading and questioning converge, and never end. Is traumatic memory, whether personal or cultural, the first and purest form of entertainment? Does the grammar of history bruise everything? Is this what time does, even as we experience it, and are we all then wax figures, gaudy and melting inside an equally gaudy museum, even as the museum melts with us? Can we pull the passing of time inside out, or pull ourselves inside out, and will this make any difference, or is the void of what happened and continues to happen the same as the reality of what happened and happens to each and every one of us? Can we exist without making dreamworlds of suffering? Is our horror our gift to each other? Will we ever be so sated on this exchange as to be immune to the Dickinsonian epiphany, in silence and anguish, those moments in which we are atomized by the flame roaring out of us, our heads blown apart?

After Yasusada

Bill Freind

In spite of the ostensible biography included in *Doubled Flowering*, Yasusada was not born in Kyoto in 1907. Neither was he born when Tosa Motokiyu, Kent Johnson, or someone else first started writing and/or publishing work attributed to that figure. Instead, I would argue, Yasusada was born when his fictive status was first revealed. At that point, Yasusada could no longer be seen as a once-living human, but neither was he merely a character or just a heteronym. Instead, Yasusada became, in Foucauldian terms, the marker of a discourse, a discourse that centered on questions of, for example, the ethical status of a (probably) white author or authors employing the voice of a *hibakusha*, the stubborn role of The Author in our modes of reading, and (much less commonly) the quality of the work itself.

How did this discourse begin? The usual story is that Eliot Weinberger's 'Can I Get a Witness?' was the first to announce Yasusada's heteronymy, but that's not accurate. The first public declaration I've found is from Lee Chapman, who was then the editor of the journal *First Intensity*. On 29 August 1995, Chapman posted a message to the Poetics Listserv at the University of Buffalo, which began:

> As one of the editors who recently published work by Araki Yasusada (Brad Morrow, *Conjunctions*, and Jean Stein, *Grand Street*, were others), I feel a responsibility to inform anyone who may have read the work (in *First Intensity* #5) that it is more than likely a hoax; that is, a person or persons unknown to me at this time concocted the bio and writings of this supposed Hiroshima poet. The person who submitted the work to me refuses to confirm or deny the rumors of fakery, and with absolutely no evidence in favor of Yasusada's existence, while there is plenty against it, I think it's safe to assume that the rumors are true. (Chapman)

The interesting part is the final clause: "the rumors are true," which indicates that others had questioned Yasusada's existence in non-public forums. Many critics have alluded to this: "rumors began to circulate" (Boully), "rumors were spreading" (Hayot), "word was leaking out"

(Perloff), "[t]he hoax lasted several months before editors became suspicious" (Rekdal), "had rumors of Yasusada's identity not begun to circulate" (Weinberger). Yasusada, as we now understand him, was born not merely from the words on the pages of the journals that published him, but also from the emails, phone calls, gossip, and articles that revealed, attacked, and celebrated his fictiveness. Obviously, many authors are creations of the discourse that surrounds them, but Yasusada isn't an author in any conventional sense of the term. The discursive nature of the Yasusada work is also indicated by the text of *Doubled Flowering* itself, which includes letters to and from Yasusada, as well as essays and interviews.

Given all of that, the publication of *Also, With My Throat, I Shall Swallow Ten Thousand Swords: Araki Yasusada's Letters in English* seems both necessary and predictable. Collections of letters often provide interesting and even crucial details about an author's life and/or aesthetics, as shown by the correspondence of John Keats, or of Robert Creeley and Charles Olson, to cite only a few examples. Because the letters in *Also, With My Throat* were ostensibly written when Yasusada was eighteen and nineteen, one might assume that they would shed some light on his poetic development.

However, far from elucidating Yasusada, the letters essentially—and, I suspect, intentionally—obscure him. Although the text is a collection of letters addressed to a mysterious correspondent named Richard, it tells us almost nothing about the writer (or character, or heteronym). Instead of biography, *Also, With My Throat* presents a complicated system of editorial squabbles and pronouncements that overwhelm the text itself. For instance, there are an extraordinary number of footnotes from Tosa Motokiyu, the nominal author of the letters, and a separate set of footnotes from both Kent Johnson and Javier Alvarez, the ostensible editors of the collection. Motokiyu, according to Johnson, is the pseudonym of the actual author of Yasusada's work. Johnson also insists "Moto" is now dead, but one could be forgiven for wondering if he ever existed, since his name echoes *The Tosa Diary*, a tenth-century Japanese text written in the voice of a woman, but whose author was probably Ki no Tsurayuki, a renowned (male) poet and governor of Kochi (formerly Tosa) Prefecture. The title page lists Motokiyu as the author, but even with those facts there's no way that

Motokiyu can replace Yasusada as either author function or heteronym. Motokiyu remains all but undefined in the text, and the copyright is held by "Kent Johnson, for the estate of Tosa Motokiyu."[1] In *Doubled Flowering*, the poems, letters, and drafts are so rich that it is possible to believe in Yasusada in the way we believe in a character in a film or play: we learn about his courtship with his wife Nomura, the cremation of his daughter, his many friendships, his Zen exercises.

That is not the case in *Also, With My Throat*. Besides the lack of biography, the writing is marked by a translationese that is even more self-conscious than in *Doubled Flowering*: it makes no attempt to simulate a voice that could be construed as an actual Japanese speaker writing in English. Instead, the complicated network of authors, editors, correspondents, and heteronyms suggests one of the most important aspects of the text: it has neither an actual nor a fictive authorial center. For instance, a letter dated May 7, 1926 reads:

Dear Richard,

What was there before your birth?

What was there after your death?

Who or what is it, at this moment, that is reading?

---

[1] Alvarez, on the other hand, is an actual person, an internationally renowned composer who was a roommate of Kent Johnson's in the 1980s. However, critics have largely ignored his role: as Alex Verdolini notes, Michael Atkinson identified him as a folksinger. (Emily Nussbaum made the same mistake.) 'Walkers with Ladle' is dedicated to "Javier Alvarez (1906–1945)," and a footnote says he was Bolivian Consul to Hiroshima and that he presumably died in the bombing. *Doubled Flowering* also includes a letter from "Javier del Azar" to Yasusada, which includes a piece of music that del Azar claims is inspired by Yasusada's poem 'Sarcophagus and Maracas.' A footnote says that the editors (Tosa Motokiyu, Ojiu Norinaga and Okura Kyojin) were unable to find any composer with that name, and they suggest that "del Azar may be a pen name for a known composer of the period" (106). The musical score included with the letter is actually 'Temazcal,' a piece for maracas and magnetic tape, composed by Javier Alvarez (the composer, not the consul). I find it striking that the one actual person besides Kent Johnson who is associated with the text's composition and/or editing has received so little attention. (I've emailed him to ask about his association with Yasusada and received no response.)

> How can we have the apricot blossoms perfuming the whole world?
>
> I am sincere,[2]
>
> Araki Yasusada (*Also* 5)

Motokiyu's note on this letter reads "[i]n our opinion, as editors and translators, this is the most mysterious and beautiful of all the letters" (5). The second person plural indicates that Motokiyu's assessment is shared with his fictive co-editors, Ojiu Norinaga and Okura Kyojin. To Motokiyu's note, Kent Johnson and Javier Alvarez respond with a note of their own: "[a]s the editors of the 'editors,' we don't necessarily concur, but that would be, of course, neither here nor there" (5). Their note amounts to a kind of passive-aggressive pulling of rank: Johnson and Alvarez don't explicitly contradict Motokiyu, et. al., but as "editor of the 'editors'" they reserve the right to do so. Additionally, the notes of Johnson and Alvarez are in bold, which seems to emphasize their prominence in the text. At the same time, some of the notes apparently don't have a reference (e.g., note 1 on page 32 and note 6 on page 33). Does it matter if these are typographical errors or intentional aspects of the text? Either way, the notes both emphasize and denigrate the roles of the various editors. *Also, With My Throat* offers a proliferation of writers, heteronymic or otherwise, in a sort of drama that simultaneously highlights and undermines the different forms of authority that occur in many edited collections.

The entire Yasusada project has always been concerned with the absent and unrecoverable; it presents a plethora of illegible sections, missing letters, missing dates on letters and poems, letters that are available only as reproductions from a carbon copy, inexplicable references, and the sections of the notebooks that aren't published. It's fair to say that one of the most striking things about *Doubled Flowering* and *Also, With My Throat* is how much of it is not there. This recalls those who perished in the bombing, many of whom would have

---

[2] "I am sincere" is the default closing to the letters, occurring thirteen times. The irony is that there is no "I" in the usual sense of the word, which would seem to make "sincerity" impossible.

literally vanished with the detonation of Little Boy; that may include his wife Nomura and younger daughter Chieko who (according to the biography) "died instantly in the atomic blast on August 6" (*DF* 10). Once his heteronymity was revealed, "Yasusada" became a marker for an author who never existed. However, the Preface to the letters indicates that Yasusada's absence becomes even more marked in that collection: "[i]f *Doubled Flowering* is, as a critic from Japan has fancifully put it, a kind of ceremonial gown enshrouding an absent Author, perhaps these letters may be taken as a kind of painted fan, snapped open now, and held up, coquettishly, to his invisible face" (*Also* xv). Obviously, this both employs and parodies stereotypes of Japan: the painted fan, the adverb "coquettishly," which feminizes this absent author. But if the fan and the gown, which are supposed to both conceal and reveal, actually surround nothing, both Yasusada and Motokiyu essentially vanish in the letters.

The biography included in *Doubled Flowering* states that "Yasusada was undertaking a work parallel to Spicer's letters and 'translations' in *After Lorca*, to be entitled *After Spicer*" (*Doubled* 10). As the scare quotes around "translations" would suggest, some of the renderings in *After Lorca* are extremely free or even wholly invented by Spicer himself. *Also, With My Throat* serves as a kind of *After Yasusada*, with the word "after" functioning in two senses. First, "after" suggests a type of imitation. If *Doubled Flowering* was sometimes characterized by a translationese that was uncharacteristic of any actual Japanese writer, the language in *Also, With My Throat* is even more implausible: it sounds like a parody of a caricature. In other words, it is a kind of unlikely copy of Yasusada. Second, "after" operates in a temporal sense: the actual text was published about eight years after *Doubled Flowering*, although it was ostensibly written eighteen years before the earliest work in *Doubled Flowering*. Obviously, the bombing of Hiroshima was central to the poetic identity of Yasusada, so *Also, With My Throat* moves beyond Yasusada in part by placing itself chronologically before the event that made Yasusada Yasusada. To be somewhat paradoxical, *Also, With My Throat* moves after *Doubled Flowering* in part by coming before *Doubled Flowering*. The things that come before Yasusada—and are in fact absolutely necessary for the initial acclaim the work received before Yasusada's heteronymity was revealed—are the assumptions and fantasies about Japan that many in the West brought to their readings of the work.

    This is suggested at the very beginning of the book, which includes a reproduction of what is supposed to be a photograph of a page from Motokiyu's notebook. With its extraordinary welter of scrawl it is clearly a parody of the tortured artist's manuscript: it is all but illegible, except for a few handwritten notes and three captions that appear to be cut and pasted onto the page. Each bears the recognizable font of captions from *National Geographic*, and they are in fact taken from the April, 1944 edition of that magazine. (This is eighteen years after Yasusada supposedly began his letters to Richard.) A caption identifies the page as an "image from the notebooks of Tosa Motokiyu," which, significantly, recalls the title of the first volume, *Doubled Flowering: From the Notebooks of Araki Yasusada*. While a drawing of Yasusada was included in both *Doubled Flowering* and with the poems by Yasusada included in *American Poetry Review* (as well as on the cover of this book), *Also, With My Throat* instead offers three captions with no images. A facsimile page from a writer's notebook would presumably offer some "authentic" view of the writing process, yet this page is almost completely illegible, except for three captions written by neither Yasusada, Motokiyu, nor Kent Johnson. If the root of "caption" is the Latin *caption-em*, "taking," what's being taken on an almost unreadable page with no images?

    One answer, I think, is that *National Geographic* works as a metonym for the preconceptions that many North Americans have brought (and sometimes continue to bring) to our readings of a *hibakusha* poet. With its striking photography of far-away places, the magazine often presented the first—or only—depictions of those places to many Americans.[3] As Catherine Lutz and Jane L. Collins write:

> If the sharp focus and conventional framing of *Geographic* photographs marked them as 'records,' it was their replication of popular understandings of the third world that made them seem neutral in their presentations and gave them the comforting feel of 'commonsense' realities captured on film.

---

[3] I would include myself in that characterization: as a child, I had a bound set of all the *National Geographic* magazines from the 1940s, which my grandparents had bought for me at a garage sale.

> In this way, the mass media's images become mirrors serving to reflect Americans' feelings, rather than windows to the complex, dynamic realities of foreign societies (Lutz 30).

As with an article in *National Geographic*, Yasusada's initial popularity stemmed from the way he seemed simultaneously familiar and irreducibly exotic: an unknown *hibakusha* who practiced Zen and wrote renga and haiku while reading Roland Barthes, Paul Celan, Jack Spicer, and the Beats.

The article from which the captions are taken is 'Japan and the Pacific' by Joseph C. Grew, who at the time was Special Assistant to the Secretary of State, and who has served as Ambassador to Japan. The opening paragraphs suggest that Japan, like Yasusada, is simultaneously exotic and familiar:

> The Japanese dress as we do, and in many respects they live and act as we do, especially in their modern business and industrial life. But they don't think as we do, and nothing can be more misleading than to try to measure by Western yardsticks the mentality of the average Japanese and his reaction to any given set of circumstances. We who have lived in Japan for 10, or 20, or even 40 years, know at least how comparatively little we really do know of the thinking processes of the Japanese (Grew 385).

In these lines, Grew makes an important double gesture. Japan was rapidly industrializing at this time, and as a result many Japanese, especially those living in and around major cities, were beginning (in Grew's words) to "live and act as we do." Immediately after that claim, Grew falls back on the all-too-familiar stereotype of the inscrutable Asian to suggest that the "Japanese mind" remains largely unknowable even to Westerners who have lived among them for four decades. While this is a very standard move in *National Geographic* articles, in the context of the second World War it has another implication: the irreducible foreignness of the Japanese means that they cannot be understood by Westerners, which at least offers the implication that the most prudent course of action in the war would be unrestrained military force. While Grew himself was opposed to the bombing of

Hiroshima and Nagasaki,[4] a number of passages seem to eerily anticipate the detonation of those bombs. For instance, Grew claims:

> The [Japanese] cities have been built to face earthquakes. The houses will burn easily, but their fire fighters are intensively trained and efficient, and, in any case, their homes will be all the easier to replace.

> The Japanese have lived in anticipation of catastrophe and fire. No blitzkrieg can compare with an erupting volcano, or with the ruptured earth. Japan has built her cities to withstand shock, fire, concussion (387).

Again, Grew employs the double gesture: the Japanese houses are simple and even primitive, but this—in combination with both their well-trained and presumably modern fire fighters, and their experiences with volcanic eruptions and earthquakes—gives them an ability to withstand military attack[5] that "we in the west" do not possess. This formulation both necessitates and excuses an excessively brutal military attack: because the Japanese are used to destruction, the United States must respond with a force that approaches or even exceeds that of a volcano or earthquake. However, doing so is forgivable, since their houses are easy to rebuild. Of course, Grew talks about the destruction of houses, not bodies or lives.

Likewise, two of the three captions included in *Also, With My Throat* seem to anticipate the bombing. One abbreviated caption reads "Mount Fuji, near Tokyo, Symbol of Japan's Natural Beauty, Will Be an Outstanding Guidepost to A." Going to the original article reveals what was cut off from the caption: Mt. Fuji, it says, will be an outstanding guidepost for "Allied Bombers" (Grew 400). While this probably refers to conventional bombers, it nonetheless foreshadows the destruction of Hiroshima and Nagasaki. Perhaps that's not a coincidence, since the map of Japan included in that issue of *National Geographic* was used for planning air attacks against Japan (Lutz 33). This caption provides

---

[4] See Grew, Joseph. "The War Could Have Been Ended Without the Bomb." In *The Atomic Bomb: The Critical Issues*. Ed. Barton J. Bernstein. Boston: Little, Brown and Company, 1976 (29-32).

[5] Note, however, that Grew uses the term "blitzkrieg" to stand for an attack that would come not from Germany but from the United States. Perhaps that anomaly stemmed from Grew's own opposition to the atomic bombing.

a perfect encapsulation of the entire thrust of the article: it provides a beautiful image that operates as perhaps the quintessential symbol of Japan, then suggests how useful that symbol will be in waging war against that country. The two are related: the othering of Japan in Grew's article serves to make the attacks on that country seem less horrific, or even necessary, Grew's opposition to the detonation of nuclear weapons notwithstanding.

Also, With My Throat operates in a similar way. In a letter dated August 21, 1926, Yasusada asks "Would you like some Hiroshima?" (11). Although the letter is nominally addressed to Richard, I see that as a rhetorical question addressed to the readers: because we're reading the letters, the question implicitly highlights the somewhat voyeuristic fascination with the suffering of others that initially led at least some to Yasusada's work. In fact, lines that appear to refer to the bombing are much more common in this volume than in *Doubled Flowering*, in spite of the fact that these letters date from the mid 1920s. For instance, the fifth sentence in the first letter states "Particularly there is hotness in my nation in August" (3). The letter is dated January 5, 1926, so it seems difficult to see this merely as small talk about the weather; instead, it recalls the fact that both Hiroshima and Nagasaki were bombed in August, 1945. Later in the same letter, Yasusada tells Richard about his girlfriend, or, at least, a woman he desires: "her sexual hair is a whole forest, smelling after rain falling. It is very dark within there. Bodies in piles are burning" (3). While the metaphor of sexual desire as flame is familiar and even clichéd, when placed in the context of a poet who was writing in Hiroshima it inevitably evokes the atomic bomb that was dropped on that city. The section is a disturbing fusion of the stereotype of the eroticized East and the image of the anonymous dead of Hiroshima; it is a kind of self-conscious pornography of violence and as readers we find ourselves caught looking.

Another of the abbreviated captions glued onto the page from Motokiyu's notebook reads "Tokyo Fraternity Hospital—Monument of American." Returning to Grew's article shows that Motokiyu omitted a single word at the end of the caption: "Generosity," complete with a concluding exclamation point (Grew 406). The hospital was built with donations from the American Red Cross after the Great Kantō Earthquake of 1923, which killed approximately 143,000 people. The hospital itself was completed in 1929, and obviously there's more than a little irony in the fact that the construction of such a monument of American generosity would be followed by bombings—both atomic and conventional—that would kill a much larger number of civilians. Additionally, the hospital was taken over by the United States Army for a decade after the end of the war, so the symbol of generosity became a visible representation of the occupation (Reconstruction).

The letters themselves also quote—or claim to quote—from the same issue of National Geographic. In a letter dated September 16, 1926, Yasusada writes "[i]n the Industrial Promotion Hall, which is in the quaint and bustling center of Hiroshima, one of Japan's largest and most cosmopolitan of cities, a wooden man shall breath [sic] a fire" (17). "A wooden man shall breath a fire" again calls to mind the atomic bombing, especially since the remains of the Promotion Hall would become the Hiroshima Peace Monument, more commonly known as the Atomic Bomb Dome. Motokiyu includes a somewhat puzzling note on those lines: "Yasusada is quoting from a war-time article on Japan published in *National Geographic* magazine, April 1944, where numerous photographs of daily life in Japan are published. In none of these photographs is a clear image of a person's face presented" (16). In fact, those lines do not appear anywhere in the article, although (with the exception of the reference to the wooden man) they certainly sound consistent with the prose found in the captions. The Industrial Promotion Hall is modern and western, especially since Hiroshima is described as "one of Japan's largest and most cosmopolitan of cities," but the center of that city is "quaint." Again, this presents a Japan that is both familiar and foreign; again a "caption" foreshadows the bombing, even if it is wholly invented. Perhaps this suggests that the *National Geographic* style is so familiar to Motokiyu—and so analogous to the Yasusada project—that he can imitate it at will. Additionally, Motokiyu's claim that "[i]n none of these photographs is a clear image of a person's face presented" is demonstrably untrue: while the article does include a surprising number of photographs in which the subjects are partially or fully turned from the camera, many pictures clearly depict faces, including the photo of the Tokyo Fraternity Hospital. However, if Motokiyu's claim does not apply to *National Geographic*, it certainly applies to both Motokiyu and Yasusada, the names of which are analogous to captions without a photograph.

Perhaps the best way of understanding *Also, With My Throat* is by looking at Jack Spicer's final letter to Lorca in *After Lorca*. In the final paragraph of that letter, Spicer writes:

> Saying goodbye to a ghost is more final than saying goodbye to a lover. Even the dead return, but a ghost, once loved, departing will never reappear.
>
> Love,
>
> Jack (51)

Yasusada haunts the pages of *Doubled Flowering*: he is a poet who became not merely dead but ghostly when his heteronymity was revealed, and he drifts like a specter among the letters, poems and biography. In *Also, With My Throat*, the editorial jousting often seems less like a series of explanatory notes than the squabbling of distant relatives over the estate of the deceased. In the midst of those comments and annotations, Yasusada's spirit slowly dissipates, leaving only the questions, critiques, and polemics that (perhaps) will continue to surround his absence.

Works Cited

Anonymous. 'Reconstruction of the Clinical Library with the Installation of LIS and LAS, The Fraternity Memorial Hospital.' http://www.aandt.co.jp/eng/labtour/doai.htm. Accessed 30 June 2011.

Anonymous. 'The Outline of the Hiroshima Peace Museum: Hiroshima in Ruins' http://www.pcf.city.hiroshima.jp/outline/index.php?l=E&id=9. Accessed 30 June 2011.

Grew, Joseph C. 'Japan and the Pacific.' *National Geographic*, April, 1944

Lutz, Catherine and Jane L. Collins. *Reading National Geographic*. Chicago: UC Press, 1993.

Motokiyu, Tosa. *Also, With My Throat, I Shall Swallow Ten Thousand Swords*. Ed. Kent Johnson and Javier Alvarez. Cumberland, RI: Combo Books, 2005.

Yasusada, Araki. *Doubled Flowering: From the Notebooks of Araki Yasusada*. Ed. and Trans by Tosa Motokiyu, Ojiu Norinaga, and Okura Kyojin. New York: Roof Books, 1997.

Biographies

Jenny Boully is the author of *not merely because of the unknown that was stalking toward them* (Tarpaulin Sky Press), *The Book of Beginnings and Endings* (Sarabande), *The Body: An Essay* (Essay Press), and *[one love affair]** (Tarpaulin Sky Press). She lives in Chicago and teaches in the nonfiction and poetry programs at Columbia College Chicago.

Martin Corless-Smith was born and raised in Worcestershire. He is a Professor of English at Boise State University where he currently directs the MFA in Creative Writing. His books include *English Fragments*, *Swallows*, *Nota*, *Complete Travels* and *Of Piscator*. He has published essays on W.G. Sebald, Richard Caddel, Thomas Traherne and Henry Howard, Earl of Surrey, among others.

Jacob Edmond is a senior lecturer in the Department of English at the University of Otago, New Zealand. He has published on cross-cultural encounter, comparative literature, generic and inter-art boundary-crossing, and avant-garde poetics, focusing on poetry in Russian, Chinese, and English. Poets he has written on include Kamau Brathwaite, Arkadii Dragomoshchenko, Yang Lian, Mayakovsky, Mandelstam, and Pushkin. He has edited special issues of the *New Zealand Journal of Asian Studies* and *Landfall* (on Russia), and edited and translated, with Hilary Chung, Yang Lian's *Unreal City: A Chinese Poet in Auckland*. His book *A Common Strangeness: Contemporary Poetry, Cross-cultural Encounter, and Comparative Literature* is under contract with Fordham University Press.

Mikhail Epstein is Samuel Candler Dobbs Professor of Cultural Theory and Russian Literature at Emory University. Born in Moscow, he moved to the USA in 1990. His research interests include cultural and literary theory, the history of Russian literature and philosophy, Western and Russian postmodernism, semiotics and linguistics, and new methods and interdisciplinary approaches in the humanities. His books include *After the Future: The Paradoxes of Postmodernism and Contemporary Russian Culture* (1995), *Russian Postmodernism: New Perspectives on Post-Soviet Culture* (with A. Genis and S. Vladiv-Glover, 1999), and *Word and Silence: The Metaphysics of Russian Literature* (in Russian, 2006).

Bill Freind is the author of *American Field Couches* (BlazeVox, 2008) and *An Anthology* (housepress, 2000). He teaches at Rowan University in Glassboro, New Jersey, and lives near an abandoned golf course.

Forrest Gander's most recent book is *Core Samples from the World*, from New Directions, a book of poetry, haibun, and collaborations with photographers. His most recent translations are *Watchword*, the Villaurrutia-Award-winning collection by Mexican poet Pura Lopez Colomé and (with Kyoko Yoshida) *Spectacle and Pigsty: Selected Poems of Kiwao Nomura*.

Eric Hayot is Professor of Comparative Literature and Asian Studies at Pennsylvania State University. He is the author of *Chinese Dreams: Pound, Brecht, Tel Quel* (Michigan, 2004) and *The Hypothetical Mandarin: Sympathy, Modernity, and Chinese Pain* (Oxford, 2009), and a co-editor of *Sinographies: Writing China* (Minnesota, 2008). He has published articles and book chapters on Asian America, virtual and literary worlds, global modernism, and comparative literature.

Hosea Hirata is currently Professor of Japanese Literature and Chair of the Department of German, Russian, and Asian Languages and Literatures at Tufts University. Previously he has taught at Pomona College and Princeton University. His major publications include *The Poetry and Poetics of Nishiwaki Junzaburô: Modernism in Translation* (Princeton University Press, 1993), and *Discourses of Seduction: History, Evil, Desire, and Modern Japanese Literature* (Harvard University Press, 2005).

Dan Hoy is a writer living in Brooklyn, NY. His collections include *Omegachurch* (Solar Luxuriance, 2010), *Polaroid* (Wrath of Dynasty, 2010), *Glory Hole* (Mal-O-Mar, 2009, published with Jon Leon's *The Hot Tub*), *Basic Instinct: Poems* (Triple Canopy, 2008), and *Outtakes* (Lamehouse, 2007). He previously co-edited *Soft Targets* (2006–2007), a magazine of art, literature, and philosophy, and his personal site is www.thepinupstakes.com.

Kent Johnson has been caretaker of the Yasusada writings of Tosa Motokiyu since the early 1990s.

Farid Matuk is the author of *This Isa Nice Neighborhood* (Letter Machine, 2010) and the chapbooks *Is It the King?* (effing press, 2006) and *Riverside* (Longhouse, 2011). His poems have appeared most recently in *The Boston Review*, *6x6*, and *Big Bridge*. New work is forthcoming in the journals *Mandorla* and *Third Coast* and online at *Esque*. Matuk serves on the editorial team at *Fence* and helps bring writers from all over into Dallas with the nonprofit WordSpace. He lives in east Dallas with the poet Susan Briante.

Brian McHale is Distinguished Humanities Professor of English at The Ohio State University. He is one of the founding members of Project Narrative at Ohio State, and current president of the Association for the Study of the Arts of the Present (*ASAP*). He is the author of three books on postmodernist fiction and poetry, including *The Obligation toward the Difficult Whole: Postmodernist Long Poems* (2004). He is co-editor, with Randall Stevenson, of the *Edinburgh Companion to Twentieth-Century Literatures in English* (2006) and, with Luc Herman and Inger Dalsgaard, of the *Cambridge Companion to Thomas Pynchon* (forthcoming). He is currently co-editing with Joe Bray and Alison Gibbon the *Routledge Companion to Experimental Literature*.

Biographies

Marjorie Perloff is Sadie D. Patek Professor Emerita of Humanities at Stanford University and currently Florence Scott Professor Emerita at the University of Southern California. She teaches courses and writes on twentieth- and now twenty-first-century poetry and poetics, both Anglo-American and from a Comparatist perspective, as well as on intermedia and the visual arts. Her many books include *Radical Artifice: Writing Poetry in the Age of Media* (1992), *21st Century Modernism* (2002), and *Wittgenstein's Ladder* (1999). She has also recently published her cultural memoir, *The Vienna Paradox* (2004). Recent publications, both from Chicago UP, are *The Sound of Poetry / The Poetry of Sound*, co-edited with Craig Dworkin (2009), and *Unoriginal Genius: Poetry by Other Means in the Twenty-First Century* (2010).

Paisley Rekdal is the author of a book of essays, *The Night My Mother Met Bruce Lee* and three books of poetry, *A Crash of Rhinos*, *Six Girls Without Pants*, and *The Invention of the Kaleidoscope*. A hybrid photo-text memoir that combines poems, nonfiction and fiction, entitled *Intimate*, and a fourth collection of poems, entitled *Animal Eye*, are forthcoming.

David Rosenberg, co-author with Harold Bloom of the *New York Times* best-seller *The Book of J*, has recently published *Abraham: The First Historical Biography*, and the diptych to it, *An Educated Man: A Dual Biography of Moses and Jesus* (2010). Also out in 2010 was *A Literary Bible: An Original Translation*, collecting and assessing over thirty years of translation work. Way back in the '60s/'70s, he edited *The Ant's Forefoot*, mainly in Toronto and New York but partly in London and Colchester (including *Voiceprint Editions* with Paul Evans). Rosenberg currently teaches creative writing at Princeton University.

Alex Verdolini is a writer and translator based in New York. His most recent project is a rendering, in English, of Hölderlin's renderings, in savage German, of Pindar's odes in Greek. He is a doctoral candidate in Comparative Literature at Yale.

Eliot Weinberger's most recent books of essays are *An Elemental Thing* and *Oranges & Peanuts for Sale*, both published by New Directions.

David Wojahn is the author of eight collections of verse, most recently *World Tree* (University of Pittsburgh Press, 2011) and *Interrogation Palace: New and Selected Poems* (Pittsburgh, 2006), which was a named finalist for the Pulitzer Prize in Poetry and winner of the O.B. Hardison Poetry Prize from the Folger Shakespeare Library. He teaches at Virginia Commonwealth University and in the MFA in Writing Program of Vermont College of the Fine Arts.

www.ingramcontent.com/pod-product-compliance
Lightning Source LLC
Chambersburg PA
CBHW032017230426
43671CB00005B/116